L. E. Chittenden

Recollections of President Lincoln and his Administration

L. E. Chittenden

Recollections of President Lincoln and his Administration

ISBN/EAN: 9783744716475

Printed in Europe, USA, Canada, Australia, Japan

Cover: Foto ©ninafisch / pixelio.de

More available books at **www.hansebooks.com**

RECOLLECTIONS

OF

PRESIDENT LINCOLN

AND

HIS ADMINISTRATION

BY

L. E. CHITTENDEN

HIS REGISTER OF THE TREASURY

NEW YORK
HARPER & BROTHERS, FRANKLIN SQUARE

THIS VOLUME

HAS GROWN OUT OF MY LOVE AND RESPECT FOR

ABRAHAM LINCOLN

AND KNOWING NO WAY IN WHICH I CAN BETTER ATTEST
THE SINCERITY OF ITS PURPOSE

¶ Dedicate it

TO HIS SON

ROBERT T. LINCOLN

MINISTER OF THE UNITED STATES TO THE COURT OF ST. JAMES

CONTENTS.

                                                            PAGE

I. PRELIMINARY AND EXPLANATORY.—ORIGIN OF THIS VOLUME.—ITS SCOPE AND PURPOSE 1

II. A GLIMPSE OF A NOTED CAMPAIGN.—THE STATE ELECTIONS EARLY IN OCTOBER, 1860, WHICH VIRTUALLY SETTLED THE PRESIDENTIAL CONTEST. 8

III. OFFICE-SEEKING BY AN INEXPERIENCED CANDIDATE.—APPOINTMENT TO THE PEACE CONFERENCE.—SENATOR FOOT, OF VERMONT.—HIS PREMONITIONS OF REBELLION. 17

IV. NOTES ON THE PEACE CONFERENCE.—THE PLANS OF THE CONSPIRATORS.—ADAM GUROWSKI.—JAMES S. WADSWORTH 23

V. AN OFFICIAL CALL UPON THE PRESIDENT.—IT UNITES THE LOYAL MEMBERS OF THE CONFERENCE. 32

VI. ANOTHER OFFICIAL CALL.—GENERAL SCOTT.—HIS LOYALTY AND ITS INFLUENCE UPON THE DECLARATION OF THE ELECTORAL VOTE 36

VII. THE 13TH OF FEBRUARY, 1861.—THE ELECTION OF PRESIDENT LINCOLN DECLARED.—FIRMNESS OF VICE-PRESIDENT BRECKINRIDGE.—ANGER OF THE SECESSIONISTS 40

VIII. ANOTHER INCIDENT OF FEBRUARY 13TH.—JUDGE SMALLEY ON TREASON.—SEIZURE OF ARMS IN NEW YORK CITY.—ACTION OF ITS MAYOR. 47

IX. AN ALTERCATION IN THE PEACE CONFERENCE.—SENATOR LOT M. MORRILL AND COMMODORE STOCKTON.—A TEST OF NORTHERN COURAGE. 50

X. THE CONSPIRACY OF ASSASSINATION.—ITS DETAILS.—MR. LINCOLN CONSENTS TO FOLLOW THE ADVICE OF HIS FRIENDS 58

CONTENTS.

		PAGE
XI.	How did Mr. Lincoln "Get through Baltimore"?	65
XII.	A Second Presidential Reception.—Mr. Lincoln Converses with Leading Southerners.—His Duty to the Constitution	68
XIII.	The Last Week of President Buchanan's Administration.	79
XIV.	The Inauguration.—A Memorable Scene	84
XV.	Some Notes upon General Scott and Robert E. Lee	93
XVI.	The Nones and Ides of March.—The New Cabinet	103
XVII.	A Novel Induction into Office	109
XVIII.	The Isolation of the Capitol.—An Alarmed Virginian	115
XIX.	Baltimore Blocks the Way	120
XX.	The First Volunteer Defenders of the Capitol.—The Plug-Uglies of Baltimore.—The Seventh New York and the Eighth Massachusetts Regiments	125
XXI.	The "Trent Affair."—Statesmanship of Mr. Seward	132
XXII.	The Antagonism of the Regular to the Volunteer Service.—The Influence of President Lincoln	149
XXIII.	The Colored People.—Their Industry in Learning to Read.—Their Implicit Confidence in President Lincoln	158
XXIV.	Secretary Cameron.—His Resignation.—General Fremont.—His Troubles in the Department of the West.—Secretary Stanton.—His Character.—The Davis Commission.—Mr. O'Neill's Report on Secretary Stanton's Services	168
XXV.	Making $10,000,000 of U. S. Bonds Under Pressure.—The Construction of Confederate Iron-clad Ships in British Ship-yards.—The Departure of Two Prevented.—An Englishman Offers a Great Service to Our Republic.—His Incognito	194

CONTENTS. vii

XXVI. PRESIDENT LINCOLN'S CONNECTION WITH THE ORIGIN OF ARMORED VESSELS.—HIS FAITH IN IRONCLADS.—THE INFLUENCE OF ASSISTANT-SECRETARY FOX.—HIS INTERVIEW WITH THE PRESIDENT ON THE 7TH OF MARCH, 1862 212

XXVII. PRESIDENT LINCOLN'S CONFIDENCE IN ARMORED VESSELS, CONTINUED.—THE "MONITOR" AND HER BATTLE WITH THE "MERRIMAC" DESCRIBED BY CAPTAIN WORDEN 222

XXVIII. JOSEPH HENRY AND ABRAHAM LINCOLN. 235

XXIX. INTER ARMA, SCIENTIA.—THE POTOMAC NATURALISTS' CLUB 239

XXX. A NIGHT WITH THE POTOMAC NATURALISTS' CLUB. —THE GIANT OCTOPUS 246

XXXI. HOSPITAL NOTES.—THE WOUNDED FROM THE WILDERNESS.—CHARITIES OF THE COLORED POOR.— SISTERS OF CHARITY.—ANÆSTHETICS 251

XXXII. PRESIDENT LINCOLN AND THE SLEEPING SENTINEL. —ERRONEOUS VERSIONS OF THE STORY.—WILLIAM SCOTT, OF THE THIRD VERMONT, SENTENCED TO DEATH FOR SLEEPING ON HIS POST.—HE IS PARDONED BY THE PRESIDENT.—HIS LAST MESSAGE TO THE PRESIDENT.—HIS DEATH AT THE BATTLE OF LEE'S MILLS 265

XXXIII. TREASURY NOTES AND NOTES ON THE TREASURY . 284

XXXIV. NEW MONEYS OF LINCOLN'S ADMINISTRATION.— DEMAND NOTES.—"SEVEN-THIRTIES."—POSTAGE CURRENCY. — FRACTIONAL CURRENCY. — LEGAL-TENDER NOTES, OR "GREENBACKS."—THEIR ORIGIN, GROWTH, AND VALUE 296

XXXV. GRANT AND MCCLELLAN. 316

XXXVI. THE CONFEDERATES EXCHANGE A PARTY OF THEIR PRISONERS OF WAR. 323

XXXVII. PRESIDENT LINCOLN'S STORY OF DANIEL WEBSTER 330

XXXVIII. PRESIDENT LINCOLN THE UNAPPRECIATED FRIEND OF THE SOUTH.—HIS OFFER OF COMPENSATED EMANCIPATION. — HE MEETS A VERMONT CONTRACTOR.—THEIR IMPRESSIONS OF EACH OTHER. 335

CONTENTS.

	PAGE
XXXIX. THE PROFESSIONAL DETECTIVE. — HIS EMPLOYMENT BY THE UNITED STATES AND ITS INFLUENCE UPON THE PEOPLE	341
XL. PUBLIC MISCONCEPTIONS OF THE VALUE OF SALARIED OFFICERS.—GENERAL STANNARD	353
XLI. WAS GENERAL THOMAS LOYAL?	360
XLII. THE IMPARTIAL JUDGMENT OF PRESIDENT LINCOLN. —THE RESIGNATION OF SECRETARY CHASE. — ITS CAUSES AND CONSEQUENCES	366
XLIII. THE CAMPAIGN AGAINST WASHINGTON IN 1864.--THE BATTLE OF MONOCACY	385
XLIV. GENERAL EARLY BEFORE WASHINGTON IN 1864.— BATTLE OF FORT STEVENS.	403
XLV. THE JUDGMENT OF PRESIDENT LINCOLN.—HIS COOLNESS IN TIMES OF EXCITEMENT.—HIS FAITH THAT THE UNION CAUSE WOULD BE PROTECTED AGAINST SERIOUS DISASTER. —FOUR OF HIS LETTERS NOW FIRST PUBLISHED	428
XLVI. ABRAHAM LINCOLN.—A SKETCH OF SOME EVENTS IN HIS LIFE	431
INDEX	455

RECOLLECTIONS OF
PRESIDENT LINCOLN
AND HIS ADMINISTRATION.

I.
PRELIMINARY AND EXPLANATORY.—ORIGIN OF THIS VOLUME.—
ITS SCOPE AND PURPOSE.

WHEN the notes were made which are now expanded into a volume, I had no purpose beyond that of recording, so far as I had time and opportunity, my personal knowledge of current events, which might afterwards possess some interest for my family and my immediate personal friends. Neither then nor for a quarter of a century afterwards had any thought of their publication occurred to me. As time passed, and many of these events were imperfectly or inaccurately described in the numerous current publications, corrections of them, which I verbally made, appeared to possess an unexpected interest to those who heard them. I have been told many times, and by those whose judgments are entitled to respect, that my version of these occurrences formed a part of the history of Mr. Lincoln's administration, and that their publication and preservation was in some sense a duty.

Accordingly, and by way of experiment, I brushed

the dust of more than a score of years from my notebooks, and acting as my own amanuensis, wrote out the article entitled "Making United States Bonds under Pressure," which was published in the number of *Harper's Monthly Magazine* for May, 1890. How that article was received the public knows. The correspondence to which it gave rise was extensive enough to become a burden. While the criticisms were generally favorable, the complaint was many times repeated that I ought to have given more details—that the article was too much condensed—that I should have given more of the conversations—what was said by the President and Secretary Chase, etc. This complaint was unexpected because I supposed that the more condensed it was, the greater was the merit of the article. It was followed by others which were not unfavorably received, and the interest excited, with the possibly too partial judgment of my friends, has resulted in the preparation of this volume.

Whatever other criticism may be made, it cannot be said that the book.has been thoughtlessly written. Thoughts have rushed upon me like a flood—the difficulty has been to avoid giving expression to them, and to restrict my pen to the record of the events. The reader will comprehend some of these reflections if he will place himself in my position. He will appreciate as he never did before, how quickly "one generation passeth away and another generation cometh." There were giants in those days. It has been a labor of love for me to recall some of their mighty works. But where are the giants now? The great war cabinet, the great soldier, and the President, greater than all combined, have all passed away. The last of the three financial secretaries of President Lincoln, stricken while I am writing, now lies upon what is feared will be his dying couch. I am the last surviving officer of the Treasury, above the grade of a clerk, connected with the issue of securities during the war. General Spinner, the incorruptible guardian of the gold of the nation, the last of my official associates, has recently passed away. In his letter to me, one of the last written by his hand, he says: " In my 89th year an incurable disease has so affected my vision that I can only write with great difficulty, and for five weeks all my letters have been written by another hand. I wish I could write you a long letter about old times, but I cannot. So, good-bye, old friend, and may God bless you!" His death sadly reminds me that if there is any importance in having this history written by one who had some part in it—some personal knowledge of its details, I am almost the only civil officer of that time upon whom the duty rests, and that I have but little time left for the performance.

It was natural that the story of the military and naval operations of the war should have been first written. This work has been comprehensively performed. It probably fills more volumes than the history of any other four years since the invention of printing. They represent both parties to the contest, and are usually written by admirers of the heroes whose achievements they record. They are interesting, but in many details they are not history; they are so far from it as to suggest a doubt whether events can be accurately described by their contemporaries. If, as I am sure he will, the reader shall find statements herein directly opposed to the assertions of the authors of some of these military histories, I ask the same charity which I will concede to others. Let the statements be judged by all the evidence, intrinsic as well as external. If they will not stand that test, they are not true and have no place in history.

When I took charge of a bureau in the Treasury, I naturally wished to understand the theory of its construction. What were the functions of the several bureaus? their relation to the secretary and to each other? I wanted a history of the institution. Mr. Hamilton was its reputed creator. What were his plans? his objects? How did he propose to secure them?

No such history existed. The memoirs of Mr. Hamilton were silent upon the details of this the greatest work of his life. The only printed book which gave any promise of the information I wanted was a work by "Robert Mayo, M.D., Compiler of a New System of Mythology," published in 1847. In these thin quartos, buried in an indigestible mass of circulars, instructions and decisions of secretaries, were a few details of the functions of the different bureaus, and that was all. Such knowledge as I acquired of the Treasury, and of all the matters referred to in this volume, was derived through my own personal experience in the operations of the government and personal contact with its officers. I am therefore solely responsible for the accuracy of my statements, where I have not given the authority upon which they are made.

I acquired, as I believe justly, a high opinion of the Treasury system and of the importance of a rigid enforcement of its regulations. By its complete control of the finances during the war it was a mighty power for evil as well as for good. The fate of the nation depended upon its competent management. Directed by an able financier who could reinforce the military and naval departments by the confidence born of a strong national credit, ours was one of the strongest governments on earth. In the hands of an incompetent secretary, careless of the national credit, the future promised was bankruptcy, defeat in the field, and a divided union.

Important as it was in the suppression of the rebellion, I do not intend to write the history of Secretary Chase's financial policy, nor any financial or other history. This volume, like the notes of which it is an extension, has no special object. It will meet all my expectations if it records facts, does no injustice, and gives credit to whomsoever credit is due.

I must protest in advance against any inference against public men whom I hold in high esteem because the truth of history requires me to mention acts of theirs which their friends have always regretted. No man is at all times entirely great. If he were, he would be a hero to his valet. In the early part of the war, the public judgment was very unreliable. Those were the days when the people were shouting, "On to Richmond!" and looking to Providence for a Moses or a Napoleon. An unimportant victory was sufficient to make them cry out, "Behold, he is a leader and a commander to the people"—a single failure and they were equally ready to crucify him. Later on they learned to tolerate errors and excuse failures, and value public men by the general balance of their services. Their judgment was more matured and reliable when Secretary Chase, after more than two years of labor, had established the public credit, when Grant would fight it out on that line if it took all summer, and Sherman was leading an army through the enemy's country on a march which commenced in November and ended with the war in May.

The sectional divisions of the country must be considered by those who would comprehend the earlier events of the war. The North believed that slavery was the sum of all villainies—the South that it was the mother of all virtues; one that it degraded, the other that it ennobled, the white race; one that it changed men into coarse, brutal tyrants, the other that deprivation of its salutary influences had converted the North into the home of a race of traders too cowardly to fight and too inferior to govern. With such extreme views, they necessarily misjudged and misunderstood each other.

Sectional differences in our republic belong to the past. By the war, slavery, its cause, has perished. There is no longer any excuse for sectional divisions. The ship of state, manned by a united crew, has turned away from the dangers of the past, and is sailing over tranquil seas towards the peaceful port of her manifest destiny, the supremacy of the nations of the Western Continent. The enterprise to secure that supremacy will be furnished by her own sons, the wealth to maintain it will be gathered from her own mines and forests, and the products of her own soil, and not from weaker nations despoiled. The sections devastated by the war have been the first to recover their strength. Manufactures are pushing southward; new towns and cities are springing up, and everywhere the sun of prosperity is shining over a reunited and reconstructed union.

Such political and industrial conditions must not be ignored by those who write of the history of the war. Such writers owe a duty to the future as well as to the past. It is plainly a part of that duty not to revive old controversies which the war has settled. No one can be made better or happier by threshing over the straw of old accusations, which only serve to awaken old animosities. There were events of the war, there are events in all wars, which good men should regret, which should as quickly as possible be blotted from the memory of man. It would be almost criminal to revive and perpetuate them. I have sought to keep this duty and these facts in mind while writing this book. On the other hand, it is not to the advantage of either section that facts should be suppressed or misinterpreted which may hereafter be of service by way of warning or instruction. I have corrected some misdescription in accounts of battles. I have spoken plainly of the treatment of Federal prisoners, and of those who I believe were responsible for that crime against humanity. But here and in every sentence I have sought to write in the temper of mind which would have controlled the martyr-President, who, especially in the closing days of his noble life, was mindful that "the end of the commandment is charity."

II.

A GLIMPSE OF A NOTED CAMPAIGN.—THE STATE ELECTIONS EARLY IN OCTOBER, 1860, WHICH VIRTUALLY SETTLED THE PRESIDENTIAL CONTEST.

VERMONT was the first state which held an election after the nomination of Mr. Lincoln. The first Tuesday in September had come, and the Republicans had carried Vermont. If doubts had existed, they were now dispelled. The Republicans were united; they had made a strong pull and a pull all together, and when they made a united effort they almost always carried Vermont. Their majority being greater than the combined vote of all their opponents, the state was considered safe for Lincoln at the presidential election in November.

As soon as the election was over I was invited by the National Committee, then in continuous session, to come to the Astor House, New York, for consultation. They wanted to know something about our Vermont methods; also what Vermont could do for other states where the contest was more doubtful. At the committee rooms I first met Judge William D. Kelley, then making his first run for Congress in Philadelphia. He had not then gained the name of "Pig-iron Kelley," nor the grateful affection of his state and the country which he afterwards earned by long, efficient, and most reputable service in the popular branch of the national legislature. We made short speeches at the same mass-meeting in Jersey City. When the meeting was over he said to me, "Your style will just suit my district. Come over to Philadelphia with me, and give us a taste of your Green Mountain quality. You may return to New York early on Monday."

I assented, with little thought of the danger of trusting myself to the friendly contact of Philadelphia politicians. I went with Judge Kelley to what was then a suburb of the city of brotherly love, Germantown by name, where I made an out-door address to ten thousand Wide-awakes and other Republicans. The newspapers said the speech was "a cracker." I had never heard the term before applied to any form of political or intellectual work. It was evidently commendatory, and indicated the partiality of the Philadelphians to what I thought was rather a dry form of edible.

On the following morning Judge Kelley introduced me to some of the campaign managers at the committee rooms. I remember two of them, for their names became afterwards pretty well known to the people of this republic. There were Andrew G. Curtin and Col. Alexander McClure. The first-named was running for governor, and Col. McClure was running him. Both greeted me with effusion. They could now tell me in person what I should have learned later by letter. They had decided that Col. Frank Blair and myself were a matched pair of speakers for the country. They had, therefore, appointed a series of meetings for us which would occupy nearly every afternoon and evening until the Friday preceding the state election in October. They had telegraphed the notices to every town and city where the meetings were to be held.

I objected that this was rather a cool proceeding; that Col. Blair and myself had never met; that I had business engagements at home; that I protested on general principles against an appropriation of my time for two or three weeks without mentioning the subject to me. They swept my objections away like cobwebs; declared that we "Vermonters did not know the first principles of running a campaign; that if they waited to arrange all the details in advance, they would never get the speakers they wanted; that the only safe way was to make the appointments and then capture the speakers; that in our case there had been no difficulty; Col. Blair and myself were both within easy reach, and they knew we would never consent to disappoint fifty thousand Republicans, disarrange the plans of the committee, and perhaps endanger the election."

Resistance appeared to be unavailing. I surrendered, telegraphed home some of the details of my capture, and that I did not anticipate an early escape out of the hands into which I had fallen. The next day two very lively young Republicans took charge of Col. Blair and myself, and carried us far into the dark regions of a Democratic county. Where we travelled, what places we visited, I never inquired. The image of that fortnight upon my memory represents a continuous procession of committees of eminent citizens, mass-meetings, torch-light processions, Wide-awakes in uniform, shouting, singing political songs, and hurrahing for the ticket. In the afternoons Col. Blair and myself usually addressed the same mass-meeting. As soon as one had concluded he was hurried away to a distant town or city, to be in time for the evening meeting. The other made his speech, and was rushed off in the opposite direction. Some nights we were hundreds of miles apart, at noon the next day together. Such sleep as we got was on the cars. We were only permitted to see Republican newspapers, which declared that our converts were numerous, our missionary work a pronounced success. We never failed to make our connections, and, as agreed, were returned to the Girard House in Philadelphia, on Friday preceding the Monday of the state election. We were a used-up pair of campaigners. We had lost our voices; could not speak above a whisper, and in desperate need of the rest and sleep to which we intended to appropriate the next forty-eight hours.

But rest and sleep were not for us. Col. Blair was hurried off somewhere, and I did not see him again until the second year of the war. John T. Nixon, afterwards a Federal judge in the southern district of New Jersey, was lying in wait for me. He was running for Congress; was having a hard fight, and there were special reasons why, he said, I must go into the southeast corner of New Jersey to a great mass-meeting and barbecue, where I had been advertised to speak. I pleaded exhaustion, loss of voice, general dilapidation and worthlessness, in vain. I could "save the district," he said. "A night's rest would set me all right. I must go and show myself, if I had to be carried on a stretcher, or he would be accused of intentionally deceiving and disappointing five thousand people in a rural community. Promptly at seven next morning he would come for me."

I was awakened out of a dream. It was early morning. From my window I saw that the street in front of the hotel was filled by a crowd of Wide-awakes, who were commencing the day by a service of music and song, which they ended by a night procession in the country, one hundred miles away. They were to form my escort to the train for Southeastern New Jersey.

Omitting the intervening details, let me say at once that, attended by Mr. Nixon and a party of his friends,

I reached the place of meeting shortly after midday. There was no town or village, scarcely a collection of houses. I do not know that the place had any name. It was near water communication with Delaware Bay, for during the afternoon four steamers arrived, bringing as many thousand Wide-awakes from Philadelphia and vicinity. Seats had been provided in a lovely grove, and these were already occupied, apparently by the population of the locality *en masse*. Fathers and mothers with their families, young persons of both sexes, to the number of six or seven thousand—the most orderly, quiet, cleanly rural population it has ever been my good-fortune to see. They had come not to shout, but to listen. Their good example reacted. Nobody could talk nonsense to such an audience. The speeches were argumentative, sensible, the best I had heard during the campaign.

The Wide-awakes attended, to close the exercises with a torch-light procession. Coming from the city on excursion steamers, a political organization, to attend a political meeting in the country, it may be anticipated that, being well provided with poor whiskey, they turned the meeting into a pandemonium, and, to use a phrase not then invented, that they "painted the place red." Nothing of the kind. There were oxen roasted entire, refreshments in abundance, but no whiskey nor evidences of whiskey. There was a grand political meeting, good, sound, creditable speeches, an attentive, respectful audience, ending with one of the most beautiful torchlight processions I ever witnessed; music, songs, but not one incident of rowdyism or disorder to mark or mar the day or the occasion. At the very close, two pre-revolutionary anvils performed duty as cannon, and made considerable noise. The whole affair was a credit to the orderly community which conducted it. Judge Nixon, referring to it during the next session of Congress, said its object was to stir up the community. It was at first feared that it had not produced the effect desired. But on election day, when he carried the county by an unheard-of majority, it was decided that an earthquake, reinforced by a cyclone, could not have done the work so thoroughly as that quiet, well-ordered meeting.

It had been arranged that I should return to Philadelphia by one of the steamers. I took the one said to be least crowded, but it turned out that there were at least two Wide-awakes for every square foot of standing-room it afforded. We got under way; ran out into the bay; also into a fog as thick as molasses, as dark as Erebus, and as cold as the shady side of an iceberg. All that long night, until two hours after daylight, we rolled and wallowed in the waters of the bay. The fog was so thick that it was unsafe to run by compass, or even to start the boat ahead. There was not a bed or a blanket on board. In my exhausted condition, with no place to lie or even to sit down, I suffered dreadfully. Some of the boys finally hunted up an old sail, wrapped it around me, and laid me away on a cushioned seat in the pilothouse. I slept through all the racket, until we reached the dock at Camden, where I was taken to the residence of a hospitable Republican, had a bath and a bed, and slept until election morning.

That was an exciting election day. It settled the presidential contest. Ohio and Indiana, if I rightly remember, then held their state elections on the same first Monday in October. I was admitted to the rooms of the committee. At frequent intervals during the day reports came from many sections that the election was very quiet, men were keeping their promises, and all seemed to be going well. But there were no results for comparison until evening, when the large hall was packed, and the street in front completely blocked by an expectant crowd, awaiting the announcement of victory or defeat in the most important election since the Declaration of Independence. It was arranged that the reports from other states should come through state committees. Those in Pennsylvania came through many sources.

The first figures were from Ohio. Names I have forgotten, nor are they material. Call this one Dover. The operator read out, "Dover, Republican first time. Seventy majority. Last year one hundred and ten Democratic." Some one started a cheer; others shouted, "Hush!" The next was from a Democratic county in Pennsylvania. It announced a Democratic majority of, say seventy. One who held the record of the last corresponding votes added instantly to the despatch, "A Democratic loss of ninety votes." The silence was still unbroken. Another Pennsylvania despatch: "C. beats D. by eighty, and is elected." The reader of the record adds, "A Republican gain of a member; a Democratic loss on the vote of nearly two hundred." A Republican, with powerful voice, exclaimed, "That means that Abraham Lincoln is the next President of the United States, and Andrew Curtin the next Governor of Pennsylvania!" The roar of triumph that went up from that crowd was enough to have started the roof from its fastenings. It was caught up outside as the signal of victory, and the sound of human voices suppressed the sound of cannon, which instantly commenced a salute of one hundred guns. It might well have been impressive, for it was Republican notice to the world that the people had decreed, in the words of Washington, that "the Union must be preserved!"

The announcement was accidental; it was dangerously

premature. Prudent men were very anxious lest it might be necessary to recall it. But the despatches came in rapid succession — as fast as the operator could read them — faster than the vote could be compared with that of preceding years. Their tenor was constant Republican gains, Democratic losses! When the returns upon the state ticket began to come in, the average improved. It was nearly ten o'clock, and not until we knew that Ohio, Pennsylvania, and Indiana, and probably Illinois, had gone Republican, that some remote little precinct, far up the Alleghany Mountains, reported the first trifling Democratic gain. There was a howl of derision, when some one said, "I know that place. It's where they are still voting for Jefferson and Burr."

As soon as it was known to a certainty that we had carried these four states, I quietly elbowed my way through the crowd to my hotel, with a thankful heart for the victory. The mighty crowd was celebrating it without the least evidence of rioting or disorder. There was but little sleep that night; all this noise and crowd was directly underneath my window. But I was so weary that a battery of artillery, engaged in target-practice in the next room, would not have kept me awake. I was asleep within a minute after my head rested on the pillow, and for ten hours nothing disturbed me. It was eight o'clock next morning when a delegation from the committee called, to ascertain what disposition I had made of myself, and, as it happened, to give me my first lesson in "Practical Politics."

"How many city members of Congress do the Republicans elect?" I asked. "When I left you last night almost everything else was settled; but the Congressional vote was the last counted, and no complete returns were in from any district. Is Judge Kelley defeated?"

"I should think not!" replied one of my visitors. "We have swept the decks. We have elected four congressmen from this city, sure. When I left the committee-rooms they were debating whether they should permit the Democrats to *count in the other*. It hadn't been decided."

"Counting in," I exclaimed—"what do you mean by *counting in* a member?" "You poor, unsophisticated Vermonter," he said, "you pretend you don't know what '*counting in*' means! You must have played the counting-out games of children! This is the same thing, only it works the other way."

Young men will better comprehend the progress backward of politics within a little more than a fourth of a century when I say that my guilelessness was not at all assumed. I was born in a community in which the casting of a ballot was regarded as a solemn and serious duty. In my boyhood, election meetings were opened with prayer, and until the vote was counted there was no act unbefitting the church in which the elections were always held. I had never heard of "counting out" or "counting in" a candidate. The suggestion dawned upon me like a suggestion of a crime. Such remarks make no impression now. I have become too familiar with the practice, professionally and otherwise. The person referred to afterwards became a Democratic leader. I still occasionally meet him, but never without recalling this observation with a sensation which is neither creditable to him nor agreeable to myself.

III.

OFFICE-SEEKING BY AN INEXPERIENCED CANDIDATE.—APPOINT-
MENT TO THE PEACE CONFERENCE.—SENATOR FOOT, OF VER-
MONT.—HIS PREMONITIONS OF REBELLION.

THE October elections decided the presidential contest. Pennsylvania was the keystone. "As goes Pennsylvania, so goes the Union!" was the slogan of all the political clans. The praises which were the reward of my services in Pennsylvania naturally increased my estimate of the value of those services, so that when I returned to my law office I looked about to see what office would suitably reward me. I had been treading out corn for a month—the Republicans would not muzzle the ox that treadeth out the corn—the laborer was worthy of his reward, and I did not doubt that I should be strongly supported as a candidate for any place in my own state for which I might apply. The collectorship of the port would, as I thought, just suit me—the salary was not large—under two thousand dollars, but it was the largest in the state in the gift of the President, and therefore best worthy of my attention.

Mindful of the success of the traditional early bird, I would take time by the forelock and secure the support of my Republican friends before any other candidate started in the race. I would not even wait for the election. I would begin now. I prepared letters to leading Republicans in all parts of the state. I am sure they were models. I put the whole responsibility upon my friends. Personally, I said, I was rather disinclined to take the office—but my friends were so persistent—they insisted that I ought to receive some substantial reward —that my appointment would do credit to the state, to myself, and the party. I had decided to take their advice. If the gentleman addressed agreed with them, would he kindly furnish me with his written recommendation to the President for my appointment?

The result was a trifle disappointing in two respects. My friends, "all with one consent, began to make excuse." Every one had pledged himself months before to some one else. Candidates were as numerous as the counties. A few answered that they would stand by me if I said so, although it would embarrass them to recede from their pledges. The general tenor of the correspondence might be poetically expressed in the solemn words, "Too late! Too late! Ye cannot enter now."

October, November, December passed; Lincoln and Hamlin were known to be elected. What power was it that closed our eyes to current events and their consequences? The people of the South were infatuated—of the North, blind! blind! Was it one of those mysterious ways in which the Almighty works his sovereign will, which led to the sealing up of Northern eyes? Day after day we saw the funds of the United States transferred to Southern depositories; cannon, small-arms, and military supplies transferred to Southern arsenals; Southern leaders seizing upon and appropriating moneys which the United States held in trust for wards of the nation. South Carolina called a convention which passed an ordinance of secession, without one dissenting vote. Her representatives and senators in Congress shook the dust of Washington from their feet and left the capital, with insult and contumely for the Union on their lips; every Southern state engaged openly in preparations for the destruction of the Union; and while all this was going on the people of the North went, one to his cattle, another to his merchandise, and if they cast a glance at the angry clouds gathering in the Southern sky, declared that they might result in a sprinkle, but that we should not have much of a shower after all! To us the Union was the ark of our covenant, men might rage and bluster and threaten, but to touch it with unhallowed hands involved a measure of depravity of which we believed no American capable.

That fine old merchant, manufacturer, and patriot, Erastus Fairbanks, was then Governor of Vermont. On Saturday, the second day of February, late in the day, he telegraphed me that he wished me to lay aside all business, and leave Burlington that evening for Washington —that I was appointed a member of a delegation—my associates would meet me on the train—one of his aids would bring us our commissions, with the few suggestions he thought proper to make to us. I obeyed his injunction. When the train reached Troy, there were on board of it Gen. H. H. Baxter, ex-Governor Hall, Messrs. Underwood, Harris, and myself. There, a letter from the governor was handed us, stating that we were delegates appointed to represent Vermont in a Peace Conference called by Governor Letcher, of Virginia, to be held in Washington on the 4th of February, only two days later. Governor Fairbanks bound us by no instructions, made but one brief recommendation. It was that we should consult with our delegation in Congress, and then represent Vermont in the conference according to her principles and her traditions, witholding nothing that ought to be surrendered, submitting to nothing that was wrong, unjust, or inconsistent with Republican principles.

We reached Washington on time; other delegates

boarding the train as it passed through New York, New Jersey, Delaware, and Maryland. We went to Willard's, then the principal hotel, owned by two young Vermonters, who informed us that the city was crowded with strangers, principally from the South.

With a brief delay to clear ourselves from the dust of travel, we drove to the Capitol. Senator Foot was the only member of the Vermont delegation we found there. We knew him at home as a prudent, cautious, rather retiring statesman, very conservative in his views, and eminently cautious in his expressions, in short, a typical Vermonter in whom all Vermonters had unlimited confidence. He met us with his usual cordiality, but the first mention of the Peace Conference appeared to enrage him.

"It is a fraud, a trick, a deception," he exclaimed, "a device of traitors and conspirators again to cheat the North and to gain time to ripen their conspiracy. I at first hoped Governor Fairbanks would pay no attention to it. I am now glad that he has sent delegates. At home they do not believe we are living here in a nest of traitors. You will be able to see and judge for yourselves!"

Ex-Governor Hall, one of the most amiable of men, was shocked by the senator's violence. "You do not mean, senator," he said, "that we are on the eve of rebellion—that there is danger?"

"That is precisely what I do mean," he said; "the plot to seize the Capitol and prevent the inauguration of Lincoln is already formed—they will prevent the counting of the votes, if they dare. Their chief present difficulty is want of time. That time you are to assist them in gaining by useless debates in a misnamed Peace Conference. But you have no need to take my word for it. Keep your eyes open and judge for yourselves!"

"We are here for consultation," continued Governor Hall; "we have decided to do nothing except upon consultation and the advice of our delegation in Congress."

"I think you are wise in that," said the senator. "There are no divided counsels in the delegation. We all think alike, but possibly I express my opinions with the least reserve."

As we were about to withdraw the senator observed: "There is one subject in addition which I ought to mention. I should speak plainly, possibly to your surprise. The city is overrun with Southerners. A few of them are gentlemen, but the large majority are roughs and adventurers, who profess great contempt for what they call the cowardice of Northern men. They are all armed—they believe that Northern men will run rather than fight—that they may be insulted with impunity. They will probably insult you. I believe street fights would be common if these fellows were not ruled with an iron hand by their leaders, who do not want any fighting until they are prepared. Northern men now carry arms who never carried them before, and are prepared to defend themselves. I think each individual must determine such matters for himself. I have decided that, so long as I represent Vermont as one of her senators, I shall express my opinions touching her interests upon all proper occasions in such language as I deem consistent with the dignity and position of a senator. If assaulted or insulted for such expressions, I shall undertake to defend the honor of Vermont. I do not believe in fighting, nor in submitting to the charge of cowardice. These men are traitors, conspirators, rebels, leagued together for the destruction of the Union. I do not hesitate to tell them so to their faces!"

"Senator!" exclaimed one of our number, astounded

at these expressions from one ordinarily so prudent and self-controlled. "Do you advise us to prepare for street fights? to carry pistols? If I had a loaded pistol in my pocket I should feel as if I were preparing to commit a burglary."

"I advise nothing," he responded, "I am merely putting you upon your guard. You are Vermonters; you know how to defend your state and yourselves. After you have been here a few days you will judge for yourselves whether it will be wise for you to carry arms."

IV.

NOTES ON THE PEACE CONFERENCE.—THE PLANS OF THE CONSPIRATORS.—ADAM GUROWSKI.—JAMES S. WADSWORTH.

I DO not aspire to the dignity of a historian. I am not writing a history of the Peace Conference. I may, however, venture to hope that the incidents I shall describe may be of use to future historians. They concern the very origin of the rebellion. The Peace Conference was a prelude to the bloody drama which followed it, and its record must be read and understood by those who would comprehend in their chronological order the events which ended all hope of a peaceful solution of the long-pending controversy between freedom and slavery by the opening gun against Fort Sumter.

Willard's great hotel, like a parasitic plant, had gradually grown around and taken in an old Washington church, which was then called Willard's Hall. Here the members of the Conference were notified to assemble. They found that its self-appointed managers had attended to all the preliminary work. Without any effort to ascertain who were commissioned as members, a temporary chairman and secretary were elected, and a Committee on Rules and Organization was appointed. An uninstructed member then moved the admission of reporters for the press, a large number of whom were then waiting at the door, directed, as the member said, to make public the proceedings of the most important conference which had been held since the adoption of the Federal Constitution.

Mr. James A. Seddon, of Virginia, who assumed the duties of managing director of the Conference, objected. He did not see that any good could possibly come of giving publicity to its proceedings. Wide differences of opinion would be found to exist at the outset; these were to be harmonized by mutual concessions and compromises. The interference and criticisms of the press, he said, would destroy every hope of success. Members would not have the courage to consent to necessary compromises if they were subjected to the daily attacks of the newspapers. If the Conference was to produce any good results, it must transact its business behind closed doors. The motion to admit the reporters, to use the Southern phrase, "passed in the negative."

The programme arranged for the three following days was followed without the slightest change. The Republicans contented themselves by looking on, without any interference with the harmony of the proceedings. Ex-President John Tyler was made permanent president, a series of rules was reported by the committee an l adopted; a Committee on Credentials was then appointed and made an immediate report; a Committee on Resolutions, consisting of one member from each state represented, to which all resolutions and propositions for the adjustment of existing difficulties between states were to be referred without debate, was *appointed by the president.*

After some informal consultations among themselves, the Republican members decided that the time had arrived for them to take a more active part in the exercises. One of them, after remarking that a record of the resolutions introduced and disposed of should be preserved for future use, moved the appointment of a recording secretary. Another insisting that every member should be accurately reported, and should be able to show to his constituents what he had said as well as how he had voted, moved the appointment of an official stenographer, who should take notes of the debates and hold them subject to the order of the Conference. Both motions were promptly rejected.

I obtained the bad distinction of casting the first firebrand into the inflammable materials of the Conference. I introduced a formal resolution for the appointment of a stenographer, which was laid on the table. I then observed that it was a part of my duty to make an accurate report of all that transpired in the Conference to the Executive of Vermont; that I was no stenographer, and did not crave the labor I was about to undertake; that, after the votes declining to make any record or to preserve the materials from which a record might afterwards be made, I intended openly to take notes and make the best report of the debates and record of the proceedings I could, and to make such use of them as I thought proper.

Then there was trouble. The Southerners and their Northern allies were furious. No member, they said, had a right to disregard the vote of the Conference. One demanded that the Committee on Rules should immediately report a vote of censure; another demanded my expulsion, unless I would promise obedience. Mr. Seddon called up an amendment he had offered to the report of the Committee on Rules, prohibiting any communication of the proceedings except by members to the states they represented, and called for a vote upon it.

There was great confusion. A dozen Southerners, each offering different remedies, were all trying to speak at the same time. There was but one remark from a Northern delegate—William Curtis Noyes, with a quiet emphasis which cut like a finely tempered sabre, said that there was a considerable body of delegates on that floor who intended to secure the rights of every individual delegate. President Tyler, whose discretion never deserted him, saw that the time for his interference had come. He sternly commanded and restored order. He announced peremptorily that the proposed attempt to control the individual conduct of an orderly member, and to interfere with his communications to his constituents, was unparliamentary and out of order. The amendment of Mr. Seddon, by the rule already adopted, must be referred to the Committee. Order was restored, the storm passed, and the skies were clear again.

Among the singular people at that time collected in Washington, perhaps the most extraordinary person was Adam Gurowski. I came to know him intimately afterwards, but neither myself nor any one else, so far as I could ascertain, ever knew anything of his previous history or of what country he was a native. He was a fine scholar and writer, with an excellent command of language; a brilliant conversationalist in all the modern European tongues. He claimed acquaintance with several crowned heads and many of the statesmen of Europe, was perfectly familiar with diplomatic usages, a gentleman in dress and carriage. Without any very definite knowledge, I formed the conclusion that he was a Russian, who had been connected with the diplomatic service, but compelled to leave Europe on account of opinions which were somewhat erratic, if they were not revolutionary and socialistic. He was unobtrusive, yet he managed to form the acquaintance of everybody of any note, and usually to secure their good opinion. Diplomatists, cabinet officers, senators, and members of the House—everybody was accessible to him and received him on a familiar footing. He was the firm friend of the North, and entertained an inveterate hatred of slavery and its influence. I mention him here, because I afterwards learned that his ability to obtain reliable information of important facts was phenomenal. His conclusions were usually accurate, though probably in great part the result of intuition. Within a week after our arrival in Washington, we found ourselves conversing with Gurowski upon the footing of an acquaintance, and I believe he had made himself known to every Northern member of the Conference.

On the evening of the day of our first flurry in the Conference, Gurowski called at the rooms where the Northern members were accustomed to confer.

"Do I intrude?" he asked. "I felt it my duty to call at once and congratulate you. You are beginning to experience the maternal cares of the 'mother of the presidents,' 'even as a hen gathereth her chickens under her wing,' etc. How do you Northern gentlemen like the experience?"

We denied his knowledge of what had been done in the Conference. He related its action, the substance of the speeches, the president's decision, with perfect accuracy.

"You will make a mess of it between you," he said. "These conspirators do not know how to conspire, and you Republicans!—I don't know how to take you. Are you lambs to be eaten up unresistingly by the wolves of secession? Or are you fishes with blood so cold that it cannot be stirred to action? Don't you know the details of the plot? I can give them to you to the dotting of every i and the crossing of every t—from the first capital to the final period. If you knew them as I do, you would not be wasting your time in Washington."

I shall give Gurowski's version, not because I think it should be accepted upon his evidence, but because it presents in a compact form a plan of which subsequent events furnished strong confirmatory proof.

"Mr. Lincoln's election," he said, "decided the question of secession. The leaders agreed that the electoral vote should not be counted, that his election should not be officially declared. General Cass was to be quarrelled out of the Cabinet. Mr. Buchanan, naturally infirm of purpose and weakened by age, could be controlled by the remaining members, while as much as possible of the national property was transferred into the Southern states. South Carolina was to secede at once—other states to follow as fast as possible—Washington was to be packed with fighting Southerners, and on the 13th of February, during the count of the electoral vote, a riot was to be started in the House, the Capitol and the departments seized, and a new confederacy proclaimed with Jefferson Davis as President *ad interim.*

"Floyd and Cobb had upset the entire plan by their premature and criminal acts, which drove them from the Cabinet, and brought in General Dix and Mr. Stanton. General Cass had been driven out as they intended, but in a brief spasm of resolution Mr. Buchanan had insisted upon putting Judge Black in his place, and Judge Black could not be trusted by the South. General Scott also had made an unexpected difficulty. Old and rheumatic as he was, he had declined to submit to temptation or control; he had smelt the danger, collected such regulars from the army as he could in Washington, and had given the plotters notice that the first one that laid a hand of force on the government should be shot down without trial, mercy, or delay. When Congress convened in December, the plot to prevent the count of the electoral vote was a failure. There had been too many rogues and fools admitted into the counsels of the conspirators.

"Then a new conspiracy had to be formed. It was agreed that Jefferson Davis should be its head and general manager. Special work might be assigned by him to individuals, but he alone should determine how far others should be admitted to a knowledge of its details. It dated from the day, or rather the night, of the 5th of January, when Judah Benjamin, Slidell, Mallory, and Mason met at the house of Mr. Davis in Washington. It was then agreed that the electoral vote should be counted and the result declared. All the senators and representatives should remain in Congress, drawing their pay, until their respective states had seceded. South Carolina was already out of the Union. In the Gulf states, secession should be hastened as much as possible. Slidell and Mallory were to prepare a plan for the confederacy and to call a convention of the seceded states to adopt it at Montgomery, Alabama, not later than the middle of February. The Border states could not be voted out of the Union in time, but they were nearest Washington, and could provide the men to seize the government on the 4th of March, to which date the rebellion was now postponed.

"Here," exclaimed Gurowski, "comes in the most disreputable part of the conspiracy. The people of the free states, their representatives in Congress, were to be played with like children. They were to be entertained by the hope of an arrangement, of some peaceful settlement of the controversy, which, at the fall election, passed irrevocably beyond the limits of peaceful settlement. This part of the plot was committed to Mr. Mason. Virginia, the home of Washington, the mother of the presidents, should apparently intervene to save the Union. Her legislature was in session; her governor should invite the states to send delegates to a conference to be held in Washington, to agree upon terms of compromise and peace. The North would respond, the conference would occupy the time until March 4th, and so long as such a conference existed the North would sleep on undisturbed, doing nothing in the way of preparation until awakened by the sound of revolutionary cannon on the morning appointed for Mr. Lincoln's inauguration.

"The rest you know," he continued. "Here you are permitting yourselves to be used as the instruments of a treasonable conspiracy, when you ought to be at home, organizing and drilling your regiments, preparing to defend the only government worth living under left upon the face of the earth.

"Adieu, gentlemen," said the old man, politely taking his leave; "I have made my little speech. I have told you plain truths, because I love this republic, how well you will never know until you have passed through my experiences, from which may the Almighty Father protect and preserve you."

There was present one of the noblest men ever produced by this or any country, who afterwards laid down his life for the Union—he was the model of an American gentleman—James S. Wadsworth, of New York.

"I suppose that man is a crazy foreigner," said Mr. Wadsworth, "but I do wish there were not so much method nor quite so much intelligence in his madness. If he is half right, our position here deserves the contempt of the world. Yet we cannot deny that, with few exceptions, the Northern press hailed the invitation of Virginia to this Conference with favor and commendation. It urged the Northern states to accept it, to send as delegates their most conservative and compromising men. It gives me a chill to think how carefully the state of New York has made up her delegation. Subtract one member from it, and the South to-day controls one half that delegation. I begin to think it is time we held a caucus, and found how many members we have upon whom we could absolutely rely."

There was swift assent to Mr. Wadsworth's suggestion. Different members undertook to notify a caucus to be held the following evening. Mr. Clay, of Kentucky, George W. Summers, of Virginia, and other Southern members came in, and there was no opportunity for further consultation.

V.

AN OFFICIAL CALL UPON THE PRESIDENT. — IT UNITES THE LOYAL MEMBERS OF THE CONFERENCE.

THERE was but little for the Conference to do until the Committee had reported their propositions for the amendment of the Constitution. President Tyler, on the 7th of February, announced that an official call upon the President was a manifest duty of the Conference, that he had made the necessary arrangements, and the President would receive us immediately upon the adjournment. This call was so clearly a part of the programme that no objection was made to it. Preceded by the Virginia delegation, with President Tyler at its head, we marched to the Executive Mansion with the solemnity of a funeral procession.

It was to the Northern members a memorable call. It would be more agreeable to omit any account of it, as I should certainly do, were it not that the Executive was a factor in the existing situation which cannot be comprehended unless the measure of his influence is understood. We went to the White House, believing that the President, the sworn defender of the Constitution, the head of the army and the navy, held in his own hands the power to command all the resources of the republic for the crushing of secession and the suppression of treason. We came away convinced that, so far as the defence of the Union depended upon him, the barrier against secession was so frail that a breath would blow it away.

We found the venerable President advanced in years, shaken in body, and uncertain in mind. He exhibited every symptom of an old man worn out by *worry*. No one doubted his personal fidelity to his country, but every action, all his conversation with the delegates, indicated that his mind was completely unsettled by apprehension and anxiety. He received every person presented with effusion, with uncontrollable emotion. His thoughts ran exclusively upon compromise and concession. It was very painful to see him throw his arms around the neck of one stranger after another, and, with streaming eyes, beg of him to yield anything to save his country from "bloody, fratricidal war." This appeared to be his favorite phrase. He used it many, many times. He had not one word of condemnation for disunion, secession, or treason. He appeared to look upon the South as a deeply injured party, to which the North owed apology and promise of better conduct in future. It was natural that the South should resent assaults upon her domestic institutions, he said, and that she should demand, if not indemnity for the past, at least security for the future. That security the Conference could give. By consenting to the amendments to the Constitution which the South demanded, because they were indispensable to satisfy the Southern people, the Conference could give peace to a distracted country, and save the Union! What a noble object! What a patriotic work! How could we stop to measure concessions which would produce such grand results?

His remarks were noticeable for what they did not, as well as for what they did, comprise. They were so nearly identical with those of the Secession delegates as to suggest consultation. They did not contain the slightest reference to his successor or to his incoming administration. When a delegate suggested that, by the election of Mr. Lincoln, the people had pronounced judgment upon the important claims now made by the South, and that the Conference had no power to reverse that judgment, there was an immediate interference in the conversation by several of the Southern delegates, and a diversion to other topics. Such a reference was evidently inconsistent with the preconcerted harmony of the visit.

"What do you think of it?" said one Northern delegate to another, after witnessing a number of repetitions of the emotional conduct of the President as different members were presented to him.

"These views are not original with President Buchanan," he said. "They are the doctrines of Sir Boyle Roche, the inimitable maker of Irish bulls. He declared emphatically that he would give up a part, and, if necessary, *the whole* of the Constitution, *to preserve the remainder !*"

This call upon the President produced an impression very different from that anticipated by those who brought it about. It was well known that disagreements in the Cabinet had arisen. General Cass had been compelled to resign. The position of Secretary Stanton was not, at that time, known to us. The despatch of General Dix to Hemphill Jones, "If any man hauls down the American flag, shoot him on the spot!" had sent a thrill through the North, showing that there was ·one member of the Cabinet who was true to his country. Now, it was plain to the delegates that a disorganized and divided Cabinet, with its President thus broken in mind and body, formed an Executive Department in no condition to cope with the adroit, energetic agents of secession. The dangers of the situation became apparent. Months of debate could not have united the Northern delegates together so firmly as the insensible influence of this formal call. Even before they left the White House, many had decided that loyal men of all shades of political opinion must now stand together in a firm purpose to maintain the integrity of an unbroken Union, and to resist all further aggressions of the slave power. That evening a caucus was held, attended by nearly every Republican delegate who had supported Mr. Lincoln. Mr. Chase was made its permanent chairman. A resolution was adopted to the effect that no action should be taken in the Conference which the Republicans could delay, until it had been first considered in the caucus. Since probably none but national questions would arise in the Conference, upon which there would be only slight differences in Northern opinion, it was decided that the co-operation of all loyal Democrats should be cordially invited. From that time the Republican delegates acted as a compactly united body.

VI.

ANOTHER OFFICIAL CALL.—GENERAL SCOTT.—HIS LOYALTY AND ITS INFLUENCE UPON THE DECLARATION OF THE ELECTORAL VOTE.

THE 13th of February, the day appointed by law for counting the electoral vote, was rapidly approaching. The impression was almost universal that the count would not be interrupted—that the project of seizing the government by force was postponed to the 4th of March, the day of inauguration. Still, there were many indications, very troublesome to patriotic minds. The influx of Southerners into Washington increased. Every available room in the hotels, boarding or private houses, was crowded with guests. They took full possession of all the saloons and places where liquor was sold. One of their favorite pastimes was to collect in front of the liquor saloons and jostle or crowd the "white-livered, black Republicans" and women into the street. The Northern visitors to the capital were careful to avoid all collision with them.

The air was filled with rumors. Few Northern men in the city doubted that a conspiracy to seize the government existed among the trusted leaders of secession; that the force to execute it was organized, armed, and to be furnished by the adjacent states of Maryland and Virginia; and that the brutal horde which at that time infested the streets of Washington was a part of that force. Whether any adequate preparations had been made for the defence of the city against such a force, we did not know. There was, consequently, a general feeling of uneasiness; and if a revolution had broken out at any time, it would not have caused much surprise. I should have mentioned that the argument for excluding the public from the debates of the Conference which had the most force with the Republicans was that the traitors might seize upon any confusion or disorder that should arise as an excuse for a riot, or an armed attack upon the officers employed to enforce order, and thus give the signal for open rebellion.

On the 8th of February, after a brief session of the Conference, filled with this feeling of anxious uncertainty, I determined, somewhat impulsively, to call upon General Scott, and learn whether any preparations had been made to secure the undisturbed counting of the electoral vote, and declaration of the result on the following Wednesday, only five days later. His headquarters were then in Winder's Building, opposite the old War Department, which at that time was under the control of Judge Holt, the loyal successor of the criminal Floyd. I sent in my card with my address written upon it, and without the least delay was shown by Colonel Townsend, one of his aides, into the private room of the lieutenant-general. The grand old man lay upon a sofa. He raised his gigantic frame to a sitting posture. There was infirmity in the movements of his body, but it was forgotten the moment he spoke, for there was no suspicion of weakness in his mind.

"A Chittenden of Vermont!" he said. "Why, that was a good name when Ethan Allen took Ticonderoga! I know the Vermonters—I have commanded them in battle. Well, Vermont must be as true to-day as she has always been. What can the commander of the army do for Vermont?"

"Very little, at present," I answered. "I called to pay you my personal respects. You may, however, do me and some others a favor. In common with many loyal men, I am anxious about the count of the electoral vote on next Wednesday. Many fear that the vote will not be counted nor the result declared."

"Pray tell me why it will not be counted?" he asked, without any apparent effort, but with a voice which rang like an order through a clear-toned trumpet. "There have been threats on that subject," he continued, "but I have heard nothing of them recently. I supposed I had suppressed that infamy. Has it been resuscitated? I have said that any man who attempted by force or unparliamentary disorder to obstruct or interfere with the lawful count of the electoral vote for President and Vice-President of the United States should be lashed to the muzzle of a twelve-pounder and fired out of a window of the Capitol. I would manure the hills of Arlington with fragments of his body, were he a senator or chief magistrate of my native state! It is my duty to suppress insurrection—*my duty!*"

It had been upon my lips to ask him whether he had any adequate force to stamp out a revolution in the capital; but it was awkward to do so. He spoke of his duty as something inevitable; its performance was not to be doubted. Accordingly, I said:

"Permit me to express my gratitude, general. There is relief, encouragement, satisfaction in your assurance. The Vermont delegation will sleep more quietly to-night when they hear it."

"I will say further," he continued, "that I do not believe there is any immediate danger of revolution. That there has been, I know. But the leaders of secession are doubtful about the result. They are satisfied that somebody would get hurt. I have the assurance of the Vice-President of the United States that he will announce the election of the President and Vice-President, and that no appeal to force will be attempted. His word is reliable. A few drunken rowdies may risk and lose their lives; there will be nothing which deserves the name of a revolution. But no promises relieve me from my duty. While I command the army there will be no revolution in the city of Washington!"

I made no secret of this interview with General Scott. It soon became known that, although he was suffering intensely from disease, he was always to be found at his quarters, and that he was the most accessible public man in Washington. His visitors were numerous. Every loyal man left his presence with his hopes for the future strengthened, his faith renewed, his confidence in the General of the Army absolute, his principal regret being that such a tried and true patriot could not exert a more powerful influence upon the administration. There was an energy in the emphatic declarations of this loyal veteran which compelled belief, even in the hearts of traitors, that he understood his duty, and had accurately estimated his own ability to insure its performance.

VII.

THE 13TH OF FEBRUARY, 1861.—THE ELECTION OF PRESIDENT LINCOLN DECLARED.—FIRMNESS OF VICE-PRESIDENT BRECKINRIDGE.—ANGER OF THE SECESSIONISTS.

ALL governments have their crises. Our republic never escaped one more alarming than that of February 13th, 1861. It was the day appointed for the seizure of Washington. Preparations had been made; armed bodies of men had been enlisted and drilled, and many of them had reported in the city pursuant to orders. When the managers were compelled to postpone the rebellion, these recruits declined to accept the necessity or to put off the opening drama. They had assembled for a revolution with its natural consequences—booty and plunder; any delay was felt to be a personal injury to each individual.

The sun rose in a cloudless sky on the morning of Wednesday, February 13th, the day appointed by law for counting the electoral vote and declaring the result. Train after train from the South, the West, and the North poured its volume of passengers into the streets of an already overcrowded city. As early as eight o'clock in the morning crowds began to climb the sides of Capitol Hill, every individual intent on securing a comfortable seat in the gallery of the hall in which the two Houses of Congress were to meet in joint assembly. They were doomed to disappointment. At every entrance to the building stood a guard of civil but inflexible soldiers, sternly barring admission. Prayers, bribes, entreaties, oaths, objurgations, were alike unavailing. No one could pass except senators and representatives, and those who had the written ticket of admission signed by the Speaker of the House or the Vice-President, the presiding officer of the Senate. Even members could not pass in their friends. Consequently the amount of profanity launched forth against the guards would have completely annihilated them if words could kill. The result was that, although solid humanity outside could have been measured by the acre, the inside of the building was less crowded than usual, and there was no difficulty in passing from room to room in all parts of the Capitol.

The members of the Conference had been, by vote, admitted to the floor of the House of Representatives. My certificate of membership enabled me to pass the guard without difficulty, and by the courtesy of a doorkeeper I secured a seat in the gallery, where my view of the hall was unobstructed.

By twelve o'clock the galleries were comfortably filled, and all the seats and standing-room in the hall were occupied, except the seats reserved for members of the two Houses. The Southerners were a vast majority; in fact, except the members, there were very few persons present from the Northern states. To one who knew nothing of the hot treason which was seething beneath the quiet exterior of the spectators, the exercises would have appeared to be tame and uninteresting.

Except the guards at the entrances, there were no soldiers visible. None were supposed to be present. A friend who resided in the city recognized me and took a seat by my side. Aware that he had organized a selected body of loyal men into a regiment, of which he was colonel, more than a month previously, I expressed my surprise at his presence in citizen's dress, and said, "I supposed you would be on duty to-day with your regiment." He smilingly replied, "We are *minute* men, you know; that is, we enter a room as private citizens, and come out of it a minute afterwards, a regiment, armed with loaded repeating-rifles. Such a thing might happen here to-day, if the necessity arose. My men are within easy call, and their rifles are not far away. Some men get excited on election day, and require control. However, I think this is to be a very quiet election."

Two large connecting committee-rooms, on the north side of the hall, were, as I had noticed, inaccessible to all persons. This observation of the colonel explained the reason why. The House was now called to order, and my attention was directed to its proceedings. First, a message was ordered to be sent by the House to the Senate, informing senators that the House was in session, awaiting their presence, so that in a joint assembly the electoral votes for President and Vice-President might be opened and counted.

There was a gathering of Southern members on the floor below me, which a young member from Virginia (whose name is omitted, because he is now, I have no doubt, an earnest friend of the Union) was addressing with much gesticulation. He was urging that then was "the best time to give them some music, before the Senate came in." At that moment the Senate of the United States was announced, and, preceded by Vice-President Breckinridge, the officers leading the way, the senators entered. The members of the House arose and remained standing, while the senators took their seats in a semicircle arranged for them in front of the clerk's desk. The Vice-President was conducted to the chair. Senator Trumbull, and Messrs. Washburn and Phelps of the House, who had been appointed tellers, were shown to seats at the clerk's desk. Absolute silence prevailed throughout the hall.

Vice-President Breckinridge rose, and in tones no louder than those of an ordinary conversation, but which were heard in the most distant corner of the gallery, announced that the two Houses were assembled, pursuant to the Constitution, in order that the electoral votes might be counted for President and Vice-President, for the term commencing on the fourth day of March, 1861. "It is my duty," he said, "to open the certificates of election in the presence of the two Houses, and I now proceed to the performance of that duty."

There is an unmeasured, latent energy in the personal presence of a strong man. If he could be remembered only for his services on that day, Vice-President Breckinridge would fill a high place in the gallery of American statesmen, and merit the permanent gratitude of the American people. He knew that the day was one of peril to the republic — that he was presiding over what appeared to be a joint meeting of two deliberative bodies, but which, beneath the surface, was a caldron of inflammable materials, heated almost to the point of explosion. But he had determined that the result of the count should be declared, and his purpose was manifested in every word and gesture. Jupiter never ruled a council on Olympus with a firmer hand. It was gloved, but there was iron beneath the glove.

One member rose—" Except questions of order, no motion can be entertained," said the presiding officer. The member exclaimed that he wished to raise a point of order. "Was the count of the electoral vote to proceed under menace? Should members be required to perform a constitutional duty before the janizaries of Scott were withdrawn from the hall?" "The point of order is not sustained," was the decision which suppressed the member, more by its emphasis than by its words. The presiding officer opened the envelope containing the electoral vote of Maine, handed it to Senator Trumbull, who read out the long certificate. The vote of Maine was announced for Lincoln and Hamlin. There was a slight ripple of applause which was instantly suppressed. Several other states followed, the reading of each record occupying some minutes. Senator Douglas suggested that the reading of the formal parts of the remaining certificates be omitted. There was no objection, and the announcement and record of the votes proceeded rapidly to the end. The only interruption was an expression of mingled contempt, respect, ridicule, and veneration when the vote of South Carolina was declared.

In a silence absolutely profound, the Vice-President arose from his seat, and, standing erect, possibly the most dignified and imposing person in that presence, declared:

"That Abraham Lincoln, of Illinois, having received a majority of the whole number of electoral votes, is duly elected President of the United States for the four years beginning on the fourth day of March, 1861; and Hannibal Hamlin, of Maine, having received a majority of the whole number of electoral votes, is duly elected Vice-President of the United States for the same term."

The work of the joint meeting was completed. The Senate retired to its own chamber. The fuse was fired, the outbreak attempted, but the hoped-for explosion did not take place. Its object had failed; the election of Abraham Lincoln by the people of the United States had been proclaimed to the world. A dozen angry, disappointed men were on their feet before the door had closed upon the last senator, clamoring for recognition by the speaker. For a few minutes the tumult was so great that it was impossible to restore order. The concentrated venom of the secessionists was ejected upon the General of the Army. There were jeers for the "rail-splitter," sharp and fierce shouts for "cheers for Jeff. Davis," and "cheers for South Carolina." But hard names and curses for "old Scott" broke out everywhere on the floor and in the gallery of the crowded hall. The quiet spectators seemed in a moment turned to madmen. "Superannuated old dotard!" "Traitor to the state of his birth!" "Coward!" "Free-state pimp!" and any number of similar epithets were showered upon him. Members called on the old traitor to remove his "minions," his "janizaries," his "hirelings," his "bluecoated slaves," from the Capitol. I glanced around me. The seat next me was empty; my military friend, and the quiet gentlemen I had noticed near by, had vanished—where and for what purpose I knew only too well. For a few moments I thought they would officiate in a revolution.

It was, however, "*vox et præterea nihil.*" The power of the human lung is limited, and howling quickly exhausts it. The speaker soon pounded the House back to order, and the danger inside had passed. I went out at the north front of the Capitol, and, entering the first carriage I found, I ordered the colored driver to take me to my hotel. He drove through the crowd on that side without difficulty. It was orderly and undemonstrative, for just beyond the Square was the old Capitol, and along the street in front of it were two batteries of artillery, quiet themselves, but none the less causes of the quiet around them. The avenue in the direction of the Treasury was choked with a howling, angry mob. We escaped through one of the cross streets to F Street, and reached the rear entrance of Willard's Hotel.

The mob had possession of the avenue far into the night. Reputable people kept in-doors, and left the patriots who were so injured by the election of Mr. Lincoln to consume bad whiskey and cheer for Jeff. Davis undisturbed. There was much street-fighting, many arrests by the police, but no revolution.

I believed at that time, and I have never since doubted, that the country was indebted for the peaceful count of the electoral vote, the proclamation of the election of Mr. Lincoln, and the suppression of an attempted revolution on that day, to the joint influence of Major-General Winfield Scott and Vice-President Breckinridge. A perfect understanding existed between them. General Scott knew that he could rely upon the promised assistance of the Vice-President, who had repeatedly declared that until the end of his term he should perform the duties of his office, under the sanction of his oath. Faithfully, without evasion or paltering with his conscience, after the manner of Cobb and Floyd, he kept his pledge. General Scott defined his purposes upon all proper occasions, especially to the apologists for secession, with emphasis, and if he was not misrepresented, sometimes with an approach to profanity. When challenged by Wigfall, whether he would dare to arrest a senator of the United States for an overt act of treason, he was reported to have answered, "No! I will blow him to h—l!" These two men, both Southern-born, on the 13th of February conducted the republic safely through one of the most imminent perils that ever threatened its existence.

VIII.

ANOTHER INCIDENT OF FEBRUARY 13TH.—JUDGE SMALLEY ON TREASON.—SEIZURE OF ARMS IN NEW YORK CITY.—ACTION OF ITS MAYOR.

ANOTHER incident of the same 13th of February illustrates the rapidity with which the spirit of national patriotism was overcoming the ties of party, and driving good men into their true relations to the coming contest. Hon. David A. Smalley, of Vermont, had, in the nominating convention, powerfully contributed to, if he had not caused, the nomination of Mr. Buchanan. He was chairman of the Democratic National Committee which conducted the successful campaign, and he had been rewarded by Mr. Buchanan with the appointment of Judge of the Federal Court for the District of Vermont. The appointment was political, and few supposed that he would exhibit any sympathies of a higher type than those for his party.

He proved a national disappointment, especially to those who imagined that he would carry his politics upon the bench, or that he would not interfere with treasonable practices, because indulged in by Southern Democrats.

Judge Smalley held the January term of the Federal Court in the Southern District of New York. In his charge to the grand jury he had defined in vigorous terms the elements of the crime of treason, and the duty of grand juries to make inquest and present every guilty person. He was the first Federal judge who mentioned the subject, and on that account and because of its energetic language the charge attracted wide attention, and one result of its influence was the seizure by the police of New York City of a consignment of arms to the state of Georgia, only a few days after the charge was delivered. This seizure was denounced in severe terms by Mayor Fernando Wood, in a correspondence with Senator Toombs of Georgia, as an unjustifiable and illegal interference with private property, for which the city of New York ought not to be held responsible, because the mayor, most unfortunately, had no control over the police, or he would have summarily punished such an outrage. This semi-proclamation of the mayor of New York had given great comfort to our Southern brethren in Washington, who regarded it as a guarantee against further interference with such shipments, and a sure indication that the commercial cities of the North, particularly New York, warmly sympathized with secession, and rejected the views of Judge Smalley.

Nor was this conclusion of the active agents of secession so remarkable as it may appear to the present generation. Some weeks before Judge Smalley hurled his judicial bolt against Northern traitors, South Carolina had defined treason to consist in adhering to the enemies of that commonwealth, and giving them aid and comfort; a crime to be punished with death and an added penalty, supposed to be especially severe where Christian observances were so universal, death *without benefit of clergy!* A leading newspaper in Alabama had announced that Mr. Lincoln's life would not be worth a week's purchase after a single gun had been fired against Fort Sumter. Mr. Benjamin had taken leave of the Senate in what he called "a conciliatory speech," in which he prophesied that the South could never be subjugated, a prediction received by the packed galleries with uproarious shouts of applause. When, after such expressions, the mayor of New York declared that interference with the shipment of guns into the South, to be used against the government, was a lawless interference with private rights of property, it is not singular that inexperienced traitors deemed it safe to continue their treasonable commerce in contempt of Judge Smalley's charge.

The announcement of the election of Mr. Lincoln was not the only act of oppression which the 13th of February imposed upon the persecuted agents of secession. They had shipped another consignment from New York, this time of fixed ammunition, on a steamer bound for the port of Charleston, and the incorrigible police, not having the fear of the mayor before their eyes, had seized and carried it away. Instead of ordering the ammunition to be released without notice and without delay, Judge Smalley had returned the papers to the lawyer who made the application, with an expression of his regret that the police "had not also seized the rascals who made the shipment." This seizure was the subject of extended comment in Washington, and among the secessionists the opinion was almost universal that they could not remain in a Union where such tyranny was tolerated.

IX.

AN ALTERCATION IN THE PEACE CONFERENCE.—SENATOR LOT
M. MORRILL AND COMMODORE STOCKTON.—A TEST OF NORTH-
ERN COURAGE.

THE Northern delegates so conducted themselves as to secure the respect of the gentlemen from the South, and were careful to avoid contact with the rougher classes. In the good-natured discussions, which sometimes occurred, of the relative fighting qualities of the representatives of the two sections, the Northerners generally admitted (at all events they did not deny) that they were not fighting men, and held with Falstaff that discretion was the better part of valor. An incident occurred in the Conference, however, which may be worth relating, for it produced an impression that some Northern men, notwithstanding their protestations, were not altogether destitute of personal courage.

Two days after the peaceable election of Mr. Lincoln had been proclaimed, and before the heated brains of many Southern visitors to the capital were reduced to their normal temperature, the Committee on Resolutions made a majority and minority report to the Conference. That of the minority may be dismissed as unimportant; that of the majority recommended amendments to the Federal Constitution, which should assert the right of the owner to transport his slave *through* any state or territory and *into* any state or territory south of latitude 36° 30′; the admission of new states north or south of that parallel with or without slavery, as the people of the new state might determine; that slavery in the District of Columbia should not be abolished without the consent of Maryland; and that, when these amendments were adopted, they, with certain other articles of the Constitution, should not be changed without the consent of all the states.

These propositions were not prolix, but they were a comprehensive abandonment of the vital principles upon which the people had just passed final, decisive judgment in the election of Mr. Lincoln. It may appear incredible, after the lapse of time, but it is the fact that many delegates from the free states—four out of the nine from the state, and one of them from the city of New York— were ready and voted to accept these drastic measures, solely to avoid a civil war, without any pledge that one of the six states which had then seceded would return to the Union. While the majority of the Committee claimed that their report presented fair terms of compromise, which all the states ought to accept as conditions of perpetual union, Mr. Seddon, of Virginia, objected to them, because they did not contain sufficient guarantees; in fact, because they did not render the humiliation of the free states sufficiently abject.

The general debate was opened by Mr. Seddon. He was the most conspicuous and active member of his delegation, which comprised several distinguished men. His personal appearance was extraordinary. His frame was fleshless as that of John Randolph, and he was equally with that statesman intense in his hatred of all forms of Northern life—from the statesman of New England to the sheep that fed upon her hillsides. The pallor of his face, his narrow chest, sunken eyes, and attenuated frame indicated the last stages of consumption. His voice, husky at first, cleared with the excitement of debate, in which he became eloquent. Notwithstanding his spectral appearance, he survived to become Secretary of War in the Confederacy. He was the most powerful debater of the Conference, skilful, adroit, cunning, the soul of the plot which the Conference was intended to execute. His speech was an arraignment of the free states for offences of which they were not guilty, a picture of the moral beauties of the domestic institution, an attempted demonstration of the equity of the demands of Virginia. He had no word of condemnation for secession, of hope for the return of South Carolina and the five other states which by that time had seceded. He struck the key-note of the debate for slavery, and many Southern speeches followed in the same key. Instead of arguing in favor of the report of the majority, the position of the speakers appeared to be opposition to any compromise which did not involve the complete humiliation of the North.

The effective answer to the speech of Mr. Seddon from a Northern Republican came from Maine, a state represented in the Conference by her Congressional delegation. It was made by Lot M. Morrill, one of her senators. His age was about sixty years, his figure rather slight, his manner retiring, and his general appearance somewhat effeminate. There was not a trace of the bully in his composition, not the slightest suspicion of aggressiveness in his character. On the contrary, he would have been selected as almost the last man in the Conference to become involved in a personal controversy —as one naturally disposed to concession, who would yield much for the sake of peace. He was never an abolitionist of the extreme type, but he was an early free-soiler, and a good representative of his state in her steadfast opposition to the extension of the territory or the political influence of slavery. His quiet, peaceful nature was deceptive to strangers; for at the bottom lay a stratum of resolution which would have carried him to the stake before he would surrender a natural right or abandon an important principle, His ideas were clear and decided. He possessed great facility in expression and a command of language which qualified him for the discussion of great questions with a power and force seldom excelled in any legislative body.

Commodore Stockton was one of the delegates from New Jersey. Imperious and overbearing by nature, his long service in the navy had accustomed him to command, and rendered him intolerant of opposition, or any contradiction of the opinions which he entertained. His age must have been above seventy years; he stood six feet high. His physique was powerful and his manner authoritative. He was a Northern man with Southern principles. He had a lofty admiration for the Southern character, and entertained pro-slavery views of a more pronounced type than those of the delegates from the Border slave-states. He would have been selected as the most fiery, Senator Morrill as the least combative, member of the Conference.

Although the Republicans had abandoned all expectation of any beneficial results from the Conference, and were not very attentive to the debate, Senator Morrill had not been many minutes on his feet before he had a large body of interested auditors. His voice, at first low and quiet, gathered volume as he proceeded, until, as he approached the real points in controversy, his lucid arguments cut like a Damascus blade.

"You tell us," he said, "that our multiplied offences are more than you can endure; that our unfriendly criticisms of slavery, our obstructions to the surrender of the fugitive slaves, our opposition to the admission of Kansas with a constitution which tolerates slavery, justify extreme measures on your part; that, although some have left the Union, the states here represented will condone our offences by one more compromise. But only upon one condition: that we consent to write it into the fundamental law that slavery is to be perpetual in the republic, and that any territory with sufficient population, wherever situated, shall, if its people so vote, come into the Union as a slave state, and its status once fixed, shall be forever unchangeable.

"I shall not now debate the issues of the past; I look to the future. I agree with you that the time has come to settle for all future time the grave questions which have disturbed our peace. You say that there is but one way to settle them. That the North must accept what you term another compromise, or the Union must perish.

"We have made compromises before, not one of which was ever broken by the North, by every one of which the South ultimately refused to abide. You proposed the Missouri Compromise. You solemnly agreed that all the states north of 36° 30' should be free. How you kept the faith let Kansas answer! You demanded the Fugitive Slave Act as a condition of preserving the Union. Your demand was conceded, and your slaves have been returned to you by Northern hands from under the shadow of Bunker Hill. Now you demand another compromise which changes a free republic into slave territory. You say the North *must* make the concession as the price of union. *Must* is a word which does not promote a settlement founded upon compromise. If we *must*, what then? There is in your propositions of amendment no pledge, no promise on the part of the South. What does the South propose to do? If we assent to the terms, will South Carolina—will the Gulf states return to the Union? Or will the South repeat her history?—do as she has always done before?—perform her agreement as long as it will serve her interests, and then violate—"

"Silence, sir!" shouted a voice from a gigantic form, which rushed towards Senator Morrill with violent and angry gesticulations. "We will not permit our Southern friends to be charged with bad faith, and with violating an agreement! No black Republican shall—"

The sentence was never completed. In a moment, by a common impulse, twenty or thirty Republicans were on the floor, and had surrounded Senator Morrill like a living wall. "Back to your seat, you bully!" exclaimed a stalwart Vermonter, the equal of Commodore Stockton in size and his superior in strength and activity. The Southerners rushed to the assistance of their volunteer defender. They could not check the impetus of his compulsory retreat, until he was forced into his seat. For an instant many believed an armed encounter was unavoidable. It was prevented by the prompt intervention of President Tyler.

"Order!" he shouted. "Shame upon the delegate who would dishonor this Conference by violence!" His command was obeyed; the danger passed as suddenly as it had arisen.

None of the actors in this scene were proud of their participation. Still, its influence was excellent. It would have surprised no one if a gentleman of Senator Morrill's delicate organization had exhibited some excitement or discomposure under such an aggressive attack, supported by an angry crowd which was restrained from bloodshed only by the effective interference of one of their number. But the senator's face was not flushed, nor his circulation apparently quickened by so much as one pulsation. Without a tremor in his voice, as soon as order was restored, he continued :

"As I was inquiring, Mr. President, is it the purpose of the representatives of the slave-power to force this compromise upon us, and then to violate it, as they have violated all former compromises? You are wasting your time, gentlemen. Until some one, having authority, will pledge the South, including the seceded states, to accept your proposed amendments as a finality, and henceforth to abide in the Union, the North will never consider the subject of their acceptance! Never! Never!"

Very soon afterwards, possibly on the following evening, in a mixed company of moderate Northern and Southern men, this occurrence was adverted to. An able and courteous Kentuckian, addressing an ex-governor of a New England state, widely known and loved as one of the purest and most amiable of men, observed :

"I do not understand why you New-Englanders so persistently repudiate the possession of personal courage. We know in Kentucky that our citizens of New England origin are destitute of fear. Senator Morrill showed to-day that he had courage enough and to spare. The men that hurried to his support were New England men. Are you quite ingenuous? Is this a time to inculcate a false estimate of Northern character? I prefer that the South should understand what I know, that, in the quality of personal courage, Northern men have no superiors, certainly not in the South. Had the South been more accurately informed on the subject, we should not have drifted so near to revolution!"

"I think you misjudge us," replied Governor H——. "Northern men do not know whether they are men of courage or not. How is one to know whether or not he is a coward until he is put to the test? The masses of

Northern men go through life without any experience on this subject. You would not have us assume a virtue which we are not certain of possessing?"

"I would have both sections form just estimates of the character and qualities of each," said the Kentuckian. "I do not regret the occurrence in the Conference. I am quite certain that it will lead to a better judgment among our people of the Northern men."

This conversation took place many years ago. I have never since heard from an intelligent Southerner any expression of doubt as to the courage of Northern men. In the first year of the war, such rabid sheets as the Baltimore *Sun* and the Charleston *Mercury* were accustomed to use vile names, and to declare that a "flunkey," a "servile follower," was a local, an unadulterated Yankee product; but the experiences of the first twelve months of rebellion relegated such expressions to the era of many other Southern errors.

X.

THE CONSPIRACY OF ASSASSINATION.—ITS DETAILS.—MR. LINCOLN CONSENTS TO FOLLOW THE ADVICE OF HIS FRIENDS.

THE 4th of March was approaching. Rumors of intended revolution multiplied; evidences of a design to seize Washington augmented daily, attended by dark hints of some event which would paralyze the North and enable the Secessionists to secure the Capitol without loss of life. Gurowski openly said to the Republicans, "Lincoln is to be assassinated—I know it. I tell you of it in time for you to prevent it. I know that wagers at heavy odds have been laid that he will never reach Washington alive. Yet you do not believe what I tell you! It is not even an independent plot; it is part of the conspiracy of secession."

A small number of younger Republicans, then temporarily in Washington, had undertaken to act as an independent committee of safety. They were in active communication by wire with the principal Northern cities. The investigation and exposure of rumors was a part of their work.

On the afternoon of Sunday, February 17th, when we knew that the President-elect was in Buffalo, a messenger, duly authenticated, from reliable friends in Baltimore, came to Washington to tell us that they wished to have two or three members of our organization return with the messenger to that city. Their purpose in inviting us, the latter stated, would be explained on our arrival. It was too important to be trusted to the

mails or the telegraph, or even to be put upon paper.
He himself did not know what it was. He was directed
to say to us that our coming over that evening was
necessary to enable the Republican party of Baltimore
to sustain itself, and to be of any service in the coming
emergency.

It was arranged that, with a single companion, I
should take a late train that evening which made a stop
at the Relay House, a few miles out of Baltimore. My
associate was a contractor, accustomed to deal with large
bodies of foreigners. I was an acquaintance and friend
of the Republican who sent the invitation, but my companion and myself were alike strangers in Baltimore.
We took the train as arranged. It was boarded at the
Relay House by my Baltimore friend, who stared me in
the face, and then passed me without apparent recognition. A few minutes after the train started, a stranger
half stumbled along the aisle of the dimly lighted car,
partially fell over me, but grasped my hand as he recovered himself and apologized for his awkwardness.
I felt that he left a paper in my hand. I went into
the dressing-room to read it. It contained these words:
"Be cautious. At the station follow a driver who
will be shouting 'Hotel Fountain,' instead of 'Fountain
Hotel.' Enter his carriage. He is reliable and has his
directions."

I destroyed the paper. We followed its directions,
and were driven—where, I never knew. It was, however,
to a private residence. A gentleman waiting outside
showed us into the house, and the driver hurried away.
Our friend of the train came soon after, and we were
taken to an upper room where were half a dozen Republicans, to whom we were presented. No time was
wasted. Mr. H——, well known to me as a true Re-

publican, said: "We want you to help us save Baltimore from disgrace, and President Lincoln from assassination. We find our work difficult. We are watched and shadowed so that we cannot leave the city without exciting suspicion. We have sent messengers to leading Republicans in Washington, notifying them of the plot against the President's life; but they will not credit the story, nor, so far as we can learn, take any action. We also learn that Mr. Lincoln declares that he will pursue his journey openly, if he loses his life in consequence. Within ten minutes after the presidential train reaches the Canton station it will be surrounded by a mob of twenty thousand roughs and plug-uglies, from which he will never escape alive. We have every detail of the plot; we know the men who have been hired to kill him; we could lay our hands upon them to-night. But what are we to do if our friends will not believe our report?"

"You call the plot a certainty. What proof have you? Direct proof, I mean?"

"We will show you some of it. The sporting men gave it away by betting at odds that Mr. Lincoln would never reach Washington. Recently they have modified it by betting that he will not pass through Maryland alive. Then a woman about to be abandoned by her lover betrayed him to us—he had no scruples, and promptly sold his associates in the plot."

"You cannot condemn reputable men upon such evidence. He is an accomplice!"

"You should hear his story and its confirmations before you say that. Bring in the fellow!" he said to one of the company.

Two men entered the room with the supposed assassin. He looked the character. He represented a genus of the human family seen in pictures of Italian bandits. His square, bull-dog jaws, ferret-like eyes, furtively looking out from holes under a low brow, covered with a coarse mat of black hair; a dark face, every line of which was hard, and an impudent swagger in his carriage, sufficiently advertised him as a low, cowardly villain. I shall not attempt to imitate his dialect, or the shameless unconcern with which he described his bargain to murder and his betrayal of his associates.

"A bad president," he said, "was coming in the cars to free the negroes and drive all the foreigners out of the country. The good Americans wanted him killed. They had employed Ruscelli to do the job; Ruscelli was a barber who called himself Orsini since he escaped from Italy, where he was in trouble for killing some men who failed to pay their ransom. There were five who were to put the president out of life, who were to have each a hundred dollars, besides twenty dollars paid when they made the promise. They were to follow Ruscelli into the car. Each was to strike the president with a knife, to make sure. Then they were to go quick away to sea. Yes, the two gold eagles which Mr. H—— had were a part of his pay."

There were more details of the fellow's story. He and his associates were the mere tools. Their employers were known—they were secessionists, pot-house politicians of a low order, with some admixture of men of a better class, some of them in the police. Our friends had an agent who had joined the conspiracy and attended all the meetings. Through him they had learned that the murder had been several times in part rehearsed to avoid mistakes.

At that time the cars were drawn through the city by horses. At the end of a certain bridge the track was to be suddenly torn up. When the President's car was stopped at the obstruction the assassins were to follow their leader into the rear of the car, pass rapidly through it, each knifing the president, out at the forward door, through the crowd to a rum shop, at the rear of which lay a schooner, with a tug under steam, which would immediately go down the bay with the schooner in tow. Clearance papers would be provided for the port of Mobile, to which the schooner would as speedily as possible make her way. If he left the cars for a carriage, its progress was to be blocked, and the President killed at the same crossing. The whole work, it was found, from arresting the car to the departure of the schooner, could be done in five or six minutes. To add to the confusion, bombs and hand-grenades, which exploded by concussion, were to be thrown into the cars through the windows.

The seven or eight gentlemen present were reliable citizens of Baltimore. They had not believed at first that the conspiracy comprised any but members of the criminal class. Now they were satisfied that there were leading Secessionists privy to the plot; some of them influential politicians and citizens who had argued themselves into the belief that this was a patriotic work which would prevent greater bloodshed and possible war. They provided the money which had been used with a free hand in purchasing the schooner and taking measures to avoid detection. The disappearance of the hired ruffian and the woman through whom the plot was first discovered had made the conspirators watchful, and some of them had not only withdrawn from the plot, but had left the city. The others held nightly meetings, and had no intention of giving up the project. Our friends were now at a standstill, because Mr. Lincoln persisted in passing through the city openly, on the day appointed, and the leading Republicans of Washington would not accept the evidences of the conspiracy.

"Why," we asked, "do not the Republicans of Baltimore arm, organize, and themselves protect the President in his journey through the city?"

"Because," they replied, "the police, from superintendent to patrolmen, would oppose us and protect the conspirators. The Plug-Uglies of Baltimore number thousands, and have been notorious for years as the worst fighting roughs in existence. If Mr. Lincoln's train reaches the Canton station, it will, within five minutes, be surrounded by a crowd of rowdies. If he takes a carriage, the crowd will block it, and have ample time to tear him to pieces. If driven to the car, as they intend he shall be, he cannot pass the bridge. What can we do, with the police, the roughs, and the Secessionists against us? It would require disciplined regiments to control them. They will surround the car or the carriage, they will swoop down upon it like vultures, or swarm over it like monkeys. No, we have done all that men can do; we have the names of the conspirators; we have agents who attend their meetings, who contribute to their expenses. We know that they are not all hired assassins. There are men among them who believe they are serving their country. One of them is an actor who recites passages from the tragedy of Julius Cæsar in their conclaves. They are abundantly supplied with money. Where does it come from, if not from men of substance? No, gentlemen, we have done everything in our power! If the government itself will not interfere, and if, as he declares he will, Mr. Lincoln insists on passing through Baltimore in open day, on the train appointed, his murder is inevitable. We have invited you here that you might convince yourselves, and to ask you to help us to convince others. Have we satisfied you?"

"I am satisfied," said my companion, "and I believe I can satisfy General Scott. But I should like first to wring the neck of that miscreant in the other room, and carry his head to Washington as a voucher of the plot!"

The consultation was prolonged until it was time for an early morning train to Washington. In the gray of the morning we drove to the house of Elihu B. Washburn, called him from his bed, and in a few words summed up our night's experience, with the statement that we had come for his assistance in precautionary measures.

He said that we might put aside our anxiety; that he knew positively that Mr. Lincoln had determined to follow the advice of his friends, and would reach Washington without risk. It was deemed wise that none but those who had charge of the President's journey should know by what route or at what time he would pass through Baltimore, but that he himself, Mr. Seward, and General Scott had become satisfied that precautions must be taken to protect his life, and they would be effectual.

XI.
HOW DID MR. LINCOLN "GET THROUGH BALTIMORE"?

THE story of Mr. Lincoln's journey through Baltimore, as recorded in history, requires some correction. Like other sufferers by the hat of the period, he was provided with a knitted woollen cap for use in the cars, particularly at night. This he wore on his night-trip to Washington. The myth of the disguise and the Scotch cap had "this extent, no more." There was no necessity for disguise. Mr. Lincoln entered the sleeping-car at Philadelphia, and slept until awakened within a few miles of Washington.

The street-lights were not yet extinguished on the early morning of the 23d of February, when Elihu B. Washburn and Senator Seward stepped from a carriage at the ladies' entrance of Willard's Hotel. A tall man, with a striking face, followed them into the hall, the swinging doors closed, and the future president and preserver of the republic was safely housed in its capital. The pledge of Mr. Washburn had been kept, and Republicans could lay aside their anxiety.

There were a few Republicans whose faces shone as they greeted each other, when they met at the opening of the Conference that day. They were in the secret of Mr. Lincoln's arrival. Members were not particular about the position of their seats, and mine then happened to be between one occupied by Mr. Seddon and that of Waldo P. Johnson, an impulsive Secessionist, afterwards a Confederate general, who then, in part, represented Missouri. The body-servant of whom Mr. Seddon was then proprietor was a man scarcely darker than himself, his equal in deportment, his superior in figure and carriage. This chattel had made himself a favorite by his civil and respectful manner, and by general consent was the only person, not a member or officer, who had the *entrée* to the sessions of the Conference.

As soon as the meeting was called to order, this servant approached his master and handed him a scrap of paper, apparently torn from an envelope. Mr. Seddon glanced at it, and passed it before me to Mr. Johnson, so near to my face that, without closing my eyes, I could not avoid reading it. The words written upon it were, "Lincoln is in this hotel!"

The Missourian was startled as by a shock of electricity. He must have forgotten himself completely, for he instantly exclaimed, "How the devil did he get through Baltimore?" With a look of utter contempt for the indiscretion of the impulsive trans-Mississippian, the Virginian growled, "What would prevent his passing through Baltimore?"

There was no reply, but the occurrence left the impression on one mind that the preparations to receive Mr. Lincoln in Baltimore were known to some who were neither Italian assassins nor Baltimore Plug-Uglies. Mr. Johnson was not the only delegate surprised by the announcement of Mr. Lincoln's presence in Washington. As the news circulated in whispers through the hall, members gathered in groups to discuss it, and were too much absorbed to hear the repeated calls of the chairman to order. No event of the Conference, not even the collision between Commodore Stockton and Senator Morrill, produced so much excitement. The member who was addressing the chair, after repeated attempts to make himself heard above the din of voices, gave up the effort and resumed his seat. It was not until some one had moved an adjournment that the burden of preparation weighing upon so many members, and the danger of losing the opportunity of delivering their speeches, combined to restore order and enable the Conference to resume its business.

But the attempt to go on with the debate was unavailing. The fact of the arrival of the President-elect was quickly known to every one. Members were not in a condition of mind to make speeches or to listen to them. There was a hurried consultation among the Republicans, which resulted in a motion by Mr. Logan, one of the delegates from Mr. Lincoln's state, that the president of the Conference wait upon the President-elect and inform him that the Conference would be pleased to visit him in a body at such a time as would suit his convenience. This motion was fiercely opposed. Waste of precious time was the open ground of opposition. There were cries of "No! no! Vote it down!" "Lay it on the table!" with exclamations, in an undertone, of "Rail-splitter!" "Ignoramus!" "Vulgar clown!" etc. Again President Tyler interfered to prevent the making of a disreputable record. He declared that "the proposal was eminently proper; that the office, and not the individual, was to be considered; that he hoped that no Southern member would decline to treat the incoming President with the same respect and attention already extended to the present incumbent of that honorable and exalted office." These appropriate observations suppressed the opposition; the motion of Mr. Logan was unanimously adopted, and the Conference, having resolved upon an evening session, adjourned.

XII.

A SECOND PRESIDENTIAL RECEPTION.—MR. LINCOLN CONVERSES WITH LEADING SOUTHERNERS.—HIS DUTY TO THE CONSTITUTION.

THE Republican members of the Conference were not pleased with the manner in which the chairman performed his duty. Instead of *waiting upon the President-elect in person*, as directed by the vote, he announced at the evening session that he had addressed him a note of inquiry, in reply to which Mr. Lincoln said that he would be happy to receive the members at nine o'clock that evening, or at such other time as might suit their convenience. As Mr. Lincoln had taken no exception to the manner of the invitation, and as President Tyler could have pleaded the communication to Mr. Buchanan as a precedent, they decided to raise no question about what was, after all, but a mere matter of form.

I thought it might prove of advantage to Mr. Lincoln to have some information in advance of the men who would meet him that evening. I therefore called upon him, with the intention of informing him who would visit him out of respect, and who would come out of curiosity, or only to jeer and ridicule. This, my first meeting with him, was an event which would have been more impressive had I then appreciated that he was the greatest of Americans, whose life-labors would restore the broken Union, and whose death would cement the foundations of the republic.

As I entered his apartment, a tall, stooping figure,

upon which his clothing hung loosely and ungracefully, advanced to meet me. His kindly eyes looked out from under a cavernous, projecting brow, with a curiously mingled expression of sadness and humor. His limbs were long, and at first sight ungainly. But in the cordial grasp of his large hands, the cheery tones of his pleasant voice, the heartiness of his welcome, in the air and presence of the great-hearted man, there was an ascendency which caused me to forget my errand, and to comprehend why it was that Abraham Lincoln won from all classes and conditions of men a love that "was wonderful, passing the love of women." "He was pleased," he said, "to have an opportunity of meeting so many representative men from different sections of the Union; the more unjust they were in their opinions of himself, the more he desired to make their acquaintance. He had been represented as an evil spirit, a goblin, the implacable enemy of Southern men and women. He did not set up for a beauty, but he was confident that, upon a close acquaintance, they would not find him so ugly nor so black as he had been painted. He hoped every delegate from the slave states would be present, especially those most prejudiced against himself. He mentioned one or two whom he had known in Congress; also Mr. Rives and Judge Ruffin, as influential statesmen whom he particularly wished to know. I left him, having said nothing I had intended to, with a conviction that he would require no guardian. From that first visit to the time when my more matured judgment and intimate knowledge of the noble qualities of his mind and heart led me to account him the greatest of Americans, he never ceased to grow in my esteem.

The hour of nine arrived; the Conference adjourned, so that those who wished might attend Mr. Lincoln's reception. Not, as when we called on President Buchanan, were we formed in procession and marshalled on our way, preceded by our presiding officer; but in straggling groups we made our way as best we might to the drawing-room, in which the President-elect was to be placed on exhibition, before what was, in the main, a most unfriendly audience. No delegate from a slave state had voted for him; many entertained for him sentiments of positive hatred. I heard him discussed as a curiosity by men as they would have spoken of a clown with whose ignorant vulgarity they were to be amused. They took him for an unlettered boor, with no fixed principles, whose nomination was an accident, and his election the victory of the ultra anti-slavery faction. A small number of more conservative men from the slave, and very nearly a majority of the delegates from the free states, were inclined to respect his office, but regarded its prospective incumbent as an extremist, with no qualification for its duties. Some queried whether, like old John Brown, he actually longed for an insurrection of the slaves. Even the small minority of his political supporters, who had resolved in their hearts that he should be inaugurated, though stanch in his defence, had not discovered his intellectual strength, and suspected few of his sterling qualities.

An experienced politician would have prepared himself for such an occasion. In fact, his friends anticipated that Mr. Lincoln would conduct himself with extreme reserve, and use great caution in the expression of his opinions.

Mr. Lincoln had not made the slightest preparation. He stood in the corner of one of the public drawing-rooms of the hotel alone, unattended. Mr. Lamon, who had accompanied him from his home, and who it was understood he would appoint marshal of the district, was not present until a later hour. No one had been provided to introduce the delegates or give any direction to the proceedings. I observed the omission as I entered the room, and, there being no time to stand upon ceremony, took a position, as if by arrangement, at Mr. Lincoln's side, and presented each member of the Conference by name. Their number was as large as that present at President Buchanan's reception. A general curiosity prevailed to witness the manner in which the incoming President would conduct himself, and many wished, by a closer observation of his appearance and awkwardness, to nourish their contempt for the "railsplitter." Many "who came to scoff" did not find the entertainment to their liking, if they did not "remain to pray."

An experienced public man, who had travelled constantly for ten consecutive days, making from one to four addresses daily, who had just escaped a conspiracy against his life, might have pleaded some excuse if, within fifteen hours after his arrival, in his first public appearance, and before a contemptuously inimical audience, he had failed to seem entirely at his ease. But it was soon discovered that the friends of Mr. Lincoln might dismiss whatever anxiety they might have felt on his account. He was able to take care of himself. The manner in which he adjusted his conversation to representatives of different sections and opinions was striking. He could not have appeared more natural or unstudied in his manner if he had been entertaining a company of neighbors in his Western home.

Mr. Lincoln's reception of the delegates was of an entirely informal character. There was no crowded approach, nor hurried disappearance; no procession of the members beyond where he stood. *There* was a point of attraction—not of repulsion. As the guests were successively and cordially received, they gathered round him in a circle, which enlarged and widened, until it comprised most of the delegates. His tall figure and animated face towered above them, the most striking in a group of noted Americans. His words arrested the attention; his wonderful vivacity surprised every spectator. He spoke apparently without premeditation, with a singular ease of manner and facility of expression. He had some apt observation for each person ready the moment he heard his name. " You are a smaller man than I supposed—I mean in person: every one is acquainted with the greatness of your intellect. It is, indeed, pleasant to meet one who has so honorably represented his country in Congress and abroad." Such was his greeting to William C. Rives, of Virginia, a most cultivated and polished gentleman. " Your name is all the endorsement you require," he said to James B. Clay. " From my boyhood the name of Henry Clay has been an inspiration to me." " You cannot be a disunionist, unless your nature has changed since we met in Congress!" he exclaimed as he recognized the strong face of Geo. W. Summers, of Western Virginia. " Does liberty still thrive in the mountains of Tennessee?" he inquired as Mr. Zollicoffer's figure, almost as tall as his own, came into view. After so many years, much that he said is forgotten, but it is remembered that he had for every delegation, almost for every man, some appropriate remark, which was forcible, and apparently unstudied.

There was only one occurrence which threatened to disturb the harmony and good humor of the reception. In reply to a complimentary remark by Mr. Lincoln, Mr. Rives had said that, although he had retired from public life, he could not decline the request of the Governor of Virginia that he should unite in this effort to save the Union. "But," he continued, "the clouds that hang over it are very dark. I have no longer the courage of my younger days. I can do little—you can do much. Everything now depends upon you."

"I cannot agree to that," replied Mr. Lincoln. "My course is as plain as a turnpike road. It is marked out by the Constitution. I am in no doubt which way to go. Suppose now we all stop discussing and try the experiment of obedience to the Constitution and the laws. Don't you think it would work?"

."Permit me to answer that suggestion," interposed Mr. Summers. "Yes, it will work. If the Constitution is your light, I will follow it with you, and the people of the South will go with us."

"It is not of your professions we complain," sharply struck in Mr. Seddon's sepulchral voice. "It is of your sins of omission—of your failure to enforce the laws— to suppress your John Browns and your Garrisons, who preach insurrection and make war upon our property!"

"I believe John Brown was hung and Mr. Garrison imprisoned," dryly remarked Mr. Lincoln. "You cannot justly charge the North with disobedience to statutes or with failing to enforce them. You have made some which were very offensive, but they have been enforced, notwithstanding."

"You do not enforce the laws," persisted Mr. Seddon. "You refuse to execute the statute for the return of fugitive slaves. Your leading men openly declare that they will not assist the marshals to capture or return slaves."

"You are wrong in your facts again," said Mr. Lincoln. "Your slaves have been returned, yes, from the shadow of Faneuil Hall in the heart of Boston. Our people do not like the work, I know. They will do what the law commands, but they will not volunteer to act as tip-staves or bum-bailiffs. The instinct is natural to the race. Is it not true of the South? Would you join in the pursuit of a fugitive slave if you could avoid it? Is such the work of gentlemen?"

"Your press is incendiary!" said Mr. Seddon, changing his base. "It advocates servile insurrection, and advises our slaves to cut their masters' throats. You do not suppress your newspapers. You encourage their violence."

"I beg your pardon, Mr. Seddon," replied Mr. Lincoln. "I intend no offence, but I will not suffer such a statement to pass unchallenged, because it is not true. No Northern newspaper, not the most ultra, has advocated a slave insurrection or advised the slaves to cut their masters' throats. A gentleman of your intelligence should not make such assertions. We do maintain the freedom of the press—we deem it necessary to a free government. Are we peculiar in that respect? Is not the same doctrine held in the South?"

It was reserved for the delegation from New York to call out from Mr. Lincoln his first expression touching the great controversy of the hour. He exchanged remarks with ex-Governor King, Judge James, William Curtis Noyes, and Francis Granger. William E. Dodge had stood, awaiting his turn. As soon as his opportunity came, he raised his voice enough to be heard by all present, and, addressing Mr. Lincoln, declared that the whole country in great anxiety was awaiting his inaugural address, and then added: "It is for you, sir, to say whether the whole nation shall be plunged into bankruptcy; whether the grass shall grow in the streets of our commercial cities."

"Then I say it shall not," he answered, with a merry twinkle of his eye. "If it depends upon me, the grass will not grow anywhere except in the fields and the meadows."

"Then you will yield to the just demands of the South. You will leave her to control her own institutions. You will admit slave states into the Union on the same conditions as free states. You will not go to war on account of slavery!"

A sad but stern expression swept over Mr. Lincoln's face. "I do not know that I understand your meaning, Mr. Dodge," he said, without raising his voice, "nor do I know what my acts or my opinions may be in the future, beyond this. If I shall ever come to the great office of President of the United States, I shall take an oath. I shall swear that I will faithfully execute the office of President of the United States, of all the United States, and that I will, to the best of my ability, preserve, protect, and defend the Constitution of the United States. This is a great and solemn duty. With the support of the people and the assistance of the Almighty I shall undertake to perform it. I have full faith that I shall perform it. It is not the Constitution as I would like to have it, but as it *is*, that is to be defended. The Constitution will not be preserved and defended until it is enforced and obeyed in every part of every one of the United States. It must be so respected, obeyed, enforced, and defended, let the grass grow where it may."

Not a word or a whisper broke the silence while these words of weighty import were slowly falling from his lips. They were so comprehensive and unstudied, they exhibited such inherent authority, that they seemed a statement of a sovereign decree, rather than one of fact which admitted of debate. Comment or criticism upon them seemed out of order. Mr. Dodge attempted no reply. The faces of the Republicans wore an expression of surprised satisfaction. Some of the more ardent Southerners silently left the room. They were unable to comprehend the situation. The ignorant countryman they had come to ridicule threatened no crime but obedience to the Constitution. This was not the entertainment to which they were invited, and it was uninteresting. For the more conservative Southern delegates, the statesmen, . Mr. Lincoln seemed to offer an attraction. They remained until he finally retired.

A delegate from New Jersey asked Mr. Lincoln pointedly if the North should not make further concessions to avoid civil war? For example, consent that the people of a territory should determine its right to authorize slavery when admitted into the Union?

"It will be time to consider that question when it arises," he replied. "Now we have other questions which we must decide. In a choice of evils, war may not always be the worst. Still I would do all in my power to avert it, except to neglect a Constitutional duty. As to slavery, it must be content with what it has. The voice of the civilized world is against it; it is opposed to its growth or extension. Freedom is the natural condition of the human race, in which the Almighty intended men to live. Those who fight the purposes of the Almighty will not succeed. They always have been, they always will be, beaten."

A general conversation followed, in which Judges Brockenbrough and Ruffin and Mr. Summers sought to draw from him some more definite expression of his views concerning the seceded states. Without exhibiting the slightest desire to conceal his opinions, he gave no further expression to them. His own duty, as defined by the Constitution, seemed to engross his mind. The Union must be maintained if the Constitution was to be enforced as the supreme law of the land. If he became President, all the executive powers of the government would be used to enforce obedience to the supreme law. Further than this, he had nothing to say.

After the reception several of the delegates commented upon the remarks of the President-elect. Mr. Rives expressed the change in his own opinions concerning him with perfect candor. "He has been both misjudged and misunderstood by the Southern people," he said. "They have looked upon him as an ignorant, self-willed man, incapable of independent judgment, full of prejudices, willing to be used as a tool by more able men. This is all wrong. He will be the head of his administration, and he will do his own thinking. He seems to have studied the Constitution, to have adopted it as his guide. I do not see that much fault can be found with the views he has expressed this evening. He is probably not so great a statesman as Mr. Madison, he may not have the will-power of General Jackson. He may combine the qualities of both. His will not be a weak administration."

Judge Ruffin regarded his pronounced opinions against concessions as a misfortune. The controversy had been carried so far that great concessions must be made to avoid actual conflict. Still, he could not find much fault with Mr. Lincoln's opinions. They were evidently founded upon the Constitution.

At the close of this interview Mr. Lincoln had not been twenty-four hours in Washington. That he had created a profound impression, favorable to himself, was undeniable. The Republican members of the Conference felt encouraged and strengthened by his presence. The sympathizers with secession were correspondingly discouraged and depressed.

XIII.
THE LAST WEEK OF PRESIDENT BUCHANAN'S ADMINISTRATION.

THE forces which change the current of public opinion are often remote and difficult of discovery. One of the most unexpected of these changes, occurring within my experience, was synchronous with Mr. Lincoln's arrival in Washington. Before that day the growth of disunion had been vigorous. True, it had met with some checks, principally caused by the indiscretion of those who should have been, and in the future would be, excluded from the higher councils of the leaders. These checks had compelled the postponement of the seizure of the capital. General Dix, Judge Holt, and Mr. Stanton had been disturbing agencies in the cabinet, and General Scott had made trouble by his contemptuous refusal to listen to or temporize with secession. On the other hand, six states were already out of the Union; others were ready to follow, a confederacy had been formed, its president and general officers elected; successive delegations had taken leave of Congress, declaring that the South could never be subjugated; military supplies, money, and other national property to a large value had been transferred from the North into the seceded states; the national credit had been undermined. Newspapers and influential leaders in Northern cities had declared against the use of force to subjugate the South; the Peace Conference had performed its allotted service, secession in Maryland and Virginia was ripening, and

Congress would soon adjourn, leaving a weakened government without means of defence or resistance. On the whole the situation was satisfactory, the future promising, and the capture of the government on the 4th of March assured. It could be accomplished without bloodshed, if General Scott and "his janizaries" would not interfere. The secessionists were confident, the friends of the Union verging towards despondency.

A change in the situation came unexpectedly. It was coextensive with the political horizon, it was written upon the faces of the people of Washington and of the strangers within her gates. It began on the morning after Mr. Lincoln's arrival, and before evening it had pervaded the community. Ten regiments of veterans, coming to reinforce General Scott's handful of soldiers, could not have more effectually annihilated the plot for armed seizure of the capital on the morning of the day of inauguration.

Nor was the arrival of Mr. Lincoln the only event which occurred to darken the prospects of the disunionists. They had counted upon the support of the Northern Democrats, and of the conservative element in the Republican party. It was a common saying among them that no regiment for the subjugation of the South would be permitted to pass through the city of New York. But now, the example of General Cass, the ringing command of General Dix for the protection of the flag, Mr. Stanton's bold declaration to the President that the surrender of the forts and property in Charleston Harbor was an indictable crime, and the far-reaching, though more quiet, influence of that patriotic Kentuckian, Judge Holt, began to call back responsive echoes from the North and West. I cannot enumerate these, but I must not omit to mention one of the first and most powerful, the letter from that tried old Democrat, General Wool. These statements proclaimed a united North: Douglass Democrats, the numerical majority and all the best elements of Democracy, together with Republicans and men of no party, declared they would give short shrift and swift execution to any who should raise the hand of treason in the capital of the republic.

It was also quickly known that Mr. Lincoln would call into his cabinet representative men like Senators Seward, Chase, and Cameron, who would unite the country if they did not constitute a united cabinet, and that he would offer one or two places to true men from the disloyal states. General Scott also was strengthening his defences. Several volunteer companies of the most loyal young men in Washington had been organized, and had received their guns and ammunition. They would be ready for service on a few moments' notice. Another type of American now became common in the streets of Washington. They were the young stalwart Republicans from all sections of the North and West who had been influential in the election of Mr. Lincoln, and who had come to give their personal attention to his inauguration. They became quite as numerous as the visitors with slouched hats from the Border states, and they had very promptly offered their services to General Scott to act as guards, as soldiers, or as policemen on the day of inauguration.

Whether the joint operation of these events was the cause of the change, or whether the actual presence of the President-elect produced it in whole or in part, the fact of the change was beyond dispute. The precautions were not relaxed, but the extreme solicitude, which had previously influenced loyal men, had completely disappeared. Instead of the excitement anticipated, the last days of the Peace Conference were positively dull. The absence of David Dudley Field when the final vote was recorded, of which an unfair advantage was taken by some of his colleagues, and the decision of the presiding officer that the vote of New York should be controlled by the delegates present, and not cast as directed by the resolution adopted by a clear majority of all the delegates from that state on the previous evening, neutralized the vote of New York, and led to the adoption of the amendments proposed by the majority of the Conference Committee on Resolutions by the slender majority of one vote. Such a result carried no weight with Congress or the country. The proposed amendments were submitted to the Senate and to the House. But it was during the last hours of the session, and neither house would permit them to be brought before it for action. They were offered in the Senate by way of an amendment to the well-known Crittenden Resolutions, and rejected by a vote of twenty-eight to seven. The Conference adjourned on the 27th of February, having served the purpose of its originators and done one good work for the country—that of uniting the Republicans and many Democrats in the defence of the Union.

From Monday, the 25th of February, to Monday, the 4th of March, a kind of paralysis appeared to have fallen upon the disunionists. They did almost nothing to attract public attention. The usual arrangements with the outgoing administration were made for the inauguration. The city was crowded with visitors, so that there was a large overflow to Georgetown and Baltimore. The event which attracted the greatest measure of public attention was an address by Senator Seward to a body of his constituents who called upon him in

Washington, and the chief point of interest in this was its omission to disclose any of the purposes of the incoming administration, of which it was understood that he was to become the premier.

XIV.
THE INAUGURATION.—A MEMORABLE SCENE.

A BRIGHT sun rose over the city of Washington on March 4th, the day appointed by law for the inauguration of President Lincoln. It was an orderly city; a stranger would not have suspected that any preparations had been made to suppress insurrection, or that the necessity for such precautions existed. The leading secessionists had taken their departure. Those who remained belonged to the reckless, disorderly class, below the average respectability of the party they served. Since the influx of Northern Republicans, these roughs had become less demonstrative, so that it was safe for ladies and gentlemen to make use of the streets and sidewalks. Some experiments had been tried in insulting and jostling the recent arrivals, which had resulted disagreeably for the assailants, who were much depressed by another postponement of the revolution. General Scott had stationed his small force of regulars and volunteers where they were inconspicuous, but could be made serviceable at very short notice. His dispositions had been so quietly made that surprise was expressed because so little had apparently been done by way of preparation.

At an early hour a dense multitude occupied both sides of the avenue from the Executive Mansion to the foot of Capitol Hill, where it divided, surrounding the grounds and filling the open space and the square on the east front of the Capitol, on the steps of which a broad platform had been erected, whence the inaugural address was to be delivered. At all the street crossings platforms with seats had been built, all of which were crowded. Every window overlooking the avenue was filled with the bright costumes of ladies and children, while many displayed the national colors. Cables had been stretched on either side of the carriage-way which was kept clear by a small force of policemen, without apparent difficulty. No shops were open; business was suspended, and the real, and not the pretended closing of the liquor saloons by the order of General Scott, essentially contributed to the order of the day.

The procession set out from the Executive Mansion. President Buchanan there entered the carriage which, drawn by four led horses, and preceded by the Marshal of the District with his aids on horseback, moved out of the grounds to the avenue. Here a selected company of the sappers and miners of the regular army, commanded by Captain Duane of the Engineers, who had sought and obtained the position of a guard of honor, formed in a hollow square, with the carriage in its centre. No body of men of finer appearance and discipline, or more trustworthy and loyal, ever guarded the great Frederick or a Roman emperor. With the surrounded carriage they moved down the avenue with the unity and precision of a machine, followed by several companies of uniformed volunteers, the whole procession comprising not more than five hundred men. In front of Willard's Hotel a halt was made. Mr. Lincoln walked out through the crowd which civilly opened a lane to permit him to pass, and entered the carriage. The venerable form, pallid face, and perfectly white hair of Mr. Buchanan contrasted powerfully with the tall figure, coal-black hair, and rugged features of Mr. Lincoln, and suggested that the exhausted energies of the old were to be followed by the vigorous strength of the new administration.

The appearance of the President-elect was the signal for a slight cheer of welcome and the waving of banners from the windows. It was time for me to leave for the Capitol. As my carriage drove rapidly down F Street, to a station where arrangements had been made to pass invited guests through the crowd to the platform, I heard the volume of cheers roll down the avenue *pari passu* with the procession. I learned afterwards that the tall form of Mr. Lincoln was exposed during the whole distance, so that a shot from a concealed assassin from any one of the thousand windows would have ended his career. But not only was no assault attempted, but, as I was assured by the marshal, no word of discourtesy or insult was heard during the progress of the procession through over a mile of the crowded streets.

A memorable spectacle lay before our eyes, after we had ascended the steps inside and come out upon the platform. North and south from the ends of the great Capitol building, the ground fell off, while on the east were the vacant Capitol grounds, a broad square, each side of which measured some five hundred yards, bounded on the farther side by a street. All this space, including the eastern portico, was filled by the multitude, patiently awaiting the arrival of the President. The people were quiet, orderly, silent. They had come to see and hear. A few policemen were present, but the only duties they performed appeared to be the directing of persons holding tickets to their seats on the platform. Not a soldier was visible. Far out on the street, in front of the building afterwards well known as the " Old Capitol Prison," was a thin line of mounted men. Had I not been informed beforehand, I should not have suspected that these horsemen were the visible parts of two batteries of horse artillery of the regular army, ready for action should any occasion arise for their services.

We were not long kept waiting. A passage had been kept open from the columns of the eastern portico, across the whole platform, to its front. From between the two central columns first appeared the marshal with a man of soldierly bearing by his side. The tall, bent form with the intellectual face of the Chief Justice of the United States followed, arm in arm with the President-elect. Senators, congressmen, officers of the army and navy brought up the rear. But the crowd had no eyes for them. All were fixed upon Mr. Lincoln. The party advanced to the front of the platform, where a small table had been placed for Mr. Lincoln's convenience. Without seating himself, the silvery voice of Senator Baker, of Oregon, rang out over the multitude with these simple words, " Fellow-citizens, I introduce to you Abraham Lincoln, the President-elect of the United States of America!"

A slight ripple of applause followed this introduction. The commanding figure of Senator Baker receded into the audience. When I next saw it, the soul had gone out of it at Ball's Bluff. It lay, torn and disfigured by a score of rebel bullets, in the east room of the White House, covered by the flag in defence of which he gave his life. With head uncovered, towering above the eminent men by whom he was surrounded, Mr. Lincoln advanced to the table and commenced the reading of his address.

There were few persons in that uncounted throng who

expected to hear, or were in a frame of mind to appreciate, the import of that address. It needed the light of subsequent events for its comprehension. I count it as one of the valued opportunities of my life, that, seated only a few yards away from the speaker, I heard distinctly every word he uttered, watched the play of his strong features, and noted the effect of his emphatic sentences upon the persons around me. A flash of light swept over the field as the faces of the multitude were turned towards Mr. Lincoln, when the words "Fellow-citizens of the United States" fell from his lips. Few of those faces were turned away until his last words had been spoken.

Mr. Lincoln's ordinary voice was pitched in a high and not unmusical key. Without effort it was heard at an unusual distance. Persons at the most distant margins of the audience said that every word he spoke was distinctly audible to them. The silence was unbroken. No speaker ever secured a more undivided attention, for almost every hearer felt a personal interest in what he was to say. His friends feared, those who were not his friends hoped, that, forgetting the dignity of his position, and the occasion, he would descend to the practices of the story-teller, and fail to rise to the level of a statesman. For he was popularly known as the "Rail-splitter;" was supposed to be uncouth in his manner, and low, if not positively vulgar, in his moral nature. If not restrained by personal fear, it was thought that he might attack those who differed with him in opinion with threats and denunciations.

But the great heart and kindly nature of the man were apparent in his opening sentence, in the tone of his voice, the expression of his face, in his whole manner and bearing. The key-note of his address might have been shown in a sentence. Distrustful of himself, and relying upon the assistance of the Almighty, he should, to the best of his ability, discharge the trust which his office imposed, of supporting the Constitution, and maintaining the Union of the states in its integrity, as it was bequeathed to us by our fathers. But he required, he desired, he besought, the coöperation of his fellow-citizens in the execution of his trust. This same duty rested alike upon himself and all his fellow-citizens. It was the defence and preservation of their joint inheritance. He was about to take an oath in their presence, before Almighty God, to protect and defend the Constitution. Would his fellow-citizens assist him to keep the oath, and execute the trust it involved? Whatever else might happen, "the Union must be, should be preserved!"

His introduction had not been welcomed by a cheer, his opening remarks elicited no response. The silence was long-continued and became positively painful. But the power of his earnest words began to show itself; the sombre cloud which seemed to hang over the audience began to fade away when he said, " I hold that in the contemplation of universal law, and of the Constitution, the Union of these states is perpetual!"—with the words "I shall take care, as the Constitution itself expressly enjoins upon me, that the '*laws of the Union shall be faithfully executed in all the states!*'" And when, with uplifted eyes and solemn accents, he said, "The power confided to me will be used to hold, occupy, and possess the property and places belonging to the government," a great wave of enthusiasm rolled over the audience, as the united voices of the immense multitude ascended heavenward in a roar of assenting applause.

From this time to the end of the address, Abraham

Lincoln controlled the audience at his will. He had gained the confidence of his hearers and secured their respect and affection. Nor did he abuse his power. There was not a trace of menace, not a word of criticism, not an unfriendly suggestion in the entire speech. Who that heard them will ever forget the influence of those affectionate sentences with which the address terminated? "I am loath to close. We are not enemies, but friends. We must not be enemies. Though passion may have strained, it must not break, our bonds of affection."

"The mystic chords of memory, stretching from every battle-field and patriot grave to every living heart and hearthstone, all over this broad land, will yet swell the chorus of the Union, when again touched, as surely they will be, by the better angels of our nature!"

There was no hesitancy in the judgment which the audience was prepared to pronounce upon this inaugural address. From end to end of the Capitol, from the farthest limits of East Capitol Square, from the distant street where General Scott and his batteries were posted as a corps of observation, and from every superficial foot of the enclosed space, a burst of applause arose which made loyal hearts beat more rapidly, and the blood in loyal arteries leap joyously to their extremities. Over and over again the cheer was repeated. Grave senators and judges "joined in the rapturous cry, and even the ranks of *slavery* could scarce forbear to cheer!"

The Chief Justice of the United States now came forward. His venerable appearance gave to what might have been a mere matter of form great dignity and impressive significance. He extended an open Bible, upon which Mr. Lincoln laid his left hand, and, uplifting his right arm, he slowly repeated after the Chief Justice the words of the Constitution. "I do solemnly swear that I will faithfully execute the office of President of the United States, and will, to the best of my ability, preserve, protect, and defend the Constitution of the United States. So help me God!"

The ceremony ended. Those upon the broad platform rose and remained standing as the President and his party passed back into the building. The procession reformed in the same order as before and returned, leaving at the White House, as President of the United States, the private citizen it had escorted from the hotel. Within the hour another carriage, in which there was a single occupant, was driven down the avenue to the only railroad-station then in Washington. It contained ex-President Buchanan, returning as a private citizen to his Pennsylvania home, bearing with him less credit for loyal service to his country than he deserved. The crowd rapidly melted away. The change was completed. Without disorder or disturbance, with the dignity befitting an act of such transcendent importance, and, as events proved, upon the very threshold of civil war, the will of the people expressed at the ballot-box was executed, the old administration had surrendered its great powers to the new, and Abraham Lincoln, with the prestige of law and order in his favor, had become the President of the Republic. To this desirable result, General Dix and Mr. Stanton had each powerfully contributed; Judge Holt and others less conspicuously. Mr. Buchanan might justly have claimed credit for patriotic intentions partly executed. It was less his fault than his misfortune that the weakness of declining years led him to repose confidence in those who were false to their country and to himself. But it was the united opinion of the closest observers that the man to whose prudence, energy, and patriotism the country was chiefly indebted for the peace of March 4th, 1861, was Winfield Scott, Lieutenant-General, Commanding the Army.

XV.

SOME NOTES UPON GENERAL SCOTT AND ROBERT E. LEE.

ACCIDENT, united with admiration for some of his sterling qualities, at this time gave me opportunities of acquaintance with General Scott and members of his military family. Disregarding the chronology of events, possibly this is as good a time as I shall have to bring together and revise the impressions made upon me by these interviews.

No man, not Mr. Lincoln himself, was at this time more intensely hated by the secessionists than General Scott. A Virginian by birth and education, he became a citizen of South Carolina, and, while residing in Charleston, left the law for the career of a soldier. He was a favorite with Southern officers throughout his long service in the army, and they confidently anticipated that he would side with the South when the hour of separation came. He had been called from New York to Washington early in December. Even before the election, correctly forecasting its results, he had urgently advised President Buchanan to reinforce the Southern forts and put them in a better condition for defence. Many times after he came to Washington he had pressed similar suggestions upon the Executive. He had become suspicious of the Secretary of War, and on one noted occasion had personally requested permission to send two hundred and fifty men, with munitions of war and supplies, to Fort Sumter without the knowledge of that officer. His request was disregarded, and he then turned his attention to the defence of Washington and its security during the inauguration. Although himself reticent upon the subject, it was known to his friends that strong influences, founded upon his attachment to his native state, had been brought to bear to detach him from the cause of the Union; that appeals to his duty to Virginia, offers of high command, and arguments of influential Virginians had failed to shake his loyalty to his flag. He was reported to have sternly informed one Virginia senator that his friendship for that gentleman would not survive a second suggestion of desertion.

Unable to obtain even the promise of his neutrality, they abandoned all hope of influencing him, and set him down as an enemy to be removed or destroyed. Then there *was* a change! The intensity of secession wrath and fury contrasted powerfully with the magnificent contempt for both with which the veteran pursued his path to duty. They exhausted the vocabulary for words of invective, and threats of assassination became so numerous that a mail which did not bring them was the exception. I shall not soil my pages with the foul epithets with which they made the city vocal.

One of their charges had some evidence in its support. "He was untrue to the South," they said, "not because he loved the Union, but because he hated Jefferson Davis. They had been enemies for thirty years. The cause grew out of General Scott's vanity, which had been wounded by changes in his "General Regulations for the Army," for which he held Mr. Davis responsible while he was connected with West Point. Mr. Davis, also, as chairman of the Senate Committee on Military Affairs, had felt bound to oppose, and had for several years succeeded in postponing, the passage of the resolution which authorized the President to confer upon General Scott the brevet rank of lieutenant-general. As a cabinet officer, he had prevented any increase of pay under the resolution, until Congress interfered by a positive declaration that it be allowed. "It was selfish interest and wounded vanity," they said, "and not patriotism or fidelity to the Stars and Stripes, that bound him to the decaying cause of the Union."

I once heard the subject of his relations with Mr. Davis, and this charge, mentioned in his presence. It was on the 9th of February, the day following the election of Mr. Davis to the Presidency of the Southern Confederacy.

"I have no quarrel with Mr. Davis," said the veteran chief; "I must decline to discuss the statements to which you refer. Possibly they may have some color of truth. For more than thirty years he has been my persistent, deadly enemy. Yet he never did me much harm. The American people took excellent care that his plots against me should not succeed. But I can give a better reason why loyal men ought not to consort with him. He is a false man — false by nature, habit, and choice. His patriotism consists in promoting the interests of Jefferson Davis and his pets. His pets are the men that he can use. General Taylor should have been a good judge of Mr. Davis, for he was his father-in-law, and had excellent opportunities of estimating his value. He despised him thoroughly."

"I am amazed," he continued, warming to his subject, "that any man of judgment should hope for the success of any cause in which Jefferson Davis is a leader. There is contamination in his touch. If secession was the 'holiest cause that tongue or sword of mortal ever lost or gained,' he would ruin it! He will bear a great amount of watching. My friends in Congress learned that he had arranged for a veto of the resolution which had passed both Houses, giving me the pay and allowances of a lieutenant-general, according to their intention, of which his machinations had deprived me for three years. Against his opposition, they then incorporated the resolution as an amendment into the Military Appropriation Bill, which he could not afford to veto. He was chairman of the Military Committee; they had to appoint a committee of their own number to watch the amendment from its adoption until it was written into the engrossed bill to *prevent its being lost!* He is not a cheap Judas. I do not think he would have sold the Saviour for thirty shillings; but for the successorship of Pontius Pilate, he would have betrayed Christ and the apostles and the whole Christian Church!"

In his intercourse with Northern men, about the time of Mr. Lincoln's inauguration, General Scott expressed his opinions without any apparent reserve. He had no sympathy with the abolitionists; his opinions were decidedly pro-slavery. Long after others had abandoned all hope of a peaceful settlement, he clung to the hope that a great Union party might be formed on the basis of the "Crittenden Resolutions," which would bring back the seceded states, and prevent war. If war became inevitable, he declared it would be long, bloody, and expensive. The North would prevail, because it was the stronger in numbers and resources; but it was hopeless to attempt to subjugate the South with an army of less than three hundred thousand men. The assertion that the South was the superior of the North in personal courage excited his contempt. He had led men in battle from every state in the Union. There was little difference in their fighting qualities. Why should there be? They were of the same race and origin. Even the immigrants were principally of the same descent. If the Southern men had more dash, the Northern had better staying qualities.

He spoke of himself with equal freedom. "His day," he said, "had passed. Age and pain had exhausted him. He had not for many months been able to walk without assistance, or to move without pain. The general commanding an army must be able to lead as well as to direct it. Successful generals, from Alexander to Napoleon, with few exceptions, had been young men. Desaix and Hoche, the youngest marshals of Napoleon, had been his most efficient generals."

Twice, in my presence, General Scott spoke in complimentary terms of Colonel Robert E. Lee. One of these occasions was previous to the day of the inauguration, immediately after Colonel Lee arrived in Washington from Texas, and about the first of March. He "knew him thoroughly. He was an accomplished soldier, equal to any position—to the command of the army." He spoke of the opinions of Colonel Lee as from personal knowledge. "He is loyal to the Union," he said, "from principle as well as birth, and his education as a soldier." He had very recent evidence that Colonel Lee was not and never would be a secessionist.

The biographer of General Lee has very recently made public the evidence which, I have no doubt, enabled General Scott to speak so positively of the opinions at that time held by Colonel Lee. He has published a letter written by the latter from Texas to his son in Washington under date of January 23d, 1861, in which secession is condemned in emphatic terms. He said: "Secession is nothing but revolution. The framers of our Constitution never would have exhausted so much labor, wisdom, and forbearance in its formation, and surrounded it with so many guards and securities, if it was intended to be broken by every member of the confederacy at will. It is intended for *perpetual union*, as expressed in the preamble, and for the establishment of a *government*, not a compact, which can only be dissolved by revolution or the consent of all the people in convention assembled. It is idle to talk of secession. Anarchy would have been established, and not a government, by Washington, Hamilton, Jefferson, Madison, and all the other patriots of the Revolution."

Within six weeks after the 4th of March, I had occasion to recall these strong expressions by General Scott, of his confidence in the loyalty of Colonel Lee. Instead of waiting for the paymaster to make his rounds, the officers of the army and navy, who resigned to take service with the Confederacy, secured an arrangement with their departments by which they were paid, to the date of their resignations, by treasury-warrants. I believe it was General Spinner, the treasurer, who suggested that, as these gentlemen were going South, we should pay them by drafts on the stolen assistant-treasuries in the seceded states. As the warrants passed my office, I marked them for such drafts when I had the necessary information.

On one of the dark days which afterwards shrouded the capital, when these officers were deserting their flag and resigning their commissions by scores—being careful to collect the last dollar of their pay—one of these warrants, payable to a member of the family of Colonel Lee, was brought to me for signature. It was on the 20th day of April, three days after the secession of Virginia. I marked it, "Pay by draft on Richmond," as there was more government money there than in the treasury at Washington. Though we knew the rebels had seized it, we thought it would serve for the payment of rebel claims. My innocent note made trouble. Several of the officer's friends called to assure me that I was doing himself and his family great injustice; that they were all loyal; that he resigned because he could not fight his native state—but he would never fight against the Union. Then it was that I heard the report that it was not Colonel Lee who was to resign; it was General Scott, and Colonel Lee was to be his successor in the command of the Union army. I was inflexible. I would not change the order except upon the written pledge of the officer not to enter the Confederate service. It is unnecessary to add that the pledge was not given.

At the time I was being urged to pay this claim, the resignation of Colonel Lee was in the hands of General Scott. "It has cost me a struggle," he wrote, "to separate from superiors and comrades who have been so kind and considerate to me." But for the republic, to the bounty of which he owed his education, his position, and the greater part of his possessions, there was no word of gratitude, obligation, or regret. "Save in defence of my native state," he said, "I never *desire* again to draw my sword." His intent and purpose did not correspond to his desire.

Three days later, in the state house in Richmond, he received from Governor Letcher the appointment of "Commander of all the military and naval forces of Virginia," as he declared, with an approving conscience, there pledging himself to her service, and asserting that, "*except in her behalf, he would never again draw his sword.*" On the 10th of May he accepted the command of "all the forces of the Confederate States in Virginia." Twice he led an invading army to meet disaster and defeat north of the Potomac; and if the republic was not destroyed and a slave-ocracy erected upon its ruins, it was not because he failed to labor diligently to that end from the date last named until rebellion was driven by loyal hands to its unlamented grave.

No loyal American desires to abate or diminish by one grain any credit gained by any participant in the rebellion. He is content that the Confederacy should rest quietly on the bloody field where it fell until it has faded from the memory of man. It had no right nor reason to be. It was a rebellion against the freest government that ever existed. It was sown in conspiracy, nourished by patriotic blood, and perished from exhaustion. The sooner it is forgotten, the better for those who caused and upheld it, for the country, and mankind.

The defection of Colonel Lee has been treated by the loyal North with exceptional charity. His conscientiousness in resigning his commission has not been questioned. His admirers should have accepted the situation and not have excited discussion by presenting his example as one worthy of imitation by patriotic men. That discussion inevitably raises the question, What would have happened if Colonel Lee had followed the example of General Scott and Major Geo. H. Thomas, and continued loyal to the Union?

For more than two centuries the Lees had been the most influential family in Virginia. It was a Lee who gave to Washington his deserved place—"First in war, first in peace, and first in the hearts of his countrymen." By his marriage, Colonel Lee had united the wealth and influence of the Washingtons and the Lees. He had been made the ward of the republic; he had been educated at its expense; he had voluntarily enlisted in its service. He had obtained his first, and every succeeding commission, by pledging himself on his honor, "to bear true faith and allegiance to the United States of America—to serve them honestly and faithfully against all their enemies whatsoever, and to obey the orders of the President of the United States, and the orders of the officers appointed over him, according to the rules and articles of war." If between the two oceans that wash its remotest limits there was one man more firmly than any other bound to the service of the republic by tradition, training, associations, pecuniary considerations, and the honor of a soldier, that man was Colonel Lee.

The final verdict of history must be that Colonel Lee had no justification for his course. A skilful casuist may sometimes break the force of an invincible argument by some bold assertion which, although it may be true, has no relevancy to the subject. The only plea of justification made by himself at the time, or his eulogists since, was that he "could not draw his sword against Virginia." To this plea I demur, for irrelevancy. There was no issue with Virginia, no question pending of drawing swords against her or in her defence. Colonel Lee came to Washington on the 1st of March, opposed to secession, as is shown by his letters. A president, whose election was admitted to have been fair and by constitutional methods, was shortly afterwards inaugurated, and became the head of the government. He was pledged to non-interference with slavery, bound by his oath to maintain the Union. He had made no threat, proposed no violent measures. Virginia was still a member of the Federal Union. At her last election the Unionists were a powerful majority. Had Colonel Lee remained loyal, had he thrown the weight of his family, his name, and his influence into the scale for the Union, had he accepted the command of the Union armies, which he says was tendered to him by the President's authority, who shall say that the balance would not have been turned—that he would not have saved the country from war and Virginia from devastation?

The ability of General Lee as a leader of armies was very great. It was acquired in the service of the United States. His character was elevated, and in many respects worthy of imitation, for its foundations were laid in the first military school of the republic. He was not unduly elated by victory, nor depressed by defeat. He was respected by his foes, admired by his intimates, beloved by his soldiers. Next after his desire to win victories was his purpose to mitigate the evils of war. Only one unsoldierly act, and that was one of omission, was ever mentioned to his discredit. It was that he did not actively interfere to suppress the horrible treatment of Union prisoners. Of that no man should be accused except upon plenary proof. He was the pride of the Confederacy, and the love which the Virginians bore him surpassed their love for Washington. Peace to his ashes, and honor to his memory! But it cannot be forgotten that his otherwise stainless life was defaced by one gigantic error, which must not be suppressed lest any man fall after the same example.

XVI.

THE NONES AND IDES OF MARCH.—THE NEW CABINET.

THE inaugural address called forth opinions as diverse as the issues which disturbed the country. The Unionists in the South received it with favor. They said its tone was pacific, and that no just complaint could be made of the evident purpose of the author to preserve the Union and to perform his constitutional duty of enforcing the laws. The organs of the Douglas Democracy declared that in its statesmanship it met the expectations of the country, and its effects would be salutary. The Secessionists denounced it as sectional and mischievous, and insisted that if the President meant what he said, it was the knell and requiem of the Union, and the death-blow of hope. The pronounced Republicans were inclined to reserve their judgment. They did not quite like his positive pledge not to interfere with slavery; but, on the other hand, with a strong tendency to conciliate, it was decided in its condemnation of secession and in its purpose to preserve the Union. The fact was that none of the parties appreciated the dignity and power of the document, nor the ability and sound sense of its author. Read by the light of subsequent events, it proved to be one of the most able state papers of its generation, and fully equal to the great demands of the emergency.

The announcement of the names of the cabinet officers for the moment diverted the public attention from other subjects. They were obviously selected upon the novel, and it was feared dangerous, principle of placing the government in the hands of those members of the successful party most in favor with the people, as shown by their strength in the nominating convention. Upon this principle Mr. Seward had no competitor for the Department of State. Mr. Chase was selected for the Treasury, Mr. Cameron for the War Department, and Mr. Bates for the Attorney-Generalship. The President desired that the slave-holding states should have a more decided representative of their interests than Mr. Bates, and places were offered to distinguished statesmen of Virginia and North Carolina. Upon their declination the vacancies remaining were filled by Montgomery Blair, of Maryland, who had considerable strength in the nominating convention, Caleb B. Smith, a moderate Republican from Indiana, and Mr. Welles, of Connecticut, a very conservative representative of New England.

In the construction of his cabinet Mr. Lincoln had obviously determined to secure strength at the sacrifice of unity. It was scarcely to be expected that the views of Mr. Seward and Mr. Chase, or Mr. Cameron and Mr. Bates, could be harmonized. On the other hand, the Cabinet comprised some of the strongest men of the party, who would administer their several departments, each in his own way, perhaps, but with force and energy. One question was settled by the announcement of their names: there would be no more concessions to slavery!

My own awakening to the proximity of war occurred on the evening of March 3d. I had been the secretary, and Governor Chase the chairman, of the caucus of Republican members of the Peace Conference. We occupied adjacent apartments at the Rugby; we were thrown together almost daily, and I had acquired a high opinion of the abilities of the Ohio statesman. On the evening in question, he called at my rooms, and in his peculiarly concise manner said: "I have consented to accept the Treasury under Mr. Lincoln. I wish to have you take one of its bureaus."

I thanked him, but said it was impossible for me to accept the offer. I was dependent upon my profession, I had a young family to educate, and I could not afford to accept office upon so small a salary.

"We are living at a time when such considerations have no weight," he said. "Within a few weeks men of your age and health will have no choice. You will be compelled to enter the service of the government. You are worth more in the Treasury than you can be in the field; therefore it is your duty to go into the Treasury."

"Is it possible," I asked, "that you think we are on the verge of war? that we are to have bloodshed?"

"There is no more doubt of it, in my opinion," he said, "than there is of your existence. There is only one way to avoid it. It is that suggested by General Scott, to say to the seceded states, 'Wayward sisters, depart in peace!' Would New England consent to that?"

"No," I answered, "not to the diminution of the Union by one square inch! But I cannot take in the possibility, the suggestion of war, with all its consequences. I must think over what you tell me. I cannot leave Vermont—it is the home of my fathers."

The words of Governor Chase were a shock as well as a surprise to me. Except our brief experience in distant Mexico, the existing generation knew nothing of war. We had all assumed that the good sense of Congress would discover some way of avoiding war—of arranging the controversy without disunion or final separation. This conviction of Mr. Chase confounded me. But I persisted that family duties and professional business forbade my acceptance of any office except the collectorship of my own district, for which I then informed him I should be an applicant.

I returned to my Vermont home and my law office. After the confirmation of the Cabinet, for nearly three weeks there was a lull in the public excitement, and negotiations on the part of the seceded states were again attempted. On the 22d of March I was summoned to Washington. I met Governor Chase, who informed me. that he had appointed a collector for the district of Vermont, and, as I thought, with very little consideration for my claims. He again pressed me to accept an appointment in the Treasury, which I was again compelled to decline. On my way home I passed the night at the Astor House, in New York city, and at breakfast, on the morning of March 26th, read in the newspapers the announcement of my confirmation as Register of the Treasury, to which office I had been appointed on the day before.

On reaching my home I found a letter from Secretary Chase, asking me to accept the office of register, at least for the time, and to return to Washington as soon as I could make arrangements for an absence of a few weeks from my business. I set about these arrangements, and for nearly three weeks was actively occupied with them.

On the 14th of April there was a whispered rumor, which found speedy confirmation. The first gun of treason had been fired against Fort Sumter. Next we heard that Sumter had fallen. The first effect of this information on the public mind was stupefying, as when a deadly blow is struck across the temples. It was nearly two days before the reaction began. Then it swept everything before it. In a moment, in the twinkling of an eye, as if at the call of a trumpet, the united voice of the loyal North denounced the treason and invoked judgment on the traitors. I have some notes of the beginning of the uprising of a great people made at the time. I will transcribe a few of them:

"Monday, April 15th, at 9 A.M., I left Burlington for Washington. Yesterday the news of the surrender of Fort Sumter to the rebels by Major Anderson swept through New England. The indignation is indescribable. With it came the answer of the President to the delegates from Virginia, that he should not depart from the principles of his inaugural address. Crowds were collected at all the stations on the railroads, even at the small country towns, thirsting for news. At Rutland we had the Troy morning papers, with the proclamation for an extra session of Congress on the 4th of July, and the President's call for seventy-five thousand men for the recapture of the Southern forts and the defence of the country. We had an hour at Troy. The crowds increased in numbers and exultation. A mass-meeting is called for to-night to arrange for enlistments. Leading citizens say that there is only one party now—the party of the Union. Gen. Wool heads the call. Passed through great crowds at every station on the railroad, and reached the Astor House at ten o'clock in the evening. City Hall Square is packed with an orderly crowd, which has made a demonstration against the *New York Herald*, and compelled it to display the Union flag. No expressions against the Union or the President are permitted."

There was little sleep that night in the lower part of the city. Cheers for President Lincoln and the Union, and patriotic songs rang through the streets. A despatch from Governor Fairbanks requested me to ascertain when the First Regiment of Vermont Volunteers would be accepted. I was unable to get any decent seat in the train until the following evening, and the cars then were crowded. I reached Washington at daybreak on Wednesday, April 17th. The enthusiasm pervaded Philadelphia, but was not apparent in Baltimore, nor visible in Washington.

If the experiences of that journey could be adequately represented on paper, they would serve as an instructive lesson to all who in future may harbor the thought of trifling with the Union, or showing any want of respect to the national flag. Men may come and men may go, but the love of Americans for the Stars and Stripes will abide forever. Never before had the flag seemed to me half so glorious. I left my home with no thought but that of returning to it as soon as I had performed any temporary service which I might be able to render to the Secretary. When I reached Washington I was willing to take any place in which I could render the best service to my country.

XVII.

A NOVEL INDUCTION INTO OFFICE.

I HAD an invitation to breakfast with Secretary Chase at the Rugby House. He had so many friends who "waited on their office according to their order," and who pursued him even to the breakfast-room, that he only had time for a few words with me. "Your commission," he said, "is in the hands of Mr. Harrington (the First Assistant Secretary). I wish you would get it, take the oath, and assume possession of your office this morning. Whatever may happen, I must have some Republicans near me upon whom I can rely."

Mr. Harrington directed me to one of the district judges, before whom I could take the oath of office. A clerk, who he said was well known to the judge, accompanied to identify me. We found "His Honor" not in a judicial temper, and evidently much tossed about in his mind. "He transacted his business in court," he said, "and not at his private residence." He declined to recognize my attendant. He did not know "why he should be annoyed by Republican office-seekers. He should not inconvenience himself to accommodate them; his court was held at the City Hall; it opened at eleven o'clock."

"I am here," I remarked, "at this early hour, at the special request of the Secretary of the Treasury. I am assured that you have often administered oaths upon the identification of the clerk sent here with me. Being myself a lawyer, I can recognize an unsound excuse for the non-performance of a judicial duty. I respectfully ask you to administer the oath, or, in plain terms, and not by inference, decline to do so."

He snatched the commission from my hand, muttering, in an undertone, something about "committal" and "for disrespect," scrawled his name upon the paper, and flung it at me in a contemptuous manner. "You have certified to what is not true," I said. "If this manner of administering an official oath suits you, I think your certificate will answer my purpose."

It was, I think, his last judicial act. He "went South" the next day, and I saw him no more. 1 refer to this incident because it illustrates the sullen anger of the Secessionists who at that time swarmed in the streets of Washington.

My predecessor in office received me courteously, and introduced me to the clerks and employés in the bureau. He had prepared for the change, and delivered the office to me in excellent working order. He soon after took his departure, offering his services should I, at any time, have occasion to need them.

My first discovery in office was that its atmosphere was one which I could not breathe, and to which I could never become accustomed. It was as fatal to personal independence as carbonic-acid gas to animal life. The clerks approached the presence of the head-officer as if he were a superior being. I never could tolerate the sight of a person who came up to me "washing his hands with invisible soap in imperceptible water." The change of a cringing, grovelling carriage in the presence of superiors was my first official decision. It had been attended with petty tyranny over inferiors.

There were but slight indications that Washington

would take any part in the answer which I knew would be returned from the North to the call of the President for seventy-five thousand men. One or two volunteer companies had tendered their services, and the War Department had accepted them. But every one seemed to be waiting to see what Virginia would do. If Virginia seceded, the prevailing opinion seemed to be that the cause of the Union was hopeless. I did not like the atmosphere nor the surroundings. My first day of official life was neither cheerful nor satisfactory.

The first papers presented for my signature, on the morning of April 18th, were certificates for the fraction of the month's salary claimed by two clerks who had resigned to take office under the Confederacy at Montgomery, Alabama. My chief clerk said that my certificates were necessary to enable them to draw their money.

"Why should they draw their money?" I asked. "Does not a deserter always forfeit any pay otherwise due him?"

He did not know, he said. It had been the custom in all the bureaus. My predecessor had always signed the certificates. He supposed I would not wish to change the practice.

I said the matter would require consideration. From the effect produced by this observation, one would have supposed desertion to be a virtue rather than an offence. The story of the "outrage" flew on the wings of the wind. The injured clerks demanded an interview. They were filled with indignation. Had they not a right to resign? Could they do otherwise than follow the fortunes of their states? The practice of paying up to the date of the acceptance was universal. This refusal deprived them of their earned wages, etc.

I made an end of the subject by the remark that, morally, I could see no distinction between their cases and that of a soldier who deserts his flag; that I had neither love nor respect for traitors or deserters, and that, with my present views, I should not sign those nor any similar certificates without the special order of the secretary.

I had scarcely disposed of these gentlemen before I received a request to attend at the office of Assistant Secretary Harrington, at two o'clock on the same day. It was a meeting of the chiefs of the bureaus of the Treasury. There were no absentees. Mr. Harrington said that the secretary would like to have our views concerning the defence of the Treasury, if an attack should be made upon it. I think General Francis E. Spinner, whom I then met for the first time, made the first answer.

"I am for defending the Treasury," he said; "but first I would put it into a condition to be defended. The building needs cleaning out. I prefer to take my secession clear, unadulterated, from the outside. We should know whom we can depend upon. The doubtful and uncertain should be excluded from the building. I do not wish to have men around me who require watching."

These views met with universal assent. In less time than is required to write the account it was agreed that the clerks and messengers of all the bureaus should be called together at four o'clock, and the number of those ascertained who would unite in the defence of the Treasury.

"I will have my say!" said one, as the indications of adjournment became pressing. "My military education was neglected. It consisted in blowing the fife one day at a June training. Why may we not have an officer from the War Department to teach us at least the drill of the awkward squad?"

"Your question, I think, justifies me in giving you information of one fact," said Mr. Harrington, addressing the meeting. "It was arranged that Captains Shiras and Franklin, from the War Department, should organize the Treasury regiment, when the secretary decided first to consult you. You will find the appearance of the Treasury changed in the morning. There will be no want of arms or instructors."

We returned to our offices. I can only speak of what took place in my own. To insure that all should be notified, I called the clerks into my room, and gave the notices in person. There was a flutter of excitement, followed by several applications for leave of absence. None were granted. At five o'clock each employé of the office had the opportunity to sign the following paper: "I will defend the Treasury, under the orders of the officer in charge of it, against all its enemies, to the best of my ability."

This was not a complicated pledge, but it was not received with enthusiasm. In fact, it reminded me of the reception of an invitation mentioned by St. Luke, for "They all, with one consent, began to make excuse." I do not know that any of them had bought a piece of ground, or five yoke of oxen, or had married a wife, but one had a sick wife, another was surrounded by Secessionist neighbors, who would make his life a burden if he openly joined any Union organization; there was a perfect epidemic of heart and nervous diseases, and one belonged to a family in which palpitation of the heart was hereditary, and always brought on by any sudden shock. I assured them that I sincerely regretted their unfortunate situations, but I could not see that it was important to the government whether it was deprived of their services by cowardice or misfortune; it was the loss of the services in defence of the Treasury which was material.

It remained for an old Southerner to put them to shame. He had been in the office almost half a century; he belonged to an old Carolina family. He had been appointed when very young, and was put in charge of surrendered ship's registers, in the basement of the Treasury, where scarcely any one ever had occasion to go, and where he had been for so long a time that connections with his family and friends had long since ceased to exist. "I never fired a gun in my life," he said. "I could not hit the side of a barn, and I have no doubt that I am a coward. But as long as the star-spangled banner waves, I have something to live for. If I am too old to be of any other use, I can at least act as a powder-monkey, and my body will stop a Secession bullet with the best of you." He seized the pen, and the name first signed to the paper was that of *Francis Lowndes.*

His example was followed by all except two or three. They were directed to report for further orders at nine o'clock on the following morning.

On the six-o'clock train between five and six hundred Pennsylvanians arrived, the first volunteers for the defence of the capital. "There is a rumor that the Virginia Convention has passed the ordinance of secession! All the cars and locomotives have been sent to Richmond. The government should have seized them ten days ago. Commodore Paulding, from Norfolk, reports no disturbance there, and that he has two ships in position to protect the government property. These reports are unsatisfactory. If Virginia has seceded, a long war seems to me inevitable." Such was my note of that day.

XVIII.

THE ISOLATION OF THE CAPITOL.—AN ALARMED VIRGINIAN.

No account of the isolation of Washington has yet been written. It began on Friday, April 19, and ended on the Thursday following. It was unpredicted, and to many as alarming as eclipses formerly were to superstitious peoples.

On Friday morning the Treasury seemed singularly metamorphosed. Armed men guarded its entrances, and excluded all but officers and employés. Stacks of rifles and boxes of cartridges occupied the halls; busy men were fitting huge beams into the openings, and piling sand-bags into exposed places. Barricades, from floor to ceiling, closed the way to the vaults, and the sharp notes of the bugle rang out at intervals. Captains Franklin and Shiras had opened an enlistment office, and were forming the Treasury regiment, and recruits in squads were already being drilled in all the unoccupied spaces.

Applications to the register for leaves of absence were numerous. The epidemic of nervous diseases was on the increase. I granted them freely. I did not expect the applicants would return, and I was not disappointed.

Colonel Lane, of Kansas, and Cassius M. Clay, of Kentucky, each formed volunteer companies from strangers temporarily in the city, which were accepted as guards of the Executive Mansion. Squads of these companies were under instruction, and were being drilled in the vacant lots and broad streets in the vicinity of the White House and the Treasury.

The first news received from the outside was that the company of regulars at Harper's Ferry had sent as many of the arms as they could place on the train to Washington, and had burned the remainder—about fourteen thousand stands. The Virginians had organized a force to capture the armory as soon as the ordinance of secession had been adopted by the Virginia Convention.

At noon another rumor convulsed the city. It was said that the Seventh New York Regiment had been cut to pieces by a mob in the streets of Baltimore. I knew that regiment had not yet left New York. But some regiment had been attacked, and it was assumed, in the excitement, that a similar attack would be made upon the few volunteers in Washington. Soon we heard that the regiment had fought its way through Baltimore, and was coming, with its dead and wounded, on a train which would arrive about six o'clock that evening.

I went to the station to await the arrival of the train. The crowd was large, and in no mood to listen to treasonable observations. I heard one man remark that the regiment was one of those sent by that d—d abolitionist, Governor Andrew. The next moment he was sprawling in the gutter. Not a word was spoken by his assailant.

The train arrived. The soldiers left the cars and formed in two lines on the street. Then a procession of men, with stretchers, came out of the station. On each lay a wounded man. I counted seventeen. Their dead they had left in Baltimore. The wounded were placed in ambulances and sent to the Washington Infirmary.

Three or four persons in citizen's dress were engaged in an excited conversation with a number of officers. They were from Baltimore, and had come to arrest the soldier who had fired from the train and killed one Davis, a Baltimore merchant. These officers claimed that they could identify the soldier, and proposed to arrest him on the spot. The colonel said that he would interpose no objection, but he would not assist them in making the arrest, because the man was cheering for Jeff. Davis when he was shot. He should leave the matter with his men. The men, with few words, convinced the officers that they could not arrest one man unless they were prepared to arrest the entire regiment, whereupon they abandoned the undertaking.

A Baltimore acquaintance described the march of the last one hundred men through the streets as an act of singular gallantry. They were cut off from the rest of the regiment, and surrounded by the mob. Forming into a square, with fixed bayonets, in double-quick time they drove their way through a howling crowd of a hundred times their number, and a shower of clubs, stones, and shots, to the train, without firing a shot in return.

The rumors flying over the city on Saturday were numerous, contradictory, and kept every one who gave them much attention in a flutter of excitement. The steamers running to Aquia Creek were ordered to Richmond, but were sent to the navy yard, and taken possession of by the War Department. The Department was closed at twelve o'clock, the keys, except of the vaults, being left in the doors to enable the engineers and two hundred regulars under their orders to complete the defences of the building. Awkward squads, belonging to the Department regiments, were being drilled wherever there was a suitable place.

Sunday morning brought a heavy crop of new rumors, but no mails or newspapers from the North. The monotony of the day was broken by one incident, which was both amusing and interesting. After church, I walked down the avenue in the direction of the Capitol. The sidewalks were crowded, and I was suddenly thrown into the carriageway by a person who, with head bowed down, was rushing madly forwards, apparently desirous of avoiding observation. Believing that I recognized an acquaintance, acting in a very strange manner, I overtook him, and, with some difficulty, identified him. It proved to be the author of the "Private Libraries of New York"—a native of Virginia, recently domiciled in New York city. He would not recognize me at first, but on my insisting, he assumed a position of entreaty and exclaimed, "Hush, hush! I must not be known. For God's sake, tell me how I can get across the river."

I thought he had gone crazy, but he proved to be only excited. I invited him, and, after much persuasion, induced him, to go to my rooms. But he insisted that he was pursued—that his life was in danger, and he should not be safe until he could reach Virginia. He was suffering from hunger as well as terror. He was an educated gentleman, naturally of a nervous temperament, who really believed the North had gone mad. From his account of the departure of the Seventh New York, and the preparations for the great meeting on Saturday, I began to gain some idea of the great uprising. After I had persuaded him to take some refreshment, which somewhat quieted his nerves, I ascertained that he had come by the way of Annapolis, and might be able to give some reliable information concerning the New York Seventh and the Massachusetts Eighth regiments, which we had last heard from at Philadelphia on Saturday, where they were taking steamers to come to Washington, either by way of Annapolis, or up the Potomac

River. He was uncommunicative, until I proposed that if he would go with me to the Executive Mansion and give the President all the information he had, I would procure him a pass across the Potomac into Virginia. He accepted the offer. I introduced him to the President, who, by a skilful cross-examination, extracted the few facts in his possession.

New York, he said, was ablaze with excitement. Nothing favorable to the South was permitted to be published or spoken. All the Southerners had been notified to leave the city within ten hours on pain of death; all their property had been seized, and several had been hung to the lamp-posts. He saw the Seventh Regiment depart. The whole city was out to see them off. They had left Philadelphia on Saturday with a Massachusetts regiment on separate steamers, and had not since been heard of. The bridges on the railroads had been burned; he saw some of them burning. He was, or claimed to be, unable to tell by what route he came. One prevailing idea filled his mind. The whole North was already on the way to the invasion and destruction of the South! They were coming down like an avalanche. General B. F. Butler was to be the leader of the invading army.

The information extorted from the doctor scarcely paid for the trouble. He received his pass, however, and disappeared, making rapid speed in the direction of the Long Bridge across the Potomac River.

XIX.
BALTIMORE BLOCKS THE WAY.

On Saturday, April 20th, Washington was detached from the loyal states. We had no mails from the North, no communication by railroad or telegraph with Philadelphia, Harrisburgh, or places north or west of either city. For news we had only rumor, which informed us that bridges had been burned on all the railroads running into Baltimore; that the steam ferry-boat at Havre-de-Grace had been sunk, and that no regiments on the way could reach the capital.

For outside information we were served with the Baltimore *Sun*. That rebel sheet declared that "Yesterday the best blood of Maryland was spilled by Northern mercenaries." It demanded that "not another soldier from the North shall desecrate the soil of Maryland." It reported a public meeting of citizens of Baltimore, one of whom, Carr by name, was "ready to shoulder his musket for the defence of Southern homes," and who demanded to be immediately informed, "whether the minions of Lincoln should cross the soil of Maryland, to subjugate our sisters of the South." And the citizens answered by unanimous shouts, "No! never!"

There has been so much written that is wrong touching the action of the officers and people of Maryland on and after the 19th of April, that I feel justified in contributing some definite facts to the literature of the subject. Maryland never seceded. Her governor, and the members of her Legislature were elected as Union men. Baltimore was a Secessionist city. With the exception of a small minority of true and daring Republicans, her people were disunionists. When the call for seventy-five thousand men was issued, for the general service of the government, Governor Hicks had undertaken to say that "no troops would be sent from Maryland unless it may be for the defence of the national capital;" and the mayor of Baltimore had joyously exclaimed "Amen!" In fact, the governor, instead of boldly placing himself on the side of the Union, had practically surrendered his authority to the officials of Baltimore.

Accordingly, no preparations were made to protect the Northern regiments, and the second one that passed through Baltimore had to fight its way through a mob of ten times its number of ruffians, who knew they had the moral support of the authorities. The newspapers said that only three soldiers were killed and eight wounded, when more than twenty, with serious injuries, were lying in the Washington Infirmary. The mayor of the city forthwith despatched to the President a committee "to explain the fearful condition of affairs," and to inform him that "the people are exasperated to the highest degree by the passage of troops, and the citizens are universally decided that no more troops should be ordered to come;" also that "the authorities of the city did their best to prevent a collision, and, but for their efforts, a fearful slaughter would have occurred." Governor Hicks fully concurred in all that was said by the mayor in the above communication. "A public meeting of citizens," continued the mayor, "has been called, and the troops of the state and the city have been called out to preserve the peace. They will be enough." The governor, the mayor, and the police board telegraphed the president of the Baltimore and Ohio Railroad to "send back the troops from Rhode Island and Massachusetts to the borders of Maryland," and President Garrett "most cordially approved the advice, and gave the necessary order."

The mayor and his committees met the President and General Scott on the 20th and 21st, and reported that the President recognized the good faith of the city and state authorities; that his sole object in concentrating troops was the defence of the capital; that he protested that none of the troops brought through Maryland were intended for any purpose "aggressive as against the Southern states," and that, while insisting that troops were necessary for the defence of the capital, both the President and General Scott agreed that they would bring them around the city, and not irritate the people by marching them through Baltimore. The report is too long for insertion here, but in substance it represented the President as satisfied with the conduct of the Baltimore authorities; that he was conscious that the "people of all classes were fully aroused, and that it was impossible for any one to answer for the consequences of the presence of Northern troops anywhere within the borders of Maryland."

Had these statements been true, had the President and General Scott been in the temper of mind here represented, Washington would have been in rebel hands within forty-eight hours. There were many official acts of President Lincoln which seem to have exerted a powerful influence upon the fortunes of the republic, but there was none more beneficial in its results, or which more clearly shows his cool judgment, than his dealing with the Secessionists of Baltimore at this time of universal excitement, almost at the beginning of his official career.

When he gave these gentlemen his answer, he knew of some events of which they were ignorant. He knew that his call for men had already been approved by the loyal nation; that more men than he had called for had been tendered by a single state; that there had been a great uprising of the people which rendered the insolent answers of some rebel governors pitiful by contrast; that every hamlet, as well as every city, from Maine to Oregon, was alive with the work of preparation, and that choice regiments from Massachusetts and New York, the advance guard of the legions to follow, were already within the waters of Maryland.

No; Abraham Lincoln did not take that moment to bargain with Secessionists. It is not impossible that these gentlemen were deceived by his apparent unconcern. In the account given by himself to Baltimore Republicans of his interview with the mayor and his friends, he said that he told them that he would do all in his power to prevent bloodshed, and that the service, for which the regiments were called, was expressed in the call itself. It was " to repossess the forts, places, and property which have been seized from the Union." He said that the defence of the capital was first to be provided for, and that the routes by which the regiments came were matters with which he had nothing to do. They concerned General Scott and his subordinates. What he was anxious about was to have the regiments get here. Virginia had now seceded; it was reported that she would close the Potomac River by her batteries. Maryland bounded Washington on the north and west. These regiments could not fly over her in a balloon or dig under her by a tunnel. How were they to get here without crossing Maryland? Those who objected to the way proposed must find some other!

The Baltimore delegation admitted the difficulties. They could not remove them, and did not come for that purpose. They proposed to relieve themselves from the responsibility for bloodshed. The Marylanders were a proud and sensitive people; the sight of these Northern invaders was offensive to them. They would not permit them to pass through Baltimore, probably not to enter the state. They would rise as one man, and defend their state from such an invasion!

The final answer of the President was that he regretted such a conclusion, and that he would have to refer them to General Scott. He supposed the War Department, like all other departments, was much engaged just then in preparing for the defence of the capital against the disloyal persons, with whom the people of Maryland were apparently in sympathy. But if the condition of public opinion in Maryland was accurately represented by the committee, he was quite certain that some means would be found of informing the people of that state that "there was no piece of American soil too good to be pressed by the foot of a loyal soldier on his march to the defence of the capital of his country."

Such was President Lincoln's account of his interviews with the mayor of Baltimore and his associates. It differs materially from the versions made public by them immediately afterwards. It was accepted by the loyal friends of the Union. It certainly had the probabilities in its favor.

XX.

THE FIRST VOLUNTEER DEFENDERS OF THE CAPITAL.—THE PLUG-UGLIES OF BALTIMORE.—THE SEVENTH NEW YORK AND THE EIGHTH MASSACHUSETTS REGIMENTS.

FORT SUMTER fell on Saturday. On Monday, April 15th, the President called for seventy-five thousand men. On Thursday Pennsylvania sent her first regiment into Washington. On Friday, at noon, the Sixth Massachusetts was fighting its way through the Baltimore mob. When it reached the capital, all the railroads through Maryland were broken, and the state for all practical purposes was under Rebel control.

At the hour when the Sixth was fighting the Secessionist rabble, the Eighth Massachusetts was speeding southward to the defence of Washington on an express train through New Jersey. A few hours later the Empire State had sent her choicest regiment, the gallant Seventh, one thousand strong, with like speed on the same errand. At Philadelphia these regiments learned that the railroad bridges had been burned, and that the steam ferry-boat, *Maryland*, the only means of crossing the Susquehanna, had been sunk. Ordinary men would have gone into camp and awaited the opening of the railroad; but General Butler pushed on to Havre-de-Grace, where he found the *Maryland* still afloat, and, placing his regiment on board, he started for Annapolis. Colonel Lefferts chartered the first steamer he could find, the Seventh boarded her in Philadelphia, and on Sunday morning was on the ocean outside the capes of Delaware. Turning into the capes of Virginia, he sailed up the bay, and, hearing that the Potomac was commanded by rebel batteries, turned northward, and at dawn on Monday dropped anchor in the harbor of Annapolis. The *Maryland* was already there; but, in towing the old *Constitution* out of danger of rebel seizure, by the treachery of the pilot she had been run aground with the regiment on board. After laboring in vain all day to get her off, just at evening the regiments were landed, disregarding the protests of the mayor and citizens, that their appearance would cause bloodshed, Colonel Lefferts observing that, if they were "let alone, they would disturb nobody."

The railroad from Annapolis to Annapolis Junction, with the main line from Baltimore to Washington, was torn up, and many of the rails were carried away and sunk in deep water. The locomotives had been dismantled, and bodies of rebels were lurking about the vicinity ready to attack the regiments if opportunity offered. Massachusetts soldiers reconstructed the engines, placed cannon and men to serve them on a platform-car in front, the baggage of the two regiments was loaded on cars in the rear, and, with the train thus made up, they took up their march, rebuilding the railroad as they advanced. Companies were detailed to forage and cook, for they lived on the country. Their progress was slow, but on Thursday morning they reached Annapolis Junction. Learning that a party of twelve or fifteen thousand rebels was preparing to attack them, the Massachusetts regiment remained at the junction to meet them. The Seventh New York took a train for Washington, where they arrived at noon on Thursday, April 23d, a little more than five days after their departure from New York.

As already mentioned, Baltimore had for some years bred a new variety of the human species called the "Plug-Ugly"—a hybrid of slavery and brutality, first developed for political purposes. Its representatives had no reason for existence, no visible means of support. They were idle, vicious, muscular, sensual brutes, who subsisted upon whiskey and crime. They were very bold in the presence of the weak, and very cowardly in contact with brave men. Their numbers had enormously multiplied with the growth of secession. Washington had caught the overflow, attracted by the hope of possible plunder when the rebellion should break out. Its postponement had made them hungry and desperate. Now that war was inevitable, they thought their time had come. They had a rude sort of organization, which enabled them to collect in great numbers at a given point on short notice.

To the "Plug-Uglies" was assigned the congenial task of burning the bridges, breaking up the railroads, and falling upon and destroying the new and inexperienced regiments on their way to Washington. They professed great contempt for the "counter-jumpers" and "kid-gloved darlings" who constituted these regiments, and regarded their destruction as a pleasant pastime.

As soon as they knew that communication was to be attempted from Annapolis, they selected the junction of the branch railroad with the main line as the best place at which to fall upon the Yankees. It was central, their friends could come by rail from Baltimore and Washington, and it was a good point at which to concentrate the bands scattered over the state. They arranged to collect there a force of fifteen thousand, and widely proclaimed that Annapolis Junction was the selected field for the destruction of the Northern invaders.

So successfully had they spread this proclamation that a battle at the junction was regarded as inevitable. It would have taken place if General Butler and Colonel Lefferts with their regiments could have been persuaded to wait a week or ten days longer. But they would not wait. These regiments expected to fight—that was the purpose of their coming. Many messengers had been sent from Washington to inform them of the rebel preparations. One or two of them escaped capture, and brought contradictory advices. Col. Landers, the last, brought such an account of the anxiety of General Scott for the safety of Washington, that Colonel Lefferts determined to push forward, though he expected to meet with a loss of a portion of his men. Annapolis Junction had been reached. The Massachusetts regiment halted there to await the promised attack, and the Seventh started for Washington without coming within musket-shot of an armed rebel.

The Eighth Massachusetts, after waiting some hours for the attack, came to the Capitol, and were comfortably quartered under its dome before the Secessionists as near as Baltimore could be convinced that they had passed the junction. Farther South they refused to credit the collapse of the plan so elaborately prepared for a victory at Annapolis Junction. A Baltimore paper of the 25th published the report, as coming from "three or four different sources," "that the Seventh had been cut to pieces at Annapolis." "It was probably true, but it would be well to wait for further confirmation."

The papers of Charleston and other cities put no such restraint upon their exultation. For some hours they gave free rein to their wild delight. They announced in bold head-lines, "Glorious news! The crack regiment of New York cut to pieces between Annapolis and Marlboro! Three times three cheers for the brave Marylanders!"

While the seceded states were giving this ludicrous exhibition of their joy over a victory before the battle was fought, I was an eye-witness of a different picture. The Seventh New York was marching between two mighty waves of cheers from the masses of loyal citizens which filled the broad streets of the capital. The regiment halted near the open space, west of the National Hotel. That space contained the Washington contingent of the species described, which their sympathizers supposed was at the junction. They had infested the streets since the previous February, and were readily recognized. For the first time I passed through them without insult. They appeared depressed. Sorrow was on their faces and blasphemy on their lips. As the Seventh halted I stood on a corner and saw that villainous multitude melt away. It was their last appearance, they were visible for the last time. That night there was a flight into the Egypt of secession of a most unholy family. The species became extinct in Washington, and everywhere north of the Potomac excessively rare.

As a frost cuts down the noxious weeds which choke the sprouting corn, so did the tread of these two regiments, as they landed upon her shores, arrest and deaden the rank growth of secession in Maryland. In one week from the time of the President's call, they had formed the front rank of the great column from the loyal states, had burst their way through rebel obstructions, and stood almost two thousand strong within the shadow of the dome of the Capitol. It was afterwards said that the President seemed pleased with their appearance; that he was very cordial to them without distinction of rank. Could they have seen him a day or two before, when his countenance wore that peculiar expression, I think the saddest ever shown upon the face of man, they would have more perfectly comprehended his estimate of the value of their services.

The citizens of Washington would have made these soldiers their guests. They felt hurt because discipline required the men to go into camp and sleep under canvas. There was not one instance in which a private of either regiment was guilty of the slightest excess or insubordination. They were gentlemen always as well as soldiers. They were overwhelmed with civilities and comforts, which they divided with less-favored regiments. A private of the Seventh lost his life by an accident. The whole city mourned his loss, and hundreds sent expressions of sympathy. Having been selected for the protection of the President and to lead the march into Virginia, the work of this regiment was accomplished. They offered to re-enlist at the expiration of their term of service, but were finally discharged with this statement, that "it is the desire of the War Department, in relinquishing the services of this gallant regiment, to make known the satisfaction that is felt at the prompt and patriotic manner in which it responded to the call for men to defend this capital when it was believed to be in peril, and to acknowledge the important service which it rendered by appearing here in an hour of dark and trying necessity."

I knew many members of the Seventh personally, and saw much of them during their thirty days' service. I thought then, and I have never since changed the opinion, that, in the succession of stirring events, the public attention was so diverted that the regiment failed to receive that full measure of appreciation which its services deserved. The debt which the republic owes for its gallant service was largely due to the cool judgment and splendid, soldierly accomplishments of Marshal Lefferts, its colonel and commander.

XXI.

THE "TRENT AFFAIR."—STATESMANSHIP OF MR. SEWARD.

IT has been stated already that no attempt would be made to arrange these notes as a connected history or in chronological order. There were weeks and sometimes months when great events were happening, but when no time could be spared for any but official duties. Occasionally it was possible to record memoranda of some occurrence of special importance of which I happened to have knowledge. One of these was the "Trent affair" as it was called, which, because it so clearly illustrates the influence and statesmanship of Secretary Seward, I thought worthy of particular notice, and which may as well be presented in the present connection.

The "Trent affair" was an incident of the war which furnished the only occasion within my recollection when the judgment of a substantial majority of the people was reversed by the publication of a single state paper.

Before the commencement of hostilities there were good reasons for anticipating the friendship of Great Britain for the loyal North. The relations of that power to slavery alone would have furnished a basis for such a hope, which was confirmed by the leading English journals. The London *Times* had declared that "the secession of states and the formation of a new confederacy are events which this journal has always declared to be impossible;" "that should the clamor of secession, by any chance, be carried too far, and the threat, uttered in jest or earnest, lead to bloodshed, . . . Mr. Lincoln will in that case command a majority in Congress, and carry with him the support of all those who, however tolerant of slavery, will not acquiesce in its becoming the basis of a hostile and illegal confederacy." The *Saturday Review* had declared that "the dissolution of the Union, so far from being hailed as a profitable transaction, will be lamented in this country (England). . . . It is a truth, absolutely certain, that any policy will miscarry which assumes that England can be coaxed or bribed into a connivance at the extension of slavery." Less influential papers teemed with similar articles.

During the first six months of the war, there was an extraordinary change in the sentiments of the English people. The *Times* proclaimed that "there must be two federations—on no other footing will peace ever be made." "In our opinion, the forcible subjugation of the South will prove a hopeless task." The *Saturday Review* said that it was "the unanimous opinion of nineteen out of twenty educated Englishmen that a more hopeless enterprise than the reconquest of the South by the Federal government has never been projected by any ancient or modern state." "The North is just as foolish for trying to reconquer the South, as Xerxes was when he led half the world against Athens, or as Napoleon was when he led Europe against Russia." Mr. Roebuck regarded "the attempt of the North in endeavoring to restore the Union by force as an immoral proceeding, totally incapable of success." And even Mr. Gladstone said that "Mr. Jefferson Davis has made of the South a nation, and separation is as certain as any event, yet future and contingent, can be."

With this change of opinion had arisen a popular demand in Great Britain for the recognition of the Southern Confederacy by the great powers of Europe. It was apparent that Great Britain was prepared for such recognition whenever France would join her, and that a very small excuse would suffice to induce her to act in the matter without further delay. There was one incident referred to by Mr. Bright in his celebrated speech at Rochdale, which almost savored of contempt of the North in the British Cabinet. Fully alive to the importance of amicable relations with Great Britain, the United States government had commissioned Mr. Charles Francis Adams, one of its first statesmen, as its representative at the Court of St. James. On the day of his arrival in London, but without waiting for any communication with him, the British Cabinet published a proclamation, intended to prepare the way for a full recognition of the Confederacy, and which unmistakably evinced the ultimate purpose in that respect of the British crown.

The defeat of Bull Run appeared to be hailed in England with delight. It apparently determined the party in power to settle the fate of the Union without further postponement. From this time, until the final capture of the army of General Lee in April, 1865, the possibility that the rebellion might be suppressed was scarcely admitted in Great Britain. Mr. Bright, and perhaps half a dozen others, were the only leading Englishmen willing to speak a friendly word for the North, and every act of our government was performed under the impending danger of a recognition of the Confederacy, a disregard of the blockade, and the actual intervention of Great Britain in our attempt to suppress an insurrection upon our own territory.

On the 17th of November, 1861, the United States steamer *San Jacinto* arrived at Fortress Monroe with Messrs. Mason and Slidell prisoners on board. Captain

Wilkes, her commander, immediately reported to the Navy Department that, learning that these parties had been appointed on some diplomatic mission from the Southern Confederacy to Great Britain and France, and had run the blockade, reaching Havana from Charleston, expecting to depart from the former place on the 7th of the month in the English steamer *Trent* for St. Thomas, on their way to England, he had intercepted the *Trent*, in the Bahama Channel, on the 8th of November, about two hundred and forty miles from Havana, brought her to by firing a shell across her bows, and had forcibly captured from her Messrs. Mason and Slidell, with their secretaries, and now held them on board his ship in Hampton Roads. Detailed reports of all the officers concerned in the capture, with the protest of the Confederate envoys, and Captain Wilkes's reply thereto, accompanied the account of the capture.

On the receipt of this report, Mr. Welles, the Secretary of the Navy, congratulated Captain Wilkes, and stated that his "conduct in seizing these public enemies was marked by intelligence, ability, decision, and firmness, and has the emphatic approval of this Department." On the first day of the December Session of Congress, the House of Representatives passed a resolution, tendering the thanks of Congress to Captain Wilkes for the capture and arrest of Mason and Slidell.

As soon as the facts reached the State Department, which was some time about the first of December, Secretary Seward addressed a note to the American Minister in London, which he was requested to read to Earl Russell, stating that the action of Captain Wilkes *was without any instructions from his government*, and that he trusted that the British government would consider the subject in a friendly temper. The first information, therefore, received by Great Britain from our government, after the capture, announced that it was made without authority, and declared the willingness of the United States to consider the questions which it involved upon settled principles of international law.

The first communication from Earl Russell in relation to the capture indicated a very different temper. It was sent by a special messenger to Lord Lyons, who was directed to inform Secretary Seward of its contents. It declared that the act of Captain Wilkes was an affront to the British flag, and a violation of international law. It announced that "the liberation of the four gentlemen named and their delivery to your lordship, together with a suitable apology for the aggression, alone would satisfy the British nation." With this demand came information of the public excitement in England upon the first reception of the news of the capture, and of the action of the British authorities, which appeared to indicate their purpose to force the two countries into a war. •

As soon as the telegram announcing the boarding of the *Trent* by a Federal vessel of war was received in Liverpool, a placard was posted on the Exchange announcing the "outrage on the British flag," and calling a public meeting. This meeting was presided over by Mr. James Spence, who, upon taking the chair, read a resolution calling upon the government to assert the dignity of the British flag by requiring prompt reparation for this outrage. The resolution offered by Mr. Spence was carried by a tremendous majority.

The English Cabinet took its cue from the Liverpool meeting. Knowing that the capture was the unauthorized act of Captain Wilkes, and that precedents were not wanting of similar acts committed by British officers, and defended as lawful by the British government, the first act of Earl Russell was to despatch the peremptory demand referred to. It was afterwards known that the demand was first framed in language so offensive that our government would have been compelled to reject it on that account, and that its terms were greatly moderated by the intervention of the amiable husband of the queen. The last note ever written by the prince consort was the one suggesting a modification of the peremptory character of the British demand, and expressing the hope that Captain Wilkes had acted without instructions, or that, if he had instructions, that he misapprehended them. An intimation from so high a quarter could not be disregarded, and the despatch was modified as Prince Albert suggested. His death occurred only a few days later. For this noble act of friendship he deserved the gratitude of all loyal Americans.

Before the messenger intrusted with Earl Russell's letter had left her shores, the ports of the United Kingdom resounded with preparations for war. Steam transports were chartered, a large number of troops ordered to Canada, the Guards were directed to prepare for immediate, active service, all the saltpetre in the British islands was seized, and every possible preparation made to attack us with the whole naval and military force of the empire the instant the demand of Earl Russell was refused. The press wrought itself up to fury. It insisted that Captain Wilkes and Lieutenant Fairfax must be reprimanded and dismissed from the United States Navy; the rebel envoys delivered up; atonement must be made for the shot and shell fired, without notice, at a steamer conveying the royal mail, and in the words of the *Morning Chronicle*, Congress "must sit down, like ancient Pistol, to eat the leek it had insultingly brandished in British faces!"

At the same time, all the Confederate sympathizers in the North were seized with a violent attack of patriotic indignation. With one voice they declared that the insult offered by England was mortal, and that even the moderate measure of self-respect which the Lincoln Cabinet was supposed to possess required the rejection of the British demand in equally insulting terms. Many newspapers of similar tendencies added fuel to the flames. Clement L. Vallandigham, on the 20th of December, 1861, introduced in the House of Representatives a resolution which recited the capture of the envoys, who were conspirators, rebel enemies, and dangerous men, for which Captain Wilkes had received the approval of the Navy Department, and the thanks of Congress, with mention of the request made to the President by the House of Representatives, that he should confine Mason and Slidell in the cells of convicted felons, until certain military officers of the United States should be treated as prisoners of war, and then resolved that it was the duty of the President firmly to maintain the stand thus taken, approving and adopting the act of Captain Wilkes, in spite of any menace or demand of the British government, and pledging to him the support of the House in thus upholding the honor and vindicating the course of the government and people of the United States against a foreign power. This resolution was referred, without debate, to the Committee of Foreign Affairs.

It must not be forgotten that over and over again Great Britain had exercised the right which she now denied to us. The London *Times* afterwards declared that "unwelcome as the truth may be, it is nevertheless a truth, that we (Great Britain) have ourselves established a system of international law which now tells against us." The *Saturday Review*, a fierce Tory sheet, said that "it must in fairness be admitted that the outrage was not so glaringly in excess of belligerent rights as to be recognized in its true character until after a careful study of precedents and legal authorities." Professor Newman, one of the highest of British authorities in international law, stated that the liberties taken by English ships against the Americans, in the war with Napoleon, were as like the act of Captain Wilkes as two peas, in a moral point of view, and that Great Britain would have to pull the beam out of her own eye before instituting a search after the mote in her neighbor's. In fact, the proof was abundant that for the last one hundred years that power had always exercised this right, especially against weaker nations.

It is also undeniable that this demand of England stirred to its depths the indignation of many patriotic citizens of the loyal states. The United States had upon its hands the most gigantic rebellion the world had ever seen; it had met with disasters in the field; every resource was being employed in raising and equipping another army; the leaders of opinion in Great Britain almost unanimously predicted defeat, and spoke of the enterprise "to restore a defunct Union" as "altogether hopeless." The demand of the English premier under these circumstances must have been intended to deliver us an insult which we could not resent, or, if we would not endure the humiliation, which would drive our people into a war, and so give Great Britain what she so much desired, a pretext for joining hands with the South and disrupting the Union. In either aspect, the act was discreditable to a nation in which loyalty to the rules of fair fighting has always been supposed to be as universal as loyalty to its sovereign.

The two countries were saved from a war which could have had none but evil consequences by the good sense of President Lincoln and of two statesmen, their respective representatives—Lord Lyons and William H. Seward. Lord Lyons was a model Englishman. His substantial frame and broad shoulders furnished a suitable support to a head well provided with solid sense. An open face and clear blue eyes indicated the sincere and generous character of the man, and his contempt for falsehood and meanness. He would have been accepted as an umpire by any contestant who relied upon justice and merit alone. He had the traditional love of the Anglo-Saxon for fair play. He thoroughly understood the controversy between North and South, and knew that upon its issue depended the supremacy in the republic of freedom or slavery. His sympathies were heartily with the North; but he was, at the same time, a faithful representative of his own nation, and watchful in the protection of her interests.

We have no special information as to what passed between the English ambassador and Secretary Seward in their private interviews. But comparing events with the character of the men, we may pretty safely assume that the reading of Earl Russell's pronunciamento did not disturb the equanimity of either. Probably, after knocking the ashes from his cigar, Lord Lyons observed, "You will give up the men, Seward, of course! As prisoners, they may be of consequence enough to cause a war; set free, they are no good to anybody. You did not authorize their capture; their surrender involves no dishonor. Say yes, and you may deliver them up at your own time, and in your own way."

"Your lordship is perfectly right," Secretary Seward probably said. "Your views are such as we had the right to anticipate from your justice, and your knowledge of the facts. We don't want these people. You know, and I am surprised that it did not occur to Earl Russell, that we could not retain them against his demand, without repudiating the principles for which we once went to war, and which we have maintained for half a century. I think I take no risk in asking your friendly co-operation. Our people will be excited by all this unnecessary parade of preparation, and the imperative tenor of Earl Russell's demand. We have mischief-makers among us who will try to arouse opposition to the surrender, especially if it is made the occasion of display in one of our larger ports, or to one of your large vessels. Suppose you name some quiet harbor on the coast of New England, into which you can safely send a fourth-class vessel, as the place of delivery. I will send the prisoners there; you can have them quietly taken on board and sent on their way."

Possibly a smile spread over the face of the noble lord as he appreciated the full import of the secretary's suggestion. I had it from good authority, at the time, that he declared his complete indifference as to the time and place of surrender, and said that it was all the same to him whether it was made in New York Bay, or in the harbor of a fishing village on Cape Cod. In fact, it impressed him as a duty to conform to the wishes of the secretary in the matter of the surrender. The only other point upon which the secretary insisted was that the despatch of Earl Russell dealt with questions of such grave international importance as to render a hasty answer highly improper, and he might find it necessary to take all the time consistent with diplomatic usages to frame a suitable reply. This was also assented to; the representatives of the two countries had come to a perfect understanding, and they separated on the best of terms. In fact, the answer of Mr. Seward was shown to Lord Lyons within twenty-four hours, although it was not made public until the 27th of December.

The general excitement increased with every hour's delay. England seized upon the excuse for war. Her government spared no pains to proclaim its warlike purposes. Tory and Liberal coalesced; Lord Derby was consulted by the government, and hastened to its support. He suggested to ship-owners to instruct the captains of outward-bound ships to signal to any English vessels they might meet that war was extremely probable, and the underwriters approved the statesmanlike suggestion. Discussion of the affair had been prevented in Congress, but British threats and warlike preparations so clearly showed a purpose to bully our government into submission that the North became a unit against the surrender of the envoys. Had any greater delay intervened it would probably have been resisted by force. The sun of December 26th set, and the night closed in over a dangerously angry people.

On the morning of December 27th the clouds had all disappeared, and the political horizon to the eastward was quiet and serene. Mr. Seward had poured upon the angry waves of popular excitement the calming oil of his answer to Earl Russell's demand, and straightway the tempest was stilled. At considerable length, with the impartiality of a judicial opinion, the secretary summed up the facts of the capture as given by the British premier, slightly modified by the report of Captain Wilkes, and then set forth the demand, divested of its imperative or disagreeable features. He then added "some facts which doubtless were omitted by Earl Russell, with the very proper and becoming motive of allowing them to be brought into the case on the part of the United States," and concluded by saying that, according to the law of nations, the capture in this case was left unfinished or was abandoned—that while Great Britain might waive the defect, if, on the contrary, she insists upon it, the United States have no right to retain the captured persons, the chief benefits of the capture, by proving them contraband. On the contrary, the voluntary release of the *Trent* must be permitted to draw after it all its legal consequences. Having thus shown, as the secretary trusted he had done, " by a very simple and natural statement of the facts, and an analysis of the law applicable to them, that this government has neither meditated, nor practised, nor approved, any deliberate wrong in the transaction to which they have called its attention, it necessarily followed that what has happened has been simply an inadvertency, consisting in a departure by a naval officer, free from any wrongful motive, from a rule uncertainly established, and probably by the several parties concerned either imperfectly understood or entirely unknown. For this error the British government has a right to expect the same reparation that we, as an independent state, should expect from Great Britain, or from any other friendly nation in a similar case."

"Nor have I been tempted at all," he continued, "by suggestions that cases might be found in history where Great Britain refused to yield to other nations, and even to ourselves, claims like that which is now before us. Those cases occurred when Great Britain, as well as the United States, was the home of generations which, with all their peculiar interests and passions, have passed away. She could in no other way so effectually disavow any such injury, as we think she does by assuming now as her own the ground upon which we then stood. . . .

"The four persons in question are now held in military custody at Fort Warren, in the State of Massachusetts. They will be cheerfully liberated. Your lordship will please indicate a time and place for receiving them."

In a second despatch to Lord Lyons, dated on the same 30th of November, and received by Lord Lyons on the 18th of December, not intended to be read to Mr. Seward, the British ambassador had been directed thus: "Should Mr. Seward ask for delay . . . you will consent to a delay not exceeding seven days. If, at the end of that time, no answer is given, or if any other answer is given except that of compliance with the demands of her majesty's government, your lordship is instructed to leave Washington, with all the members of your legation, and to repair immediately to London." Lord Lyons was also directed to communicate Mr. Seward's answer to Vice-admiral Sir A. Milne, and to the governors of Canada, Nova Scotia, New Brunswick, Jamaica, Bermuda, and such other of her majesty's possessions as might be within his reach.

Mr. Seward's letter went to its mark with the force and directness of a pointed projectile from one of Sir William Armstrong's steel guns. A war with Great Britain in defence of the act of Captain Wilkes would have been a war resulting from the direct opposite of the cause for which we waged against the same power the war of 1812. It, therefore, logically followed that the menaces, the elaborate preparations to strike us when we could not return the blow, and the wrath and anger of the British lion, all were founded upon a sudden and complete abandonment, without notice, of the principles of international law, for which Great Britain had always contended, and to which we intended to remain loyal. Without comment or objection, Mr. Seward left to her whatever of honor or credit such conduct might gain, but his recommendation to his own country was the pursuit of its own policy without variableness or shadow of turning.

Contemporaneously with Mr. Seward's letter, suggestions were published which might have had the same origin. Attention was called to the fact that, to decline the surrender of the prisoners, and so make them a *casus belli*, would enable them to pose in the character of martyrs, and give them an importance which they could not otherwise secure. But, if they were surrendered, they would drop into obscurity as soon as their admirers discovered that no profit was to be made from them, and not be heard of again. This prediction was completely verified.

From the publication of Mr. Seward's letter there was no objection heard in the loyal states to its reasoning or its conclusions. Citizens saw its wisdom; some of the newspapers which had been most earnest against the surrender of the envoys hastened to retract their error, and range themselves on the side of the secretary and the country. The Confederate sympathizers saw that the current of opinion was too strong to be stemmed, and stood dumb. The course of the English press was as singular as before the demand. It would have been scarcely decent not to show some satisfaction at the removal of such threatening differences between the two countries, and two or three of the leading journals promptly recognized the statesmanship of Secretary Seward and the value of the influence of Lord Lyons.

The London *Times*, the *Saturday Review*, and other sheets hostile to the North, attributed the surrender of the prisoners to American cowardice and fear. Their success was not encouraging. They were noticed only to be ridiculed, and very soon subsided into a mortified silence, occasionally broken by grumbling denials of our successes in the field. The feeling of sympathy with the South and hostility to the North continued to exist in many British minds, but it was more cautious in its manifestations, and never again had such an opportunity for development as it found in the case of the *Trent*. Not many months afterwards France kindly offered her mediation between the American belligerents, but was promptly informed by Mr. Seward that no war between belligerents, but only an armed insurrection, existed, which the United States was vigorously and triumphantly putting down; that we were obliged to our ancient ally for her good intentions, but as for her mediation, or that of any other power, we would have none of it. After this the powers of Europe left us to settle our own controversies in our own way.

It was found convenient for Lord Lyons to send a small English steamer to the quiet harbor of Provincetown, on the Massachusetts coast, where our government undertook to deliver the prisoners, previously confined at Fort Warren, near Boston. The season and the circumstances subjected them to some inconveniences. Our larger steamers were all on duty, and it was therefore necessary to send the envoys from Fort Warren on board a tug, not provided with passenger accommodations. They were sent in charge of Mr. Webster, a subordinate in the State Department. From him I learned that the weather was unusually tempestuous, even for December; that, in fact, the trip was made in a furious northeast gale.

The prisoners were not good sailors; the tug rolled and pitched fearfully, so that the unfortunate envoys were extremely sea-sick all the way to the rendezvous. There were times when he feared he would be unable to deliver them, for they claimed vehemently that life, under such disagreeable conditions, was undesirable. But, notwithstanding the difficulties, they succeeded at last in making the harbor; the prisoners were delivered into the charge of the British ship, which they declared was no better than the tug, and altogether unfit for diplomatic service. This spirit of captiousness was annoying to the officers of the ship, who maintained that a vessel which served as the home of officers of the Royal Navy was good enough for Confederate prisoners. Their voyage across the Atlantic did not begin under favorable auspices, but was finally accomplished, and thus closed this much-talked-of incident in American history. As the secretary had predicted, the mission of the envoys to the great powers of Europe was a failure, and their proceedings never afterwards disturbed our peace.

President Lincoln's views upon the "Trent affair" were promptly expressed with his customary common-sense and brevity. As soon as the capture was reported, he said that "it did not look right for Captain Wilkes to stop the vessel of a friendly power on the high seas, and take out of her, by force, passengers who went on board in one neutral port to be carried to another. And if it was, he did not understand whence Captain Wilkes got the authority to turn his own quarter-deck into a court of admiralty." With the people, it is not improbable that this plain, forcible view was as convincing as the able legal argument of Mr. Seward.

• After Mr. Seward's death, Mr. Gideon Welles, Mr. Lincoln's Secretary of the Navy, published several magazine articles, afterwards collected in a volume, in which he claimed that Mr. Seward at first opposed, and only consented to the surrender of the prisoners when he was overruled by the President and a majority of the Cabinet, and consequently was entitled to no credit in the premises. It is unpleasant to take issue with Mr. Welles, but the first despatch to Mr. Adams, to which I have referred, shows Mr. Seward's position; and I know that his opinion was unchanged from the first report of the capture to the surrender.

XXII.

THE ANTAGONISM OF THE REGULAR TO THE VOLUNTEER SERVICE.—THE INFLUENCE OF PRESIDENT LINCOLN.

THE events of the War of the Rebellion followed each other in such rapid succession that there was no time for contemporary examination of their relative importance. Those who were then in the public service will remember how, before one occurrence could be dealt with, another pressed upon their attention, so that any event outside the line of their duties necessarily passed without particular observation. As the general picture of those terrible years recedes into the past, some of its points, before unnoticed, rise into prominence. There were several such incidents which attracted slight attention while the war was in progress, which, regarded from a later standpoint, singularly illustrate the powerful influence for the maintenance of the Union, always exerted by the strong, native common-sense of Abraham Lincoln.

The heads of bureaus and of divisions in the bureaus seldom changed with the administration before the year 1864. In the spring of 1861 these positions in the War and Navy Departments were filled by officers of those services, usually more than sixty years of age. They had had but little experience in war. Such as they had was restricted to the war with Mexico, in which the fighting was wholly on land and in another country, besides a few local contests with the Indian tribes. There had been no fighting in the navy since 1815. It was the fact, however, that officers whose names were scarcely known to the country were at the head of these bureaus at the beginning of the War of the Rebellion, and controlled the subjects of arms, munitions, equipment, clothing, medicine and surgery, hospitals, the construction of vessels, steam-machinery, and engineering; in short, the administration of all the military and naval resources of the nation. In these bureaus everything was provided for by "regulations." An application made to the secretary for the introduction of any new arm, invention, or proposed improvement was by rule referred to the bureau with which it was connected for a report. All the traditions of these bureaus assumed that their respective regulations were perfect, that all known sources of information respecting them were to be there found, and that any change for the better was impossible. Add to these traditions contempt for popular ideas as crude and impracticable, and it is obvious that the accomplishment of any change in the theory or practice of one of these departments was a work to be accomplished, if at all, only by great perseverance and patience.

At the commencement of the war, except a small number of Colt's revolvers for the cavalry, there was not a breech-loading gun in the service. The old smooth-bore musket of the Revolution, modified by a few changes made in the armories of the United States, was the arm of the infantry. When the first call for seventy-five thousand men was made, it became necessary to purchase guns for their use. A large number of muskets, which Belgium had discarded for an improved weapon, had been sent over to New York city, where they were offered to the Government at a very low price—about three dollars each. As these afforded an economical means of arming the Volunteer Infantry at a small expense, they were promptly purchased, and issued to the regiments first mustered into service. Complaint of them was general. Men who were accustomed to handle the rifle declared that the least dangerous point of their effective field was in front of their muzzles.

The First Vermont Regiment was one of the earliest regiments mustered into service after the call. It comprised several uniformed companies, drilled and disciplined, in which were to be found merchants, manufacturers — in short, the very best native Vermonters. Its colonel (Phelps) had been educated at West Point; after long and gallant service in the regular army he had resigned, leaving a most creditable record. Governor Fairbanks, who was aware that the *personnel* of the regiment was well known to me, sent one of his aides to say that it was rumored that the regiment was to be armed with the Belgian muskets; that Colonel Phelps was of opinion that they were unfit for use; that the government had new Enfield rifles, then on shipboard in the harbor of New York, of which the First Vermont would make as good use as any other regiment; that he respectfully requested the delivery of one thousand of these rifles to the regiment; that if this request could not be complied with, the state preferred to purchase good arms for the regiment if the Secretary of War would authorize him to do so. He added that immediate action was necessary, as the regiment would arrive in New York city on the following day.

Taking a personal interest in the regiment, and desiring to promote the object of Governor Fairbanks, I immediately laid the facts before Secretary Cameron, who referred me to Colonel Thomas A. Scott, then the Assistant Secretary of War. Colonel Scott said that I must know that such a request was required by the regulations to be made in writing to the secretary, who must have a report upon it from the proper bureau, before he could either grant or reject it, adding that an officer of one department ought not to request an official of another to violate its rules. I replied that I would have taken the usual course if I had wished to have Governor Fairbanks's request denied, as applications from civilians invariably were, but that, as I wanted the rifles, I had applied to those who had the power and sometimes the will to grant such requests; and that, moreover, I had no time to waste in applications which we both knew would be refused. Finding that I was rather persistent, Colonel Scott finally said that the application must be made to the Chief of the Bureau of Ordnance, but if he refused it I might return, and he would see what could be done! I told him that I would go through the formality if I must, but that I should certainly return within half an hour.

I found the Chief of the Ordnance hedged in by more successive guards than the Secretary of War. Disregarding their remonstrances, I went directly to the chief official, apologizing that my own duties prevented me from giving time to the usual formalities of his approach. I found an elderly gentleman, who would never see seventy again, with very white hair and a very red face. I replied to his inquiry, "What I wanted," in the fewest possible words: "An order from the War Department on the proper office in New York, to deliver one thousand Enfield rifles to the governor for the use of the First Vermont Regiment." The scarlet hue of his face deepened into crimson, as he exclaimed: "Such an application was never heard of! Why was it not made regularly through the Secretary of War?" "Because there was no time," I was about to say, when he fiercely continued: "It is too late. The guns for that regiment have been issued and the orders signed. They will not now be changed."

"I supposed the order had been issued," I said, "and that it was to arm the regiment with the Belgian muskets. It is that order which I wish to have changed. I know that the Department has Enfield rifles; the Vermonters want them. The emergency is pressing, and I cannot waste any time in mere formalities. I have come to you at the request of Colonel Scott, who, I understood, was your superior officer. I assured him that my application to this bureau would be unavailing; but the Vermonters must have the rifles. If I cannot get the order for them here or elsewhere, I must go to the President."

The shock of the intimation that an order of his bureau, once signed, could be recalled, or of the proposition to ask the President to overrule it, appeared for a moment to arrest the action of his organs of speech, or I am certain he would not have listened to so long a statement. His face and hands turned to a dark purple, as his words vainly struggled for expression. He bounded from his chair and made a rush, which I thought was intended for my person. But the impetus carried him by me to a corner of the room, where stood a musket of the old Springfield pattern, the stock of which was held to the barrel by the well-known iron-bands. Except that it had a percussion lock, it was the identical arm which frightened the crows from the cornfields in my boyhood. This gun he seized with both hands, raised it above his head, and shook it furiously. He had gained command of his voice now, for he roared, rather than exclaimed: "These volunteers don't know what they want! There is the best arm that was ever put into the hands of a raw volunteer! When he throws that away, as they generally do, he does not throw away twenty-five dollars' worth of government property!"

I remarked that the Vermonters had no use for guns to be thrown away, and retired. Returning to Colonel Scott, I related my experience, and obtained the order for the rifles without further difficulty. The fact that President Lincoln could be reached in this case was controlling. But for that the First Vermont would have carried Belgian muskets through their nine months' campaign.

I had taken note of the excited bureau-chief's remark, that "the First Vermont had already got its orders." This might mean that they had been ordered to some disagreeable post, when I knew that they preferred active service. I therefore, before leaving the department, determined to call on General Scott, and see whether I could not influence the destination of the regiment. I obtained access to him without any delay. The gallant old hero of Lundy's Lane at once recognized the name of Colonel Phelps, and said: "Write to Colonel Phelps that I have not forgotten him; your request in behalf of his regiment shall be attended to." As I was taking my leave Colonel Townsend requested me to wait a few moments in his office. He was one of the aides of the Commander of the Army. His consultation with General Scott occupied but a few moments. He then came to me in his own room, and said: "I cannot inform you where the regiment of Colonel Phelps will be sent. He will receive his orders to-morrow in New York, and he will be quite satisfied with them." The regiment was ordered to Fortress Monroe, the post which Colonel Phelps would himself have selected.

In this instance the accessibility of the President and the use of his name sufficed to overcome the hard-shelled formalities of the War Office. In other instances that Department resisted every influence but the active intervention of Mr. Lincoln's common-sense. The next experience in attempting to introduce a change was with the bureau of the Surgeon-General of the Army.

If seventy-five thousand volunteers were suddenly called into active service in the swamps and marshes of the South, subject to the diseases incidental to constant exposure in a new climate, together with the casualties of battle, it was obvious to everybody except the Surgeon-General that the ordinary resources at his command would be wholly inadequate to preserve their health or secure their comfort. The recent experiences of European nations in war, which had availed themselves to the fullest extent of the assistance of private organizations to supplement the deficiencies of a better service than our own, had demonstrated the great value of such organizations, if any proof had been needed. As if by a common impulse, the charitable and benevolent of all the loyal states contributed large sums of money, and organized that magnificent charity, now well-known in history by its excellent work in saving lives, the Sanitary Commission. Dr. Bellows, of New York, accompanied by equally eminent citizens from other large cities, proceeded to Washington, and tendered their organization, with its abundant resources and supplies already accumulated, to the War Department for the use of the army. In the regular course of such human events their offer was referred to the bureau of the Surgeon-General of the Army. To their surprise and confusion, their offer was rejected with undisguised contempt. They were told, in substance, that they were interfering with matters which did not concern them, about which they knew nothing; that the Department was able to perform its own duties, and wanted none of their assistance. In short, they were, figuratively, turned out of the office and told to go home and attend to their own affairs, for their volunteered assistance was an annoyance, the repetition of which would not be tolerated.

The indignant mortification of these eminent citizens may be imagined. They had previously supposed themselves engaged in an honorable public service—they were told now that they were impertinent intermeddlers with matters beyond their sphere. Upon one conclusion they were agreed: they would shake the dust of the War Office from their feet, go home, and supply their comforts directly to the soldiers, without the endorsement or intervention of the fossils of that department.

They were about to depart from the capital, when some happy thought or fortunate suggestion turned their minds to Abraham Lincoln. They called upon him and related their experience. He "sent for" the Surgeon-General. A request for his immediate attendance at the Executive Mansion was one which even that exalted official did not think it prudent to decline. "These gentlemen tell me," said the President, "that they have raised a large amount of money, and organized a parent and many subordinate societies throughout the loyal states to provide the soldier with comforts, with materials to preserve his health, to shelter him, to cure his wounds and diseases, which the regulations of the War Department do not permit your office to supply—that they offer to do all this without cost to the government or any interference with the action of your department or the good order and discipline of the army, and that you have declined this offer. With my limited information I should suppose that this government would wish to avail itself of every such offer that was made. I wish to have you tell me why you have rejected the proposals of these gentlemen?"

Had the President realized the cruelty of confronting an old bureau officer of the War Department, encrusted with all the traditions of "how-not-to-do-it," suddenly and without previous opportunity to frame an•excuse, with the hard, inflexible sense of such a question, he would have been more merciful. The officer was confounded. He could only mumble some indefinite objections to outside interference with the management of the War Office, and claim that the Department could take care of its own sick and wounded—in short, his attempts at excuse were failures. "If that is all you can say," remarked the President, "I think you will have to accept the offer, and co-operate to the extent of your ability with these gentlemen in securing its benefits to the army." Bureaucracy struggled against common-sense no longer. The Sanitary Commission was the greatest, the most active charity of the war. Tens of thousands of saved lives, of naked men clothed, of wounded men sheltered and made comfortable, had good reason to bless the name of Abraham Lincoln, whose common-sense secured for them the benefits of such an invaluable organization.

XXIII.

THE COLORED PEOPLE.—THEIR INDUSTRY IN LEARNING TO READ.—THEIR IMPLICIT CONFIDENCE IN PRESIDENT LINCOLN.

I HAD some opportunities, particularly during the first few months of my residence in Washington, of observing the influence upon the colored race of their prospective emancipation, which were very interesting at the time. I transcribe from my journals some of the notes which I thought were worthy of preservation.

In the first month of my official life, an old resident and former official of the city, Ex-Mayor Wallach, called to ask me to appoint a colored man as a laborer in the register's office. He was a slave, whose master was a Virginia Secessionist; he was out of employment, and in absolute want. Mr. Wallach recommended him highly, saying that, besides making himself useful in the office, he was perfectly competent to assist, if any one wished to entertain dinner or other company, by taking charge of the entire affair — making provision for, cooking, and serving a dinner to the satisfaction of the most exacting. Besides, he was thoroughly honest, for the ex-mayor and his friends had employed and trusted him for many years. In view of so high a recommendation, I promised to give him a trial. His name, Mr. Wallach said, was Walker Lewis.

The next morning Lewis called upon me. He was about forty years of age, and, except for his color, had few of the characteristics of the negro. He was erect, rather slim, with a face and lips which would not have discredited any white man. He was neatly dressed, and in manner and conversation a gentleman. I addressed a few inquiries to him, and by degrees drew from him the history of his life. From boyhood his master had hired him out as a servant at hotels and watering-places. He had been for many seasons at the White Sulphur Springs and Old Point Comfort, and during the sessions of Congress he had been employed by one of the Washington hotels patronized by Southerners. He had been married once, when quite young, but his family had become separated, and he never expected to see them again. Asked if his master allowed him to have any part of his wages, he replied no, that he had to pay to him not only his wages, but all the gratuities which gentlemen gave him. He was acquainted with many leading Southern statesmen, and had served some of them. He had been steward for President Tyler and several others. When I asked him what his last employment had been, he answered, without the slightest hesitation, that he had been the steward of Major H——'s gambling-house, until the war broke out, when, all the gentlemen having gone South, business was dull, and the house had been closed. He was, therefore, out of employment, had no money, and, if I would give him a place, he would serve me very faithfully.

"But, Lewis," I said, "if I secure you a place in the Treasury, your work would be carrying money, bonds, and securities, in large amounts, from one room or office to another. Do you think it would be safe to put a man in such a position whose last employment was in a gambling-house?"

An expression passed over his face that touched me. It was pitiful. His voice trembled, and his eyes filled with tears as he said, "I wish you would only try me, master! I never gambled; I never drink liquor; I don't think I am any worse for working in a gambling-house. If I had had any choice about it, it might have been different. But I never had any choice of employment in my life. I have had to go where my master hired me out, and do what I was told to do. Seems a little hard, master, that I can't have one trial!"

"It is hard, Lewis!" I said, "and you shall have one trial. Come here to-morrow, and your name shall be placed on the roll. But the first time you go wrong you will probably go to prison; and you must drop that word 'master,' which you have used so many times. Every man in this bureau who does his duty and obeys the rules is his own master, and will have no other."

"But, master," he exclaimed, "I can't help it. I kind of forget myself. I was never spoken to so before. No! no white man ever treated me like you do. I should like to call you master. Seems like I must do something to show you how grateful I am."

Lewis's name was borne on the pay-roll of the register's office for many years after I left it; until, indeed, his hair was white, and he had accumulated a modest competence. He married, and became in time one of the leading citizens of his race in Washington. When I left the Treasury I was of the opinion that, in the three or four past years, Lewis had handled more money and securities than any other person in that department or outside of it. He was a model of industry, gratitude, and integrity. I never could break him of the use of the word "master."

Long after his appointment I noticed that, whenever I met Lewis in one of the halls of the Treasury, he would invariably cross over to the other side, and pass me as far away as possible. This was so often repeated that I saw it was intentional, and I insisted upon an explanation. I said that his conduct indicated that he was afraid of me.

"Oh, no, master," he exclaimed, "I am not afraid of you, the best friend I ever had! I will tell you about it. If I lost one of these bundles, or anybody got one away from me, I would be ruined; you would think I was dishonest. When I first began to carry money, I said to myself, 'Now, if I never let anybody get within ten feet of me when I am carrying a Treasury bundle, I will be sure that nobody gets that bundle.' So I just made a little rule, only for myself, you see, and it is this: 'Walker, when you have a Treasury bundle in your hands, never let anybody, not your best friend, not the register, come within ten feet of you, until you have put that bundle where it belongs!'"

It would have been to the profit of many treasuries if other messengers had adopted the Walker Lewis rule.

There was, at the corner of Eleventh and K Streets, a colored church, the oldest, I believe, in Washington. I passed it every day on my way to the Treasury, and frequently attended its meetings. At first, minister and members were reserved in my presence, and I saw little which might not have taken place in the churches of Drs. Gurley and Sunderland. But on one occasion it was my fortune to listen to a plain discussion of my character and relations to the colored race, which ended in an expression of confidence, and a conclusion that, since I had recommended colored men to office, and was the friend of Massa Linkum, there was no reason why I should not be admitted to their most secret councils. Afterwards their services were conducted without any apparent notice of my presence.

Meetings were held in this church almost every evening. Once or twice a week discussions were held of public questions in which the colored people were interested. The debates were usually opened by the pastor, but participated in by members of the church of both sexes. When it is remembered that the pastor was a slave, who worked for his master six days in the week, and that the members, with few exceptions, were born in slavery, and had no knowledge of freedom save the hope of it in the future, through the influence of "Massa Linkum," my readers will not wonder at the interest I felt in these debates, nor at my surprise at the manner in which they were conducted.

I was once invited to act as umpire, or judge, at one of these discussions. The question was, "What makes the white man the superior of the colored man?" I excused myself on the ground that I was interested in the question, and could not trust my own impartiality. But I did not fail to attend the meeting at which the subject was to be discussed.

The principal remarks were made by the minister. The report is deprived of much of its interest, and all of its genuine pathos, by my inability to give the dialect of the speakers. I shall only attempt to show by a few extracts the good sense which was a prominent feature of the discussion, the accuracy with which these people, whom we called ignorant, appreciated the situation, and the intelligence with which they set about preparing themselves for the coming change in their condition.

The white man, the pastor said, was their superior. This must be so, or he would not have been able to keep them for generations in slavery, and he would not now be able to live upon their labor. "He makes the world believe that we are a careless, thriftless race; that, like the grasshopper, we will not lay up anything for the future, and would starve when winter comes, if he did not take care of us. We know this is not true. How many men can I count in this congregation who are supporting the families of their white masters with the wages of their labor, besides taking care of their own wives and children? I am doing it, for one, and I do not know of any income which my master has had for a long time except the earnings of his slaves. If we support ourselves and our masters while we are slaves, we can surely take care of ourselves when we are free.

"Brethren, the great God has been very kind and merciful to us and our generation. Just like as he saved Moses from the crocodiles, and raised him up to lead his people out of the land of Egypt and out of the house of bondage; just like as he saved the dear Lord from the butchers of old wicked Herod, and bred him up to give every sinful black or white man or woman one chance to repent and escape out of the hands of old Satan, so he has now raised up Massa Linkum, and preserved his life, so that he might give us freedom. If we don't do our part towards getting ready for freedom, we don't deserve to be set free. One thing that we must do in getting ready is, to show the world that we can take care of ourselves, and that the superiority of the white man is not given him by the Almighty, and that he cannot hold it, if we do our duty.

"For the power and control of the white man over us comes from his education. He can make books and newspapers, and he can use them for his advantage. He can read history, and profit by it; he can carry on trade, make bargains, and use us to build houses and railroads, because he is educated, and can read and write and make figures. We cannot do all that he does, because we cannot read and write. What can he do with his arms and hands that we cannot do? And, if we had his education, why could we not do all these other things as well as he? Brethren, this is not a question. A question has two sides to it—this has got only one. You know that an ignorant white man is a poorer creature than an ignorant colored man. A poor white in the South is lower down than any slave. Who supports the rum-shops in this city? Is it the ignorant whites or the ignorant colored men? Yet these white men go every week from the grog-shops to the penitentiary, claiming how much better they are than the 'niggers,' with whom they are too respectable to associate!

"Oh, my dear brethren, I have only just now learned to read. Until we heard that Massa Linkum was elected I never had a spelling-book or learned my letters. I was sixty-five years old before I knew the difference between A and B. I thank the Lord that now I can read the news; that I can read the Bible. I am learning every day. Every hour that I can save from my work I give to my Reader, Geography, and Arithmetic. I want to see every colored man and woman, and every colored child, with a spelling-book or a primer or some other book always in their hands. Pretty soon now we shall have our freedom. I don't know just when, but the Lord and Massa Linkum knows, and they will tell us in their own good time. Freedom will come before we are ready. Let us get ready as fast as we can. Getting ready means learning to read and write, and make figures. When we all learn to do these things—when we educate ourselves and our children, we shall be the equals of any white race on the face of the earth; we shall become a credit to our race, to the country, and to that great and good man who has been raised up by the Lord to give us freedom. The Bible is all full of directions to get wisdom, to get education. It tells how one poor man saved a city when a great king, with a mighty army, tried to take it, because he had wisdom."

Suddenly the old man dropped upon his knees, and, raising his clasped hands in the most unstudied attitude of supplication, exclaimed, " Oh, Lord, teach my people! teach my people!" I never heard a more earnest and touching prayer. Every person in the crowded church was kneeling, and spontaneously their musical voices, pitched to the same key, swelled a mighty refrain— " Hear him, good Lord! hear him!" A single voice sang, " Praise God!" and with an effect almost indescribable the old doxology rang through the church from floor to roof-tree. I came away while the influence of the scene was upon me, humbled and abashed by the lesson which the old colored preacher had taught me of the injustice of my race, and deeply impressed by the earnest simplicity of this effort of a simple-minded man to prepare his people for emancipation.

At this period observing men could not have failed to notice that many colored men had become students of the spelling-book and primer. Porters at the hotels were poring over the well-thumbed pages whenever they had a moment of spare time. One of the laborers in my office, an old, white-haired man, had arranged to perform his service with promptness, and then to be called whenever he should be wanted. His mysterious disappearances led me to make inquiry, and, through a clerk, I soon discovered the old man's occupation during the intervals of work. The files-room of the register was in the basement of the Treasury. In a recess, formed by a window at the farther end of the room, was a space large enough to seat four persons. It was a corner seldom visited, and far away from the hall or passage.

Here four colored employés of the Treasury had improvised a school-room. Not one of them was under sixty-five years of age; the man employed in the Register's Office must have been fully threescore and ten. They had arranged narrow seats facing each other, and at the time of my entrance their teacher, a colored boy of about ten years, was hearing their lessons. My old laborer, through an enormous pair of horn spectacles, was reading out his lesson in words of three letters. He attacked his task with great earnestness, shaking his white, woolly head as he came to a hard place in it, but finally spelled out, without assistance, "The-dog-can-run." His teacher praised his improvement, and said he should soon put him in words of four letters. His old, wrinkled face beamed with delight as he asked, "Do you t'ink I can manage 'em, sonny? Dey're drefful hard!" The teacher assured him that he could, and that before very long he would be able to read the newspaper, which appeared to be the universal *desideratum*.

The colored people frequently had the latest and freshest news. How they got it I never ascertained. When armies were fighting, they used to assemble in parties of a dozen or twenty, when one would read aloud to the others all the news from the morning journals. They had other sources of information of which we knew nothing. Several times my colored messengers brought me intelligence in advance of the press. It had been decided to issue the Emancipation Proclamation before the battle of Antietam. I was first informed of its intended postponement by one of these messengers, who said that the President would not issue it until we had gained a victory; that, if issued at that time, it might be regarded as a desperate act, resorted to because we despaired of success in the field. His information was perfectly accurate. To my inquiry whether the delay would not prove a disappointment to the negro race, he made the answer which was so frequently repeated, and which illustrated their absolute confidence in the President, " Why, no, sir! Of course Massa Linkum knows best!"

XXIV.

SECRETARY CAMERON.—HIS RESIGNATION.—GENERAL FREMONT.
—HIS TROUBLES IN THE DEPARTMENT OF THE WEST.—SECRETARY STANTON.—HIS CHARACTER.—THE DAVIS COMMISSION.
—MR. O'NEILL'S REPORT ON SECRETARY STANTON'S SERVICES.

The circumstances which led to the resignation of the War Department by Secretary Cameron, and the selection of Mr. Stanton as his successor, have never been fairly presented to the public. They form a complicated chapter of our war history; they are numerous and deserve greater space than I can afford to give them. I have long felt that the general estimate entertained by the American people of the character and services of Mr. Stanton was much less favorable than it should be. Some of the facts within my knowledge may tend to a more correct appreciation of the great War Secretary, and to remove public misapprehensions, which but for his strong peculiarities Mr. Stanton would have himself rendered impossible.

In December, 1861, our republic was passing through a very trying period of its existence. There had been no successes in the field to compensate for the disaster of Bull Run. The country was putting forth a mighty effort to raise and organize an army, under a young and untried general; the Confederates, united and defiant, had suppressed every expression of loyalty in the revolted states, and their sympathizers in the North were holding conventions and resolving that the war was a failure. Just at this time Great Britain had found in the

"Trent affair" an excuse to deal us a blow which we had not the strength to return, and the Treasury, taxed to its utmost capacity, and struggling under its burdens, had reached a point where it must be relieved from the demands with which it was flooded from the "Department of the West," or publicly confess its inability to carry them.

Secretary Cameron, as the result of his own experience, had decided that the War Department required the services of a more energetic secretary. No friend of the Union doubted the loyalty or the patriotism of this eminent Pennsylvanian. His long connection with, and administration of, large corporations gave him most excellent business qualifications for the War Office. Then, as now, the Pennsylvania Railroad Company was generally accepted as a model for the business management of a great institution. Colonel Thomas A. Scott was credited with originating its business system. He was then in the prime of life, and, with his corps of lieutenants in the railroad service, followed his old chief into the War Department. So far as its business management was concerned, this Department was supposed to be better equipped than any other in the government. And so it was. The quick perception and energy of Colonel Scott, in which his aides participated, rapidly revealed the time-sanctified obstructions, and so cleared away the dead-wood of the office that it was brought to the highest state of efficiency.

But Colonel Scott encountered one obstruction which he could not overcome. It was the contempt of the officers of the regular army for the appointments from civil life. At that time every head of a bureau in the War Office was an officer of the regular army, with a very limited experience in the field. They sincerely believed that all good things came out of West Point, and that four years there, followed by twenty-five years of theoretical service in the army, were the indispensable qualifications of a bureau officer. These men never openly opposed efforts at improvement. They were always apparently ready to correct abuses, avoid procrastination, and co-operate in making the Department a model of business efficiency.

But, somehow, it always happened that when it was proposed to carry a new rule into practice, and cut off some venerable excrescence, it could not be done. No one openly objected—the difficulties arose spontaneously. If the change was pressed, objections multiplied, and the endeavor was sure to encounter the opposition of every employé, reinforced by whatever outside influence he could control. That the existing system was perfection itself was the principal article of faith of the bureau clerk. The result commonly was, that the enthusiasm for reform waned, as objections multiplied, and, after continuing the contest for a few weeks without accomplishing any good result, the advocate for improvement gave it up, and the bureau settled down into its former quiet inefficiency, much to the comfort of the official in command and his subordinates. It is true that public indignation eventually interfered, but how many lives were lost, what an aggregate of suffering and waste of money were entailed, by the hostility of the regular service to anything proposed by civilians cannot readily be estimated.

The custom of the heads of some military departments to make contracts without regard to the ability of the Treasury to meet their payments more than once brought the Treasury to the verge of bankruptcy. A very brief experience satisfied Colonel Scott of the imminence of this danger, and the total lack of necessity for the same. He proposed a change, which would still have left to such commander a limited discretion, but would have restricted his powers within safe limits. He met with the united resistance of the whole Department. It was declared an insult to military officers to subject them to such rules. Had these bureau officers seconded the wise proposals of Colonel Scott an enormous waste of money would have been avoided and the necessity for a change of secretaries would not have arisen. Finding that all his efforts at reform only served to excite opposition, and as his wish to assist his old chief had been his only reason for coming into the Department, Colonel Scott left it, and returned to his railroad, whither all his lieutenants followed him.

In June, 1861, General Fremont, just returned from abroad, was appointed to the command of the "Department of the West," with his headquarters at St. Louis. Missouri had been saved to the Union by the vigorous loyalty of her citizens. There was, therefore, some excuse for giving to General Fremont powers in addition to those usually vested in the head of a military department. He was authorized to purchase or construct vessels for use upon the Western rivers; in effect to create a navy.

During April and May there had been much looseness in the allowance of claims upon the national Treasury from St. Louis and its vicinity; the War Department had assumed some claims created by citizens without previous authority. The apology for this gross irregularity, if any such apology existed, was that the government property could not be otherwise protected. The consequences were not slow in making their appearance.

Men are apt to be liberal with the money of others, and the loyal citizens of Missouri were much like other men. As soon as the precedent was established, these claims increased to a frightful aggregate, which led to the creation of the Department of the West, and an order, that thereafter all the moneys of the United States must be disbursed by the regularly appointed officers of the government.

This order produced no diminution in the claims. To every remonstrance General Fremont replied that the claims originated before his appointment, and that he was not responsible for them. During the summer and autumn they reached an amount which it was difficult for the Treasury to meet, and some disposition must be made of them, or their continued payment be openly refused. Suspicions of their honesty began to arise. For example, an account for army blankets of a well-known description had been allowed, and a warrant drawn for its payment. The register caused the list to be copied, without the prices, and submitted to two Washington dealers, who were requested to name the prices at which they would furnish five or ten pairs of like blankets to the Treasury. Both named the same price, which was only 32 per cent. of that paid at St. Louis. The facts were communicated immediately to Secretary Chase. The subject was considered in Cabinet meeting, where it was determined that payment of all claims against the Military Department of the West which originated prior to the appointment of General Fremont should be suspended until they were examined by a commission which should report the facts, with its opinion upon the amount equitably due. The order first applied only to "unsettled claims," but before its labors finally terminated the commission's jurisdiction was extended to claims which had been approved by the accounting officers.

Towards the end of October the President appointed David Davis, of Illinois, Joseph Holt, of Kentucky, and Hugh Campbell, of Missouri, members of this commission. These gentlemen, were eminently fitted for the stern duties they were required to perform. They were just men, who would as readily reduce to its true value the claim of the most influential citizen as of the most insignificant person.

Before this commission was appointed, General Fremont had involved himself in complications which seriously interfered with his efficiency. He had issued a proclamation manumitting the slaves of rebels, which President Lincoln found it necessary to modify. A man of great amiability of character, he had too great confidence in the statements of others, and thus was easily influenced by designing men. His personal integrity was unquestioned, but his amiable weaknesses were so well known that the President had been unwilling to place him in command of such an important department, and had only been induced to do so by the persistence of the general's influential relatives and friends. His appointment was the signal for the gathering at St. Louis of the clans of the speculative, the unprincipled, and the dishonest. These men applauded him in the newspapers and extolled him to his face. They lost no opportunity of assuring him that he was the greatest military leader, the most distinguished statesman of his generation; in short, that the finger of destiny pointed to him as the coming President, the inevitable successor of Mr. Lincoln. There are few men, and General Fremont was not of the number, who do not like to be praised. The interested persons referred to were extremely vigilant. They took almost entire possession of the general, and made it very difficult for others to approach him, or to get his attention to the most urgent public business. A profitable contract was the one thing needful, the single reward which every one of these persons was seeking. The demands upon the Treasury indicated that few of them sought it in vain.

The criticisms upon the conduct of General Fremont culminated in charges against him, preferred by General Frank Blair. Although the confidence of loyal citizens in his fidelity to the Union remained unshaken, President Lincoln determined that the good of the service required his removal from his command. The order to that effect reached him at Springfield, Missouri, on the 2d of November. His conduct upon that occasion should always be remembered to his credit. He was in hourly expectation of a Confederate attack. His body-guard, which was devoted to him, was excited and indignant. But instead of sulking in his tent, he continued his preparations to meet the enemy, and spent the night in watchful inspection of the defences, ready to lead the army if the anticipated attack should be made. His brief address to his men, written during that night, is a model of its kind. It contains no trace of sullenness. It urges the army principally to make him proud of them by continuing to his successor the cordial support which had so much encouraged him. His single regret was that he could not have the honor of leading them to the victory they were about to win, but he should claim the right to share in the joy of their triumph, and to be always remembered by his companions in arms. He will be a cold-hearted American, who in after-times shall read that letter and fail to recognize the fervent patriotism of its distinguished author.

The first experiences of the commission in the investigation of these claims in St. Louis produced discoveries which led to the enlargement of its jurisdiction to all the claims in the Department, whatever their date or origin, which had not passed the accounting officers of the Treasury. But this increase of its powers was among the least important results of the commission. By the end of the year the amount of these claims allowed by the accounting officers became so large as to again threaten the solvency of the Treasury. By their allowance they became a part of the admitted national debt. What was to be done with them? There were many anxious Cabinet consultations for the purpose of devising some means of refusing payment of these claims, without subjecting the Treasury justly to the charge of repudiation. There was but one way discovered in which it could be done. Possibly there was but one man in the nation who had the moral courage to do it. The way was for the Secretary of War to undertake the personal examination of the facts in each case, and to refuse to send any claim to the Treasury for payment until he had become satisfied of its justice and equity. In this way the aggregate daily demands upon the Treasury might be kept within its ability to pay.

At this time another subject was demanding the greatest possible efficiency in the administration of the War Office. Treasonable utterances in the loyal states from newspapers and individuals were becoming bold and frequent. The fact that such newspapers were allowed freely to continue their objectionable publications was certainly one form of giving aid and comfort to the enemy, and made it difficult to call, with success, upon the country for volunteers, money, and materials. The voice of loyalty to the Union was suppressed in the

Confederate States on pain of death. To permit the advocacy of Secession principles in the loyal states was to place them at an insufferable disadvantage.

The Habeas Corpus Act had not yet been passed, and the measures for the suppression of open disloyalty must necessarily originate in the War Department. The excellent judgment of Mr. Cameron determined that he was not the secretary who could enforce such measures with the greatest success. He was conservative, deliberate, strongly averse to going beyond the bounds of lawful authority. If the writ of Habeas Corpus was to be suspended, certain Northern newspapers suppressed, and Northern men of disloyal tendencies imprisoned by military authority, the exigency demanded at the head of the War Department a bold, fearless man, prompt to assume responsibility in doubtful cases.

The immediate cause, however, of the secretary's resignation was the decision of the Cabinet to decline payment of claims from the Department of the West which arose out of contracts lawfully made and for which the government was liable according to established rules of law, and especially such as had been allowed by the accounting officers. He had no doubt that, in fact, the claims were grossly exaggerated, but the method proposed for dealing with them he regarded as undignified, or, as he expressed it, too much like pretending to pay specie by counting out dimes and half-dimes when bills were presented for redemption. Such a proceeding, he did not think, would be successful under a secretary entertaining his views, and he therefore tendered his resignation, which was accepted on the 14th of January, 1862.

I think I was in a position to know that Mr. Cameron retained the full confidence of the President and of his associates in the Cabinet, notwithstanding some criticisms made at the time by his enemies upon his official conduct. These criticisms produced considerable impression. One act of his led to the passage by the popular branch of Congress of a resolution of censure, some months subsequent to his resignation. The charge was that he had intrusted Mr. Alexander Cumming with the custody of large amounts of the public money, and authority to purchase military supplies, without taking any security. But the President was too just a man to permit an act to be exclusively imputed to Mr. Cameron for which himself and the whole Cabinet were responsible. He promptly answered the resolution by a message, in which he stated that on the 20th of April, 1861, after the fall of Sumter, and while the capital was in a state of siege, he authorized Governor Morgan and Alexander Cumming to make all necessary arrangements for the transportation of troops and munitions of war, and generally to assist the officers of the army in its movements, until communications should be re-established; and directed the Secretary of the Treasury to advance, without security, two millions of dollars to John A. Dix, George Opdyke, and Richard M. Blatchford, of New York, to be used in meeting requisitions for the public defence. Every dollar of the money had been accounted for, and Mr. Cameron was no more responsible than himself and the other members of the Cabinet for whatever fault had been committed in the premises. This vigorous language ended all further criticism, and no more attacks were made upon the late secretary. So long as the President lived he entertained the kindliest feeling for Mr. Cameron, and gave him a large measure of his confidence.

Edwin M. Stanton belonged to a class of men whose

public acts seem to invite misinterpretation. There was no man in a conspicuous position during the war whose objects were more universally misunderstood or whose motives were more harshly criticised. These results, equally unjust to himself and unfortunate for the country, were more his fault than his misfortune. They were induced by his own carelessness of speech and contempt for public opinion; they might have been at any time corrected. He had been so long accustomed to uncharitable criticism that it had ceased to annoy him or even to attract his attention.

In the year 1861, Mr. Stanton was in the very prime of his intellectual and physical life. He was about five feet eight inches in height, his figure being slightly inclined to corpulence. His face was dark, and the lower portion of it was completely covered with a long, heavy, dark beard. His eyes were small, dark, and piercing. His movements were quick. Vigorous alertness was indicated by every change of his countenance and movement of his body. His mind was as active as his person. It was original and mechanical rather than philosophic or thoughtful. Its type was indicated by his success at the bar, where he had attained an enviable reputation as an advocate in patent cases, with but little celebrity in the investigation or discussion of abstract principles. His perceptions were too quick to be always accurate; his ideas seemed to burst forth from his brain like a torrent from a mountain-side, with a force of current which swept along with it obstructions of every description. He impressed those who knew him best with a sense of his own personal courage, the existence of which was denied by his numerous enemies. Whatever he may have been in the presence of danger to his person, his whole official life was a witness to his complete insensibility to the opinions of others upon his actions. These qualities constituted a character eminently aggressive; a man capable of lofty purposes, which, once formed, were to be pursued to failure or success. He was, or at least appeared to be, insensible to all influences outside of his own construction of the law. He had the capacity of so shutting in his own consciousness that he was as impervious to external influences as if he had been made of metal or stone.

The circumstances under which Mr. Stanton had entered the Cabinet of the last administration were as trying to himself as his services there were invaluable to the country. The crimes of Floyd, the machinations of Cobb and his associates, had driven that loyal old Democratic soldier, General Cass, from the chair of state. Cobb had resigned; Floyd and Thompson were still there, with the new Secretary of State, whose opinion, as Attorney-General, "that Congress had no power to make war upon a state," still dominated the Cabinet. Stanton was tendered the office of Attorney-General, as the successor of General Black, whose political faith he was supposed to have embraced. He had decided to decline the appointment. There was nothing of reputation to be gained in the office during the fraction of the term which remained; there was but one loyal member left, and he was a Kentuckian. Mr. Stanton went to the Executive Mansion to thank the President and explain his declination. He saw and appreciated that the only defence of the Union against Secession for the moment was the wavering President who had called him to his aid. The picture changed his determination. Instead of declining, he then and there accepted the appointment.

The circumstances of the first Cabinet meeting he attended should be recalled by those who care to deal justly with the reputation of Mr. Stanton. In addition to those already mentioned, they were reported to be as follows: The meeting occurred on an unfortunate day for Secession. It was the 8th of January, the anniversary of the battle of New Orleans. Floyd had made the refusal of the President to withdraw the troops from Charleston Harbor the pretext for tendering his resignation, which had not been accepted. Cobb, after dealing a deadly blow at the national credit, had been succeeded by a man of no positive opinions from a Border state. The only member present known to be true to the Union was Judge Holt. All the other members were in sympathy with Secession, or, like the President, were struggling to maintain a neutral position, when neutrality was little better than treason.

"Should Major Anderson be reinforced or withdrawn from Fort Sumter?" was then the burning question. The discussion was fierce and long, and almost wholly on the Secession side. It ended by a motion made by Secretary Thompson that Major Anderson be *commanded* to retire and abandon Fort Sumter. The only voice raised against it was the single one of Judge Holt. Floyd, Thompson, Thomas were openly, Judge Black and the President secretly inclined in its favor.

The occasion demanded a man of courage, and he was there. It was the first Cabinet experience of Mr. Stanton. The proprieties of the occasion, the traditions of Cabinet action, and his own inclinations combined to secure his silence. But he was not the man to become an accomplice in crime. It is a public misfortune that the words of burning denunciation which constituted the first remarks of Secretary Stanton in a Cabinet meeting were not recorded at the time; that, to recall them, we are constrained to rely upon the memory of Judge Holt, the only other loyal member among traitors in intention, to whom the whip of his stinging scorn was applied. From him we learn that the words were, in substance, these:

"Mr. President: At your solicitation I have consented to become, for a very brief time, your constitutional adviser in matters of law. It is an office I did not seek, but while I hold it I shall perform its duties. The motion of your Secretary of the Interior presents my first official duty. That motion is, that you surrender the soldiers and abandon the property of the United States to its enemies. When that motion passes, its author, its supporters, every member of your Cabinet present, and yourself, if you and they do not oppose it, will have committed a crime as high as that of treason!"

Had a bomb exploded, the party would not have been more astounded. Such words had never been heard in that presence. Thompson and Floyd, their voices paralyzed with anger, vented their wrath in threatening gestures. Judge Holt moved around the end of the table to Stanton's side. Menaces were not replied to in kind by him, but, if contempt could have burned, his look would have scorched the traitors. Thompson first controlled his voice into intelligible speech. "Who," he almost screamed, "will dare to arrest me for treason? And what army officer will assist him in his Black Republican work? There are two hundred men in my own department who will protect me if I call on them!"

"If the officer appointed by law calls for assistance to arrest you or any other traitor, I will render it, for one," replied Mr. Stanton, "and one of the oldest and bravest of our generals has publicly declared that, if Fort Sumter is surrendered, he will, within twenty days, lead two hundred thousand men to take vengeance on all the betrayers of the Union!"

The meeting dispersed while the President was waiting for mutual concessions. Within a few hours the frauds of Floyd became public, and compelled the acceptance of his resignation. Thomas also made way in the Treasury for General Dix, who, within the month, had written an order which will carry his name to the last page of the latest history of patriotism, and enough of stamina was infused into the enervated administration to carry it through its expiring hours without any very humiliating concessions to disunion.

With the undeniably strong and valuable qualities which controlled the mind of Mr. Stanton were mingled others which were injurious to his reputation and a detriment to his usefulness. His judgment of other men was as partial as that of Secretary Chase. But while the latter did not resist the influence of personal admiration and praises of himself, Mr. Stanton was extremely suspicious of anything like personal commendation. Probably no man ever repeated the attempt to praise him. The first almost certainly produced either a shaft of satire or a glance of contempt. Other great faults were mixed with his great powers. He acquired permanent prejudices against others without an effort and often without a cause, and, once imbibed, they became indelible. His temperament was censorious and rather gloomy. He was parsimonious of his commendations of others, but not sparing in his criticisms. Men of his very peculiar nature are constantly making enemies, who are retained without effort, while they make but few friends, and those are not to be retained without watchful attention.

Cant, pretence, and hypocrisy were the *Parcae* which

never passed the door of Mr. Stanton's favor. He could not endure the breath of either. It irritated him to hear any one speak of his own patriotism or his sacrifices. Such men, he maintained, were necessarily hypocrites, and it must be admitted that herein his estimate was seldom at fault. There was one sin for which, before the bar of his judgment, there was neither excuse, pardon, nor remission : it was fraud or peculation in the public service. In the catalogue of crimes, as he would have arranged it, these were more iniquitous than openly bearing arms against the government.

This was no hasty or superficial conclusion of his mind—it was reached by a process of logical reasoning. To him the republic was like a woman whom we professed to love, assailed on every side by some of the children she had borne and nourished; herself defenceless, with her life depending upon the loyalty of those who were still faithful. While these, by thousands, were shedding their blood and laying down their lives to save hers, there were a few clothed in her uniform and sworn to defend her flag who were treacherous enough to make profit of her necessities by selling the arms, the food, the clothing of their sick, wounded, and dying brothers. In such a stress and strain there could be no abstraction from the national resources by unjust profit or by fraud, which did not in some way diminish the arms, supplies, the clothing or comforts of our soldiers in the field. A defrauding contractor was a greater criminal than an open, willing rebel. And there was one superlative type of unmitigated rascal, and that was a man who, wearing the uniform or invested with the authority of the United States, could use his rank, his office, or his position for his own secret, unlawful, personal gain !

An actual occurrence will illustrate both the carelessness of expression in which Secretary Stanton indulged, and the intensity of his feeling towards men of this class. At a reception one evening he was engaged in conversation with an officer when a person passed them. Turning the subject, he suddenly exclaimed:

"Do you know that person?" at the same time indicating the individual who had passed, who still stood within hearing but for the sound of conversation.

"Know him? Certainly. He is Mr. ———, chief of the ——— bureau in your own Department. Why do you ask?"

"Because he is a pretender, a humbug, and a fraud," said Mr. Stanton. "Did you ever in all your life see the head of a human being which so closely resembled that of a cod-fish?"

"He is not responsible for his head or his face. But why do you say he is a fraud? The newspapers call him a reformer, and give him credit for great efficiency."

"I deny your conclusions," he replied. "A man of fifty is responsible for his face! Yes, I know he is courting the newspapers: that proves him a humbug and presumptively a fraud."

A few months later the official in question was found guilty by a court-martial of peculation and fraud in the management of his bureau, and dishonorably expelled from the service.

Mr. Stanton's unpopularity, if the term is permissible, was due to his own neglect and carelessness. It was owing to his negligence that he never cared to give any one a favorable impression of himself—it was his fault that his dislikes were caused by slight circumstances, and often inexplicable. When he made an unpleasant remark about another it was seldom forgotten, for he could put more caustic bitterness into a brief sentence of personal criticism than Carlyle, or any known master of the vocabulary of denunciation. But, perhaps, enough has been said to indicate the qualities which led to his selection by President Lincoln as the successor in the War Office of Secretary Cameron.

Men of Mr. Stanton's temperament could not be the favorites of President Lincoln. There were also reasons of a personal character which would have barred his entrance into the Cabinet, if Mr. Lincoln had been an ordinary man. They were known to each other before the war. Both had been counsel for the same party in an action in which, by professional courtesy, Mr. Lincoln was entitled to make the argument, unless he voluntarily waived his right. It was an action in which he took a deep interest professionally, and for which he had made thorough preparation, and was, consequently, certain to have made a better argument than his associate. But Mr. Stanton, without consulting his colleague, in a domineering manner not uncommon with him in similar cases, although he was the younger man, coolly assumed control and crowded Mr. Lincoln out of his own case. The latter felt deeply hurt at the slight, which was the more remarkable since it is the only recorded instance in which he seems ever to have claimed in his own favor any question of precedence. No lawyer would have expected Mr. Lincoln to overlook such a gross discourtesy, or to take its author into confidence, without the most ample apology.

But when did any personal consideration weigh a feather in the mind of President Lincoln if the public safety was in question? Oblivion of himself on such occasions was the indisputable demonstration of his moral greatness. He who, two years later, could say of one who, without excuse, had added to the heavy burden of his cares, "If I have the opportunity I will make him chief justice," and kept the promise, now recognizing in Mr. Stanton the qualities which the War Office required, invited him into his Cabinet as cordially as if they had been old friends. From that time, through dark and evil days, through nights of solicitude and fearful responsibility, they together carried the burden of war, until, and largely owing to their joint labors, the rebellion was crushed and the republic saved.

In the dark night of another day of evil the most sorrowful heart by the bedside of the murdered President throbbed in the bosom of his Secretary of War, and his voice it was which spoke his grandest eulogy in the words, "There lies the most perfect ruler of men the world has ever seen!"

On the 14th of January, 1862, Mr. Stanton was invited into the Cabinet and accepted his nomination as Secretary of War. He was expected to diminish the demands of the Department of the West upon the Treasury, but it was not supposed that he would wholly arrest them. There were numerous monthly requisitions from the War Department upon the Treasury, authorized by statutes, which it was necessary to provide for, in order to carry on the regular operations of the government. For almost a fortnight none of these were made. The delay became so embarrassing to the daily operations of the government that the Secretary of the Treasury requested one of his bureau chiefs to call upon Secretary Stanton and ascertain the reason for the delay. This officer solicited an interview, and the Secretary of War named *six o'clock P.M.* on January 28th as a convenient time. Two hours after the close of business on January 28th this officer found Secretary Stanton literally buried in accumulated heaps of requisitions on the Treasury, each paper of which was an account, upon which some one was, by the judgment of the War Office, lawfully entitled to a Treasury warrant for its payment. There were, literally, *cords* of these requisitions. The piles surrounded the Secretary's desk, and were higher than his person when he stood erect. He was carefully examining each account with its vouchers. The result of his day's work lay by his side, possibly a dozen requisitions approved, and five times as many reserved for further investigation. The Treasury officer asked him whether he was discharging the functions of an "auditor" of these claims.

"I am discharging a duty imposed by statute," he replied. "No further payments will be made by the Treasury on the requisitions of this Department until I know that they ought to be made!"

"You are undertaking an impossibility," said the representative of the Treasury. "You will stop the wheels of government. No five men can do what you are undertaking!"

"I am not responsible for that," said the Secretary. "I am responsible for aiding the payment of fraudulent claims. You yourself have put me upon inquiry. You arrested a warrant for the payment of $26 each for muskets, previously offered to this Department for less than $4 each, and the offer was declined. Such claims are scandalous as well as fraudulent. I intend to arrest them!"

He would not be moved from this position. He would not approve the formal requisitions, which were unquestionably just, out of their regular order. He would do nothing but take up each account in its order, and either approve or reject it, as the facts seemed to warrant. To every argument or statement of the evil consequences that must follow from this practical suspension of the payment of war claims, his answer was that the statute and not the secretary was responsible.

In a few days the Department of the West was in an uproar—there was a rebellion within the loyal states. Every Western man, of any *influence*, hurried to Washington. The War Office was in a state of siege—the Secretary was waylaid in the streets, at his residence, even in his bed. No combination so powerful had been made since the fall of Sumter as that which now beset the White House and all the departments to induce Secretary Stanton to change his policy, and permit these claims to be presented to the Treasury for payment. Every conceivable means, influence, effort, and endeavor, every imaginable prediction of calamity, mischance, and disaster, even denunciations, menaces, and threats were brought to bear to persuade or to drive him to remove the obstruction, and permit the current of public money into the Department of the West to resume its flow.

But all in vain. The Washington Monument was not more insensible to the breath of a summer wind than was Secretary Stanton to all these supposed influences. He labored diligently, through the night-watches as well as in the daytime. Possibly a tenth of the average number of requisitions were made daily by his Department upon the Treasury; but when the average was once established, it never increased, nor had the Treasury any difficulty in meeting the moderate aggregate of his demands.

Many weeks of this delay did not elapse before the claimants began to implore for some measure of relief. Was no compromise possible? Was there no way of obtaining payment of such portion of these demands as was clearly just? Secretary Stanton had one uniform reply. The Court of Claims was open. It was the tribunal provided by law for claimants not satisfied with the proceedings of the Department. At length, when all other resources had failed, the claimants in the Department of the West voluntarily offered to submit their claims to the Davis Commission, if the Treasury would pay such amounts as that commission found was equitably due. To this Mr. Stanton would assent, provided the claimants would accept the amount so found justly due in full payment, but not otherwise. After a vain effort to move him from this position, the claimants consented, and the whole accumulated mass of unpaid war claims in the Department of the West was sent to the commission for investigation. They were so numerous that it was more convenient to measure them by the cubic foot than otherwise.

The commission dealt with them justly, and with all practicable despatch. It was readily proved that, as a rule, claimants and contractors had been permitted to fix their own prices. Blankets, tents, provisions, and numerous other articles had been accepted at four and six times the ordinary retail prices, and the account certified as just. Many of the claims were allowed at twenty and thirty per cent. of the amounts claimed, and the final result was that the amount of all the claims allowed by the commission was about one half the aggregate allowed by the accounting officers. As fast as the claims were liquidated they were paid by the Treasury. The claimants accepted payment of these reduced amounts under protest and, as they claimed, upon compulsion. Suits to recover the amounts reduced were brought in the Court of Claims, and that court rendered judgment in favor of the claimants; but, upon appeal, the Supreme Court of the

United States reversed these judgments, on the ground that the acceptance of the amounts allowed by the Commission operated in law to discharge the entire claim.

The official reputation of Mr. Stanton was essentially established by these early acts of his public career. They were fiercely denounced at the time as unjust and arbitrary. As he never defended his acts—as no one was interested to justify them—his reputation has necessarily suffered. Now that the supposed sense of personal injury has passed away, a more just judgment of these acts may be formed. It should be remembered that the Treasury could not have paid these claims. The scale of prices they introduced would have bankrupted the nation during any six months of the war. The claims were fraudulently excessive. The equity of the Commission was never challenged—it would not have reduced the claims one half without good reason. The net result, then, of this conduct of the Secretary of War was to save the Treasury from bankruptcy, the country from the payment of unjust claims to a very large amount, and from the introduction of a ruinous standard of prices, and to administer a stinging rebuke to the pretended patriots who were robbing the Treasury while vaunting their loyalty.

It was the common opinion that the nature of Mr. Stanton was pitiless, that he was insensible to all appeals for mercy, or for the relief of human suffering or sorrow. This opinion has outlived him, and still darkens his memory. There are individuals who have undertaken to write history who have recorded dark hints that the torments of a conscience, awakened too late to undo the miseries he had inflicted, actually drove him to end his own life. While these persons have earned nothing but contempt for their prurient vagaries, it is time that this injustice should be corrected.

I will call a single witness to the accuracy of this imperfect sketch of the character of Mr. Stanton. Charles O'Neill, of Philadelphia, entered Congress before the war, and his term of useful service is not yet ended. No man knew Mr. Stanton better than Mr. O'Neill. As chairman of a committee which reported a bill for the erection of a monument to Mr. Stanton, Mr. O'Neill's committee made the following record:

"To the intense patriotism and great personal force manifested by Mr. Stanton in 1860–61 was due his appointment as Secretary of War, Jan. 20, 1862. He was thus made chief of staff of President Lincoln, who was by virtue of his office the commander-in-chief of the military forces of the United States; and, although that great magistrate never abdicated his authority, the world knows that the confidence he reposed in Mr. Stanton made the latter mainly responsible for the placing of armies in the field and for the selection of the generals who finally led them to victory.

"From the day of his entrance into the War Office the change in the conduct of affairs was most marked. His organizing power was felt at once in every bureau of the Department. To the raising of men and the supplying of them with the munitions of war, clothing, subsistence, medicines, and transportation, he gave his great capacity for organization, his restless energy, and his wonderful powers of endurance. He was a prodigy for work.

"He had a resolute will to do what his judgment told him was necessary, and struck out new paths when the old ones led only to pitfalls, and the moral courage to pursue the course thus marked out.

"His faith in the national cause was never shaken, and he had the magnetism which enabled him to communicate it to those with whom he came in contact.

"Laggards and absentees from the army, contract brokers, and purveyors of contraband news were made to feel his righteous anger. Called upon to perform labors which would have exhausted a dozen men, taking but little sleep, and his nerves constantly wrought up to the highest tension, it would have been strange if he had not often been abrupt and impatient while engaged in the rapid despatching of business, and especially with people who insisted upon consuming time which could not properly be given them.

"The leaders of Congress had the most unbounded confidence in his wisdom as well as in his integrity, and treated him as one of themselves. The committee which had to deal with questions connected with the war gave great weight to his recommendations. The vast levies of troops and the enormous appropriations for their movement and support were in the main measured by him under advice of the generals of the army.

"When Congress had given the authority asked, he directed the marshalling of the great resources of the country thus made available. From his executive mind came the organization of the work by which two millions and a half of soldiers were enlisted to fight the battles of the Union. He was the impersonation of honesty, and, after controlling the expenditure of $3,000,000,000, he died poor as he had lived.

"President Lincoln had in him an absolute trust. When the chief-justiceship was vacant, and the good Bishop Simpson was urging Stanton for the place, Mr. Lincoln replied that he would gladly place him there if he would find him another such Secretary of War.

"When the nation made General Grant President, he appointed Mr. Stanton to a place on the Supreme Bench. He received his commission, but disease prevented him from entering upon the duties of the office. The mighty strain of the war upon him impaired his constitution and caused his death. He was a martyr as well as a hero.

"To perpetuate by enduring monuments the memory of the great few who are thus raised up in great crises for the salvation of a nation is a duty and a privilege, sanctioned by custom and demanded by the natural feelings of grateful patriotism."

XXV.

MAKING $10,000,000 OF UNITED STATES BONDS UNDER PRESSURE.—THE CONSTRUCTION OF CONFEDERATE IRON-CLAD SHIPS IN BRITISH SHIP-YARDS.—THE DEPARTURE OF TWO PREVENTED.—AN ENGLISHMAN OFFERS A GREAT SERVICE TO OUR REPUBLIC.—HIS INCOGNITO.

TEN millions are "a good many" things of any kind. They seemed to be more than a good many to the officer who had to sign coupon-bonds to that amount in denominations of $1000 and less, within the time and under the pressure of the circumstances about to be described. Except upon this single occasion, it is questionable whether so large an amount of coupon securities, of the same issue, of our government were ever brought together.

Communication between the United States and Great Britain was much more irregular and required longer time in 1862 than in 1891. Now, on regular sailing-days, twice every week, as many as ten large steamships leave New York for English ports on a single tide. Telegraphic communication between Washington and London is almost as frequent as between New York and Philadelphia, and it is not interrupted unless four cable-lines are simultaneously broken. Then there were fewer lines of steamships, and during the war the sailing-days of some of them were irregular; only one cable had been laid across the Atlantic, and that was not in working order. Special messengers carried all the important despatches between our country and Great Britain; there was time for a revolution to break out and be suppressed on the Continent before we heard of its existence. It was such a messenger who brought the first news to America of the furious rage of our transatlantic cousins excited by the capture by Captain Wilkes of those Confederate (almost) protomartyrs Mason and Slidell.

About eleven o'clock on a well-remembered Friday morning, in 1862, the Register of the Treasury was requested to go to the Executive Mansion immediately, without a moment's delay. He obeyed the summons, and found there Secretaries Chase and Seward, in anxious consultation with the President. They wished to know what was the shortest time within which $10,000,000 in coupon "five-twenties" could be prepared, signed, and issued. They were informed that the correct answer to that inquiry would depend upon the denominations already printed; that if a sufficient number of the largest denomination, of $1000, were on hand, they might be issued within four or five days; if the denominations were smaller, longer time would be required; that the number printed could be ascertained by sending to the Register's Office, for there was a report from the custodian of unissued bonds made every day. Both Mr. Chase and Mr. Seward said that so much time could not be given; that these bonds must be regularly issued, and placed on board a steamer which was to leave New York for Liverpool at twelve o'clock on the following Monday, if this could possibly be done; that the register could command all the resources of the government, if necessary, but he must see that the bonds were on board the steamer at the hour named. There was one condition —the bonds must be regularly and lawfully issued, with nothing on their face to indicate that the issue was not made in the regular course of business.

By the act of Congress which authorized the issue of these bonds it was declared that they should be signed by the register. The construction given to the act in the department was that the register must sign them in person, and that he could not delegate his authority. Any number of clerks could be employed in their preparation and entry, but the point of difficulty was whether the register could sign them within the time. There were seventy hours between the time of the discussion and the hour when the securities must be on board the special train that would carry them to the steamer. The time was long enough. Ten thousand signatures and a greater number could be made in seventy hours, with proper seasons of rest and sleep. But could the physical strength of one man hold out to the end of such a dreary, monotonous work without sleep or rest? The question was one of physical endurance, only to be determined by a trial. But a few moments could be spared for discussion. It was speedily settled that the register would set about the task at once; that he would sign until his strength gave out. He would then resign his office; the President would appoint another register, who would complete the issue. This would lead to complications, and was otherwise objectionable; but the faith of the government was involved; the emergency justified extreme measures.

The immediate occasion of this sudden determination to issue these securities was a despatch just received by Mr. Seward, by special messenger, from Mr. Charles Francis Adams, our minister to the court of St. James. As already intimated, the cable was not in working order, and no suggestion of the facts had been made to the State Department previous to the arrival of the messenger. Its importance was obvious to the two secretaries, but will not be understood by the reader without an explanation covering a considerable period of time and events which are now for the first time made public.

Mr. Adams had for several weeks been aware, and had communicated the fact to his government, that the Messrs. Laird, extensive ship-builders, were building at their yards in Birkenhead, near Liverpool, two armored vessels for the Confederate government. They were to be furnished with powerful engines, and capable of great speed. When completed, they were to proceed to a small, unfrequented British island in the West Indies, where they were to be delivered to the agents of the Confederacy. They were then to receive their armament, previously sent thither, take their crews on board, and then set forth on their piratical cruises, after the example of the *Alabama*. After sweeping our remaining commerce from the seas, by burning and sinking every merchant-ship bearing our flag, they were to come upon our own coast, scatter our blockading fleet, and open all the Southern ports to British commerce, which would no longer be required to take the great risk of breaking the blockade. This feat was to be accomplished by vessels which had never entered a Confederate port, nor, indeed, any harbor which was not covered by the British or some other flag which protected the iron-clads against pursuit or capture by vessels of the United States navy.

Greater danger than these vessels never threatened the safety of the Union. In tonnage, armament, and speed they were intended to be superior to the *Kearsarge* and every vessel of our navy. Their armor was supposed to render them invulnerable. If the blockade was not maintained, an immediate recognition of the belligerent character of the rebels by Great Britain was anticipated. Even if that did not take place, all the cotton gathered in Confederate ports would be released and find a profitable market; while the old wooden vessels, now principally constituting the blockading fleet, would not resist one of these iron-clad vessels long enough for a second broadside.

The impending danger was fully appreciated by Mr. Adams. With his accustomed energy, notwithstanding the secrecy in which all the Confederate movements in Great Britain were shrouded, he had collected and laid before the English authorities clear proofs of the rebel ownership and intended unlawful purpose of these vessels. He had even procured copies of the contracts under which the Messrs. Laird were building them, and had ascertained the fact that payments on their account had been made from proceeds of cotton owned by the Confederacy. He had represented that the evidence furnished by him, verified by the oaths of credible witnesses, was sufficient not only to justify their seizure, but to secure their condemnation in the courts, and he had insisted, with a force apparently unanswerable, that it was the duty of Great Britain to prevent the vessels from leaving the Mersey, and setting forth upon their piratical career.

But, unfortunately, the sympathies of the party in power in England were not with the Union cause. It suited the view of the law-officers of the crown not to interfere, and to excuse their inaction by raising objections to the legal sufficiency of the evidence. The situation was perfectly comprehended by the President and his Cabinet, but remonstrance appeared to be unavailing, and the departure of the vessels was expected at an early day.

Hopeless as the task appeared to be, neither Mr. Adams nor his active agents relaxed their efforts for a moment. Their recent investigations had been prosecuted with such energy that the minister had finally been able to furnish the British premier with the sworn affidavits of some of the officers and men actually enlisted in Liverpool and other English cities for service on these vessels; that the advance payments to these men had been made by Confederate agents; that the ships were to leave the Mersey at an early appointed date for an island near Bermuda; that their guns and ammunition had already been sent thither. Mr. Adams had also secured the names of several of the ship's officers, with copies of their commissions, bearing the signature of President Davis and the seal of the Confederacy.

The last instalment of affidavits forwarded by our minister proved to be more than the crown lawyers could digest. They covered every defect named in their former objections; they could not be answered even by a special demurrer. They were reinforced by the caustic pen of Mr. Adams, whose argument so clearly pointed out the duty of the English government in the premises that it would obviously be regarded as conclusive by every one but these lawyers, who possessed the exclusive power to move the slow authorities of the customs to action. The crown lawyers finally decided that the demand of Mr. Adams must be complied with, and that an order must issue, prohibiting the departure of these vessels from the Mersey, until the charges of the American minister had been judicially investigated.

There were, however, some incidents attending this most important decision which prevented its communication from giving to Mr. Adams a satisfaction wholly unalloyed. The decision had been withheld until the vessels were on the very eve of departure. The order must be immediately served, and possession taken by the customs authorities, or the vessels would escape. The crown lawyers, properly enough, observed that the affidavits furnished by Mr. Adams were *ex parte*—the witnesses had not been cross-examined. If Mr. Adams should fail to prove his charges by evidence which would satisfy the judicial mind, and the vessels be released, the damages caused by arresting them might be very heavy. It was a settled rule of procedure in the courts in such cases to secure the payment of such damages beyond any peradventure. The restraining order would, therefore, be issued, but it would not be enforced against the vessels until these damages had been secured by a deposit of £1,000,000 *sterling in gold coin*.

The situation was well known to be critical. Within three days the vessels were to sail for their destination; if necessary, they might sail forthwith. The cable was useless—broken or disabled—and Mr. Adams could not communicate with his own government. Without such communication he had no authority to bind his government as an indemnitor, or to repay the money if he could borrow it. Even if he had the fullest authority, where was the patriotic Briton who would furnish a million pounds on the spur of the moment to a government which was believed by the party in power in Great Britain to be *in articulo mortis?* Unless, therefore, the crown lawyers supposed our minister to have anticipated their decision by providing himself with this money, they must have known that this condition could not be complied with, and that they might just as well have declined to interfere. If they had intended that these ships should not be prevented from making their intended crusade against our commerce and our cause, no better arrangement could possibly have been devised. It is not to be denied that suspicions existed that such was their purpose.

But the unexpected sometimes happens. The event

which prevented these floating engines of destruction from entering upon their intended work was as unanticipated as a miracle. It constituted, possibly, the most signal service ever rendered by a citizen of one country to the government of another. It was all the more noble because it was intended to be anonymous. The eminently unselfish man who performed it made a positive condition that it should not be made public; that not so much as his name should be disclosed, except to the officers of our government, whose co-operation was required, in order to transact the business in a proper manner and upon correct principles. So earnest was his injunction of secrecy that his identity will not even now be disclosed, although he has long since gone to his reward.

Within the hour after the crown lawyers' decision, with its conditions, had been made known to Mr. Adams, and when he had given up all hope of arresting these vessels, a quiet gentleman called upon him and asked if he might be favored with the opportunity of making the deposit of coin required by the order? He observed "that it had occurred to him that, if the United States had that amount to its credit in London, some question of authority might arise, or Mr. Adams might otherwise be embarrassed in complying with the condition, especially as communication with his government might involve delay; so that the shortest way to avoid all difficulty would be for him to deposite the coin, which he was quite prepared to do."

Had a messenger descended from the skies in a chariot of fire, with $5,000,000 in gold in his hands, and offered to leave it at the embassy without any security, Mr. Adams could not have been more profoundly surprised. He had accepted the condition as fatal to his efforts;

he had concluded that nothing short of a miracle could prevent the departure of the vessels; and here, if not a miracle, was something much like one. He made no secret of the pleasure with which he accepted the munificent offer, provided some method of securing the liberal Englishman could be found. The latter seemed indisposed to make any suggestions on the subject. "It might be proper," he said, "that some obligation should be entered into, showing that the American government recognized the deposit as made on its account; beyond that he should leave the matter wholly in the hands of Mr. Adams."

The existing premium on gold was then about sixty per cent. in the United States. It would have been largely increased by the departure of these iron-clads. The "five-twenties" or "sixes" of 1861, as they were popularly called, were then being issued, and were the only securities upon "long time" then authorized by Congress. The best arrangement that occurred to Mr. Adams, and which he then proposed, was that $10,000,000, or £2,000,000, in these bonds, to be held as collateral security for the loan of £1,000,000 in gold, should be delivered to the lender, to be returned when the loan was paid, or the order itself was discharged and the coin returned to the depositor. The proposition of Mr. Adams was satisfactory to the gentleman, but he said that to prevent the disclosure of his name the deposit should be made in coupon and not in registered bonds. The coupons were payable to bearer; the registered were required to be inscribed on the books of the Treasury in the owner's name. Mr. Adams then volunteered the assurance that these bonds, to the amount of $10,000,000, should be transmitted to London by the first steamer which left New York after his despatch concerning the transaction was received in the State Department at Washington.

It was this assurance of Mr. Adams which the President and both of the secretaries desired should be made good. They regarded the faith of the government as pledged for its performance, and that faith they proposed should not be violated.

All the details of this transaction were not then disclosed. They reached the government in private, confidential despatches from Mr. Adams, some of them long afterwards. The despatch in question was understood to be confidential; certainly that part of it which related to the deposit and security proposed. It was necessarily brief, for in order to reach the steamer the special messenger had to leave London within a very few hours after the proposition of the deposit was made. There was enough in it to show that an inestimable service had been rendered to the country by some one to whom Mr. Adams had pledged the faith of the nation for the transmission of these bonds by the next steamer which left New York. There was no dissent from the conclusion that the pledge of Mr. Adams, if it were in the power of the government, must be performed.

The transmission of the securities of the United States to London, in large amounts, would be a very different problem now, after the subsequent experience of the Treasury in such transactions. Now, the blank bonds would be taken on board an ocean steamer in the custody of officers authorized to prepare, sign, and issue them, and the entire labor could be performed on the voyage. In 1862, the Treasury had had no such experience, and in the brief time spared for consultation there was no way of meeting the emergency suggested, except the regular process of filling up, signing, and sealing the bonds within the Treasury, entering them upon the proper books, and delivering them as perfected obligations of the United States.

No time was wasted in discussion. It was suggested as a precautionary measure that a request to delay the sailing of the steamer should be made, and the consultation ended. It may as well be mentioned here that the effort to secure delay was unsuccessful. It could not be complied with except with the consent of the officers of the company in Liverpool, and they could not be reached by cable. The steamer would sail at twelve o'clock on Monday.

It was next ascertained that only $7,500,000 in coupon bonds of the denomination of $1000 had been printed. The remaining $2,500,000 must be made up from denominations of $500. This involved an increase of two thousand five hundred, making an aggregate of twelve thousand five hundred bonds to be signed between twelve o'clock on Friday and four o'clock A.M. on Monday.

The theory of the statute which required a bond to be signed by the head of the bureau from which it issued originally was that the signature was some safeguard against forgery, was an evidence of authenticity, and a check against unauthorized issues. In issues of so large amounts as were made during the war, it was found to have a trifling if any value. But the labor imposed was continuous and severe; in the present instance it became dangerous to health and life; for there is no muscular exertion more severe, certainly none so inexpressibly dreary, as that of writing one's own name hour after hour, day after day, over and over again. Such, however, was the law; it was necessary to the legality of the issue that all the requirements of the law should be complied with. It will be seen in this instance at what cost obedience to this provision of the statute was secured.

When the bond issues of the Treasury required an average of two or three thousand signatures daily, every means of doing the work rapidly was necessarily employed. The signature itself was changed. If each initial letter had been written separately, in the ordinary way, the day was not long enough to finish the task. The whole name was then written at a single movement, without raising the pen from the paper, or once arresting its motion. The bonds were laid before the officer in piles; the instant the pen was raised at the end of the name, an experienced messenger removed the bond, leaving another exposed for signature. In this way it was possible to write ten signatures in a minute. If any one is inclined to doubt the rapidity or the exertion involved in doing this, he is advised to try the experiment.

In the present instance the register knew from experience that serious work was before him, which would affect his health, and might endanger his life. He endeavored to set about it with judgment and discretion. He called in an experienced army surgeon, informed him that he intended to continue to sign his name for just as many consecutive hours as his strength would permit; that he was desired to remain in constant attendance, administering such food and stimulants as would secure endurance for the longest possible time. The necessary supplies were procured, the arrangements perfected, and the register was ready to begin his work at twelve o'clock on Friday.

The first seven hours passed without any unusual sensations. He had signed for that length of time so frequently that it had become a custom to which the muscles had adapted themselves, so that they worked uncomplainingly. In these first seven hours three thousand seven hundred signatures were made. But within the first half of the eighth hour there were evidences of great muscular discontent, which soon threatened to break out into open rebellion. As the time slowly wore on, in the forenoon of Saturday, every muscle on the right side connected with the movement of the hand and arm became inflamed, and the pain was almost beyond endurance. It was necessary to continue the work, for if it should be suspended for any considerable length of time the inflammation might become so great that control over the motion of the arm and its further use would become impossible. In the slight pauses which were made, rubbing, the application of hot water, and other remedies were resorted to, in order to alleviate the pain and reduce the inflammation. They were comparatively ineffectual, and the hours dragged on without bringing much relief.

During the course of Saturday afternoon the acuteness of the pain sensibly diminished. The muscles, finding that resistance was unavailing, had to give up the contest. A series of sensations followed which, though less difficult to endure, were still more alarming. A feeling of numbness commenced in the hand, and slowly crept up the arm to the shoulder, producing an effect as if the hand and arm were dead. With this came a distortion of the fingers, so that the pen, instead of being held in the usual manner, was placed between the first finger and the thumb. It might have been expected that this condition of the muscles would have changed the form of the signature. It did not to any great extent. The constant repetition of the same movements seemed to result in their continuance, independently of the will. The signature was still a fair one.

It is unnecessary to describe all the details of the devices and means resorted to to prevent sleep and to continue the work. Changes of position, violent exercise, going out into the open air and walking rapidly for ten minutes, concentrated extracts, prepared food, stimulants more in kind and number than can now be recalled—every imaginable means was employed during the night of Saturday. Notwithstanding their use with a liberal hand, it became evident that weakness was gradually asserting itself, and that the time was approaching when the work must cease from pure exhaustion. The surgeon decided that within two or three hours at the latest the strength would give out, and that the time had come when the officer should resign, and another register be appointed.

It is quite probable that the long-continued exertion had to some extent influenced the mind of the register, and that his objections to the change proposed were more imaginary than real. The names of two registers appearing on the same issue of bonds was an apparent irregularity which might require explanations and involve delay. Calling on the President to appoint another register on Sunday was, to say the least, an impropriety which would excite public comment, even if the act itself were legal, of which some doubt was entertained. It was four o'clock on Sunday morning; only a few more than two thousand signatures would complete the labor. The register determined he would finish the task, although the surgeon earnestly advised him that it would involve a considerable danger to his life.

I have not had at any time since a very accurate memory of the events of that Sunday morning. That I could not remain in the same position for more than a few moments, that the bonds were carried from desk to table and from place to place to enable me to make ten signatures at a time, that my fingers and hand were twisted and drawn out of their natural shape — these and other facts are faintly remembered. The memory is more distinct that at about twelve o'clock, noon, the last bond was reached and signed, and the work was finished, the last hundred bonds requiring more time than the first thousand. One fact I have special cause to remember. This abuse of muscular energy eventually caused my resignation from the Treasury, and cost me several years of physical pain.

After the bonds were signed I suffered more than at any other time during the process. My nervous system was so thoroughly shattered that during the night of Sunday sleep was impossible. On Monday night, after three full days and nights during which I had not lost consciousness for a moment, I fell asleep from pure exhaustion. My subsequent experience can only be interesting to myself; certainly not to the general reader.

The bonds reached the steamer in time, and the promise of our minister was faithfully kept. But in the meantime Mr. Adams had given notice to the authorities of his readiness to make the deposit, and then some disposition of the matter was made, which avoided the necessity of making it. What this disposition was, I do not know; but it was understood at the time, by Secretary Chase, to have been made without the knowledge or privity of our minister. From the published statements at the time it appeared that no effort to deliver the vessels was made after the objections of the government were made known. In fact the iron-clads were shortly after sold to one of the Eastern powers, and their field of operations was the Mediterranean instead of the American coasts. The ability of Mr. Adams to comply with the condition and furnish the security was accepted as the end of the controversy. It *is* known that a few months later $6,000,000 of the $10,000,000 of the bonds issued were returned to the Treasury in the original packages, with the seals of the Treasury unbroken. The remaining $4,000,000 were afterwards sold for the benefit of the Treasury.

Many years elapsed before the register atoned for this violation of natural laws, which never fail to punish those who break them. While he remained in office there was no day in which he was not reminded by a sharp rheumatic twinge of the events of that Sunday morning. After he had left the Treasury there were five long years in which he could never promise that he could perform any professional labor at any fixed date in the future.

The issue of these bonds afforded an opportunity for some measurements, showing the great bulk of paper used in the whole issue of $513,000,000. I did not leave the Treasury that Sunday morning until I had seen these measurements made. The denominations of the coupon "five-twenties" were "fifties," "one hundreds," "five hundreds," and "one thousands." Of the registered the denominations were the same, with the addition of "five thousands" and "ten thousands." Only a small fraction of the issue was registered, and the certificates used were ordinarily "one thousand" and under. The twelve thousand five hundred bonds, representing $10,000,000 of the present issue, were a reasonably accurate average of the whole issue. These $10,000,000 were made into packages of $1,000,000 each, of the same length and breadth of the bonds themselves, one bond being laid, without folding, upon another. Each package was covered with one thickness of wrapping-paper, and then bound as closely as possible with strong cord, rendering each package as thin as it could be made. The ten packages were then laid in a single pile, one above the other. They measured six feet four inches in height. From these data each one can compute for himself the height of the pile of paper used in an issue of $513,000,000.

Since the publication of the foregoing facts in *Harper's Magazine* for May, 1890, I have been solicited by many correspondents to give the name of the gentleman who offered to perform such a signal service to our country. It must be obvious that nothing could give me greater pleasure than to publish his name, and to secure for him the enduring gratitude of the American people. I have, however, a special reason for my present determination not to disclose it, nor to permit myself to speculate upon the consequences of the disclosure. When we were informed that the emergency had passed, it became necessary to make a change in the entries of this large amount upon the books of the register. This was found to be a difficult matter, unless a plain statement of the issue, to the gentleman in question, and its purpose, was made with its subsequent cancellation. This course I proposed to Secretary Chase. He was decided in his opinion that the value of the service would not have been enhanced if an actual deposit of the money had been required, and that, as the gentleman himself had imposed the obligation, he was the only authority who could possibly release it. While I regarded his conclusion as incontrovertible, I did suggest that our first duty was the official one, to our own obligation to conceal nothing, and to make our official records strictly conform to the fact.

"We should have thought of that at the time," said

the secretary. "We might have declined his offer, coupled as it was with the obligation to conceal his name. But I do not remember that we considered that question. Do you?"

"No," I said. "Nothing was discussed in my presence except the possibility of compliance with his conditions, to the letter."

"Then, I think, we must continue to keep his secret, whatever the consequences may be, until he releases us from the obligation," was the final conclusion of the secretary.

I am, I believe, the only survivor of those to whom this gentleman's name was known. I have hitherto declined to discuss the question of his name or its disclosure. I depart from my practice far enough to say that I do not believe he was interested in the price of cotton, or that he was moved in the slightest degree by pecuniary motives, in making his offer. More than this, at present, I do not think I have the moral right to say. If I should at any time hereafter see my way clear to a different conclusion, I shall leave his name to be communicated to the Secretary of the Treasury, who will determine for himself the propriety of its disclosure.

XXVI.

PRESIDENT LINCOLN'S CONNECTION WITH THE ORIGIN OF ARMORED VESSELS.—HIS FAITH IN IRON-CLADS.—THE INFLUENCE OF ASSISTANT-SECRETARY FOX.—HIS INTERVIEW WITH THE PRESIDENT ON THE 7TH OF MARCH, 1862.

So many of the facts involved in the origin of armored or iron-clad vessels are in controversy, that it is a delicate matter now to meddle with the subject. But President Lincoln was a factor in this, as he was in all the great improvements made in the naval and military service during his administration. To understand how far he promoted the introduction of iron-clad vessels, it is necessary to give some facts as they were understood and acted upon by the President and others at the time, without much regard to their bearing upon other interests or questions.

Suggestions of the necessity of armored vessels for harbor defence were strongly pressed by Major Robert Anderson, very soon after he arrived in Washington from Fort Sumter. He reported that one of the Confederate batteries in Charleston harbor was covered with bars of railroad iron, in such a way that the guns of the fort made no impression upon it. Having learned from experience that a battery so protected was impregnable, and there being no reason why like armor could not be applied to a floating as well as to a land battery, Major Anderson argued that the Confederates would almost certainly undertake the construction of iron-clad vessels, and if we were not provided with similar vessels to resist them, they would take and hold possession of our navigable rivers and harbors, and so inflict an irremediable injury on our seaport cities and their commerce. The action of the Confederate Congress in May, in appointing a commission to adopt plans for raising the *Merrimac*, then sunk in Norfolk harbor, and her conversion into an armored vessel, added force to the views of Major Anderson, and produced a strong impression upon Mr. Welles, our Secretary of the Navy, and one at least of his most competent subordinates. Gustavus V. Fox was one of the President's favorites. He had acquired Mr. Lincoln's confidence by his intelligent views relating to the proposed reinforcement of Fort Sumter, immediately after the inauguration, and had accepted the office of Assistant Secretary of the Navy at his special request. He was an experienced retired naval officer, he possessed attractive personal qualities, his judgment was conservative, and he was always a welcome guest at the Executive Mansion. I was so fortunate as to have secured his friendship, and I have made several visits to the President in his company. On one of these visits, in May, I heard the President ask Mr. Fox his opinion of armored vessels, and of Major Anderson's suggestion. Mr. Fox replied, in substance, that the subject was under active consideration in the Navy Department, but that it was novel; it was very important, and though generally impressed with the practicability of such vessels, he was not yet prepared to commit himself to any fixed opinion. The President, somewhat earnestly, observed that "we must not let the rebels get ahead of us in such an important matter," and asked what Mr. Fox regarded as the principal difficulty in the way of their use. Mr. Fox replied that naval officers doubted their stability, and feared that an armor heavy enough to make them effective, would sink them as soon as they were launched. "But is not that a sum in arithmetic?" quickly asked the President. "On our Western rivers we can figure just how many tons will sink a flatboat. Can't your clerks do the same for an armored vessel?"

"I suppose they can," replied Mr. Fox. "But there are other difficulties. With such a weight, a single shot, piercing the armor, would sink the vessel so quickly that no one could escape."

"Now, as the very object of the armor is to get something that the best projectile cannot pierce, that objection does not appear to be sound," said the President.

Mr. Fox again observed that the subject was under active examination, and he hoped soon to be able to consider it intelligently, and the conversation turned upon other matters.

When we left the White House, Mr. Fox observed that the President appeared to be deeply interested in the subject of iron-clads; that it was most important, but it was new, and would encounter all the prejudices of the naval service. But its importance was such that its investigation would be pressed as fast as possible, with a view of at least trying the experiment.

Within a few days there was a rumor that the Bureau of Construction in the Navy Department, through the influence of Mr. Fox, was engaged upon plans for an iron-clad vessel. As soon as Congress met, on the 4th of July, a bill was introduced which authorized the Secretary of the Navy to appoint a Board of Construction of three naval officers, to whom the plans for an iron-clad vessel were to be submitted, and, if the board approved them, the secretary was authorized to contract for its construction.

It was a matter of common knowledge that Cornelius S. Bushnell, of Connecticut, a friend of the secretary's, was the promoter of the bill, and that through his active labors the bill passed Congress and became a law in the early days of August. The board was immediately appointed. It consisted of Commodore Paulding, Admiral Smith, and Captain Davis. The board approved the plans; the contract was given to Mr. Bushnell for the first iron-clad built on the Western Continent. She was to be built at Mystic, Connecticut, and to be completed as speedily as possible. She was to be called the *Galena*, and as many workmen as could find room were at work upon her hull before the ink of the signatures to the contract was fairly dry.

In the autumn there was a great newspaper outcry over the *Galena*. The Department, the contractor, everybody concerned, was charged with peculation and fraud. It was asserted that the *Galena* would do everything a good ship ought not, and nothing that such a vessel ought to do; that she had no stability, that she would not stand up, that she would not answer her rudder, that she would not resist even grape-shot, that she would sink like a bar of lead the moment she was launched. The President and Secretary Fox were the only officers of the government who would speak a good word for the *Galena*. Even the contractor was despondent, and almost lost faith in the vessel.

It was at this time that the name of Captain Ericsson was first heard in connection with an iron-clad vessel. The rumor was that he had pronounced in favor of the *Galena's* plans, her stability, and her ability to resist a six-pound shot, etc., and had furnished contractor Bushnell with plans for a vessel which would resist the impact of any projectile which could be thrown by any gun then invented. It was called a floating battery. Mr. Bushnell had presented these plans to the Board of Construction, and the board had rejected them. He had then carried them to the President, whose decision upon them was expressed in a very pointed story, many times since repeated, but almost invariably with the point omitted. What the President said, after the plans were exhibited and explained to him, was, "As the darkey said, in putting on his boot, into which some one had put a Canada thistle, 'I guess dar's something in it.'"

There is no doubt that, after Captain Ericsson's plans had been submitted to the Board of Construction, and the captain had been induced to visit Washington and explain them, that the President became the warm advocate of the construction of his proposed battery, as it was then called. Captain Fox was the adviser upon whom he principally relied. There were several sessions of the Board of Construction; Captain Davis, who had strongly opposed the project, finally gave way, making the board unanimous, and the contract was awarded to Mr. Bushnell, and Messrs. Corning, Winslow, & Griswold, his associates. It is only just to Mr. Bushnell to say that, in all the preliminary work of clearing away the obstructions, securing the co-operation of the President, and overcoming the objections of the board, he alone was known, and that when the contract was awarded it was understood in Washington to have been secured through the labor and energy of Mr. Bushnell. The contract required the greatest practicable expedition in completing the vessel, and the contractors pushed the work with great energy. The *Monitor*, with her engines on board, was launched on the 30th of January, and, to the great disappointment of those who had opposed the experiment, instead of sinking, as they had predicted, she drew less water by some inches than Captain Ericsson had calculated.

Her battery was put on board, and she was fitted for sea with the greatest possible expedition. Captain Fox had daily reliable reports from Norfolk. The *Merrimac* was also rapidly approaching completion, and when she was reported to be ready for use the *Monitor* was still in the waters of New York harbor. It was not until the 27th of February that she put to sea, in an unfinished state, without having made the usual trips, for some unknown destination.

Early on Friday morning, March 7th, Secretary Fox invited me to accompany him in a call he was about to make, by appointment, upon President Lincoln. Captain Fox was an officer of infinite coolness and self-command. He did not exhibit the slightest evidence of emotion or apprehension while unfolding to me a story which gave me great uneasiness during the next three days. No one else was present at our interview with the President, and I cannot now undertake to give the precise words used, but the substance of the conversation I shall probably never forget. It was obvious that the President had received a recent communication from Captain Fox, and had been informed of the object of his visit. The latter observed that, from his latest information, which he believed was reliable, he did not expect that the *Merrimac* would make her appearance before Sunday, the 9th of March. She might, however, come out at any time, for her engines appeared to be working well at the dock, and, so far as his agent could discover, her armor was completed, and the work still going on was not connected with her motive-power or with her batteries. He said that he intended to leave the city immediately, for he wanted to be there when she made her attack. He asked the President whether he had any further suggestions or instructions, and received a negative reply. After some general conversation, in which the President said but few words, Captain Fox, quite in his ordinary tone, observed that he supposed that the President was prepared for very disastrous results from the expected encounter. "No," said Mr. Lincoln; "why should I be? We have three of our most effective war-vessels in Hampton Roads, and any number of small craft that will hang on to the stern of the *Merrimac* like small dogs on the haunches of a bear. They may not be able to tear her down, but they will interfere with the comfort of her voyage. Her trial-trip will not be a pleasure-trip, I am certain."

"I think you do not take into account all the possibilities of the *Merrimac*," said Captain Fox. "True, she may break down, she may accomplish nothing, she may not be shot-proof, but she will be commanded by a skilled naval officer. The engineers who have had charge of her construction are as competent as any in their profession. If they risk her in action, you may be sure she will do good work."

"Suppose she does. Have we not three good ships against her?"

"But if she proves invulnerable?" persisted the captain. "Suppose our heaviest shot and shell rebound from her armor as harmless as rubber balls? Suppose she strikes our ships, one after the other, with her ram, and opens a hole in them as large as a barn-door or a turnpike gate? Suppose they are powerless to resist her, and she sinks them all in a half-hour?"

"You are looking for great disasters, captain," said the President, with a smile. "We have had a big share of bad luck already, but I do not believe the future has any such misfortunes in store for us as you anticipate."

"I anticipate nothing which may not happen from the coming encounter," said Captain Fox, "nor have I mentioned the worst possibilities. If the *Merrimac* proves invulnerable, if she meets the expectations of her officers, although she may not be able to go outside the capes, she can do an immense damage without going to sea. If she sinks our ships, who is to prevent her dropping her anchor in the Potomac, where that steamer lies," pointing to a steamer at anchor below the long bridge, "and throwing her hundred-pound shells into this room, or battering down the walls of the Capitol?"

"The Almighty, captain," answered the President, decidedly, but without the least affectation. "I expect set-backs, defeats; we have had them, and shall have them. They are common to all wars. But I have not the slightest fear of any result which shall fatally impair our military and naval strength, or give other powers any right to interfere in our quarrel. The destruction of the Capitol would do both. I do not fear it, for this is God's fight, and he will win it in his own good time. He will take care that our enemies do not push us too far."

"I do most sincerely hope you are right, Mr. President," said Captain Fox, "but it is my duty, as one of your officers, to use to the best advantage my own judgment as well as the materials which the country places in our hands. The iron-clad is a new element in naval warfare. We know neither its power nor its effectiveness. It is prudent to fear what we do not understand. It is perfectly natural for naval officers to distrust the iron-clad. Frankly, we cannot even guess what the *Merrimac* will do."

"Speaking of iron-clads, you do not seem to take our little *Monitor* into the account," said the President. "I believe in the *Monitor*, and her commander. If Captain Worden does not give a good account of the *Monitor* and of himself, I shall have made a mistake in following my judgment for the first time since I have been here, captain. I have not made a mistake in following my clear judgment of men since this war began. I followed that judgment when I gave Worden the command of the *Monitor*. I would make the appointment over again to-day. The *Monitor* should be in Hampton Roads now. She left New York eight days ago."

"It is not prudent to place any reliance on the *Monitor*," responded the captain; "she is an experiment, wholly untried. She may be already at the bottom of the ocean. She may be at anchor somewhere, disabled. We know nothing about her. She may not have stood heavy weather at all, and we have had strong gales since she sailed. She is very liable to break down; she went to sea without one thorough trial-trip, when she should have had several. We ought not to be disappointed if she does not reach the mouth of the James. If she arrives, she may break down with the firing of her first gun, or be sunk or disabled by the first gun from the enemy. The clear dictate of prudence is to place no reliance on her, and if she proves of service, give the credit to our good fortune."

"No, no, captain," said the President, with more emphasis than he had previously used; "I respect your judgment, as you have good reason to know, but this time you are all wrong. The *Monitor* was one of my inspirations; I believed in her firmly when that energetic contractor first showed me Ericsson's plans. Captain Ericsson's plain but rather enthusiastic demonstration made my conversion permanent. It was called a floating battery then; I called it a raft. I caught some of the inventor's enthusiasm, and it has been growing upon me. I thought then, and I am confident now, it is just what we want. I am sure that the *Monitor* is still afloat, and that she will yet give a good account of herself. Sometimes I think she may be the veritable sling with a stone that shall yet smite the *Merrimac* Philistine in the forehead."

There was more of the conversation, but I do not know that it would further illustrate the attitude or the confidence of the President. We took our leave, and walked to the west entrance of the Treasury slowly and in silence. At the door the assistant secretary said, " Is not our Lincoln the truest man, an example of the most genuine manhood, you have ever seen—of whom you have ever read? How sincere he is! He seems to have imparted some of his faith to me. I have avoided reliance upon the *Monitor*. Perhaps she may yet prove the good angel who will take us out of the Slough of Despond."

We separated; I to the labors of forty-eight slow and anxious hours, he to witness the battle which changed all the conditions of naval warfare.

XXVII.

PRESIDENT LINCOLN'S CONFIDENCE IN ARMORED VESSELS CONTINUED.—THE *MONITOR* AND HER BATTLE WITH THE *MERRIMAC* DESCRIBED BY CAPTAIN WORDEN.

SATURDAY, March 8th, was a day of calamities. The news came over the wires that the *Merrimac* had come out of Norfolk, attended by a numerous body-guard of smaller vessels, and at one o'clock was leisurely entering upon her brief career of destruction. Within two hours we knew that projectiles from our heaviest guns had realized the apprehensions of Captain Fox, by rebounding from her uninjured side like rubber balls; that she had sent the fine sloop-of-war, the *Cumberland*, to the bottom of the James River; that she had torn the frigate *Congress* in pieces with her shot and shell, and left her a grounded wreck on the shore; that two brave ships' companies had been immolated to the demon of rebellion, and that the iron-clad destroyer, satisfied with her labors for that afternoon, had retired into the harbor of Norfolk, leaving our third and most valuable frigate, the *Minnesota*, aground and ready for the next morning's sacrifice. There had been no former day of such disaster. As I left the Treasury I involuntarily walked in the direction of the War Department, where I supposed the President would be found. At the door I met him returning to the Executive Mansion.

He was as cheerful as he had been on the morning of the previous day. The battle was over for the day, he said, and the *Merrimac* had gone into port, probably to repair some temporary damages. Nothing had been heard from Captain Fox or the *Monitor*. He regretted deeply the loss of so many brave men; our first lesson in the value of iron-clads for fighting purposes had been costly, but the Almighty ruled, and it would all come right somehow. I remember most distinctly, for it made a deep impression at the time, that he said that we should probably find that the *Merrimac* was at the end of her destructive mission, and would not sink another vessel.

Aware that it would be useless to expect sleep that night, and anxious for news from Captain Fox, I returned late in the evening to the Navy Department. It was nearly midnight before his despatch came. It was in cipher, and, being translated, informed us that he reached Newport News about nine o'clock, and went immediately on board the *Minnesota*. Every one on the vessel was demoralized. She had been stripped; it had been decided to burn her, and in a few moments more the torch would have been applied. Captain Fox's arrival had saved the vessel. His inquiry whether it would not be wiser to wait until it was seen whether the *Merrimac* came out of Norfolk again before setting on fire the finest ship in the navy, and destroying property to the value of a million and a half of dollars, recalled the officers to their senses, and the conclusion to defer the application of the torch was speedily reached. I remained at the Department until after two o'clock, when, receiving no news from the *Monitor* nor any further despatches from Captain Fox, all left the Naval Office for their respective homes.

The next Sunday forenoon was as gloomy as any that Washington had experienced since the beginning of the war. There was no excitement, but all seemed to be overwhelmed with despondency and vague apprehension. I went to Dr. Gurley's church, where his audience was made still more uncomfortable by a very gloomy sermon. After service I called upon Secretary Chase. He had no news, and could give me no comfort. Since the President seemed to be the only officer of the government who could see any hope in the future, I went to the War Office, where he was usually to be found when any serious fighting was going on. There I found him with quite a large party, including two members of his Cabinet.

It was evident, from the general excitement, that news had been received from the James River. As I entered the room some one was saying, "Would it not be fortunate if the *Monitor* should sink her?" "It would be nothing more than I have expected," calmly observed President Lincoln. "If she does not, something else will. Many providential things are happening in this war, and this may be one of them. The loss of two good ships is an expensive lesson, but it will teach us all the value of iron-clads. I have not believed at any time during the last twenty-four hours that the *Merrimac* would go right on destroying right and left without any obstruction. Since we knew that the *Monitor* had got there, I have felt that she was the vessel we wanted." I then learned that the *Monitor* had arrived at Fortress Monroe on Saturday evening; without waiting for any preparation, she had steamed up to Newport News, and laid herself alongside the grounded *Minnesota*. The *Merrimac* had made her appearance shortly after daylight; Captain Worden had promptly advanced to make her acquaintance, and had ever since been sticking to her closer than a brother. It was also reported that the two fighters had ever since been pounding each other terrifically, and that the *Monitor* as yet showed no signs of weakness. Time passes quickly in such an excitement. Very soon came a message that evoked cheers from everybody. Its substance was that the *Merrimac* had withdrawn, and was again steaming for Norfolk. Even this news, which stirred the enthusiasm of every one else, so that all burst into a long-continued volley of applause, did not seem to elate the President. "I am glad the *Monitor* has done herself credit for Worden's sake—for all our sakes," was all he said. He then walked slowly to the White House.

When Captain Fox returned, his graphic account of the battle was given to the press, and seemed to settle the policy of the country in relation to armored vessels. He gave the highest credit to Captain Worden and his second in command, Lieutenant Green. The fearlessness with which they advanced the *Monitor* to the attack, the persistence with which she clung to her enemy during all that long forenoon, turning away from her in a circuit only just large enough to give time to load her guns, he said was a grand exhibition of judgment, courage, and seamanship, beautifully responded to by the vessel in the ease with which she answered her helm, and the even, regular movement of her power. He had ordered the *Monitor* to Washington for repairs, he said, and convenience of inspection, for henceforth the energies of the Navy Department would be largely devoted to the building and equipment of monitors.

Some weeks later we were the witnesses of a dramatic scene at the Navy Yard, on board the *Monitor*. The vessel came to Washington unchanged, in the same condition as when she discharged her parting shot at the *Merrimac*. There she lay until her heroic commander had so far recovered from his injuries as to be able to rejoin his vessel. All leaves of absence had been revoked, the absentees had returned, and were ready to welcome their captain. The President, Captain Fox, and a limited number of Captain Worden's personal friends had been invited to his informal reception. Lieutenant Green received the President and the guests. He was a boy in years, not too young to volunteer, however, when volunteers were scarce, and to fight the *Merrimac* during the last half of the battle, after the captain was disabled. Then, when the success and safety of the *Monitor* were both proved, an officer was promoted over his head, on the ground that he was too young to bear so great a responsibility. This was a most unjust act, for which the Navy Department was never forgiven by the American people.

The President and the other guests stood on the deck, near the turret. The men were formed in lines, with their officers a little in advance, when Captain Worden ascended the gangway. The heavy guns in the Navy Yard began firing the customary salute when he stepped upon the deck. One side of his face was permanently blackened by the powder shot into it from the muzzle of a cannon carrying a shell of one hundred pounds' weight, discharged less than twenty yards away. The President advanced to welcome him, introduced him to the few strangers present, the officers and men passed in review and were dismissed. Then there was a scene worth witnessing. The old tars swarmed around their loved captain, they grasped his hand, crowded to touch him, thanked God for his recovery and return, and invoked blessings upon his head in the name of all the saints in the calendar. He called them by their names, had a pleasant word for each of them, and for a few moments we looked upon an exhibition of a species of affection that could only have been the product of a common danger.

When order was restored, the President gave a brief sketch of Captain Worden's career. Commodore Paulding had been the first, Captain Worden the second officer of the navy, he said, to give an unqualified opinion in favor of armored vessels. Their opinions had been influential with him and with the Board of Construction. Captain Worden had volunteered to take the command of the *Monitor*, at the risk of his life and reputation, before her keel was laid. He had watched her construction, and his energy had made it possible to send her to sea in time to arrest the destructive operations of the *Merrimac*. What he had done with a new crew, and a vessel of novel construction, we all knew. He, the President, cordially acknowledged his indebtedness to Captain Worden, and he hoped the whole country would unite in the feeling of obligation. The debt was a heavy one, and would not be repudiated when its nature was understood. The details of the first battle between iron-clads would interest every one. At the request of Captain Fox, Captain Worden had consented to give an account of his voyage from New York to Hampton Roads, and of what had afterwards happened there on board the *Monitor*.

In an easy conversational manner, without any effort at display, Captain Worden told the story, of which the following is the substance :

"I suppose," he began, "that every one knows that we left New York Harbor in some haste. We had information that the *Merrimac* was nearly completed, and if we were to fight her on her first appearance, we must be on the ground. The *Monitor* had been hurried from the laying of her keel. Her engines were new, and her machinery did not move smoothly. Never was a vessel launched that so much needed trial trips, some of them to sea, to test her machinery, and get her crew accustomed to their novel duties. We went to sea practically without them. No part of the vessel was finished; there was one omission that was serious, and came very near causing her failure and the loss of many lives. In heavy weather it was intended that her hatches and all her openings should be closed and battened down. In that case all the men would be below, and would have to depend upon artificial ventilation. Our machinery for that purpose proved wholly inadequate.

"We were in a heavy gale of wind as soon as we passed Sandy Hook. The vessel behaved splendidly. The seas rolled over her, and we found her the most comfortable vessel we had ever seen, except for the ventilation, which gave us more trouble than I have time to tell you about. We had to run into port and anchor on account of the weather, and, as you know, it was two o'clock in the morning of Sunday before we were alongside the *Minnesota*. Captain Van Brunt gave us an account of Saturday's experience. He was very glad to make our acquaintance, and notified us that we must be prepared to receive the *Merrimac* at daylight. We had had a very hard trip down the coast, and officers and men were weary and sleepy. But when informed that our fight would probably open at daylight, and that the *Monitor* must be put in order, every man went to his post with a cheer. That night there was no sleep on board the *Monitor*.

"In the gray of the early morning we saw a vessel approaching, which our friends on the *Minnesota* said was the *Merrimac*. Our fastenings were cast off, our machinery started, and we moved out to meet her halfway. We had come a long way to fight her, and did not intend to lose our opportunity.

"Before showing you over the vessel, let me say that there were three possible points of weakness in the *Monitor*, two of which might have been guarded against in her construction, if there had been more time to perfect her plans. One of them was in the turret, which, as you see, is constructed of eight plates of inch iron—on the side of the ports, nine—set on end so as to break joints, and firmly bolted together, making a hollow cylinder eight inches thick. It rests on a metal ring on a vertical shaft, which is revolved by power from the boilers. If a projectile struck the turret at an acute angle, it was expected to glance off without doing damage. But what would happen if it was fired in a straight line to the centre of the turret, which in that case would receive the whole force of the blow? It might break off the bolt-heads on the interior, which, flying across, would kill the men at the guns; it might disarrange the revolving mechanism, and then we would be wholly disabled.

"I laid the *Monitor* close alongside the *Merrimac*, and gave her a shot. She returned our compliment by a shell, weighing one hundred and fifty pounds, fired when we were close together, which struck the turret so squarely that it received the whole force. Here you see the scar, two and a half inches deep in the wrought iron, a perfect mould of the shell. If anything could test the turret, it was that shot. It did not start a rivet-head or a nut! It stunned the two men who were nearest where the ball struck, and that was all. I touched the lever— the turret revolved as smoothly as before. The turret had stood the test; I could mark that point of weakness off my list forever.

"You notice that the deck is joined to the side of the hull by a right angle, at what sailors call the 'plank-shear.' If a projectile struck that angle, what would happen? It would not be deflected; its whole force would be expended there. It might open a seam in the hull below the water-line, or pierce the wooden hull, and sink us. Here was our second point of weakness.

"I had decided how I would fight her in advance. I would keep the *Monitor* moving in a circle, just large enough to give time for loading the guns. At the point where the circle impinged upon the *Merrimac* our guns should be fired, and loaded while we were moving around the circuit. Evidently the *Merrimac* would return the compliment every time. At our second exchange of shots, she returning six or eight to our two, another of her large shells struck our 'plank-shear' at its angle, and tore up one of the deck-plates, as you see. The shell had struck what I believed to be the weakest point in the *Monitor*. We had already learned that the *Merrimac* swarmed with sharp-shooters, for their bullets were constantly spattering against our turret and our deck. If a man showed himself on deck he would draw their fire. But I did not much consider the sharp-shooters. It was my duty to investigate the effects of that shot. I ordered one of the pendulums to be hauled aside, and, crawling out of the port, walked to the side, laid down upon my chest, and examined it thoroughly. The hull was uninjured, except for a few splinters in the wood. I walked back and crawled into the turret—the bullets were falling on the iron deck all about me as thick as hail-stones in a storm. None struck me, I suppose because the vessel was moving, and at the angle lying on the deck, my body made a small mark difficult to hit. We gave them two more guns, and then I told the men what was true, that the *Merrimac* could not sink us if we let her pound us for a month. The men cheered; the knowledge put new life into all.

"We had more exchanges, and then the *Merrimac* tried new tactics. She endeavored to ram us, to run us down. Once she struck us about amidships with her iron ram. Here you see its mark. It gave us a shock, pushed us around, and that was all the harm. But the movement placed our sides together. I gave her two guns, which I think lodged in her side, for, from my lookout crack, I could not see that either shot rebounded. Ours being the smaller vessel, and more easily handled, I had no difficulty in avoiding her ram. I ran around her several times, planting our shot in what seemed to be the most vulnerable places. In this way, reserving my fire until I got the range and the mark, I planted two more shots almost in the very spot I had hit when she tried to ram us. Those shots must have been effective, for they were followed by a shower of bars of iron.

"The third weak spot was our pilot-house. You see that it is built a little more than three feet above the deck, of bars of iron, ten by twelve inches square, built up like a log-house, bolted with very large bolts at the corners where the bars interlock. The pilot stands upon a platform below, his head and shoulders in the pilot-house. The upper tier of bars is separated from the second by an open space of an inch, through which the pilot may look out at every point of the compass. The pilot-house, as you see, is a four-square mass of iron, provided with no means of deflecting a ball. I expected trouble from it, and I was not disappointed. Until my accident happened, as we approached the enemy I stood in the pilot-house and gave the signals. Lieutenant Greene fired the guns, and Engineer Stimers, here, revolved the turret.

"I was below the deck when the corner of the pilothouse was first struck by a shot or a shell. It either burst or was broken, and no harm was done. A short time after I had given the signal, and with my eye close against the lookout crack, was watching the effect of our shot, when something happened to me;—my part in the fight was ended. Lieutenant Green, who fought the *Merrimac* until she had no longer stomach for fighting, will tell you the rest of the story."

Can it be possible that this beardless boy fought one of the historic battles of the world? was the thought of every one, as the modest, diffident young Green was half pushed forward into the circle. "I cannot add much to the captain's story," he began. "He had cut out the work for us, and we had only to follow his pattern. I kept the *Monitor* either moving around the circle or around the enemy, and endeavored to place our shots as near her amidships as possible, where Captain Worden believed he had already broken through her armor. We knew that she could not sink us, and I thought I would keep right on pounding her as long as she would stand it. There is really nothing new to be added to Captain Worden's account. We could strike her wherever we chose; weary as they must have been, our men were full of enthusiasm, and I do not think we wasted a shot. Once we ran out of the circle for a moment to adjust a piece of machinery, and I learn that some of our friends feared that we were drawing out of the fight. The *Merrimac* took the opportunity to start for Norfolk. As soon as our machinery was adjusted we followed her, and got near enough to give her a parting shot. But I was not familiar with the locality; there might be torpedoes planted in the channel, and I did not wish to take any risk of losing our vessel, so I came back to the company of our friends. But except that we were, all of us, tired and hungry when we came back to the *Minnesota* at half-past twelve P. M., the *Monitor* was just as well prepared to fight as she was at eight o'clock in the morning when she fired her first gun."

We were then shown the injury to the pilot-house. The mark of the ball was plain upon the two upper bars, the principal impact being upon the lower of the two. This huge bar was broken in the middle, but held firmly at either end. The further it was pressed in, the stronger was the resistance on the exterior. On the inside the fracture in the bar was half an inch wide. Captain Worden's eye was very near to the lookout crack, so that when the gun was discharged the shock of the ball knocked him senseless, while the mass of flame filled one side of his face with coarse grains of powder. He remained insensible for some hours.

"Have you heard what Captain Worden's first inquiry was when he recovered his senses after the general shock to his system ?" asked Captain Fox of the President.

"I think I have," replied Mr. Lincoln, "but it is worth relating to these gentlemen."

"His question was," said Captain Fox, "'Have I saved the *Minnesota ?*'"

"Yes, and whipped the *Merrimac !*" some one answered.

"Then," said Captain Worden, "I don't care what becomes of me."

Captain Worden apologized for his inability to provide for the President and his guests the usual refreshments of a vessel of the navy. The haste of departure from her port had led to the omission of everything that did not improve the fighting qualities of his vessel.

"Some uncharitable people say that old Bourbon is an

indispensable element in the fighting qualities of some of our generals in the field," smilingly responded the President. "But, captain, after the account that we have heard to-day, no one will say that any Dutch courage is needed on board the *Monitor*."

"It never has been, sir," modestly observed the captain.

"Mr. President," said Captain Fox, "not much of the history to which we have listened is new to me. I saw this battle from eight o'clock until midday. There was one marvel in it which has not been mentioned—the splendid handling of the *Monitor* throughout the battle. The first bold advance of this diminutive vessel against a giant like the *Merrimac* was superlatively grand. She seemed inspired by Nelson's order at Trafalgar: 'He will make no mistake who lays his vessel alongside the enemy.' One would have thought the *Monitor* a living thing. No man was visible. You saw her moving around that circle, delivering her fire invariably at the point of contact, and heard the crash of the missile against her enemy's armor above the thunder of her guns, on the bank where we stood. It was indescribably grand!"

"Now," he continued, "standing here on the deck of this battle-scarred vessel, the first genuine iron-clad—the victor in the first fight of iron-clads—let me make a confession, and perform an act of simple justice. I never fully believed in armored vessels until I saw this battle. I know all the facts which united to give us the *Monitor*. I withhold no credit from Captain Ericsson, her inventor, but I know that the country is principally indebted for the construction of this vessel to President Lincoln, and for the success of her trial to Captain Worden, her commander."

XXVIII.

JOSEPH HENRY AND ABRAHAM LINCOLN.

In the spring of 1862, I had an opportunity of comparing and contrasting two striking characters; one, a philosopher, trained in the schools, matured by a life of study and original investigation which would have made him the equal of Plato and Aristotle had he been their contemporary; the other, the product of Nature, with his strong common-sense developed by the experiences of human life under hard and trying conditions.

Professor Joseph Henry, Secretary of the Smithsonian Institution, called at the office of the register on business connected with the Light-House Board, of which he was the official head. He would have taken high rank in any circle of learned men, from the Stoics to the scientists of his own time. He was an eminent physicist before he was called to his present position. His original investigations, especially in light and electricity, were of great value, and but for his inborn modesty would have credited him with the invention of the art of telegraphy. After he was placed in charge of Smithson's great trust, he devoted himself to its care and development, and to the advancement of the interests of the republic whose servant he had become. With what fidelity he preserved the principal of that trust, and with its interest built up an institution for scientific work on a scale of magnitude of which Smithson never dreamed, is known to his country and the world. The value to the republic of his researches into the science of illumination had already been very great and was increasing with every passing year. To these good works, add an unassuming modesty, complete unselfishness, and an unvarying purpose to make every one the better and happier for his acquaintance, and it becomes apparent that Joseph Henry was a great man with a very beautiful character.

"Do you often see the President?" asked Dr. Henry, when his business was completed.

"Occasionally," I answered. "He sometimes visits this office, as I presume he does many others. He is always welcome here, but his visits are by no means as frequent as I would make them if I could."

"I have only recently come to know the President, except from a passing introduction," he said. "I have lately met him five or six times. He is producing a powerful impression upon me, more powerful than any one I can now recall. It increases with every interview. I think it my duty to take philosophic views of men and things, but the President upsets me. If I did not resist the inclination, I might even fall in love with him."

It was my opportunity to lure him on. Any views of his about President Lincoln could not fail to be of interest. "Yes?" I said. "Possibly you do not differ from the rest of us. I know of nobody in this department who knows the President who fails to respect and admire him. What do you find in him so attractive?"

"I have not yet arranged my thoughts about him in a form to warrant their expression," he replied. "But I can say so much as this: President Lincoln impresses me as a man whose honesty of purpose is transparent, who has no mental reservations, who may be said to wear his heart upon his sleeve. He has been called coarse. In my interviews with him he converses with apparent freedom, and without a trace of coarseness. He has been called ignorant. He has shown a comprehensive grasp of every subject on which he has conversed with me. His views of the present situation are somewhat novel, but seem to me unanswerable. He has read many books and remembers their contents better than I do. He is associated with men who I know are great. He impresses me as their equal, if not their superior. I desired to induce him to understand, and look favorably upon, a change which I wish to make in the policy of the Light-House Board in a matter requiring some scientific knowledge. He professed his ignorance, or, rather, he ridiculed his knowledge of it, and yet he discussed it as intelligently—"

"The President!" here interrupted a messenger, opening the door to admit President Lincoln.

"You have interrupted an interesting commentary," I began, laughingly, as I rose to welcome him.

"Do not! You will not say another word!" exclaimed the doctor, blushing like a school-girl. "You will mortify me excessively if you do." I saw that he took the matter seriously, and hastened to change the conversation.

These two great Americans seated themselves side by side. They had a long conversation. I took no part in the conversation, and shall not attempt to recall it. It began with the subject of the destruction by the Confederates of all the lights, buoys, and signal stations along their coast; their purpose in such acts, and how our own vessels could best dispense with these aids to navigation. It diverged to the subject of illuminating oils of different kinds. I inferred that the professor was experimenting with lard oils, with a view to their introduction on account of the saving of expense in their use. I could not discover that the President was at a loss for a moment, and that he conversed in any particular less intelligently than the professor. The latter looked at his watch, apologized for keeping Mr. Lincoln so long, and with the air of having done something very reprehensible, abruptly took his leave.

"Do you often see Professor Henry?" inquired the President, as soon as the door had closed.

I smiled, for it was the identical question which the professor had asked me about the President.

"My visits to the Smithsonian, to Dr. Henry, and his able lieutenant, Professor Baird, are the chief recreations of my life," I said. "These men are missionaries to excite scientific research and promote scientific knowledge. The country has no more faithful servants, though it may have to wait another century to appreciate the value of their labors."

"I had an impression," said Mr. Lincoln, "that the Smithsonian was printing a great amount of useless information. Professor Henry has convinced me of my error. It must be a grand school if it produces such thinkers as he is. He is one of the pleasantest men I have ever met; so unassuming, simple, and sincere. I wish we had a few thousand more such men!"

It was not strange that these two great men were attracted towards each other. In their natural qualities of sterling honesty, simplicity, and unselfishness, they were much alike. It was in their acquisitions that they differed, and these did not constitute the foundations of their characters.

XXIX.
INTER ARMA, SCIENTIA.—THE POTOMAC NATURALISTS' CLUB.

THE Smithsonian recalls almost the only recreation which we permitted ourselves to enjoy. After the first Bull Run, there was no time when some of our friends were not suffering from wounds or sickness, in the hospitals or in our own households. Victories were infrequent; there was a strange incongruity between so much suffering and pleasure of any description.

In the early autumn of 1861, Professor Baird suggested that we should resist the general tendency to depression, by occasional meetings of the resident naturalists of Washington. Out of this suggestion grew the Potomac Club, with its fortnightly meetings at the homes of members, and its memories are still fresh and delightful after thirty years. Time has dealt hardly with its members: only three or four of them survive. I cannot forego this opportunity for a brief notice of some of the most conspicuous, to whom we were indebted for many pleasant hours, in what would otherwise have been a dark and depressing period of Washington life.

First, and by our unanimous opinion, *facile princeps*, was Spencer F. Baird, Assistant Secretary of the Smithsonian Institute, our president. A greater number of talents were delivered to him than to any other member, but he was at all times ready to be reckoned with concerning them. The science of the world was his witness how fruitful he had made them. From boyhood he was the friend of every living creature. At the age of forty-five he had written and published a description of the form, habits, and specific characters of every known American mammal, bird, fish, reptile, and many of the mollusks and insects. He had taught his countrymen the useful lesson that a bountiful Creator had given these creatures life for some good purpose. He had brought together that gigantic collection in the Smithsonian, and distributed specimens by the hundred thousand to the museums of the world. He had trained a multitude of useful workers in science all over the country, who, but for him, would have been ignorant of its uses and its pleasures. He had created the Fish Commission, with an army of unpaid assistants, now by precept and now by example, restoring to our coasts and inland waters the great fish families almost exterminated by the reckless improvidence of man. With the resources of Smithson's legacy at his command, he was as poor as when he left his Pennsylvania home. He had certainly buried none of his talents in the earth; I think he had done more scientific work than any naturalist who had preceded him. It was not strange that Professor Baird and Professor Henry had labored so long and so cordially together, for the former was just as delightful as, and possibly more genial than, his superior officer. The Baird evenings of our club, when we met at his residence, were the most memorable in its history.

I open the pages of a dilapidated photograph-album of the period. Who is this, shod with moccasins, clad in furs, with knitted pointed cap, a blanket over his shoulders, and a dog whip with its trailing lash in his right hand? It is Robert Kennicott, just returned from his three years' exploration of the great marshes of the Yucon, the Arctic coasts reached by the Coppermine

River, and the regions round about Fort Mackenzie. He has brought back with him from their breeding-grounds, before unknown, the eggs of the canvas-back and red-head duck, and of many other birds new to science. He has increased the collection in the museum by many new specimens, and added many new facts to scientific lore. He insists that at Fort Churchill, where he acquired celebrity as a great medicine man, human beings hibernate as truly as the plantigrades. During his three years' absence he was cut off from home as effectually as if he had been in another planet.

Kennicott was born on an Illinois prairie. How energetic and black-eyed and queer he was! The playmates of his childhood belonged to the *Crotalus* family. No rattlesnake, he said, had any venom for him. He collected them in a bag, and handled them as if they were eels. None ever struck or attempted to strike at him. He was a favorite student of Professor Baird, and the very life of our social meetings. His early death was a loss to science and a personal grief to all who knew him.

William Simpson was another of our members—one of the most promising young naturalists of his time. He had labored diligently in the field. Chicago, charmed by his enthusiasm, had made him her pet. The citizens built a fine edifice for his collection, put him in charge of it with a liberal salary, and it was growing marvellously, when in an hour the fire-fiend touched it with the finger of annihilation. He had inherited tubercular disease, against which he had fought with the courage of a soldier. But this collection was the treasure of his heart, the jewel of his eye. When he lost it he withered and died, and science lost a votary and a martyr.

Count Pourtalis was another interesting member of

the club. He belonged to the French nobility. He differed in opinion with his family, and they cut him off because he insisted upon marrying the portionless girl whom he loved, and devoting himself to the study of the physical sciences. He wedded his love, both came to the United States, and he presented himself, with an empty purse and a heart devoted to science, to his massive-brained countryman, Agassiz. Through him the count obtained a position in the Coast Survey. There he proved a most useful worker, was promoted according to his merit, and was then living modestly and happily with his wife and boys in Washington. A few years later, the noble Pourtalis family were glad enough to invite him to return with his wife and children, and a national reputation as a scientist, to his paternal halls.

The subject is very tempting, but must not be further pursued in detail. Yet I cannot wholly pass over Baron Osten-Sacken, of the Russian Legation. The *Diptera*, or Cuvier's twelfth order of insects, was his *forte*. Very learned he was too, and, if I am not mistaken, his monograph on the *Diptera*, a large quarto, was printed by the Smithsonian as one of its contributions to science. He was a genial, kind-hearted, unassuming student of nature. The club had not a more popular member; but owing to his diminutive size, he acquired a name which clung to him ever afterwards.

"Pray, what are the *Diptera?*" asked a member, whose studies had not been entomological, of another member, when Osten-Sacken was mentioned.

"*Diptera?* Well, I suppose a *Culex* belongs to the *Diptera.*"

"What is a *Culex*, then?" pursued his questioner.

"A *Culex!*" was the reply. "A *Culex* is an insect with a double pair of wings, abounding in moist localities, which, thirsting for human gore, invades the habitations of man with an irritating buzzing sound, pierces the cuticle with his lancet-shaped proboscis, and discharges into the wound a poisonous fluid."

"Confound the man! He means a mosquito!" exclaimed an irreverent auditor. "Osten-Sacken would naturally write about the species. Don't you see the family resemblance?"

This was sufficient to fasten an undeserved nick-name upon the good-natured little entomologist.

I can only mention the names of others. Jillson and Peale, from the Art Departments; Shaeffer, the Librarian of the Patent Office. Peale was the brother of Rembrandt Peale, the artist, with many of his accomplishments; Shaeffer was one of the most learned of Germans. Then there was Hayden, who led an exploring-party every spring beyond the one hundredth meridian, and returned in the autumn laden with fossils and other specimens, to worry Congress into granting his appropriation for the coming year. He must have understood the business, for he never failed. Another of our members was A. B. Meek, the most conscientious geologist who ever described a fossil, whose mind was as clean and pure as that of an infant, whom we all loved and honored, but who was so intensely mortified by his deafness that he could be drawn but seldom to our meetings. Theodore Gill was our ichthyologist. He was charged with creating more new species than ever scientific enthusiast was responsible for before. S. M. Clarke, then of the Bureau of Engraving and Printing in the Treasury, whose microscope, with its collection of lenses, was our envy, and who was an accomplished manipulator of the instrument, and Schott, the mathematician of the Coast Survey, eminent in his work, and the owner of a breed of Pomeranian dogs of pure blood, close the list of our regular members.

Among our occasional visitors was Cope, who had not then commenced his warfare upon Marsh, and Dr. Newberry, who has since done such magnificent work for the spread of scientific instruction, and who was then not only a director, but a hard worker of the Sanitary Commission. Those were sessions of great interest, when, just returning from some field of bloody conflict, he told us of the lives and the pain and suffering saved by the judicious administration of that, the noblest of all the charities of the war. O. C. Marsh was always a welcome guest, able to contribute his full share to the science or pleasure of the evening.

It is fit that this notice of the members and visitors of our club should close with the name of Professor Agassiz. Three nights he was with us. Those were evenings when we wanted to omit refreshments, because they interrupted Agassiz, so eager were we to listen to the words of this giant of science. His facility of expression would have been considered remarkable in his native tongue—in English, a foreign language to him, it was marvellous. He was as willing to converse as we were to listen. And how perfectly unassuming he was! He pretended to nothing that he did not know. I had long desired to ascertain his views on one subject. One evening I had my opportunity. "Professor Agassiz," I said, "you have studied the Ice Period more exhaustively than any other physicist. Tell us what it was that changed the temperature so as to permit the ice-sheet to cover so large a part of our continent."

He answered, without the slightest hesitation: "I do not believe that the science of to-day can give a satisfactory answer to that question, simply because we know of no conditions which could vaporize as large a quantity of water as was necessary to form the ice-sheet. Its answer may be found in the great Rocky and Sierra Nevada ranges, or in the basin between, but it has not yet been discovered."

I have addressed this inquiry to many other physicists. They have almost invariably attempted some unsatisfactory reply. Professor Agassiz was great enough to say that he did not know.

XXX.

A NIGHT WITH THE POTOMAC NATURALISTS' CLUB.—THE GIANT OCTOPUS.

THE slogan "On to Richmond!" was no longer heard in our land. Its latest notes had receded into silence over the field of Bull Run. The dispirited men who, in broken ranks, straggled into Washington, had heard enough of it. They would be contented now to wait for discipline and preparation before that or any other note of inexperience was raised again.

Now it was that the anaconda was taken as the popular model for the coming campaign. With a firm attachment to Washington as its base, it was to encircle the whole Confederate army, and when the time for muscular tension came, not a single soldier of the enemy was to escape from the deadly constriction of its folds. The anaconda contrivance appeared to be safe, simple, and very popular.

At one of our club-meetings a member incidentally referred to the anaconda model suggested by our young and popular military chieftain. It was criticised as an unfortunate suggestion. These boas were a sluggish, cowardly race, said the member. They lurked in foul recesses; they struck from behind. It was essential to capture that the quarry should be standing quiet at the moment of attack. The rebels were a restless race, continually moving about, and could not be counted on to stand still long enough for the process of constriction.

The rattlesnake was a better model. He was a fighter *ab ovo*. He gave notice before he struck, and rather preferred to hit his enemy in the face.

"Why would not the giant octopus answer for a military model?" said another member. "He has claims that are not to be overlooked—that is, if his existence is not wholly fabulous."

"I believe in the giant octopus," said Count Pourtalis. "I have had occasion recently to investigate his history, and there is very satisfactory evidence of his existence. I cannot discuss him as a military model, but as an existing species he is a fact which I am prepared to prove."

The count was the expert of the Coast Survey in deep-sea soundings. His reputation as an investigator was established. He readily acceded to the universal demand of the members, that he should give them the latest facts about, as well as the natural history of, the giant octopus.

"Gentlemen," he began, "I think I shall be able to show you that the cuttle-fish is not to be ridiculed. He belongs to the squid family, and has a lot of names. He is called a cephalopod, an octopus, a loligo, a teuthis, as well as a cuttle-fish and a squid. He cuts an important figure in the early literature of natural science. In the 'Historiæ Naturalis,' of Dr. Johannes Jonstonus, published, in two huge folios, at Amsterdam, in 1657, you will find him figured in five gigantic forms. The learned doctor has collected all that the naturalists have written on the subject from Aristotle and Elian, Plutarch and Hippocrates, to the writers of his own time. Pliny describes one captured at Carteia, the dried remains of which weighed seven hundred pounds. Its arms were thirty feet long, with suckers as big as an urn. All the writers agree on its enormous size and its destructiveness to man. But it is in the Arctic seas that it is largest and most ferocious. Olaus Magnus figures one in the act of taking a sailor from the deck of a vessel. Montfort represented one pulling a three-masted ship under the waves. It remained for the pious old Bishop Pontoppidan, as recently as the last half of the seventeenth century, to describe it as 'the largest of all living creatures.' 'He never shows his whole body out of the water, but shows a portion about an English mile and a half in circumference.' 'If this, creature's arms were to lay hold of the largest man-of-war, he would drag it down to the bottom.' 'When he sinks, he creates a whirlpool which draws everything down with it.' Perhaps," continued the count, "this is enough to show you that the old naturalists thought him an animal of some magnitude." To which the club readily assented.

"Then," he resumed, "we will take some more recent evidence. In a late number of the *Comptes Rendus* of the French Academy is an account of a battle between the crew of a French man-of-war and a huge loligo, which occurred in the Indian Ocean less than two years ago. This battle is authenticated by the oaths of the officers. It continued for more than four hours. The squid escaped, for their harpoons and hooks drew out of its soft body. But they cut off some of its arms, over thirty feet in length, exclusive of the paddle, which measured ten feet more. Travellers in Japan report paintings of the squid, tearing fishermen from their boats, and on the coast of Newfoundland huge masses of one which had been killed were found, with the tentacles attached, over forty feet in length. Upon this evidence, I am a believer in the existence of the giant cuttle-fish."

The count having concluded, Professor Baird took up the discussion. "Suppose, now, that, in the words of Mrs.

Partington, we 'cease to refrain from odorous comparisons,' and look the octopus squarely in the face. His eyes are like saucers, but as he is not provided with eyelids, he carries them under his arms. He is well fixed in the matter of arms, having anywhere from eight to twenty, which, for convenience in feeding, are arranged in a circle around his mouth, which is directly on top of his head. His jaws are horny and triangular, and work up and down like the knife of a guillotine. Having such a supply of arms, he dispenses with legs altogether, and walks on his head, tail upwards. Along these tentacles, forty or fifty feet in length, are arranged rows of cup-shaped suckers. When they grasp their prey, a single muscular contraction creates a vacuum in these suckers, and every cup is made as fast as a limpet to a rock, so that it is easier to tear off than to detach the arm. They have a fair brain, in a well-protected skull, a fine sense of hearing, and they handle their arms with the quickness of a monkey. They move sideways by means of their arms, or backwards by squirting the water in advance. They are provided with supplies of paint in cells under the skin, and by pressing these cells they can paint themselves in other colors. Like an army correspondent, they always carry their ink-bag, and, whenever they wish to retire from the public or any other view, a gentle pressure upon the ink-bag surrounds them with a black curtain which no vision can penetrate, and they can then make their retreat invisible to an enemy. Obviously such invisibility would be of great advantage to a retreating army."

The subject was then open for general discussion, which was continued on a scientific basis, but in a similar temper. We decided that the squid was a fact, if not a factor, and that he was well arranged for a predatory life at the expense of the enemy. After a sarcastic notice of this discussion by the press nothing more was heard of the anaconda as a model for our army.

To these notes I may add an incident in my own experience. Years after the close of the war, I was one day walking along the Pacific coast of the Mexican territory of Lower California, near Magdalena Bay. The tide was low, and in a cavity of the rock I saw what I supposed to be a star-fish or a holothurian, and carelessly thrust the long staff I was using as a walking-stick into it. Like a flash the tentacles of the animal grasped it, reaching nearly to my hand. My companion, an intelligent Ecuadorian, well acquainted with that coast, shrieked to me to let the creature alone. I pulled it out, as it adhered to the staff, and found it to be a squid, weighing thirty or forty pounds. I had to kill the animal before he would leave the staff. My companion then gave me the following account, as of a fact which occurred within his own knowledge. The Chinese from San Francisco were accustomed to visit that coast to collect a bivalve mollusk, which they dried and used for food. One day a man belonging to one of their schooners disappeared, and was not to be found. He was finally discovered adhering, apparently, to the face of a perpendicular rock, two or three fathoms above the surface of the water. He was quite dead, in the grasp of a squid, which was already feasting on his body. The squid occupied a cavity in the rock, and had seized the Chinaman in his tentacles, drawn him to the mouth of his den, and there crushed him. That animal was supposed to weigh about four hundred pounds.

XXXI.

HOSPITAL NOTES.—THE WOUNDED FROM THE WILDERNESS.—
CHARITIES OF THE COLORED POOR.—SISTERS OF CHARITY.—
ANÆSTHETICS.

Was the whole of Grant's army being sent back wounded to Washington? It appeared so, in those early days of May, 1864. Ample hospitals had been provided for the wounded and disabled from a great battle. Many swift steamers were constantly plying between Aquia Creek and Washington. Mattresses spread side by side covered the decks and the cabin floor, on each of which, at the beginning of the voyage, lay a wounded man. As they neared its end, and came to the Sixth Street Landing, some of these were vacant. Their tenants lay in the bow of the steamer; their faces were covered, and they were very still. Attendants moved gently among them, for they were asleep. Many in that short voyage had fallen into the sleep that knows no waking.

At the landing the survivors were placed by careful hands in ambulances, which took their places in a procession constantly moving on one line out to the hospitals on the hills back of the city, and then returning by another route to the Sixth Street Landing. This procession of laden ambulances was more than three miles long, and the vehicles ran quite near each other; the return route was somewhat longer.

For three days and as many nights the procession had been moving up and down its course, never ceasing its progress, save when the breaking of a carriage caused a temporary delay. Was it never to stop? Was the entire army to be returned in this disabled condition?

The silent patience with which these soldiers endured their sufferings was most impressive. Wounded as many were unto death, tortured by the agony of thirst which always follows the loss of blood in gun-shot wounds, some with limbs amputated on the field, and the severed stumps still undressed, scarcely a sigh or a groan escaped their parched lips. It was discovered by those who lived along the route that water, or any liquid which would quench thirst, was the most grateful relief that could be afforded them. The colored people were the first to make the discovery. They built little stands by the roadside, and from these, little darkies, with vessels of every form and dimension, trotted along by the ambulances, and served out the contents to the suffering men. Soon tables were set out before many of the dwellings, and coffee, tea, and light eatables were given to all soldiers who would accept them. Almost every residence became a house of refreshments, managed by patriotic women. The gratitude which some could express only by a look was the only compensation demanded.

After midnight on May 10th, there suddenly gathered over the city one of those heavy rain clouds not uncommon in that locality. This cloud appeared to embrace the earth, the darkness was complete; its density was almost palpable to the sense of feeling. When the condensation began, the rain fell in torrents, like water from a cascade, bringing with it thunder, and lightning in flashes so frequent as to seem almost continuous. All objects were sharply illuminated and brought into bold relief. The thunder came in crashes rather than in reverberations.

The procession of the ambulances could not move in

that storm and darkness, and had come to a halt. Looking down Eleventh from M Street to Pennsylvania Avenue, one could see by the lightning flashes for a distance of half a mile. There was presented a singular and unusual spectacle. Around every vehicle was a fringe of white objects, projecting outward. They were of irregular forms and sizes, and it puzzled the observer to know what they were. They proved to be the limbs and portions of the bodies of the wounded — their legs, arms, shoulders, faces, heads, necks, every part which it was possible to expose to the falling shower of rain. It was a weird and curious picture, another of the myriad forms in which are exhibited the pains and miseries of war.

The war had its full complement of miseries; its scenes of suffering were very numerous, and painful beyond description. On the other hand, it developed some of the finer qualities of our humanity in a remarkable degree, from unexpected sources. There were occasions when everybody, the poor equally with the rich, seemed to be moved by a common impulse to works of benevolence and charity. This statement is especially true of the colored race, of which some proofs will be elsewhere given.

Bull Run, the first great battle of the war, had proved the miserable inadequacy of the hospital accommodations of the army. The churches, all the public buildings which could possibly be vacated, were filled with sick and wounded men. Citizens received their wounded friends into their own homes; tents were pitched upon the vacant squares, and yet there were hundreds who, for a day or two, lay upon the streets, exposed to the sun, the rain, the heat, the insects, and all the inconveniences of an unsheltered situation. Even when a great enlargement of hospital accommodations was undertaken, so little attention was paid to sanitary conditions that the hospitals were built wherever there was a vacant square. One of the largest was located near the Smithsonian Institution, along the border of the old canal, which, receiving the surface drainage of half the city, in the heat of summer became eventually little less than a noisome cesspool. It seems incredible that such negligence should have been permitted. The inevitable result, as any one could have foreseen, was that this hospital became the slaughter-house of the soldier. Death from blood-poisoning became so certain that the simplest incised wounds, and even scratches, were fatal, if the sufferer was sent to that hospital.

Experience and the newspapers soon brought about a reform. The Sanitary Commission made its voice heard and its influence felt. Instead of erecting hospitals in the heart of the city, the authorities began to locate them upon the hills surrounding it, where there was pure air and abundant room for the tents, which were more healthy than enclosed structures. Upon these hills were the forts which defended the capital. By the autumn of 1864 there was a succession of hospitals in a circle just outside the city limits, with large accommodations, and a greater number of tenants than were comprised in all these forts and their outworks.

Our Sunday afternoons were. generally devoted to visiting these hospitals. The occasions were infrequent when there were not sufferers from the green hills of Vermont in some of them, to whom the sight of a friendly face seemed to be the best of medicines. The grateful looks of these wounded boys always well repaid the trouble of a visit. We often found the poor fellows craving, or rather intensely suffering, for the want of something which the service did not furnish, but which a few cents and a friendly hand could supply. The gift of diamonds and sapphires would not have elicited the gratitude I have seen drawn out by the contents of a hand-basket. We saw much suffering in these visits, but we also saw much that illustrated the better side of human nature.

On one occasion I was visiting a Vermont cavalry-man, who lay in a large hospital near Columbia College, on the continuation of Fourteenth Street. He had a splendid record for bravery in the field, and now in the hospital he was fighting death with equal courage and fortitude. He was in a ward filled with the wounded from a battle in the valley some weeks before. Only those whose wounds were particularly severe had been brought there, and at the time of my visit most of those who remained had been there some three or four weeks, slowly recovering from what seemed to me terrible injuries.

I was writing at the dictation of the Vermonter a letter to his wife, when, from my camp-stool at his bedside, I saw a colored woman enter the ward. She was old, decrepit, and poorly clad, so lame that she could scarcely walk, but managed to hobble along by the aid of a staff. Except a basket, covered by a clean white cloth, which hung upon her arm, everything about her indicated extreme poverty.

The entrance of this unattractive person produced a commotion. A dozen men, my cavalry-man included, shouted their welcome, and even the faces of those too weak to raise their heads from their pillow were lighted up with joy. "Here's mammy!" "Come here first, mammy!" "Don't forget me, mammy!"—these and similar expressions came from all parts of the ward. I have seen the wife of a President enter a ward without exciting any such expressions of interest.

"Yes! ole mammy's heah, chilluns, jes' as I tole you. She's got two apiece for ebery one of ye! I had to borry some from a fren'. It's been offul dry, an' de new vines ha'n't come on like as I 'spected. But dey's doin' well now. Nex' Sunday I 'spect I'll have three apiece, an' a big one for doctor. Now you all jes' be quiet; I won't forgit one of ye!"

She hobbled up to a bed. It was vacant. "Why, where's Mass' Frank?" she exclaimed, with unmistakable surprise. "Why don't you tell me? Where's Mass' Frank, I say?"

"Poor Frank has gone home, mammy! He got his discharge yesterday," said one who lay near by, in a voice which trembled a little in spite of himself.

"I was afeerd on't! I was afeerd on't. He tole me he was goin' away!" And the poor old creature sobbed as if she had a heart as tender as one of whiter skin. "Poor Mass' Frank! I reckon he's better now. He read me his mammy's letter. Poor mammy! She's done got a heap o' trouble. She lose her boy. Poor mammy! Poor Mass' Frank! He was a brave one! His hurt was offul! Seemed like you could jes' see his heart in dat great red hole!"

She dried her tears, took up her basket, and went from cot to cot, making her distribution of its contents. The weakest of the wounded boys put out his thin hand eagerly, as if what she gave was very precious. The very last was my cavalryman, who was just as eager as the rest. And then I saw that she had been distributing *small cucumbers pickled in vinegar!*

"Dat's all to-day, my chilluns! Nex' Lord's-day I'll be here, shore! De weather's done been good, and I 'spect I'll have more an' bigger uns. Yes, I'll come, shore!"

"Bring your basket here, mammy," said one, "I have something that the boys want to put into it, which you must not look at nor open until you get home. Will you promise?"

"No, Mass' George! You can't fool ole mammy dat way. I can't make dat promise. I know yo' tricks. Dat's money, dat is. Mass' George, I'm ole, an' all broke up wid rheumatiz, workin' in de rice-field. I've got jes' one boy left. He takes good care o' his ole mammy. All de rest is sold—all gone Souf to de cane-fields or de cotton-fields! I 'spect I shall never see 'em again. But, Mass' George" (here a joyful light flashed over her wrinkled face), "I'se free now, bress de Lord an' Mass' Linkum! I reckon all I'se good for is to raise pickles for de boys. But I can't sell 'em for money! No, no!"

She shook her head in the most decided manner and went out of the ward, followed by shouts of "Good-bye, mammy!" "God bless you!" "Come again!"

The cavalryman informed me, and the statement has since been confirmed by surgeons, that there was nothing so much craved by the wounded, especially those who had lost much blood, as sharp, pickled cucumbers. He had seen the time when his longing for them was intolerable, when he would have given a month's pay for even one small pickle. I have no idea why more of them were not provided, when such complete provision was made for all hospital supplies. My informant said that one of the highest ladies in the land had visited that ward, and asked what the boys most wanted. The answer was, pickled cucumbers. She immediately told them that she would supply that want, and would order a whole barrel of the coveted delicacies from a wholesale grocery-house. The pickles never came, and the boys were cruelly disappointed. The lady probably forgot her promise, or found it inconvenient to keep it. "Old mammy isn't much on promises," said the cavalryman, "but she always fetches the pickles!"

Of all the forms of charity and benevolence seen in the crowded wards of the hospitals, those of some Catholic sisters were among the most efficient. I never knew whence they came, or what was the name of their order. They wore the ordinary plain black dress of some worsted stuff, but not the white band about the forehead. One instance illustrates the value of these volunteer nurses. In one of the wards was a gigantic soldier, severely wounded in the head. He had suddenly become delirious, and was raging up and down the ward, furious against those who had robbed him, of what I could not make out. He cast off the attendants who attempted to seize him as if they had been children. The surgeon was called in, and with several officers was consulting how they should seize and bind him, when a small figure in black entered the room. With a shout of joyous recognition the soldier rushed to his cot, and drew the blanket over him, as if ashamed of his half-dressed appearance. The sister seated herself at his bedside, and placed her white hand upon the soldier's heated brow. His chest was heaving with excitement, but the sight of her face had restored his reason. "I must have dreamed it," he said, "but it was so real! I thought they had taken you away, and said I should never see you again. Oh, I could have killed them all!"

"You must sleep now," she said, very gently. "I shall stay if you are good, and you have been so excited—"

"Yes," he murmured, "I will sleep. I will do anything for you if they will not take you away. I could not bear that, you know."

He closed his eyes, holding one of her hands clasped in both of his, and, while we were looking on, slept as peacefully as a child.

Late in that terrible battle summer, when Grant was forcing his resistless march towards Richmond, the hospitals were not only overcrowded, but for a time there was no proper separation of the wounded from those sick from other causes. In a single ward were men with freshly amputated limbs, and gunshot wounds of every kind, and men burning with many fevers. Erysipelas was silently sapping the vital forces of one, consumption undermining the lungs of another, an angry cutaneous disease absorbing the surface moisture of a third—all stretched upon cots so close together that there was scarcely room to pass between them. What seemed especially horrible to me were the surgical operations carried on in the wards, because the operating-rooms were so constantly in use. For these suffering men, in addition to their own ills, to see one of their number stretched upon a table, where the surgeon's knife severed the living muscle and the resisting bone, with a display of all the suggestive machinery of the surgeon's profession, seemed too much for weak humanity to endure.

These scenes, altogether the most painful I have ever witnessed, have nevertheless in my memory a beautiful side. More lovely than anything I have ever seen in art, so long devoted to illustrations of love, mercy, and charity, are the pictures that remain of those modest sisters going on their errands of mercy among the suffering and the dying. Gentle and womanly, yet with the courage of soldiers leading a forlorn hope, to sustain them in contact with such horrors. As they went from cot to cot, distributing the medicines prescribed, or administering the cooling, strengthening draughts as directed, they were veritable angels of mercy. Their words were suited to every sufferer. One they incited and encouraged, another they calmed and soothed. With every soldier they conversed about his home, his wife, his children, all the loved ones he was soon to see again if he was obedient and patient. How many times have I seen them exorcise pain by their presence or their words! How often has the hot forehead of the soldier grown cool as one of these sisters bathed it! How often has he been refreshed, encouraged, and assisted along the road to convalescence, when he would otherwise have fallen by the way, by the home memories with which these unpaid nurses filled his heart!

"Are there any means by which I can overcome the unpleasant sensations which I always feel on my visits to your hospital-wards?" I asked of an experienced surgeon. "It is a duty to make them, as long as I can be of any use to the boys, but I am made sick every time. I have a feeling of nausea which continues for hours."

"It is the effect of your imagination," he responded. "You are unused to wounds. You exaggerate their symptoms. These men do not suffer as you imagine; if they did, we should relieve them. Wounded men endure great suffering on the field, and on their way to the hospital, but very little after they come under our hands. They suffer more from thirst than any other cause. Loss of blood makes the whole machinery of life dry and thirsty. After they reach the hospital, relief is speedy."

"Yes, it must be," I said, ironically. "Relief by being hacked and cut and sawn in sections must be painless!"

"You should see an operation," said the surgeon. "It would cure your nausea, and correct some of your erroneous ideas. I am perfectly serious. I am to do rather a difficult piece of work now, as soon as the operating-room is put in order. Come and see it, and judge for yourself."

"I know it will irritate every nerve in my body, like a shock of electricity! But it would be cowardly to decline. Surely, if the poor soldier can endure it, I ought to be able to stand the sight of it. Yes, I will come," I said.

I was shown into a small room adjoining the ward, with windows opening on two sides, through which the green fields and peach orchards, laden with young fruit, were visible. The room had just been scoured, and was fresh and odorless. On one side of the apartment were washing conveniences with a stream of running water. A plain, heavy table stood in the centre, covered by a rubber cloth which extended nearly to the floor on its four sides. The only suspicious objects visible were several large mahogany boxes, standing upon shelves in one corner, but these were closed. If the removal of the cover had disclosed a proper table, the room might have been as well suited to billiards as to surgical operations.

Four strong men now brought in a stretcher, on which was a bed with white linen sheets, containing a wounded soldier. The stretcher was laid upon the table. An attendant quickly applied a sponge, which he pressed to the mouth of the patient. I detected the odor of ether, and in less time than it has taken to write the account the soldier lay quietly unconscious and passive. His clothing, the bed, and everything under him was then quickly removed, so that his naked chest was in contact with the rubber covering. His torso was as splendidly muscular as that of a gladiator. He was a Dane, apparently about twenty-five years of age, a blond, with blue eyes, fair hair, and a transparent skin, under which the strong muscles of his chest and right arm were plainly visible. The upper portion of his left arm and the entire left shoulder were of a deep purple color, angry and dark by contrast. Marching with his regiment through a rocky dell, far down the valley, below Luray, he had been shot by a bushwhacker ambushed in the rocks above him. A minie bullet had crashed through his shoulder at the joint, shattering the humerus to the elbow. He was far away from any hospital. Lying on the straw in an army wagon, he had been carted over the stony roads more than sixty miles to Harper's Ferry, where he had been placed with other wounded in a box freight-car on the railroad, and so had reached Washington and been carried to the hospital. It was now several days since he received his wound. The shoulder and arm were swollen, an angry circle of dark purple surrounding the opening where the ball had entered. It was a terrible wound, rendered fatal, to all appearance, by the long fatigue, neglect, and exposure.

The surgeon, with a small-bladed knife, laid open the arm from the shoulder to the elbow-joint, and began to separate the muscle from the shattered bone. Piece after piece of bone was taken out until the entire length, in six fragments, lay upon the table. The muscle was then turned out like the finger of a glove, exposing the shoulder-joint, also badly fractured. The pieces were removed, and the projecting points cut off. The whole mass of muscle was then cleansed from blood, washed with some lotion of an antiseptic nature, and the entire cut, from elbow to shoulder, carefully stitched together. The remains of the arm were then laid along the side of the chest, and firmly fastened to it with bandages. The operation occupied nearly an hour. All the bones and blood were removed, the table again washed, and clean linen placed upon the soldier. He was laid between the clean white sheets, the ether was taken away, and he was restored to consciousness.

During all this horrible operation the patient appeared to be living in a pleasant dream of the farm in Iowa, where he had made his home. He was driving his oxen at the plough, reproving the awkwardness of his farm hands, playing with his children, and consulting with his wife about their schools, and other domestic matters. He talked and laughed and sang. He had been mercifully spared all pain and suffering, so that when he recovered consciousness it was a considerable time before he could be convinced that he had been subjected to any surgical operation.

He was removed to his cot. I gave him my address, and asked him to write to me if he wanted anything which the hospital could not provide. We subsequently furnished him with a few delicacies; new cases engrossed our attention, and the Dane was forgotten.

Four or five months later, a stout, rugged man, in the uniform of a soldier, called at my office in the Treasury. I did not recognize him, though his face impressed me as one that I had seen somewhere. " I am B——, from the 4th Iowa, to whom your lady was so kind in the hospital," he said. " I have just got my discharge, and am on my way home." Upon my inquiry whether his arm was at all useful to him, he took hold of a large scuttle filled with coal, and carried it across the room. He made a fair signature with a pen, and showed that he could make good use of his arm, except that he could not raise it above the level of his shoulder. I have since heard of him as a respected farmer in easy circumstances in Iowa.

The pain and suffering spared to the soldier by the intelligent use of anæsthetics during the war was beyond measure. Although the history belongs to the profession of those who used them, I saw so much of their blessed influence that I could not forbear giving this testimony to their value.

XXXII.

PRESIDENT LINCOLN AND THE SLEEPING SENTINEL.—ERRONEOUS VERSIONS OF THE STORY.—WILLIAM SCOTT, A MEMBER OF THE THIRD VERMONT, SENTENCED TO DEATH FOR SLEEPING ON HIS POST.—HE IS PARDONED BY THE PRESIDENT.—HIS LAST MESSAGE TO THE PRESIDENT.—HIS DEATH AT THE BATTLE OF LEE'S MILLS.

The story of the President and the sleeping sentinel has been so many times sung in song and described in story that its repetition may seem like the relation of a thrice-told tale. The substantial facts are common to all its versions. A soldier named Scott, condemned to be shot for the crime of sleeping on his post, was pardoned by President Lincoln, only to be killed afterwards at the battle of Lee's Mills, on the Peninsula. The incidental facts are varied according to the taste, the fancy, or the imagination of the writer of each version. The number of persons who claim to have procured the intervention of the President to save the life of the soldier nearly equals that of the different versions. As these persons worked independently of each other, and one did not know what another had done, it is not improbable that several of them are entitled to some measure of credit, of which I should be most unwilling to deprive them.

The truth is always and everywhere attractive. The child loves, and never outgrows its love, for a real true story. The story of this young soldier, as it was presented to me, so touchingly reveals some of the kindlier qualities of the President's character that it seldom fails to charm those to whom it is related. I shall give its facts as I understood them, and I think I can guarantee their general accuracy.

On a dark September morning, in 1861, when I reached my office, I found waiting there a party of soldiers, none of whom I personally knew. They were greatly excited, all speaking at the same time, and consequently unintelligible. One of them wore the bars of a captain. I said to them, pleasantly, "Boys, I cannot understand you. Pray, let your captain say what you want, and what I can do for you." They complied, and the captain put me in possession of the following facts:

They belonged to the Third Vermont Regiment, raised, with the exception of one company, on the eastern slope of the Green Mountains, and mustered into service while the battle of Bull Run was progressing. They were immediately sent to Washington, and since their arrival, during the last days of July, had been stationed at the Chain Bridge, some three miles above Georgetown. Company K, to which most of them belonged, was largely made up of farmer-boys, many of them still in their minority.

The sterile flanks of the mountains of Vermont have, to some extent, been abandoned for the more fertile regions of the West, and are now open to immigration from the more barren soils of Scandinavia and the Alps. Fifty years ago these Vermont mountains reared men who have since left their impress upon the enterprise of the world. The hard conditions of life in these mountains then required the most unbroken regularity in the continuous struggle for existence. To rise and retire with the sun, working through all the hours of daylight, sleeping through all the hours of night, was the universal rule. Such industry, practised from childhood, united to a thrift and economy no longer known in the republic, enabled the Vermonter to pay his taxes and train up his family in obedience to the laws of God and his country. Nowhere under the sun were charity, benevolence, mutual help, and similar virtues more finely developed or universally practised than among these hard-handed, kind-hearted mountaineers.

The story which I extracted from the "boys" was, in substance, this: William Scott, one of these mountain-boys, just of age, had enlisted in Company K. Accustomed to his regular sound and healthy sleep, not yet inured to the life of the camp, he had volunteered to take the place of a sick comrade who had been detailed for picket duty, and had passed the night as a sentinel on guard. The next day he was himself detailed for the same duty, and undertook its performance. But he found it impossible to keep awake for two nights in succession, and had been found by the relief sound asleep on his post. For this offence he had been tried by a court-martial, found guilty, and sentenced to be shot within twenty-four hours after his trial, and on the second morning after his offence was committed.

Scott's comrades had set about saving him in a characteristic way. They had called a meeting, appointed a committee, with power to use all the resources of the regiment in his behalf. Strangers in Washington, the committee had resolved to call on me for advice, because I was a Vermonter, and they had already marched from the camp to my office since daylight that morning.

The captain took all the blame from Scott upon himself. Scott's mother opposed his enlistment on the ground of his inexperience, and had only consented on the captain's promise to look after him as if he were his own son. This he had wholly failed to do. He must have been asleep or stupid himself, he said, when he paid no attention to the boy's statement that he had fallen asleep during the day, and feared he could not keep awake the second night on picket. Instead of sending some one, or going himself in Scott's place, as he should, he had let him go to his death. He alone was guilty—"if any one ought to be shot, I am the fellow, and everybody at home would have the right to say so." "There must be some way to save him, judge!" (They all called me judge.) "He is as good a boy as there is in the army, and he ain't to blame. You will help us, now, won't you?" he said, almost with tears.

The other members of the committee had a definite, if not a practicable, plan. They insisted that Scott had not been tried, and gave this account of the proceeding. He was asked what he had to say to the charge, and said he would tell them just how it all happened. He had never been up all night that he remembered. He was "all beat out" by the night before, and knew he should have a hard fight to keep awake; he thought of hiring one of the boys to go in his place, but they might think he was afraid to do his duty, and he decided to "chance it." Twice he went to sleep and woke himself while he was marching, and then—he could not tell anything about it—all he knew was that he was sound asleep when the guard came. It was very wrong, he knew. He wanted to be a good soldier, and do all his duty. What else did he enlist for? They could shoot him, and perhaps they ought to, but he could not have tried harder; and if he was in the same place again, he could no more help going to sleep than he could fly.

One must have been made of sterner stuff than I was not to be touched by the earnest manner with which these men offered to devote even their farms to the aid of their comrade. The captain and the others had no need of words to express their emotions. I saw that the situation was surrounded by difficulties of which they knew nothing. They had subscribed a sum of money to pay counsel, and offered to pledge their credit to any amount necessary to secure him a fair trial.

"Put up your money," I said. "It will be long after this when one of my name takes money for helping a Vermont soldier. I know facts which touch this case of which you know nothing. I fear that nothing effectual can be done for your comrade. The courts and lawyers can do nothing. I fear that we can do no more; but we can try."

I must digress here to say that the Chain Bridge across the Potomac was one of the positions upon which the safety of Washington depended. The Confederates had fortified the approach to it on the Virginia side, and the Federals on the hills of Maryland opposite. Here, for months, the opposing forces had confronted each other. There had been no fighting; the men, and even the officers, had gradually contracted an intimacy, and, having nothing better to do, had swapped stories and other property until they had come to live upon the footing of good neighbors rather than mortal enemies. This relation was equally inconsistent with the safety of Washington and the stern discipline of war. Its discovery had excited alarm, and immediate measures were taken to break it up. General W. F. Smith, better known as "Baldy" Smith, had been appointed colonel of the Third Vermont Regiment, placed in command of the post, and undertook to correct the irregularity.

General Smith, a Vermonter by birth, a West-Pointer by education, was a soldier from spur to crown. Possibly he had natural sympathies, but they were so subordinated to the demands of his profession that they might as well not have existed. He regarded a soldier as so much valuable material, to be used with economy, like powder and lead, to the best advantage. The soldier was not worth much to him until his individuality was suppressed and converted into the unit of an army. He must be taught obedience; discipline must never be relaxed. In the demoralization which existed at the Chain Bridge, in his opinion, the occasional execution of a soldier would tend to enforce discipline, and in the end promote economy of life. He had issued orders declaring the penalty of death for military offences, among others that of a sentinel sleeping upon his post. His orders were made to be obeyed. Scott was, apparently, their first victim. It went without saying that any appeal in his behalf to General Smith would lead to nothing but loss of time.

The more I reflected upon what I was to do, the more hopeless the case appeared. Thought was useless. I must act upon impulse, or I should not act at all.

"Come," I said, "there is only one man on earth who can save your comrade. Fortunately, he is the best man on the continent. We will go to President Lincoln."

I went swiftly out of the Treasury over to the White House, and up the stairway to the little office where the President was writing. The boys followed in a procession. I did not give the thought time to get any hold on me that I, an officer of the government, was committing an impropriety in thus rushing a matter upon the President's attention. The President was the first to speak.

"What is this?" he asked. "An expedition to kidnap somebody, or to get another brigadier appointed, or for a furlough to go home to vote? I cannot do it, gentlemen. Brigadiers are thicker than drum-majors, and I couldn't get a furlough for myself if I asked it from the War Department."

There was hope in the tone in which he spoke. I went straight to my point. "Mr. President," I said, "these men want nothing for themselves. They are Green Mountain boys of the Third Vermont, who have come to stay as long as you need good soldiers. They don't want promotion until they earn it. But they do want something that you alone can give them—the life of a comrade."

"What has he done?" asked the President. "You Vermonters are not a bad lot, generally. Has he committed murder or mutiny, or what other felony?"

"Tell him," I whispered to the captain.

"I cannot! I cannot! I should stammer like a fool! You can do it better!"

"Captain," I said, pushing him forward, "Scott's life depends on you. You must tell the President the story. I only know it from hearsay."

He commenced like the man by the Sea of Galilee, who had an impediment in his speech; but very soon the string of his tongue was loosened, and he spoke plain. He began to word-paint a picture with the hand of a master. As the words burst from his lips they stirred my own blood. He gave a graphic account of the whole story, and ended by saying, "He is as brave a boy as there is in your army, sir. Scott is no coward. Our mountains breed no cowards. They are the homes of thirty thousand men who voted for Abraham Lincoln. They will not be able to see that the best thing to be done with William Scott will be to shoot him like a traitor and bury him like a dog! Oh, Mr. Lincoln, can you?"

"No, I can't!" exclaimed the President. It was one of the moments when his countenance became such a remarkable study. It had become very earnest as the captain rose with his subject; then it took on that melancholy expression which, later in his life, became so infinitely touching. I thought I could detect a mist in the deep cavities of his eyes. Then, in a flash, there was a total change. He smiled, and finally broke into a hearty laugh, as he asked me,

"Do your Green Mountain boys fight as well as they talk? If they do, I don't wonder at the legends about Ethan Allen." Then his face softened as he said, "But what can I do? What do you expect me to do? As you know, I have not much influence with the departments?"

"I have not thought the matter out," I said. "I feel a deep interest in saving young Scott's life. I think I knew the boy's father. It is useless to apply to General Smith. An application to Secretary Stanton would only be referred to General Smith. The only thing to be done was to apply to you. It seems to me that, if you would sign an order suspending Scott's execution until his friends can have his case examined, I might carry it to the War Department, and so insure the delivery of the order to General Smith to-day, through the regular channels of the War Office."

"No! I do not think that course would be safe. You do not know these officers of the regular army. They are a law unto themselves. They sincerely think that it is good policy occasionally to shoot a soldier. I can see it, where a soldier deserts or commits a crime, but I cannot in such a case as Scott's. They say that I am always interfering with the discipline of the army, and being cruel to the soldiers. Well, I can't help it, so I shall have to go right on doing wrong. I do not think an honest, brave soldier, conscious of no crime but sleeping when he was weary, ought to be shot or hung. The country has better uses for him."

"Captain," continued the President, "your boy shall not be shot—that is, not to-morrow, nor until I know more about his case." To me he said, "I will have to attend to this matter myself. I have for some time intended to go up to the Chain Bridge. I will do so today. I shall then know that there is no mistake in suspending the execution."

I remarked that he was undertaking a burden which we had no right to impose; that it was asking too much of the President in behalf of a private soldier.

"Scott's life is as valuable to him as that of any person in the land," he said. "You remember the remark of a Scotchman about the head of a nobleman who was decapitated. 'It was a small matter of a head, but it was valuable to him, poor fellow, for it was the only one he had.'"

I saw that remonstrance was vain. I suppressed the rising gratitude of the soldiers, and we took our leave. Two members of "the committee" remained to watch events in the city, while the others returned to carry the news of their success to Scott and to the camp. Later in the day the two members reported that the President had started in the direction of the camp; that their work here was ended, and they proposed to return to their quarters.

Within a day or two the newspapers reported that a soldier, sentenced to be shot for sleeping on his post, had been pardoned by the President and returned to his regiment. Other duties pressed me, and it was December before I heard anything further from Scott. Then an-

18

other elderly soldier of the same company, whose health
had failed, and who was arranging for his own discharge,
called upon me, and I made inquiry about Scott. The
soldier gave an enthusiastic account of him. He was in
splendid health, was very athletic, popular with everybody, and had the reputation of being the best all-around
soldier in the company, if not in the regiment. His mate
was the elderly soldier who had visited me with the party
in September, who would be able to tell me all about
him. To him I sent a message, asking him to see me
when he was next in the city. His name was Ellis or
Evans.

Not long afterwards he called at my office, and, as his
leave permitted, I kept him overnight at my house, and
gathered from him the following facts about Scott. He
said that, as we supposed, the President went to the
camp, had a long conversation with Scott, at the end of
which he was sent back to his company a free man. The
President had given him a paper, which he preserved
very carefully, which was supposed to be his discharge
from the sentence. A regular order for his pardon had
been read in the presence of the regiment, signed by
General McClellan, but every one knew that his life had
been saved by the President.

From that day Scott was the most industrious man in
the company. He was always at work, generally helping some other soldier. His arms and his dress were
neat and cleanly; he took charge of policing the company's quarters; was never absent at roll-call, unless he
was sent away, and always on hand if there was any
work to be done. He was very strong, and practised
feats of strength until he could pick up a man lying on
the ground and carry him away on his shoulders. He
was of great use in the hospital, and in all the serious

cases sought employment as a nurse, because it trained him in night-work and keeping awake at night. He soon attracted attention. He was offered promotion, which, for some reason, he declined.

It was a long time before he would speak of his interview with Mr. Lincoln. One night, when he had received a long letter from home, Scott opened his heart, and told Evans the story.

Scott said: "The President was the kindest man I had ever seen; I knew him at once, by a Lincoln medal I had long worn. I was scared at first, for I had never before talked with a great man. But Mr. Lincoln was so easy with me, so gentle, that I soon forgot my fright. He asked me all about the people at home, the neighbors, the farm, and where I went to school, and who my schoolmates were. Then he asked me about mother, and how she looked, and I was glad I could take her photograph from my bosom and show it to him. He said how thankful I ought to be that my mother still lived, and how, if he was in my place, he would try to make her a proud mother, and never cause her a sorrow or a tear. I cannot remember it all, but every word was so kind.

"He had said nothing yet about that dreadful next morning. I thought it must be that he was so kind-hearted that he didn't like to speak of it. But why did he say so much about my mother, and my not causing her a sorrow or a tear when I knew that I must die the next morning? But I supposed that was something that would have to go unexplained, and so I determined to brace up, and tell him that I did not feel a bit guilty, and ask him wouldn't he fix it so that the firing-party would not be from our regiment! That was going to be the hardest of all—to die by the hands of my comrades. Just as I was going to ask him this favor, he stood up, and he says to me, 'My boy, stand up here and look me in the face.' I did as he bade me. 'My boy,' he said, 'you are not going to be shot to-morrow. I believe you when you tell me that you could not keep awake. I am going to trust you, and send you back to your regiment. But I have been put to a good deal of trouble on your account. I have had to come up here from Washington when I have got a great deal to do; and what I want to know is, how you are going to pay my bill?' There was a big lump in my throat; I could scarcely speak. I had expected to die, you see, and had kind of got used to thinking that way. To have it all changed in a minute! But I got it crowded down, and managed to say, I am grateful, Mr. Lincoln! I hope I am as grateful as ever a man can be to you for saving my life. But it comes upon me sudden and unexpected like. I didn't lay out for it at all. But there is some way to pay you, and I will find it after a little. There is the bounty in the savings-bank. I guess we could borrow some money on the mortgage of the farm. There was my pay was something, and if he would wait until pay-day I was sure the boys would help, so I thought we could make it up, if it wasn't more than five or six hundred dollars. 'But it is a great deal more than that,' he said. Then I said I didn't just see how, but I was sure I would find some way—if I lived.

"Then Mr. Lincoln put his hands on my shoulders and looked into my face as if he was sorry, and said, 'My boy, my bill is a very large one. Your friends cannot pay it, nor your bounty, nor the farm, nor all your comrades! There is only one man in all the world who can pay it, and his name is William Scott! If from this day William Scott does his duty, so that, if I was there when he comes to die, he can look me in the face as he does now, and say, I have kept my promise, and I have done my duty as a soldier, then my debt will be paid. Will you make that promise and try to keep it ?'

"I said I would make the promise, and, with God's help, I would keep it. I could not say any more. I wanted to tell him how hard I would try to do all he wanted; but the words would not come, so I had to let it all go unsaid. He went away, out of my sight forever. I know I shall never see him again; but may God forget me if I ever forget his kind words or my promise."

This was the end of the story of Evans, who got his discharge, and went home at the close of the year. I heard from Scott occasionally afterwards. He was gaining a wonderful reputation as an athlete. He was the strongest man in the regiment. The regiment was engaged in two or three reconnoissances in force, in which he performed the most exposed service with singular bravery. If any man was in trouble, Scott was his good Samaritan; if any soldier was sick, Scott was his nurse. He was ready to volunteer for any extra service or labor —he had done some difficult and useful scouting. He still refused promotion, saying that he had done nothing worthy of it. The final result was that he was the general favorite of all his comrades, the most popular man in the regiment, and modest, unassuming, and unspoiled by his success.

The next scene in this drama opens on the Peninsula, between the York and the James rivers, in March, 1862. The sluggish Warwick River runs from its source, near Yorktown, across the Peninsula to its discharge. It formed at that time a line of defence, which had been fortified by General Magruder, and was held by him with a force of some twelve thousand Confederates. Yorktown was an important position to the Confederates.

On the 15th of April the division of General Smith was ordered to stop the enemy's work on the entrenchments at Lee's Mills, the strongest position on the Warwick River. His force consisted of the Vermont brigade of five regiments, and three batteries of artillery. After a lively skirmish, which occupied the greater part of the forenoon, this order was executed, and should have ended the movement.

But about noon General McClellan with his staff, including the French princes, came upon the scene, and ordered General Smith to assault and capture the rebel works on the opposite bank. Some discretion was given to General Smith, who was directed not to bring on a general engagement, but to withdraw his men if he found the defence too strong to be overcome. This discretion cost many lives when the moment came for its exercise.

General Smith disposed his forces for the assault, which was made by Companies D, E, F, and K of the Third Vermont Regiment, covered by the artillery, with the Vermont brigade in reserve. About four o'clock in the afternoon the charge was ordered. Unclasping their belts, and holding their guns and cartridge-boxes above their heads, the Vermonters dashed into and across the stream at Dam Number One, the strongest position in the Confederate line, and cleared out the rifle-pits. But the earthworks were held by an overwhelming force of rebels, and proved impregnable. After a dashing attack upon them the Vermonters were repulsed, and were ordered to retire across the river. They retreated under a heavy fire, leaving nearly half their number dead or wounded in the river and on the opposite shore.

Every member of these four companies was a brave man. But all the eye-witnesses agreed that among those who in this, their first hard battle, faced death without blenching, there was none braver or more efficient than William Scott, of Company K, debtor for his own life to President Lincoln. He was almost the first to reach the south bank of the river, the first in the rifle-pits, and the last to retreat. He recrossed the river with a wounded officer on his back—he carried him to a place of safety, and returned to assist his comrades, who did not agree on the number of wounded men saved by him from drowning or capture, but all agreed that he had carried the last wounded man from the south bank, and was nearly across the stream, when the fire of the rebels was concentrated upon him; he staggered with his living burden to the shore and fell.

An account of the closing scene in the life of William Scott was given me by a wounded comrade, as he lay upon his cot in a hospital tent, near Columbia College, in Washington, after the retreat of the army from the Peninsula. "He was shot all to pieces," said private H. "We carried him back, out of the line of fire, and laid him on the grass to die. His body was shot through and through, and the blood was pouring from his many wounds. But his strength was great, and such a powerful man was hard to kill. The surgeons checked the flow of blood—they said he had rallied from the shock; we laid him on a cot in a hospital tent, and the boys crowded around him, until the doctors said they must leave if he was to have any chance at all. We all knew he must die. We dropped on to the ground wherever we could, and fell into a broken slumber—wounded and well side by side. Just at daylight the word was passed that Scott wanted to see us all. We went into his tent and stood around his cot. His face was bright and his voice cheerful. 'Boys,' he said, 'I shall never see another battle. I supposed this would be my last. I haven't much to say. You all know what you can tell them at home about me. I have *tried* to do the right thing! I am almost certain you will all say *that*.' Then while his strength was failing, his life ebbing away, and we looked to see his voice sink into a whisper, his face lighted up and his voice came out natural and clear as he said: 'If any of you ever have the chance, I wish you would tell President Lincoln that I have never forgotten the kind words he said to me at the Chain Bridge—that I have tried to be a good soldier and true to the flag—that I should have paid my whole debt to him if I had lived; and that now, when I know that I am dying, I think of his kind face and thank him again, because he gave me the chance to fall like a soldier in battle, and not like a coward by the hands of my comrades.'

"His face, as he uttered these words, was that of a happy man. Not a groan or an expression of pain, not a word of complaint or regret came from his lips. 'Good-bye, boys,' he said, cheerily. Then he closed his own eyes, crossed his hands on his breast, and—and—that was all. His face was at rest, and we all said it was beautiful.* Strong men stood around his bed; they had seen their comrades fall, and had been very near to death themselves: such men are accustomed to control their feelings; but now they wept like children. One only spoke, as if to himself, 'Thank God, I know now how a brave man dies.'

"Scott would have been satisfied to rest in the same grave with his comrades," the wounded soldier continued. "But we wanted to know where he lay. There was a small grove of cherry-trees just in the rear of the camp, with a noble oak in its centre. At the foot of this oak we dug his grave. There we laid him, with his empty rifle and accoutrements by his side. Deep into the oak we cut the initials, W. S., and under it the words, 'A brave soldier.' Our chaplain said a short prayer. We fired a volley over his grave. Will you carry his last message to the President?" I answered, "Yes."

Some days passed before I again met the President. When I saw him I asked if he remembered William Scott?

"Of Company K, Third Vermont Volunteers?" he answered. "Certainly I do. He was the boy that Baldy Smith wanted to shoot at the Chain Bridge. What about William Scott?"

"He is dead. He was killed on the Peninsula," I answered. "I have a message from him for you, which I have promised one of his comrades to deliver."

A look of tenderness swept over his face as he exclaimed, "Poor boy! Poor boy! And so he is dead. And he sent me a message! Well, I think I will not have it now. I will come and see you."

He kept his promise. Before many days he made one of his welcome visits to my office. He said he had come to hear Scott's message. I gave it as nearly as possible in Scott's own words. Mr. Lincoln had perfect control of his own countenance: when he chose, he could make it a blank; when he did not care to control it, his was the most readable of speaking human faces. He drew out from me all I knew about Scott and about the people among whom he lived. When I spoke of the intensity of their sympathies, especially in sorrow and trouble, as a characteristic trait of mountaineers, he interrupted me and said, "It is equally common on the prairies. It is the privilege of the poor. I know all about it from experience, and I hope I have my full share of it. Yes, I can sympathize with sorrow."

"Mr. President," I said, "I have never ceased to reproach myself for thrusting Scott's case so unceremoniously before you—for causing you to take so much trouble for a private soldier. But I gave way to an impulse—I could not endure the thought that Scott should be shot. He was a fellow-Vermonter—and I knew there was no other way to save his life."

"I advise you always to yield to such impulses," he said. "You did me as great a favor as the boy. It was a new experience for me—a study that was interesting, though I have had more to do with people of his class than any other. Did you know that Scott and I had a long visit? I was much interested in the boy. I am truly sorry that he is dead, for he was a good boy—too good a boy to be shot for obeying nature. I am glad I interfered."

"Mr. Lincoln, I wish your treatment of this matter could be written into history."

"Tut! Tut!" he broke in; "none of that. By the way, do you remember what Jeanie Deans said to Queen Caroline when the Duke of Argyle procured her an opportunity to beg for her sister's life?"

"I remember the incident well, but not the language."

"I remember both. This is the paragraph in point: 'It is not when we sleep soft and wake merrily ourselves that we think on other people's sufferings. Our hearts are waxed light within us then, and we are for righting our ain wrangs and fighting our ain battles. But when the hour of trouble comes to the mind or to the body—and when the hour of death comes, that comes to high and low — oh, then it isna what we hae dune for oursells, but what we hae dune for others, that we think on maist pleasantly. And the thoughts that ye hae intervened to spare the puir thing's life will be sweeter in that hour, come when it may, than if a word of your mouth could hang the whole Porteous mob at the tail of ae tow."

XXXIII.

TREASURY NOTES AND NOTES ON THE TREASURY.

No nation has a better Treasury system than the United States. When its regulations are enforced, it practically guarantees the government against loss by error or fraud. It involves the division of the department into bureaus, each directly responsible to the secretary, having little connection with each other, and at least three of which must approve a claim before it can be paid, each thus acting as a check upon the other. It recognizes the fact that the subordinates in a bureau, subject to removal by its chief, will obey the orders of that chief, although they may involve a violation of law, so that checks within a bureau are unreliable. But if the payment of a claim requires an examination by three persons in as many bureaus, and the approval of the heads of each, a conspiracy to defraud becomes difficult and practically impossible. Frauds upon the Treasury proper have been extremely rare. The Assistant Treasuries are abnormal growths, not subject to these checks, and frauds upon them, involving large losses, have consequently been perpetrated. The manufacture and issue of the postal and fractional currency was another excrescence permitted to attach itself to the system, and the account of that issue cannot be verified. It was the only issue of the war about which there existed any doubt. The account may be correct, but it is possible that some millions of dollars of that currency more than the amount shown by the books of the Treasurer were put in circulation. It might have been done without detection, for the white paper was turned into money, ready for issue by a single department, under a single head, without supervision or the co-operation of any other department or person.

Originally adapted to an expenditure of $25,000,000 per annum, the Treasury system had the capacity of indefinite expansion without impairing its security. In March, 1861, it regulated an expenditure averaging about $8,000,000 per month. Within sixty days it increased to more than $2,000,000 per day, and ultimately to more than $1,000,000,000 per annum. Yet the system required no change except an increase of clerical force. Thus it happened that during four years of war more than $3,000,000,000 was received and covered into the Treasury, and an equal value of securities issued and delivered to those who were entitled to receive them, without the loss of one dollar by error or fraud. This statement rests upon absolute demonstration, and not upon evidence alone. The amount is as far as infinity beyond ordinary human comprehension. The statement and the system which verifies it are wonders of finance in a country convulsed by civil war.

The Treasury was the creation of Alexander Hamilton. It will live as long as the nation exists, and every one who comprehends it will accept it as a monument of the financial ability of its author. It may be criticised by those who do not understand it as an institution of red tape, but no experienced Treasury officer ever advised the removal of one of its checks, or the relaxation of one of its stringent provisions.

There were three frauds attempted during the secretaryship of Mr. Chase. Two of them came as near success as the Treasury system would permit, and perhaps their frustration must in some degree be attributed to the merits of the system, united with good fortune.

Among the inheritances from the administration of Mr. Buchanan was an application for the reissue of a lot of coupon bonds alleged to have been destroyed. The claimants proved the facts as clearly as human testimony could—that these bonds, each with six coupons attached, were deposited in a locked mail-bag in Frankfort, transported to Liverpool, and there delivered into the hands of an agent of the post-office on board a steamship which was wrecked by collision, and went, with all its mails, and all but two or three of those on board, to the bottom of the sea. The completeness of the evidence was itself a source of suspicion, and, much to the chagrin of the claimants, Secretary Chase affirmed the decision of a bureau officer, that the duplicates should not be issued except by the direction of Congress. On the application of the claimants at the next session, Congress passed an act directing the issue of the duplicates. The claim was again presented with the act, and the duplicates were demanded. The same bureau officer again represented his suspicions to the secretary, and, with the sanction of the latter, the present regulation was adopted, interposing a delay of twelve months after proof of the claim before the actual issue. This rule was vehemently assailed by the claimants through the press; they even charged the officer with intentionally nullifying the authority of Congress.

At this time the coupons of bonds redeemed were in packages in the Register's file-room. There was little need of their examination, and no attempt had been made to arrange them in consecutive order. Books were now made with one page appropriated to each bond, and a space for each coupon, while a force of clerks was detailed to place each redeemed coupon in its appropriate space.

At the expiration of the year the claimants came for their duplicates. They were assured that they would now be issued unless some satisfactory reason could be shown for further delay. The books were sent for, and in their proper spaces *were found all the coupons which had been proved to have sunk to the bottom of the sea!* A few months later the bonds themselves were presented for redemption, and, no adverse claims being made, they were paid.

What was the explanation of this mystery? I do not know. The pressure of official duties, and the anxieties of war which occupied us so incessantly, prevented any further investigation, and the inquiry will probably never be answered.

The next fraud which I recall was a success as far as the department was concerned. The loss of the money was prevented by an accident.

The course of proceeding for the collection of a claim for army supplies was usually this: The contractor made his collections through his banker. His monthly account was made up in conformity with all the rules of the War Office, and transmitted to that office with a letter of directions where the draft should be sent. The War Office approved the claim if correct, and transmitted the account, the letter, and the action of the War Department to the Secretary of the Treasury, by whom it was sent to the proper auditor, whose duty it was to audit the claim. If he decided that the claim was a proper one, it was sent to the comptroller, who revised the action of the auditor, and, if correct, approved it, sending the account with the accompanying documents to the secretary, who issued the warrant for its payment. This warrant was countersigned by the comptroller, and entered on the books of the Register; the treasurer then drew his draft upon one of the depositories for its payment, and the draft was sent by mail, according to the original letter of instruction, which constituted one of the file papers. The file was then sent to the Register's file-room, and there remained. It comprised all the papers, showing a complete history of the transaction.

On the occasion in question the cashier of one of the Washington banks came to the office of the Register with a draft just issued for more than $80,000, payable to a well-known Massachusetts contractor, and regularly endorsed. It had been presented by the head porter of Willard's Hotel, a reliable man, who said that the payee was ill and unable to leave his room. He had therefore requested him to collect the draft in notes, if possible, of $1000 each. Without any apparent reason the cashier said his suspicions were excited, and he went with the porter to the hotel to see the payee, and be sure that the transaction was all right. But the sick gentleman had disappeared. He had probably watched the porter, and, finding that there was delay in the payment, had vanished.

The file was sent for, and the letter found, directing that the draft be sent to the contractor at Willard's Hotel. He was communicated with by telegraph, and said that the letter was a forgery. He had given the same directions in this case as in his former collections.

This fraud was consummated by an outsider with the assistance of a clerk in the Treasury. No outsider could have obtained access to the files in order to remove the true letter and substitute the forgery. Such a fraud could not be prevented by any system. Fortunately the suspicions or the prudence of the cashier prevented any loss.

In another instance the fraud was successful, but its fruits were wholly recovered and returned to the Treasury. It had some interesting features. One of the most difficult subjects which engaged our attention was the complete destruction of the Treasury notes withdrawn from circulation, or so worn or mutilated that they were unfit to be reissued. The bulk of these issues was very great. The first so withdrawn were called the "demand notes." They were issued under a special act, and, being receivable for duties, bore a premium nearly equal to gold. There were sixty million dollars of them in small denominations, and their issue involved the use of many cords of paper. After the financial system authorized by the act of February 25, 1862, had been instituted, this issue was redeemed, and the notes corded up in the treasurer's vaults. The problem was to count these notes, destroy them beyond the possibility of a reissue, and give the treasurer credit for them without any opportunity for reissue or fraud.

After much deliberation the following plan was devised: The notes were separated into denominations, and made into packages uniform in amount, and each package was cut into halves, lengthwise. The upper halves were delivered to the superintendent of a force of counters in the office of the treasurer; the lower halves to the head of a like force in the office of the register. These two forces had no communication with each other. Each counted their respective packages, and made a record of each one. The records were compared in another office, and, if they agreed, the *count* was supposed to be correct. The counted packages were then delivered to a committee of citizens, and by them placed in a furnace in the basement of the Treasury, which had been heated to a white heat; the door was locked, and the combustion watched by the committee through openings, until they were entirely consumed. The committee then verified the facts by affidavit, upon which a warrant was issued to the treasurer to credit his account with the notes so destroyed. Receipts were given whenever the packages changed hands. The process was expensive, complex, and supposed to be reliable.

The burning of a cord or less of notes daily was a subject of general curiosity. Applications to witness it became so frequent that an iron railing was built around the furnace, within which no one was admitted except the committee of citizens. A colored messenger one day applied for a permit for his boy of ten years to see the process. On the following day the messenger told me that his boy had asked him a singular question: "Whether it was right for Mr. Cornwell, when throwing the packages into the furnace, to drop one of them in the side pocket of his overcoat?"

Cornwell was a clerk in the bureau of General Spinner, the treasurer, whose duty it was to see the packages cut in halves by the machine, and deliver them to the chiefs of the two divisions of counters. He had no right to touch them afterwards. His assisting in the work of the citizens' committee was an impertinent interference with their duties which destroyed the value of the system, and was probably tolerated because of his official connection with the work of the treasurer's bureau, where he was a trusted clerk, I believe of the third class.

The messenger was directed to go to his home and bring his son to the register's office. He proved to be a modest, intelligent lad, and greatly alarmed at the consequences of his question. "He was not certain," he said, "that he saw anything. But Mr. Cornwell worked very hard, and threw more packages into the furnace than all the other gentlemen. He wore an overcoat with a side pocket having a large opening, and once, as he was quickly passing his hand with the package from the basket toward the furnace door, he thought he saw one package drop into the large open pocket. He was not certain of this, however, and might be mistaken."

The boy was sent home in charge of his father, who was told to keep him indoors, and not permit him to communicate with or see any other person. Without attempting to ascertain how any use could be made of these packages of half-notes, I directed the heads of the counting divisions not to permit any of their counters to leave the room, but to send for me when their day's work was finished. About four o'clock the accounts of the day were made up, and the aggregates appeared to agree. I then directed the counters in the two divisions to bring their packages together into one room, and place each package of upper with the corresponding package of lower halves. If there was no irregularity, as the day's work commenced with packages of entire bills, a package of lower should be found for every package of upper halves. But when the last two packages were reached, to the amazement and alarm of every counter, they would not match at all. Every counter knew that something was wrong, and each was in terror lest he or she should be the one suspected. Some of the young women were in tears, and one or two gave indications of hysterics. They were dismissed with the assurance that no suspicion rested upon them, and that they would have no trouble if they kept the facts to themselves for the next twenty-four hours.

The next morning Cornwell was called into the private room of the register and shown to a chair directly in front of that officer, who, without noticing him, went on with his regular work. Cornwell soon became nervous, and in an excited manner asked what was wanted of him. I replied that I had an impression that there was something which he ought to disclose to me, and that I wanted him to consider thoroughly, without interruption. He insisted that he must return to his duties. I said that I had had him excused for the day, in order that he might assist me in the investigation of an irregularity. He soon became excited, and as he appeared to be summoning his fortitude to meet an emergency, I suddenly said to him,

"Cornwell, you have been stealing, and your thefts have been detected!"

I should fail if I attempted to describe the effect of these few words. His emotion was pitiable. A deathly pallor covered his face, and he seemed to be trying to swallow something which he could not. As commonly happens, Satan deserted his victim, and his first words were a fatal confession. After a supreme effort at self-control he said:

"How did you find it out?"

"That is of no importance," I said. "What I want of you is to tell me how much you have taken, and where it is."

He made no effort or struggle, but gave up at once. He took from his pocket a small blank-book, in which he had entered, from day to day, in regular order, the amount of his stealings. The following had been his method of procedure: He received from the treasurer daily, for example, $100,000, in ten packages of $10,000 each, and became accountable for them. After seeing the whole bills divided in the machine, it was his duty to deliver and take a receipt for an equal number of packages of upper halves from one division and of lower halves from the other division of the counters, so that the same number of packages of divided bills should be sent to the counting divisions which he had received in entire bills from the treasurer. Having abstracted a package of upper halves at one time and of lower halves at another while the bills, after having been counted, were being thrown into the furnace, he could then take a package of whole bills from those he received from the treasurer, and by substituting the packages of stolen halves for them in the delivery to the counters, his account would appear to be correct. He would deliver to the counters just as many divided packages as he had received whole ones. But the two stolen packages would not fit or match together, as had been shown in the investigation of the preceding day.

I called a carriage; he entered it with me, and we drove to his house in Georgetown. On one of the upper floors he unlocked a small room, in which there was a new safe with a combination lock. This he also opened, took from it and delivered to me one package of $100,000 in coupon 5-20 bonds, into which he had converted a portion of his booty through a firm of brokers in New York; $50,000 in whole demand notes; and packages of halves representing $20,000 more, making in the aggregate $170,000. Except a difference of a few dollars, caused by converting the demand notes at a premium into bonds, this aggregate agreed with the account of his abstractions, entered from day to day as they were made, upon his account-book. He strenuously insisted that this amount comprised every dollar of his thefts, and we never had the slightest reason to doubt his statement.

He was indicted, and, upon his own confession, sentenced to ten years in the penitentiary, where I lost sight of him, and have no knowledge of his subsequent career. He maintained to the last that he never intended to wrong the United States. These notes, he said, had been issued at par, the government having received 100 cents for each dollar of them. If they were redeemed at the same rate, the government was no loser. They happened to be worth a premium of sixty per cent.; he thought he had as good a right to make that premium as the government. He had always intended to restore the par of these notes to the Treasury. To that end he had converted enough of them to purchase $100,000 in coupon bonds, which he intended to place to the credit of the Treasury conscience fund. His appropriation of the sixty per cent. premium, he insisted, was no crime, and he thought it was not even prohibited by the Treasury regulations. It is scarcely necessary to say that this reasoning neither satisfied the Treasury officers nor did it save him from the penitentiary.

No loss to the Treasury could possibly have occurred in two of the instances above mentioned.

After the close of the war there were many members of Congress and others who did not believe it possible that so large an amount of money as $3,000,000,000 could possibly have been received into the Treasury, securities issued for it, and placed in the hands of the large number of persons entitled to them, without error or fraud, or any loss to the government. It was even suspected that the officers connected with the issue of these securities must in some manner have profited thereby. Accordingly one of the first acts of each of the two or three succeeding Congresses was to raise a special committee to investigate the Treasury. The Treasury officers well knew that no fraud or irregularity could have occurred without immediate detection in the Treasury. They therefore regarded the proceedings of the committees with quiet unconcern. In the early days of the investigation cases were found which were supposed to involve the integrity of some of these officers, and they were notified that their immediate appearance before the committee was necessary to their reputations. They did not appear, however, and in every case the committee found the explanation. These investigations were, as they should have been, thorough and exhaustive. But neither committee discovered any error, fraud, or loss to the government in the department of the Treasury proper. No credit belongs to or was ever claimed by the officers of the Treasury for this result; but it should at least be regarded as most satisfactory evidence of the perfection of the Treasury system.

XXXIV.

NEW MONEYS OF LINCOLN'S ADMINISTRATION.—DEMAND NOTES.
—SEVEN-THIRTIES.—POSTAGE CURRENCY.—FRACTIONAL CUR-
RENCY.—LEGAL-TENDER NOTES, OR "GREENBACKS."—THEIR
ORIGIN, GROWTH, AND VALUE.

THE generation which elected President Lincoln had known only two kinds of money—the notes of the state banks and the coins authorized by Congress. There were many varieties of the state bank-notes, variable in appearance as in value. The policy of Secretary Chase destroyed the circulation of the state bank-notes, and substituted for them the notes of the national banks, under which the holder was absolutely secured against loss. The necessities of war created several new kinds of paper money, and in some cases invented new names for them, such as "demand notes," "seven-thirties," "postage currency," "fractional currency," and finally "legal tenders," popularly known as "greenbacks."

The "Treasury notes," authorized by statutes in force on the 4th of March, 1861, did not circulate as money. They bore interest at the rate of six per cent., were payable one year after date, and issued in denominations of not less than fifty dollars. Before the extra session of Congress on July 4, 1861, the secretary had contrived to sell six and a half million dollars in these notes at par by offering with them a like amount in bonds on twenty years' time at six per cent. interest, at rates varying from 85 to 92 per cent. of their par value. These amounts relieved the wants of the Treasury in a very slight degree, and made no impression upon the circulation of the country.

As the 4th of July approached it became apparent that some provision for the pay of the army and navy and other pressing demands must be made without waiting for the negotiation of a loan. The secretary accordingly recommended in his first report, and Congress by the act of July 17th authorized, the immediate issue of Treasury notes to the amount of fifty, afterwards increased to sixty million dollars, in denominations of not less than ten dollars, payable on demand without interest. On the 5th of August a supplemental act was passed, authorizing the issue in denominations as low as five dollars, and making these notes receivable for public dues. They were required to be signed by the treasurer and the register, or by some persons authorized by the secretary to sign for each of said officers.

As soon as the plates could be engraved and the notes printed, a force of clerks was detailed to sign them, and their issue commenced. They were receivable for duties, and therefore almost equivalent in value to gold; they were used in payment of the army and the navy, and of other pressing obligations; they relieved the wants of the secretary for October and November as fully as the same amount in coin; and they added so much to the circulating money of the country. They were of the same size, and in appearance closely resembled bank-notes.

The passage of the legal-tender act of February 25, 1862, which required the payment of duties in coin, in order to provide the gold for the payment of the interest upon the funded debt, made it necessary to redeem and cancel the notes so issued, because as long as they were outstanding they would take the place of an equal amount in gold. This act provided for their immediate redemption and cancellation. The issue began in October; their redemption commenced in the following March; after which they were not reissued, but cancelled and destroyed as fast as they flowed into the Treasury. The whole amount authorized, $60,000,000, was issued, and after twenty-eight years, on the 31st of May, 1890, there were still outstanding, unredeemed, of these notes, $56,445.00, or about one tenth of one per cent. of the issue. These notes acquired the name of, and have always been known as, the "demand notes."

An incident occurred during the brief period of their circulation which, for a few hours, occasioned no little anxiety in the offices of the treasurer and the register. A small package of these notes, less than $100 in value, which were apparently unsigned, was presented for redemption. They were not of consecutive numbers, but from several different sheets. If any were issued unsigned, it indicated an irregularity, and possibly a loss, the amount of which could not be ascertained. I was not willing to concede the fact without further investigation. The two names of the clerks who were deputed to sign for the treasurer and register were the only words written on the face of the notes. Upon examining them with a powerful glass, I could trace on the surface the whole signatures, although every particle of the ink had disappeared. Fortunately, the person who presented them for payment was known. He was sent for, and proved to be a soldier who had received the notes from the paymaster. I asked him whether he had submitted them to any manipulation. He replied that he had carried them in a money-belt upon his person through a campaign through the swamps of Carolina. They had been saturated with perspiration, with rain, fogs, and other moisture many times, and this usage had obliterated the signatures. This discovery did more than relieve our anxiety. It effectually disposed of the claim that the written signature was any check against fraud or forgery, so that when the legal-tender notes were under consideration it was decided that all the signatures should be engraved.

The same act of July, 1861, authorized the issue of Treasury notes bearing interest at the rate of seven and three tenths per cent. per annum, payable three years from their date. The rate of interest, equal to one cent on $50 for every day, would, it was hoped, from its convenience of computation, give these notes some circulation as currency. This hope was not realized, and these notes belong to the investment rather than the currency issues of the Treasury. They were known by the name of "seven-thirties" from their rate of interest.

The suspension of specie payment by the banks in December, 1861, caused a disappearance of the gold and silver coins from circulation with marvellous celerity. They seemed to vanish in a day; probably into the private hoards of the people, since the specie of the banks failed to show any considerable increase. War existed, no one could predict the future, the thrift and caution of the people led them to lay something aside which could not lose its purchasing power. They hastened to lay hold of these coins, and secrete them where they could be found when other means of subsistence failed.

The scarcity of these coins produced great inconvenience in business. It became almost impossible to make change in the ordinary purchases from dealers and merchants. Shinplasters began to make their appearance to supply the deficiency. In the rebellious states these were not only issued by individuals and private corporations, but by states, counties, cities, towns, and all other municipal corporations. A collection of these rebel shinplasters, upon all kinds of paper, from white writing to brown wrapping, would now be an interesting memento of the war, but in a pecuniary sense absolutely worthless.

The credit of devising a lawful and adequate remedy for this inconvenience belongs to General Francis E. Spinner, Treasurer of the United States. He found it impossible to facilitate, as he desired to do, the payment of the soldiers and sailors, and to conduct the business of the Treasury with the small coins at his command. He therefore arranged with the Post-office Department to redeem in unused stamps such postage-stamps as might be used for currency. In a short time his department manufactured and introduced a new issue. All the denominations were of uniform size. A piece of paper, with one stamp pasted on it, was five cents; one with two stamps, ten cents; five stamps, twenty-five cents; and ten stamps, fifty cents. In this way, at the cost of a little labor, a considerable amount of small change was manufactured. This currency became so popular that, instead of using stamps, plates were engraved for each denomination, in imitation of the manufactured notes, the impressions from which had the same legal qualities and were used for the same purposes. These impressions were called the "postage currency." They were afterwards authorized by the act of July 17, 1862, which directed the secretary to furnish to the assistant treasurers "the postage and other stamps of the United States, to be exchanged by them on application for United States notes." These stamps were receivable in payment of all dues to the United States of less than five dollars, and could be exchanged for United States notes when presented in sums of not less than five dollars. The same act put an end to the further issue of shinplasters, by making the issue or circulation, by private persons or corporations, of notes or tokens for less than one dollar, punishable by fine and imprisonment.

Although it did not come under my notice at the time, it appears from articles by Mr. C. Gregory, in the *Philatelic Journal*, in the year 1888, that there was prepared, and there have been recently submitted to me, specimens of an ingenious device for utilizing postage stamps as currency. It was invented by Mr. J. Gault, of New York city, and was patented in August, 1862. It consisted in encasing the stamp, with a thin sheet of mica covering its face, in a sheet of copper, neatly turned over its edges, and the mica cover, in the form of a circular plaque, having the dimensions of the ordinary twenty-five-cent piece. To hold the stamp more firmly in place, side-pieces of copper were added, which were turned over a small portion of the face in such a manner as not to interfere with its legibility, the denomination being plainly visible. The stamp thus encased could be carried in the pocket, and had all the conveniences, and almost the durability, of a copper coin. Trading and business firms were quick to appreciate its advantages. By stamping their business card, or any other legend of the firm, in the copper which covered the reverse of the stamp, it was made to serve as an advertisement. Its value as an advertisement was sufficient to pay the considerable expense of encasing the stamp.

But for the act of March 3, 1863, which prohibited the use of these and all similar devices, the encased stamp must have had a considerable circulation. According to Mr. Gregory, Mr. Gault received so many orders for them that he could not supply the demand, although his shop was in operation night and day. He encased the eight denominations, from one cent to ninety cents each. It is of some interest, as showing the actual demands of commerce for fractional coins, to know that more of the one-cent value were ordered than of all the others; the three cent came next; those of five cents and ten cents taking third and fourth places. Thirty cents was the highest denomination ordered, and these only by one firm. A very small number of the denomination of ninety cents were made, and sold as specimens, which are now extremely rare.

These stamps were ordered by firms in the retail dry-goods, grocery, jewellery, and other trades, insurance companies, owners of hotels, wine-stores, restaurants, and proprietary articles, more in number being required for the latter than for all the other trades combined. They were ordered by one firm of private bankers located in Montreal. They appear to have been circulated in New York, Boston, Philadelphia, Detroit, Chicago, Cincinnati, and several smaller Northern cities.

It is also of interest that the limited use of this device should be known and preserved. I therefore describe the specimen now before me, for which I am indebted to Mr. Charles Gregory. It is the form in which, I think, stamps will be used as currency, if the restrictive act should be repealed and the necessity hereafter arise. The stamp is the blue one-cent stamp of the time, with the engraved head of Franklin, over which are the words "U. S. Postage," under it the words "One Cent." Over the face is a thin sheet of colorless mica, so transparent that its presence is not apparent to the eye. The copper covering, or frame, covers the reverse, the circular periphery, a space a sixty-fourth of an inch wide, around the face, with two oval side-pieces extending a fourth of an inch towards the centre. Stamped in the reverse of the copper frame is the advertisement of a proprietary article, and under that the words "Pat. Aug. 12, 1862. J. Gault."

The convenience of the postage currency was great, and the amount called for increased to an extent which became troublesome to the Post-office Department, and the secretary decided to take it into the Treasury, where it legitimately belonged. Accordingly an act was passed which suspended its further issue, and substituted in its place currency of another description.

The act of March 3, 1863, authorized the Secretary of the Treasury to issue "fractional notes," in such form as he deemed expedient, in lieu of postage and revenue stamps and of the fractional notes commonly called postage currency, and to provide for the engraving, preparation, and issue thereof in the Treasury Department building. Such notes were exchangeable for Treasury notes in sums of not less than three dollars, were receivable for postage and revenue stamps and in payment of any dues to the United States less than five dollars, and were redeemable at the Treasury under regulations to be established by the secretary. The amount of the issue, including postage and revenue stamps issued as currency, was limited to $50,000,000.

No currency issue of the government has ever accomplished so much public convenience in proportion to its amount as the fractional currency. Its use was uninterrupted until May 16, 1866, when the coining of five-cent pieces of copper and nickel was authorized, the further issue of fractional notes of a less denomination than ten cents was prohibited, and the five-cent notes outstanding were directed to be redeemed and cancelled. The act of the 14th of January, 1875, authorized the coinage of silver coins of the value of ten, twenty-five, and fifty cents, to be issued in redemption of the fractional currency until the whole of it was redeemed. The whole amount issued, including the reissues in the place of worn and mutilated notes, has reached the enormous aggregate of $368,724,079.45. In other words, the amount authorized of $50,000,000 has been reissued more than seven times. The act of June 21, 1879, provided for the redemption of the fractional currency then outstanding with any money in the Treasury, and for its destruction. Under this act there was carried into the statement of the public debt, as fractional currency lost or destroyed, $8,375,934. This amount has proved far below the actual loss or destruction. On the 31st of May, 1890, after making this deduction, the amount still outstanding was $6,912,010.97. Of this amount it is safe to assume that seventy per cent., or $4,838,407, has been so far lost that it will not be presented for redemption. There is thus shown a clear profit to the United States on the issue of the fractional currency of more than $13,000,000, or more than twenty-six per cent. of the $50,000,000 to which the issue at any one time was limited.

Why has this large proportion failed to be returned for redemption? The answer is necessarily speculative. Collectors of stamps and other memorabilia of the epoch have absorbed some of it. But it has happened, in the experience of many, that each has become possessed of a fractional note so worn or mutilated that it was declined by the person to whom he offered it. The name of the person from whom he received it was forgotten, the amount was too small to pay for the trouble of sending it to Washington for redemption; he laid it aside in some corner of his pocket-book, where it remained to be further worn, until, tired of seeing it, he at length threw it away. Such has been my own experience. It has been multiplied by that of others, possibly in instances numerous enough to account for the loss.

If the public convenience were alone in question, there would be a reissue of the fractional currency. It was, and would still be, universally preferred to small silver coins. So long as it could be had in a cleanly condition, institutions were willing to incur expense to obtain it, especially for their lady customers. If the silver, instead of being coined, could be deposited in some out-of-the-way place in bars too heavy for asportation, and the cost of coinage applied to the cost of issuing fractional currency, the public would be better accommodated, and the silver bars could rest undisturbed until some convulsion should subvert all existing financial conditions.

There was much complaint at the time, and the reputation of the secretary suffered, from his persistence in allowing the engraving, printing, and complete manufacture of the white paper into the money of the fractional currency, ready for issue, to be done in the Bureau of Engraving and Printing without any oversight or supervision. The bureau itself had grown from nothing to very large proportions, as an annex or convenience to the office of the secretary. It was subject to none of the checks which the Treasury system imposed upon other bureaus, and an unauthorized issue of currency was quite possible, which might never be detected if it were not greater than the percentage of notes not returned for redemption. There was so much criticism of the secretary's action that he appointed a commission, which reported the danger, and earnestly recommended that the bureau should be brought under the general Treasury regulations. But no change was made by Secretary Chase. His view of the matter was, that naked stealing could not be prevented by checks; that confidence must be reposed in somebody; and it was safer to trust one man than a great number. One of the first acts of his successor, Mr. Fessenden, was to comply with the recommendations of the commission. Since that time checks have been added which now make the bureau safe, and render any fraud as nearly impossible as it can be under human management.

Justice to all at any time concerned in the management of the Bureau of Engraving and Printing requires the statement that neither investigation, lapse of time, nor the subsequent redemption of its issues has produced any evidence whatever of fraud or wrong in that bureau down to the close of the war. On the contrary, the very large amount now outstanding indicates that there has been no unauthorized issue. Such, I am glad to know, is the opinion of experienced officers still remaining in the department.

There is an act of Congress which prohibits the engraving upon any of the Treasury issues of any portrait the original of which is living. It originated in the fact that the head of the Bureau of Engraving, in 1864, placed his own portrait upon the plate of the five-cent note. It was a presumptuous act, so fiercely denounced by the press that only a single issue from the plate was made. To prevent its repetition, the act was afterwards passed. This five-cent note is much sought after by collectors, and is much the scarcest of the Treasury issues during the war.

The fight of legal tender had been won, and won on the ground stated by Thaddeus Stevens in the opening sentence of his speech: "This bill is a measure of necessity, not of choice." The act had been passed and approved. We could issue $150,000,000 in currency at once, $60,000,000 would pay the demand notes, leaving $90,000,000 to pay our soldiers and carry on the war for some months to come.

We had also gained our first military success. Grant had captured forts Henry and Donelson, and was pushing for Nashville. The clouds seemed to be breaking away, and the future to look more hopeful.

I was therefore surprised when one afternoon, late in February, 1862, President Lincoln entered the register's room with as sad a look as I ever saw upon his careworn face. He dropped wearily into a seat he had previously chosen, and after a short silence exclaimed:

"What have you to say about this legal-tender act? Here is a committee of great financiers from the great cities who say that, by approving this act, I have wrecked the country. They know all about it—or they are mistaken."

"You have done nothing of the kind," I said. "The time for argument has passed. Legal tender is inevitable. The gentlemen you mention have made it a necessity. The people would take our notes without the legal-tender clause. The banks and the copperheads will not. We cannot risk the country in their hands. You have followed your own good judgment in signing the act. The people will sustain you and Secretary Chase and Congress."

"I do not see that I am exclusively responsible," he continued. "I say to these gentlemen, 'Go to Secretary Chase; he is managing the finances.' They persist, and have argued me almost blind. I am worse off than Saint Paul. He was in a strait betwixt two. I am in a strait betwixt twenty, and they are bankers and financiers."

"You are right in signing the act," I said; "that point has passed debate."

"Now that is just where my mind is troubled," he continued. "We owe a lot of money which we cannot pay; we have got to run in debt still deeper. Our creditors think we are honest, and will pay in the future. They will take our notes, but they want small notes which they can use among themselves. So far I see no objection, but I do not like to say to a creditor you shall accept in payment of your debt something that was not money when it was contracted. That doesn't seem honest, and I do not believe the Constitution sanctions dishonesty."

"No more do I," I replied. "I do not claim that legal tender can be upheld as an abstract right under the Constitution. But self-preservation is a right higher than the Constitution. We are warranted in making any sacrifice of property or political right to save the Union. Gold and silver are beyond our reach; our soldiers must be paid and fed and clothed. We can issue Treasury notes, and circulate them as currency. It is right and honest that we should give them the quality of legal tender, provided we return to specie as soon as the necessity has passed. I have watched the debates in Congress. I have read the opinion of your attorney-general. There are those who hint and suggest that legal tender is provided for in the Constitution. I have read no speech in which that right is broadly asserted. I believe it safer to defend our position on the ground of necessity."

"I understand that is Chase's ground, though he does not put it so strongly. We shall see. We will wait to hear from the country districts, from the people."

He again relapsed into silence, which I did not interrupt. Then he said, "When the old monks had tired themselves out in fighting the devil, did they not have places to which they retired for rest, which were called *retreats ?*"

"They did," I answered; "though I understand they were for spiritual rather than bodily recuperation."

"I think of making this office one of my *retreats*," he said. "It is so quiet and restful here. Do you never get discouraged?"

"I shall be delighted to have you," I said, ignoring his question. "I only wish I could say of it, as Father Prout sang of the Groves of Blarney,

"'There's gravel-walks there for speculation,
And conversation in sweet solitude.'"

"Tell me more of that ballad," he exclaimed, cheerily. "I like its jingle. What an Irish conceit that is—
'conversation *in sweet solitude.*'"

"I fear I cannot. I must send you the book. I only remember,

"'There's statues gracing this noble place in,
All heathen goddesses so fair,
Bold Neptune, Plutarch, and Nicodaymus,
A-standing naked in the open air.'"

"I must have that book to-night," he said. "A good Irish bull is medicine for the blues."

He left the office actually to the sound of his own musical laugh. He sent for the book—a copy of Crofton Croker's "Popular Songs of Ireland." It is before me now; priceless almost, when I remember that it once gave Abraham Lincoln some pleasure, some respite from his cares.

I have several reasons for this prelude to a sketch of the greenback. It suggests what every American ought to know—that it was resorted to in a very dark period of the war; that it was accepted by the President on his faith in the financial policy of Secretary Chase, who advocated it not as a constitutional right *per se*, but as a right, like the proclamation of freedom to the slaves, founded upon military necessity. The story may possibly be regarded as trivial, but it tends to show with what intense earnestness the President bore his grave responsibilities, and that he seized upon an amusing story or volume because it diverted him for the moment, and strengthened rather than weakened his capacity for his graver duties. I think it tends also to illustrate the simple honesty of his mind. Had Mr. Lincoln been preserved to the republic, I do not believe that the question of legal tender would have been carried into the Supreme Court of the United States. The weight of his influence, never so powerful as on the day of his death, would have been thrown in favor of commencing the retirement of the legal-tender notes at the close of the war, and the return to a specie basis at the earliest date consistent with prudence and discretion.

A "greenback" is a statement engraved and printed in the similitude of a bank-note that "the United States will pay to the bearer —— dollars." It bears on its face the engraved signatures of the register and treasurer of the United States; a memorandum that it is issued under the act of March 3, 1863; and that it is a legal tender for —— dollars. A fac-simile of the Treasury seal is printed upon it in red ink and by a separate impression. In an open space on the back is a statement that "this note is a legal tender at its face value for all debts, public or private, except duties on imports and interest on the public debt," with a note of the punishment denounced against its counterfeiting or alteration. Originally it bore a certificate of its right to be converted into bonds of the United States, bearing interest at the rate of six per cent. per annum. This right was withdrawn by the act of March 3, 1863, as to all notes not presented for exchange before the 1st day of July in that year.

The greenback, then, is the naked promise of the United States to pay the bearer a certain number of dollars, unsecured except by the national credit, without date or time of payment, which, for all ordinary purposes, is money, equal to the gold and silver coins authorized by law.

The alteration and counterfeiting of bank-notes, crimes almost unknown to the present generation, were common when the state-bank issues existed. The bank-note companies owned a patented green ink, which they claimed was a protection against photography, that it was difficult to erase, the composition of which was a secret unknown to the criminal classes. Secretary Chase decided that the backs of the legal-tender notes should be printed with this patented green ink, giving to such notes literally green backs. The soldiers, quick to seize upon an appropriate name, on the first visit of the paymaster with these notes, gave them the name of "greenbacks." This name was universally adopted, and became as permanent as the notes themselves.

The authority for the issue of greenbacks was conferred by three acts of Congress, passed respectively on February 25 and July 11, 1862, and March 3, 1863. The first act authorized the issue of $150,000,000; but $60,000,000 of these were to be in lieu of the $60,000,000 of demand notes authorized by the act of July 17, 1861.

Each of the other acts authorized the issue of $150,000,-000, making the whole amount authorized $450,000,000.

The largest amount of greenbacks outstanding at one time was on the 3d of February, 1864, less than one year after the passage of the last act. The aggregate then reached was $449,479,222, or within a little more than half a million dollars of the full amount authorized.

The act of June 30, 1865, restricted the amounts of greenbacks issued and to be issued to $400,000,000, and "such additional sum, not exceeding $50,000,000, as may be temporarily required for the redemption of temporary loan" (sic). The aggregate in circulation on the 31st of August, 1865, which may be taken as the close of the war, was $432,553,912, and on the 1st day of January, 1866, $425,839,313.

This large amount, however, was not an addition of so much money to the circulation of the country. Had it been, the inflation of prices and the activity of speculation would have been greater. The net increase of the circulating money at any time during the war would require a computation more complicated than is suited to this sketch. It may be mentioned, however, that the circulation of the state banks, estimated in the loyal states at $150,000,000, had been withdrawn, and that issued to national banks was not large enough to take its place. The difference between these two amounts, with the whole amount of coin, had disappeared. The outstanding fractional currency must be added to the greenbacks, and the loss of state bank circulation and coin deducted, in order to ascertain the net increase. It affected values, no doubt, but probably not so much, as the value of greenbacks was diminished by depriving them of the right of exchange into interest-bearing bonds under the act of March, 1863.

At the close of the war there was a worthy successor of Secretary Chase at the head of the Treasury. Republics are fortunate which in periods of financial difficulty are able to secure the services of such men as Salmon P. Chase and Hugh McCulloch. We had, by the bullet of the assassin, lost the potential personality of Abraham Lincoln. His secretary, McCulloch, in the true spirit of the legal-tender legislation, as soon as the necessity had passed, turned his energies towards a return to a sound specie basis, and to the retirement of the greenbacks as the first and proper step towards that desirable goal. The national debt had then reached the gigantic amount of more than $2,800,000,000. To form an accurate judgment of the progress of which the republic was capable when it was relieved of the incubus of slavery and permitted to expand under the influences of peace; to preserve the national credit; to provide for and pay the debt due to the soldiers and sailors who had crushed the rebellion; and promptly, without delay, to lay out and enter upon the shortest safe road to specie payment, required not only a man able to comprehend the financial situation, but who had the boldness and courage to act upon his convictions. They have an expression on the Pacific coast which conveys a world of meaning. They say of a man who has shown great abilities wherever he has been placed that he is a "scopy" man. Secretary McCulloch was evidently a "scopy" man. In his first report to Congress after the close of the war, on the 4th of December, 1865, he declared in plain terms that the legal-tender acts were war measures passed in a great emergency, that they should be regarded only as temporary, that they ought not to remain in force a day longer than would be necessary to enable the people to prepare for a return to the gold standard, and that the work of retiring the greenbacks which had been issued should be commenced without delay, and carefully and persistently continued until all were retired. Such words were powerful because of their sense and justice. By the act of April 12, 1866, Congress authorized the secretary to commence the withdrawal of the greenbacks from circulation, to retire $10,000,000 within six months from the passage of the act, and thereafter to continue the process at the rate of $4,000,000 per month. The unanimity with which the secretary's policy was supported was shown by the vote in the House of Representatives on the passage of this act. There were 144 votes in the affirmative, and only 6 in the opposition.

Secretary McCulloch immediately instituted the process of retirement, and conducted it with quiet and eminent discretion. By the end of the year 1866 he had reduced the greenbacks outstanding from $425,000,000 to $380,000,000, and was proceeding quietly to continue the process at the rate of $4,000,000 per month.

But suddenly there was a change in the political atmosphere. A multitude of impecunious patriots, scattered over the North and West, discovered that they were being oppressed and afflicted beyond endurance by the contraction of the currency. They made the country resound with their moanings of distress. The speculators of the "bull" party joined in the cry. Together they organized a political party called the Greenback Party. It attracted the same class of recruits that went down to David in the cave of Adullam. Every one that was in distress and every one that was in debt and every one that was discontented joined the party, and began to cry out with a loud voice against contraction, against the dreadful tyranny of Secretary McCulloch. Then it was that the republic wanted Abraham Lincoln. Had he been alive to support his secretary, there would have been no such weak yielding to noisy clamor as then occurred. That tower and stronghold no longer existed. The secretary continued his work until he had reduced the volume of the greenbacks to $356,000,000, when, on the 4th of February, 1868, Congress suspended further reduction. The amount in circulation has since been subjected to some variation, in 1875 rising as high as $382,000,000, and in 1879 being reduced below $347,000,-000. But it is accurate enough for all practical purposes to say that since the suspension in 1868, a term of more than twenty-two years of profound peace, the amount of legal-tender notes in circulation has been $356,000,000.

If the republic shall again be involved in war there are many facts in the history of the currency issues here briefly described which will be useful to its financial minister. Secretary Chase had no experience of the past for his guide. The Continental currency of the Revolution was made a legal tender by state laws only. His judgment devised, Congress authorized, and the people loyally accepted the novelties in currency to which this chapter refers. In his financial policy he had the confidence and the support of President Lincoln. His policy was criticised; in one or two respects it may have been erroneous. But he was a statesman and a great financier. He was stationed at the weakest point in the national defences, where defeat or retreat would have been ruin. He preserved the credit of the republic; he was supported by a patriotic people; and by his administration of the Treasury he fairly earned the gratitude of posterity.

XXXV.
GRANT AND McCLELLAN.

ONE morning, in the summer of 1862, there was a procession in the streets of Washington. It passed along Fifteenth Street in front of the Treasury, down the avenue, turned to the right, and, moving over the long bridge across the Potomac, disappeared among the hills of Virginia. It was led by four bay horses; they were fine animals, matched and spirited. Their harnesses and trappings were new and glossy, but plain, and furnished with dark trimmings. They were driven by a colored man in blue livery. On the seat with him was another man of color, wearing a similar livery. The horses were harnessed to a four-wheeled vehicle called a box-wagon; *i. e.*, a wagon the body of which was an oblong box about six feet wide and high, and eight or nine feet in length. The running-gear and box were painted a dark-brown color, and varnished so that they shone in the rays of the morning sun. Twenty-four other wagons followed, each a duplicate of the first. Each had its colored driver and attendant in uniform, and each was drawn by four matched, spirited bay horses. On the sides of each box, in large gold letters, was the inscription in three lines:

"Baggage.
Headquarters
Army of the Potomac."

These one hundred matched horses, fifty attendants, and twenty-five wagons constituted the train provided to transport the baggage of General George B. McClellan, Commander-in-Chief of the Army of the Potomac, and his staff. It was said at the time that this army was perfect in its organization. This train for use at headquarters was the only part of it I, personally, saw. If the army was as well provided for as its general, this statement was incontrovertible.

I remember another morning in Washington. It was in the early days of spring, and I was living at Willard's. The outlook was discouraging, and occurrences in the Treasury had been very depressing to friends of the Union. I had risen early, had left my room before dawn, and, seated by a window which overlooked the avenue, in the main office, I began to read the morning paper. The passengers from the Western trains had not yet arrived. The gas-lights were turned down, and that potentate, the hotel-clerk, who had not yet put on his daily air of omnipotence, was peacefully sleeping in his cushioned arm-chair. Two omnibuses were driven to the entrance on Fourteenth Street, with the railroad passengers from the West. The crowd made the usual rush for the register; the clerk condescended to open his eyes and assign them rooms on the upper floor (there was no elevator), as though he felt an acute pleasure in compelling them to make the ascent, and for a few moments there was bustle and confusion. It was soon over; the clerk resumed his arm-chair, closed his eyes, and his weary soul appeared to be at rest.

There were two passengers who did not appear to be in such frantic haste. One was a sunburned man of middle age, who wore an army hat and a linen duster, below which, where a small section of his trousers were visible, I caught a glimpse of the narrow stripe of the army uniform. He held the younger traveller, a lad of ten years, by the hand, and carried a small leather bag.

As they modestly approached the counter, the temporary lord of that part of creation, without deigning to rise from his chair, gave the register a practised whirl, so that the open page was presented to the elder traveller, observing as he did so, "I suppose you will want a room together."

He named a room with a high number, gave the usual call "Front!" while the guest proceeded to write his name without making any observation. The clerk removed the pen from behind his ear; gave another whirl to the register, and was about to enter the number of the room, when—he was suddenly transfixed as with a bolt of lightning! His imperial majesty became a servile menial, thoroughly awake, and ready to grovel before the stranger. He bowed, scraped, twisted, wriggled. "He begged a thousand pardons; the traveller's arrival had been expected—parlor A, on the shady side of the house, the very best apartment in the hotel, had been prepared for his reception—it was on the first floor, only one flight of stairs! Might he be allowed to relieve him of his travelling convenience?" and the lordly creature actually disappeared up the stairway, like Judas, carrying the bag.

My curiosity was excited to ascertain who it was that had wrought such a sudden transformation. I walked to the counter, and there read the last entry on the register. It was " U. S. Grant and son, Galena, Ill."

It was the name of the General of the Western Army, who, after the capture of Vicksburg and the other mighty victories in the division of the Mississippi, had been called to the capital, to receive his commission of lieutenant-general, and to become commander-in-chief of all the armies of the republic. He was on his first visit to Washington, for what purpose I did not then know; but I have ever since been glad that I witnessed the simple and unostentatious manner in which the commander of two hundred thousand men indicated his arrival at the capital.

I depart from my purpose of writing only conversations with the President when I was present, to mention an interview between General Grant and the President, which preceded the advance of the Army of the Potomac in the spring of 1864. The account was given to me on the day, or day but one, after the conversation took place, by a senator of the United States, who was present at the interview, and whose veracity is beyond question.

The senator was with the President when General Grant was announced. After a few observations upon general subjects, he said that as that was his last day in Washington for the time, he was unwilling to leave the city until he had thanked the President for his compliance with every wish he had expressed. He said the President had given him all that he had asked for, and consequently if the campaign should not prove a successful one, its failure could not be charged to any neglect or omission of President Lincoln's. He added that he was satisfied with the army, its discipline, and its officers, and that he did not believe a better army was ever organized.

The President was pleased by the general's remarks, and cordially thanked him for his thoughtfulness in making his parting call.

"I have thought much," he said, "about this army. I always do think much about every army, particularly when it is about to open a campaign. I look upon this campaign as of great importance, and hope it may prove decisive. I have, therefore, tried to think of all the wants of this army, and, as far as it is in my power, to cause them to be provided for. I can only act through others, with some of whom, it is charged, I have not much influence. It pleases me to know that in this instance my directions appear to have been carried out."

"Now, there is one subject," continued the President, "which I ought to mention to you. Heretofore we have always had to provide a large amount of transportation on the river, in connection with the advance of this army—enough in the event of defeat to transfer the whole army to the north bank of the Potomac. This time I have heard nothing said about transportation. Have you provided it? and have you a sufficient number of vessels?"

"I think so," answered the general. "We have a good many vessels—more, I think, than will be needed if the army is compelled to cross the river. I do not intend any reflection upon the past," he continued, "either upon the army or its generals, but I have an impression that the Army of the Potomac has never been fought up to its capacity—until its military effectiveness was exhausted. This time it will be; and if it is defeated, its numbers will be so reduced that it will not need a large amount of transportation."

The senator declared that it was quite impossible to describe the quiet firmness and resolute determination with which these sentences were uttered. The President congratulated the general upon his firmness of purpose, and said that it promised as great victories in the East as had been gained in the West.

"The country should be cautioned," said General Grant, "against hoping for great successes. The loyal and the rebel armies, East and West, are made up of men of the same races. They have had about the same experience in war. Neither can justly claim any great superiority over the other in endurance, courage, or discipline. One may be more skilfully handled than the other; accidents have sometimes won victories and caused defeats. But where two such armies meet on common ground, about equal in numbers, and equally well handled, I do not know why any better result should be expected from one than from the other. In the coming campaign, in one respect, the rebels have the advantage. We shall be in their territory, with which they are perfectly familiar, and we shall be upon strange ground. Their arms are equal to ours, they claim superior discipline and greater endurance. While I hope and expect to defeat them, I do not know why this war should not end as wars generally do, by the exhaustion of the strength and resources of the weaker party."

I cannot tell how this conversation may impress others. At the time, it gave me entirely new views of the character of General Grant, and greater confidence in his ability as a military leader. Its influence was the same upon the limited circle to which it was communicated after its occurrence. Had he not touched the very point and centre of the subject? Was it not true that Lee and the rebels would fight, as Montcalm and the French did, until the resources of the country were completely exhausted? If so, it was almost idle to hope for a great and conclusive victory. The chances of such a result were not as good as they were at Gettysburg and Antietam, where the rebel army was in peril of destruction until it had reached the south bank of the Potomac. In this campaign General Lee's army would not be exposed to any such risk or danger. When, a few days later, battle was joined in the Wilderness, and so many of the vessels on the river began to be employed in transporting the wounded to Washington; when for a week there were no despatches from General Grant; when only one fact seemed assured—that instead of retiring, as it always had before, the army was all the time advancing, it was a great comfort to loyal men to recall this conversation, and to feel that General Grant had measured the work in advance, and was engaged in its performance with the resolute purpose indicated by the interview. His despatch to the Secretary of War, of the 11th of May, in the light of that conversation, seemed to be the fulfilment of prophecy—"We have now ended the sixth day of very heavy fighting. The result to this time is much in our favor. Our losses have been heavy as well as those of the enemy. I think the loss of the enemy must be greater. . . . I propose to fight it out on this line if it takes all summer."

XXXVI.
THE CONFEDERATES EXCHANGE A PARTY OF THEIR PRISONERS OF WAR.

I AM about to describe a visit to a hospital, which many will say might better have been omitted. All who make any public reference to such scenes are charged with intensifying and perpetuating sectional differences which ought to have ended with the war, and which must be buried out of memory if we are to have a country thoroughly reunited. But does not the truth of history require that some account be preserved of those melancholy events which are facts as essential to a correct record of the war as its less repulsive features?

On the evening of the 3d of May, 1864, the President said to me, "Can you leave your office for to-morrow, and go over to Annapolis?"

"Certainly," I replied, "with the permission of Secretary Chase."

"I will obtain that permission," said the President, "or, if there is any difficulty, I will inform you so that you may return immediately. A party of about four hundred officers and men out of rebel prisons arrived there yesterday. Their condition will be investigated by Congress; but that will take time. An intelligent lady, whom you know, has given me such an account of their sad state that I should like to know the truth at once from one who will neither exaggerate nor suppress any of the facts. Will you go and see them and bring me back your report?"

I promised to do so. He seemed unwilling to state what had been the report of the lady he had mentioned, for he appeared to think that her sympathies might have influenced her judgment. Still, he seemed much disturbed, and some expressions fell from him which indicated that his own sympathies had been thoroughly aroused. I remarked that this lady had a clear head, sound judgment, and much experience in the hospitals, and that it was very improbable that she should be deceived or overcome by any sentiment. "I know it," he said. "I know of few men who are more reliable. Yet she was so completely overwhelmed that she had great difficulty in telling her story. There must be some mistake about it! It is too horrible! too horrible! Yet Stanton had the same story, and believes every word of it."

I went to Annapolis that evening, and saw in the hospitals a memorable spectacle of all that remained of a party of over three hundred enlisted men. They were men no longer—they were skeletons! With few exceptions they were Americans, representing almost every one of the loyal states. Their minds had gone with their strength. It was almost impossible to get an intelligent answer to a question from one of them. I asked one his name. With a vacant, wandering expression in his eyes he answered, "I guess it is Mason!" The rags in which they had arrived three days before had been taken from their bodies and burned. The hair had been shaved from their heads, and kind hands were washing the grime from the spaces between their festering sores. Many had only stumps where their fingers and toes had been frozen off. All that could converse told the same story. They had been robbed of their blankets, clothes, and money, and then left on Belle Isle in the winter storms to starve and die. Their destruction was well-nigh completed. Eight died on the voyage. The surgeons were of opinion that at least thirty-three per cent. of them had no chance of life, and that the recovery of others would be slow and painful.

I will not distress myself nor the reader by a further description. Those who doubt the facts may consult Report 67 of the first session of the Thirty-eighth Congress. It is the report of the Joint Committee on the Conduct of the War, written by Mr. Gooch, of Massachusetts, a clear-headed, conservative man. Portraits of the patients, the testimony given by them, and scores of other reliable witnesses, seem to point to the correctness of the conclusion drawn by that committee, that exposure and starvation, and the inhuman practices so indicated, "were the result of a determination by the rebel authorities to reduce our soldiers in their power to such a condition that those who survive shall never recover so as to be able to render any effectual service in the field."

The horrors of Andersonville and Salisbury came later. They were farther away, and the proof is not so overwhelming. The proportion chargeable to Wirz and Winder, and that for which the Confederate authorities were responsible, may not in this world be known. The conduct of these wretches, repeatedly denounced to their superiors by the more humane officers of the Confederacy, upon official examination, is probably not to be charged to any direct orders from the rebel authorities. In the case of the poor victims at Annapolis, there is less excuse. They were robbed and frozen and starved in the city of Richmond, in the capital of the Confederacy, under the very windows of the Executive Mansion, under the eye of Jefferson Davis and the rebel congress. Scarcity of food, fuel, and clothing never existed in Richmond; they were abundant at the collapse of the Confederacy almost a year later. It is difficult to find excuse or apology for the treatment of the prisoners at Belle Isle, and I doubt if such will ever be attempted.

The evidence need not be strained in order to extend the responsibility for these atrocities to others than the notoriously guilty. His admirers claim that no part of it rests upon General Lee, and as we have no record that any word or remonstrance or objection ever came from him, it is to be fervently hoped that he was ignorant of the whole damning story.

It was a Boston woman of wealth and culture who went with me from cot to cot during the visit of that evening. In the preceding forty-eight hours every comfort which her wealth and energy could procure had been provided for these poor sufferers with a bountiful hand. Even their dull minds seemed to recognize in her the instrument of a kind Providence, and I could not determine whether their tears of gratitude or hers of pity were the more abundant. I did not see them at their worst, but even at the time of my visit the scene transcended description. It sickened me; and the recollection of its sad and tragic features served to keep sleep from my eyes during the greater part of the ensuing night.

At early dawn I hurried back to the hospital to convince myself that my imagination had exaggerated the horrors of my previous visit. But no such result ensued. Attendants were removing those who during the night watches had forgotten their pains and should remember their miseries no more. Death had harvested seventeen victims.

I returned to Washington by the earliest train. It

was scarcely seven o'clock when I reached the Executive Mansion. I was not kept waiting.

"Well ?" said the President, as he entered the well-known room, with a world of interrogation in his face.

"Mr. President," I responded, "all the way from Annapolis I have been studying the formula for an answer to your question. It is useless! You would like to know what I have seen? I cannot tell you. Imagine, if you can, a body of stalwart, strong men, such as you may see in any of our camps, robbed of their money, blankets, overcoats, boots and clothing, covered with rags, driven like foxes into holes on an island, exposed there to frost and cold until their frozen extremities drop from their bleeding stumps; fed upon husks, such as the swine in the parable would have rejected, until, by exhaustion, their manhood is crushed out, their minds destroyed, and their bodies, foul with filth and disease, are brought to the very borders of the grave, which will close upon more than half of them, and you may get some faint conception of what may be seen at Annapolis. But it will be very faint. The picture cannot be comprehended even when it is seen!"

"Can such things be possible?" he exclaimed, "and you are the fourth who has given me the same account! I cannot believe it! There must be some explanation for it. The Richmond people are Americans—of the same race as ourselves. It is incredible!"

"No, no!" I exclaimed, "I saw these poor unfortunates last evening. I went again this morning to find something which would relieve the horror of the first impression. I did not find it. I have conversed with men who know that they are dying, and that they have been brought to the very edge of their open graves by neglect. They all tell the same story, and but one conclusion is possible. A frightful weight of responsibility and guilt rests upon the authorities at Richmond for these crimes against humanity!"

"I feel all your sympathy," he said; "nothing has occurred in the war which causes me to suffer like this. I know it seems impossible to account for the treatment of these poor fellows, except on the theory that somebody is guilty. But the world will be slow to believe that the Confederate authorities intend to destroy their prisoners by starvation. We should be slow to believe it ourselves. It must be that they have some claim of excuse! Why, the Indians torture their prisoners, but I never heard that they froze them or starved them!"

"It seems to me," I said, "that a parallel to these cruelties would be hard to find even in the conduct of the Spaniards towards the Indians of Central and South America, which Las Casas so graphically sets before us."

"And yet we may not know all the facts, the whole inside history. They may have excuses of which we know nothing," said the President.

"Make the case your own," I persisted. "Washington is larger than Richmond; your duties are quite as absorbing as those of Mr. Jefferson Davis. Could Confederate prisoners of war be dying by hundreds of exposure and starvation on an island in the Potomac, between this city and Alexandria, and you not know it? Why, the newsboys in the streets would publish it, and the authorities could not remain ignorant of it if they were deaf and dumb."

"Well, well!" he said, "you have the best of the argument, I admit. But do me a favor. Retain your opinions, if you must, but say nothing about them at present, until we are compelled to make the charge, until there is no alternative, and the world is forced to think as we do."

"I will do as you request," I responded, "but we cannot control our judgments. It is plain where the responsibility of these enormities should rest, and condemnation of those who permitted them must follow from any right-minded and humane person."

The President's face wore that sad expression which I have so often referred to, as he said, "Let us hope for the best! We shall have enough to answer for if we survive this war. Let us hope, at least, that the crime of murdering prisoners by exposure and starvation may not be fastened on any of our people."

XXXVII.

PRESIDENT LINCOLN'S STORY OF DANIEL WEBSTER.

The story of Daniel Webster's school-days, as related by Mr. Lincoln, was imperfectly given by Mr. B. F. Carpenter, the artist, in his anecdotes and reminiscences appended to Raymond's "Life and Public Services of Abraham Lincoln," published soon after his assassination. The value of the story as an interesting illustration of certain qualities in the President's character depends, in a great degree, upon the circumstances under which it was told. These are in part omitted, and in part misdescribed, in the published account. The following is a correct version, as I can affirm from personal knowledge:

The colored people, from the hour of his inauguration, regarded Mr. Lincoln as the promised saviour of their race. Their faith in his wisdom and power was unbounded. It was most fully expressed in their churches and religious services by a singular combination of reverence and trust. They had no doubt whatever of his ability to set them free, and that he would do so whenever it was to their advantage that the blessing of freedom should be bestowed. They were content to wait until that time arrived. Their duty, as impressed by their ministers, was to prepare themselves for the great impending change in their condition, by learning to read and write, and by leading good and honest lives. Whenever Mr. Lincoln's name was mentioned, or when they saw him or heard him speak, they exhibited much the same reverence as we may imagine was shown by sincere believers at the sight of the Saviour of men.

In May, 1862, there was a Sunday-school celebration of the colored children of Washington. The bright contrasts of striking colors of which the race is so fond, with their genius for display, enabled the parents to dress and arrange their children in a procession of a memorable character at a small expense. The young, black, merry faces, the simple dresses of white with a red shawl or sash worn over them with native grace, the girls carrying bouquets of crimson roses, and the boys waving colored banners, arranged in a procession, with their teachers and parents walking solemnly by their side, all occupied in a vain effort to suppress their enthusiasm, was a pleasant picture to behold. The procession was a long one, and must have comprised most of the colored children in the city. It was the season of flowers, and the large bunches carried by the girls lent an added brightness to the scene.

The route of the procession brought it in front of the Executive Mansion about ten o'clock on a bright May morning. President Lincoln stood at one of the windows on the second floor, and the procession passed within a few yards, so that every child in it had a full view of his person. At the head of the column were forty or fifty colored ministers and teachers, who set an excellent example of sober dignity to their young followers. Their injunctions of silence to the children were emphatic and often repeated.

But it would have been no more difficult to suppress so many explosions of powder with the match applied than to quell the involuntary outburst of enthusiasm which came from every child in that long procession as he or she recognized the well-known face and figure of Abraham Lincoln. It would be useless to attempt to repeat their exclamations. From the boys there were shouts of enthusiastic delight; from the girls a more suppressed form of reverential wonder. Boys and girls alike wanted the fact to be known that they had seen the President. "I seen him!" "I seen him my own self!" "Dat's Massa Linkum!" "Look at him! Look at him!" "Oh, don't he look just the same as the Lord!" Every boy would swing his flag, and shout his hurrahs as he came near the President, and each was frantic with joy when, as often happened, he appeared to notice him. The girls, not so demonstrative, clasped their hands and blessed "Massa Linkum" in every imaginable form of expression. Scores of them tossed their bunches of roses into the Mansion, so that the floor was carpeted with them.

For a full hour the President stood at the window, giving the last child as good an opportunity to see him as the first. There is not much of the pathetic in the account, but there was something very touching in this universal reverence for Abraham Lincoln. It did not fail to affect every spectator, the President, apparently, most of all. His sad, melancholy face could not have been more expressive if he had felt a sense of personal responsibility for every human being in that numerous crowd. The scene was so touching that there were some eyes which were not entirely dry, and I thought, at the time, that the President's were among the number.

When the procession had passed, and the last of the innumerable "God bless him's" had died away, without breaking the silence which he had maintained for an hour, Mr. Lincoln turned from the window and walked slowly back towards the well-known little room in which he had received so many visitors, followed by those who had with him witnessed the exhibition. When the President entered the room, his face wore that look of melancholy so habitual to it; so different from that of any other human being.

Suddenly he stopped and turned about. In an instant the whole aspect of the man had changed; the melancholy look had disappeared, and his sad eyes sparkled with humor. Without addressing any one in particular, he exclaimed:

"Did you ever hear the story of Daniel Webster and the school-master?"

No one answered. "Well," he said, "this is the story: Daniel was a very careless, some called him a dirty boy. His teacher had many times reproved him for not washing his hands. He had coaxed and scolded him, but it was useless; Daniel would come to school with dirty hands. Out of all patience with him, one day he called Daniel to his desk, made him hold up his hands in the presence of the whole school, and solemnly warned him that if he ever came to school again with his hands in that condition he would give him a ferruling which he would long remember.

"Daniel promised better behavior, and for two or three days there was great improvement in his appearance. His hands looked as if they were washed daily. But the reformation was not permanent. In a few days his hands were as dirty as ever. The teacher's sharp eyes detected them, and, as soon as school had opened for the day, with a stern voice he said, 'Daniel, come here!' the guilty culprit knew what was coming. His palms began to tingle in anticipation. He stealthily brought the palm of his right hand into contact with his tongue, and, as he walked slowly towards the master's desk, rubbed the same upon his pantaloons, in the effort to remove some of the dirt. 'Hold out your hand, sir!' said the master. Daniel extended his right hand palm upward. 'Do you call that a clean hand?' demanded the teacher. 'Not very, sir,' modestly replied the offender. 'I should think *not very!*' said the master. 'I promised you a ferruling; but if you will show a dirtier hand in this school-room, I will let you off for this time.' 'There it is, sir!' exclaimed Daniel, quickly extending his left hand, which had not undergone the summary cleansing of the right.''

Mr. Lincoln seldom laughed at his own stories, but usually left his auditors, for whose benefit they were told, to enjoy them. But the quickness with which the school-boy had seized upon the weak point in the master's offer seemed to touch his keen sense of humor, and at the conclusion of the story he laughed as heartily as any one present. The story was a good one, but what there had been in the procession just witnessed to bring it to the President's mind was difficult to discover.

XXXVIII.

PRESIDENT LINCOLN THE UNAPPRECIATED FRIEND OF THE SOUTH.—HIS OFFER OF COMPENSATED EMANCIPATION.—HE MEETS A VERMONT CONTRACTOR.—THEIR IMPRESSIONS OF EACH OTHER.

To those who were in almost daily intercourse with President Lincoln, who knew his inmost thoughts, it was surprising that the slaveholders could not see that he wanted to be their friend. When the war was fairly begun, I believe he gave up all thought that slavery could be saved. I know that he began to formulate plans to secure to the slaveholders payment for their slaves, and if the Border states had come to his assistance there was a time when they could have secured it. As early as September, 1861, I heard him discuss the subject frequently. He spoke of the poverty and distress which emancipation would bring upon the slaveholders. He hoped that Congress would propose some plan of co-operation with the Border states in abolishing slavery. Immediately after our first military successes in the winter of 1862, and early in March, he sent a special message to Congress, proposing a joint resolution offering such co-operation, and that Congress should offer at least partial payment. In July he transmitted a bill to Congress, which provided that bonds of the United States at a fixed rate per head, according to the census of 1860, should be issued to any state that abolished slavery.

This liberal proposal received considerable support at the North. Mr. Greely advocated it in the *Tribune*, and the leading Republican papers followed his lead. Mr. Lincoln personally invited his friends to interest themselves in the subject.

But the proposition met with no support in the Border states, where it ought to have been received with enthusiasm, and in the seceded states it was ridiculed. The London *Times* scoffed at it, and in all England only the *Daily News* gave it a cold support. Mr. Lincoln quite took its failure to heart, and declared that it still remained true that, whom the gods wished to destroy they first made mad. He became discouraged almost to the point of abandoning the project, when a suggestion was made which attracted some attention, and promised to acquire some strength in the Border states. The proposition was not only to pay for the slaves, but to remove them bodily to some territory which should be wholly given up to them, and where they should try the experiment of self-government.

Unfortunately the source of this suggestion gave it little political strength. The fact that Mr. Lincoln consented to entertain and consider it at all showed how far he was willing to go for the protection of the slave owners, and how unwilling he was to give up all hope of success. The proposition seemed to his friends absurd and impossible. If it were not, it was hopeless; for no Northern state would consent to pay for the slave property, incur the expense of removing it, and also become responsible for its future management. The author of the scheme was ex-Senator Pomeroy, and its promoters were speculators rather than statesmen.

It was very close to the new year of 1863 that the suggestion was tentatively given to the newspapers, in the form of a rumor that parties were ready to undertake the removal of the slaves to Western Texas. It attracted but little attention, and it became evident that some other impulse must be given to it if it was to succeed.

During one of his welcome visits to my office, the President appeared to be buried in thought over some subject of great interest. After long reflection he abruptly exclaimed that he wanted to ask me a question.

"Do you know any energetic contractor?" he inquired. "One who would be willing to take a large contract, attended with some risk?"

"I know New England contractors," I replied, "who would not be frightened by the magnitude or risk of any contract. The element of prospective profit is the only one which would interest them. If there was a fair prospect of profit, they would not hesitate to contract to suppress the rebellion within ninety days!"

"There will be profit and reputation in the contract I may propose," he said. "It is to remove the whole colored race of the slave states into Texas. If you have any acquaintance who would take that contract, I would like to see him."

"I know a man who would take that contract and perform it. I would be willing to put him into communication with you, so that you might form your own opinion about him. He is so connected with my family that I would not endorse him further than to say that he has energy enough to remove a nation."

By the President's direction I requested John Bradley, a well-known Vermonter, then temporarily in New York, to come to Washington. He was at my office when the Treasury opened, the morning after I sent the telegram. I declined to give him any hint of the purpose of his invitation, but took him directly to the Pres-
22

ident. When I presented him, I said: "Here, Mr. President, is the contractor whom I named to you yesterday. Please understand that if I endorse him it must be 'without recourse.' You must take him upon your own judgment, if at all. His plans are too comprehensive for me to make good if he should fail."

I left them together. Two hours later Mr. Bradley returned to the Register's Office, overflowing with admiration for the President and enthusiasm for his proposed work. "The proposition is," he said, "to remove the whole colored race into Texas, there to establish a republic of their own. The subject has political bearings, of which I am no judge, and upon which the President has not yet made up his mind. But I have shown him that it is practicable. I will undertake to remove them all within a year."

"What do you think of the President?" I asked.

"I think he is the greatest man of the century!" he answered. "He has the intellect of Webster and the hard common-sense of Silas Wright. I can understand now his power over other men. He is thoroughly honest and unselfish. He has sound judgment; he can command all my resources for anything he wishes to do. He is greater than Washington, and the world will eventually so decide."

"But is not this project for the deportation of the negroes rather impracticable? Is it not an act of rashness to favor it?"

"He has not decided to favor it. It is the project of Senator Pomeroy, of Kansas, and a few others. The President has it under examination. I do not understand the political questions involved in it, and I think it is very doubtful whether President Lincoln approves it. But if he does, it will be a success, and I shall do all in my power to favor it. Mr. Lincoln is great, because he is honest. The people must follow such a leader! They cannot do otherwise. I cannot do otherwise. If he decides upon this wholesale transfer of the colored race, they will be in Texas within a year. I would like to take the contract for their removal. All the assistance I want is the approval of President Lincoln."

"What is your opinion of Mr. Bradley?" I asked the President at my next opportunity.

"He is equal to any enterprise, even the removal of a race from one continent to another," the President answered. "He poured a flood of information over the entire subject. He had built a railroad through the state of Texas; he knew all about the soil, the climate, all the conditions which control the problem. He was a veritable mine of information. He was even ready to take the contract for the deportation of the negroes at so much a head. But he also had powerful reasons against the project. If it is undertaken, he will have a hand in it. Have you many such men in Vermont? Why would they not make great soldiers? A dozen such men combined ought to control the resources of the state."

"There is one defect in Mr. Bradley's character," I said. "He will carry any enterprise through its difficulties, but when these are overcome, the project ceases to have any attraction for him."

"I think I understand you. As they say in the hayfield, he requires a good man to 'rake after him.' I asked him if he had had any military experience. He said that he had not, but that he could learn military science in two months. On my word, I believe he could."

"If such men were in command, there would be a movement at the front," he continued. "I can find men enough who can rake after; but the men with long arms and broad shoulders, who swing a scythe in long sweeps, cutting a smooth swath ten feet wide, are much more difficult to find."

The project for the removal of the colored race was soon after abandoned. I doubt whether it was ever seriously entertained by the President. The plan was favorably considered by others, and his rejection of it serves to illustrate the practical judgment by which the President decided every question presented for his consideration.

XXXIX.

THE PROFESSIONAL DETECTIVE.—HIS EMPLOYMENT BY THE UNITED STATES AND ITS INFLUENCE UPON THE PEOPLE.

WAR is a crime against humanity. Criminals who transgress laws made by man sometimes escape the penalty; those who break the laws ordained of God, never. Whether nation or individual, their punishment is inevitable.

After the War of the Rebellion was over, and the great wrong of slavery had been expiated in blood, there were those who hoped that the nation might be restored to the soundness of *ante-bellum* days, and escape the demoralizing results which have followed all wars from that one waged in heaven by the first rebel against his omnipotent Master. It was a thrice-vain hope. We who lived before the war are able to compare the tone of legislation, the purity of the judiciary, the integrity of public officers, and the conscience which regulated the intercourse of men in those peaceful days, with the insane speculations, the monopolies, the thirst for office and the greed of riches of the present day, and require no other proofs of the extent of the national demoralization. It is not an agreeable picture. More closely than anything in history, it tends toward the condition of the empire when Rome, by her conquests, had accumulated, in the Eternal City, the corruptions as well as the riches of the world.

Much of this degradation of the public morals was the inevitable result of war. It arose from causes probably beyond human control, under the wisest of governments. Upon these causes it is useless to enter. But there were others which might have been prevented or suppressed. Their evils were anticipated and discussed; there was opportunity to employ or reject them. I will give a short sketch of one of them, and some of the incidents of its operation.

Secretary Chase was opposed upon principle to any system of direct taxation which required a force of revenue officers for its collection. His chief objection was, that it would create an inquisition into the private affairs of the people to which they were unused, and which could not fail to become disagreeable and offensive. To the cases cited of Great Britain and other powers, where a large revenue was collected under such a system, he replied that the revenue was obtained from but few articles or sources; that this kind of taxation had been so long in use that its evils had been reformed; the people had become accustomed to it and its burdens were light. Whereas here, the whole subject was novel, and the tax would necessarily be laid upon a much larger number of articles.

But Secretary Chase had constantly before him one controlling fact, to which the general public gave but little attention. The Treasury was the weakest point in the national defences and the constant source of impending peril. The national credit was as necessary to a restoration of the Union as oxygen to life. If that became bankrupt, a divided union and a confederacy founded upon negro slavery were as inevitable as death.

The battle of Bull Run, however, settled several open questions. One of them was, that every practicable means of supplying the Treasury with money must be employed without longer delay. Customs duties must be increased to an extent which made illicit importations immensely profitable, and all manufactured products, the professions, and the incomes of the people must be taxed to an extent before uncontemplated. An internal revenue system, reaching into every village and hamlet of the loyal states, had become an immediate necessity.

The secretary invited suggestions from a number of gentlemen for the structure of the Internal Revenue Statutes. These suggestions arranged themselves in two classes. One class proceeded upon the assumption that men were naturally dishonest, and that they would regard a fraud upon the United States as an evidence of shrewdness rather than a crime, as a credit rather than a stigma. The other insisted that the nation was now experiencing a grand and most creditable development of patriotism, which led it to regard the payment of necessary taxes as a duty, and which would no more tolerate frauds upon the Treasury than it would any other form of treason.

The first of these classes consequently proposed an internal revenue system which should enforce the collection of taxes by heavy fines, penalties, and forfeitures, which should be divided with informers and spies. As these informers would require instruction in their labors, in order to become experts, they proposed a bureau of detectives in the Treasury, presided over by a chief, with such a number of subordinates as should be found necessary, all to be salaried officers of the United States.

The general plan of the second class proposed considerable rewards for prompt returns and payments, in deductions from the amount of the tax. Their principal reliance, however, was upon the honesty of a patriotic people, who, if properly encouraged by the Treasury, would constitute a great army of unpaid agents for the collection of the taxes, besides paying their own, since no man who bore his own share of the burdens of war would permit his neighbor to escape from the same burdens by fraud or dishonesty. This plan wholly dispensed with detectives and paid informers.

I took a somewhat active part in the discussion of the subject, and, at the request of the secretary, prepared a written argument, in which it was claimed that the employment of an army of detectives was inconsistent with the dignity of the government, and would exert a corrupting influence upon the people. I also stated that in my experience as a lawyer I could not remember that I had ever met with a professional detective who could be trusted; that the reason was probably to be found in the fact that a man who used deception and falsehood as the tools of his trade became incapable of distinguishing them from truth, so that he would use either, as at the moment seemed most expedient. Such a man's mind was not likely to be controlled by conscience, nor were perfect candor and sincerity towards an employer to be expected from one whose ordinary line of action in the pursuit of a criminal must necessarily involve a constant exercise of the opposite qualities. It was also stated that the people, knowing that such agents were employed by the Treasury, would infer that honesty and integrity were no longer appreciated, and would lose all interest in the honest execution of the laws, concluding that, as they got no credit for fair payment of their taxes, they might just as well evade them whenever they could. The results would necessarily be a general demoralization of the public service and a thorough corruption of the public mind.

The advice of the class first mentioned finally prevailed. After long hesitation the secretary decided upon the employment of detectives, and the first internal revenue act of 1862 was framed upon the theory that the taxpayers were the natural enemies of the government, who would avail themselves of every opportunity to defraud it, and evade the payment of their taxes. The laws for the collection of duties upon imports were amended so as to conform to the same theory. Heavy penalties were imposed by the internal revenue and the tariff laws, which were to be enforced by the official power of the United States, but the penalties, when collected, were to be divided between the government and the informers. Statutes were enacted which gave to irresponsible detectives powers of visitation and inquisition into the business of the citizen which were intolerable enough to have provoked a revolution if the country had not been already involved in war.

The Detective Bureau was established as one of the regular bureaus, not under the control of the commissioner of internal revenue, or the commissioner of the customs, as it should have been, if permitted to exist, but as an annex to the office of the secretary. One L. C. Baker, who had acquired some notoriety as a detective, was appointed its chief. By some means, never clearly understood, his jurisdiction was extended to the army, and he exercised his authority in all the departments and throughout the United States.

Baker wore the uniform, and probably had authority to assume the rank, of a colonel in the army. He took into his service, from all parts of the country, men who claimed to have any aptitude for detective work, without recommendation, investigation, or any inquiry, beyond his own inspection, which he claimed immediately disclosed to him the character and abilities of the applicant. How large his regiment ultimately grew is uncertain, but at one time he asserted that it exceeded two thousand men.

With this force at his command, protected against interference from the judicial authorities, Baker became a law unto himself. He instituted a veritable Reign of Terror. He dealt with every accused person in the same manner; with a reputable citizen as with a deserter or petty thief. He did not require the formality of a written charge; it was quite sufficient for any person to suggest to Baker that a citizen might be doing something that was against law. He was immediately arrested, handcuffed, and brought to Baker's office, at that time in the basement of the Treasury. There he was subjected to a brow-beating examination, in which Baker was said to rival in impudence some heads of the criminal bar. This examination was repeated as often as he chose. Men were kept in his rooms for weeks, without warrant, affidavit, or other semblance of authority. If the accused took any measures for his own protection, he was hurried into the Old Capitol Prison, where he was beyond the reach of the civil authorities. Baker's subordinates in other cities emulated and often surpassed the example of their chief. Powers such as they exercised were never similarly conferred by law under any government claiming to be enlightened.

Corruption spread like a contagious disease, wherever the operations of these detectives extended. It soon became known that impunity for frauds against the government could be procured for money. Men who, but for the detective system, would never have thought of such enterprises, went into the regular business of illicit distilling, bounty-jumping, smuggling, defrauding the customs, and other similar practices. Honest manufacturers and dealers, who paid their taxes, were pursued without mercy for the most technical breaches of the law, and were quickly driven out of business. The dishonest rapidly accumulated wealth, which they could well afford to share with their protectors. Good citizens became discouraged, and ceased to take any interest in the administration of justice, or the suppression of fraud. The worst predictions of the opponents of the detective system were speedily verified.

The methods of Chief Baker were shown by actual occurrences, one of which I will relate. It became evident that certain contractors were receiving preferences in the payment of their claims, in violation of an imperative rule of the department. Evidence of repeated infractions of this rule was produced. Brokers in New York would, for a commission, not only undertake to secure payment of claims by certain dates, but would inform claimants, in advance, of the date on which they would receive their money. This favoritism could only be accomplished in one of two ways; either by changing the order of issuing the warrants for the payment of settled claims, or by changing the warrants on their way through the Treasury. If the first was the case, the fraud was in the secretary's office; if the second, it was probably in the office of the register. I was satisfied that the warrant clerk in the office of the secretary was the guilty party, but he had the secretary's confidence, and regarded his position as impregnable.

Baker undertook the investigation of this fraud with great enthusiasm. He announced that he should report to me twice every day; that my suspicions had fallen upon the right person, but that he was operating with another clerk, and that the two were criminals of such experience and skill that nothing short of the machinery of his office would suffice for their detection. His reports were made with great detail, and finally announced that the guilty parties had become alarmed, and were on the point of taking flight with their plunder. The secretary, however, would not authorize their arrest, unless I would certify that a *prima facie* case against them was made out.

I declined to make this certificate. Baker's next report was, that the two clerks had become so suspicious that they did not speak to each other, nor correspond through the post-office; that each sent his letters to a hollow tree in Georgetown, where they were deposited; that he had already opened and read two of their letters and replaced them, and that, very soon, he expected to have proof of their criminality under their own hands.

One day, while I was reading one of his rambling reports, Baker, on the opposite side of the table, was printing words with a pen on a loose sheet of paper, and had nearly covered a half-sheet with his own name, and other words, in imitation of printed capitals. This sheet he left on the table, and I, without any purpose in my mind, swept it into a drawer. Shortly afterwards, he came to inform me that the suspected persons were about to attempt a flight to Havana, and that one of them had written to the other, fixing upon the train by which they were to abscond, and asking for an answer, which answer he expected every moment to receive from one of his men who was on the watch at the hollow tree.

While he was giving me this account, he was called out of the office in an excited manner by one of his men. He soon returned, and, with an air of mystery, threw a letter on the table, observing that, "If we could see the inside of that, I would probably be willing to consent to the arrest, for we should have the scoundrels, sure!"

My eye had caught the direction. I took up the letter and began deliberately to open it.

"Hold! hold!" he exclaimed. "Don't you know that it is a felony to open a letter addressed to another without his authority?"

"I think I will take the risk," I said. I opened and read from it a long farrago about steamers from Cuba, the register's suspicions, Baker's unrelenting pursuit and watchfulness, the writer's danger, etc.

"Are you not willing to give the order for their arrest upon that evidence?" he asked.

I smoothed the letter upon the table, and laid by its side his own scribbled sheet, taken from my drawer, and asked somewhat sternly,

"Colonel Baker, do you not think both these documents were written by the same hand?"

Perfectly unabashed, without a blush, the fellow smiled as he looked me in the face and said,

"That game didn't work, did it? It was a good one, but the best plans will sometimes fail. If I could have got your consent to an arrest, I would have had their confessions before morning. We must now try another plan."

"No," I said. "I suspected you were a fraud, and now I know it! You are of the same pattern with almost every detective I ever knew. You were willing to involve me in your scheme of deceit, in order to get an opportunity of frightening these men into confession. You may have the poor excuse of having practised falsehood so long that you have forgotten how to be honest. However that may be, I shall end all communication with you by reporting you to the secretary.

I knew he was armed, but I was very sure that he was a coward, and would not resent a kick, if I chose to administer it. He took no offence whatever.

"I always did like a frank man," he observed. "I think we now understand each other, and shall get along admirably. You will like me when you know me better."

I satisfied him that the conversation could not be protracted. But from this time forward he always insisted that we were the best of friends. An accident soon afterwards led to the exposure of the guilty clerk.

I never did understand under what authority Baker exercised his unendurable tyranny. He never hesitated to arrest men of good position, put them in irons, and keep them imprisoned for weeks. He seemed to control the Old Capitol Prison, and one of his deputies was its keeper. He always lived at the first hotels, had an abundance of money, and I am sure did more to disgust good citizens and bring the government into disrepute than the strongest opponents of the system had ever predicted. He opened an office in the Astor House in New York, formed a partnership with a notorious person called "The. Allen," who enlisted twelve hundred vagrants and tramps, promising them an opportunity to desert. Instead of being permitted to desert, the recruits were hurried to the front. They were worthless as soldiers, having been enlisted by deception, and the whole scheme was a detestable fraud. This was Baker's method of breaking up "bounty-jumping," and may be taken as an average illustration of his practices. He managed to appropriate the credit due to a party of cavalrymen in the pursuit and capture of the assassins of the President, and maintained his rank and office to the end of the war.

It is probably too late now to dispense with the detective system. The system itself created a class of criminals who now require its continuance. Training and attention have developed a better class of officers for the secret service of the Treasury. Here and there a few men of ability have taken up the detection of crime as a science, and among them the Pinkertons, and Inspector Byrnes, of New York city, may be recognized as useful officers of great ability. But they are conspicuous exceptions to a very general rule, and do not affect the estimate of conservative men with old ideas of integrity and principle in regard to the system as a whole. Such men will not approve the use of such means, although the multitude may cry out, "Let us do evil, that good may come!"

The guilty clerk whom Baker was pursuing was not long in exposing his methods. His New York associates now openly offered their facilities for securing prompt payment of claims, for a commission, to contractors. The suspected clerk set up his carriage, became a patron of *coryphées* of the ballet, and indulged in other luxuries quite inconsistent with his salary of $1600 per year. I carried the next warrant, marked "special," that was presented for signature to the secretary. As I suspected, he knew nothing about it. In as few words as possible I pointed out the circumstances, and the secretary instantly sent for the warrant clerk. It was too late. He must have seen me enter the secretary's office with the warrant in my hand—he had taken the alarm and fled. He was not arrested. For such a piece of work as the arrest of a real criminal Baker was worthless. The practice, however, was broken up.

Some years afterwards, in my office in New York, I was told that a person wished to see me who bore every appearance of a "tramp." In the outer office I found a poor palsied, ragged creature, having every mark of poverty and destitution. He extended his hand in a furtive manner, then withdrew it, and in a broken voice said, "You don't remember me. I am H——, once warrant clerk in the Treasury. I was discharged from the hospital yesterday. I have eaten nothing since. I am weak and hungry. Will you not lend me two shillings to get a breakfast?" It was the man who once kept his carriage, and was the confidential clerk of the Secretary of the Treasury. "How much money will take you to your home and your friends?" I asked. "I have no home and no friends," he said, despairingly. I relieved his necessities; he went from my office and I saw him no more.

XL.
PUBLIC MISCONCEPTIONS OF THE VALUE OF SALARIED OFFICES.—GENERAL STANNARD.

IF civil offices were estimated at their actual instead of their imaginary value, those who dispense them would not be troubled by the pertinacity of the office-seeker. Civil officers of the United States of all grades, with few exceptions, are underpaid. The amount and character of the service required, given to almost any of the pursuits of private life, would be much better rewarded. Why, then, do so many good citizens enter this mad race for office at every opportunity? It is a race in which scores are beaten and endure the shame and mortification of defeat where one succeeds; in which the winner is in the end the loser, and deserves commiseration rather than congratulations for his success.

There is a certain glamour over public office which is extremely deceptive. This is particularly the case with offices which have to do with the receipt and disbursement of money. Many times I have pointed out to applicants for these offices the inadequacy of their salaries, and the impossibility of increasing their income in any honest way. They see, but will not be convinced. They are certain that handling so much money must be profitable. If they can once get the place, they are sure that they can find a way to make it lucrative.

From the days when Hamilton was the Secretary of the Treasury to the present time, the ingenuity of financial officers and members of Congress has been taxed to render impossible the very results for which the office-seeker is hoping. They have so surrounded official life with checks, guards, and penalties that it may now be stated as an axiom that, except by stealing, there is no way known among men of making an office profitable beyond its appointed salary.

Errors in judgment in this respect have been the ruin of many worthy men. The subject is important. An actual occurrence, which fell under my own observation, will serve as an illustration.

The War of the Rebellion created or developed many brave and brilliant soldiers. None of them had a better record than Major-General George J. Stannard. On the 15th of April, 1861, he was the superintendent of an iron foundry in St. Albans, Vermont, and an officer of a company of uniformed militia in that town. He entered the service as a colonel, and was rapidly promoted through all the grades to the rank of a major-general. He never failed in his duty, and seldom omitted to distinguish himself in battle. He was several times wounded, and finally lost an arm. He appeared to be destitute of fear, and was at once the pride and admiration of his men. An account of the battle of Gettysburg will never be read which does not contain a conspicuous notice of General Stannard. It was his brigade which held the front line on the left centre of the Union forces, on which General Lee, for more than two hours, concentrated the fire of 140 pieces of artillery, and against which the famous charge of Pickett's division was directed. It was his inspiration that caught the instant when that mad rush of a charging army was defeated to order out upon its flank two regiments which, at the distance of a pistol-shot, poured their deadly volleys into the mass of Confederates, which so demoralized them that they never halted until three or four thousand of them passed to the rear as prisoners of war. It was conceded by military critics to have been one of the most brilliant military acts of the war—to have been almost without a parallel in its history. In the final campaign he commanded a division of the Eighteenth Corps, which captured and held Fort Harrison, and it was in defending it against an attempt made by ten brigades to recapture it that he lost his arm.

When General Grant was elected President, General Stannard became a candidate for the office of collector of the district of Vermont. He asked me to sign his recommendations. I declined, on the ground that I esteemed him too highly to promote his ruin. I argued with him, I pointed him to the statute which limited the annual pay of the office to $2500. I showed him that it might not amount to half that sum, and that none but a close business man, who would rigidly obey the law, and touch no dollar of the government money, could take the office without peril to himself and to the friends who became his sureties. I failed to make the slightest impression upon him. Somebody had told him that a former incumbent had cleared annually $10,000 from the office; that what had been done could be done. He went away offended, and for some months treated me as his personal enemy.

He obtained the appointment. His intimate friends became his sureties, and for something like a year he was a most popular collector. To the rigid rules of the Treasury he paid not much attention. As the receipts of the office flowed in, they were deposited in the Treasury, or in the pocket of the collector, as happened at the time to be most convenient. Money was abundant with him, and, with the open hand of a soldier, when he had a dollar he gave half of it to any friend who had none. In short, he administered the office under a code of rules of his own invention. Everybody was delighted. He was the friend of everybody, and he naturally had a larger circle of friends than any of his predecessors in the office.

Very gentle is the first letter of the first auditor to a collector when his quarterly accounts show a balance on the wrong side. The error is attributed to accident, to inadvertence, of course. The collector is referred to certain rules, which he will observe in future; one of these is that every dollar received be deposited in the Treasury. But under its most courteous concluding words the collector will discover, upon close examination, a most positive direction to deposit the balance immediately!

Woe to the collector if, instead of acting upon the hint, he lays the letter aside to be attended to at some more convenient season, until perhaps some friend pays his loan, or money flows in from some other quarter. He may have a short grace of a few days at first, but never afterwards. These letters require attention. No doubt there is a "First Auditor's Complete Letter Writer," with progressive examples, each sharper and more pointed than the last, to enforce upon the delinquent the conviction that he is the servant of a department which has rules that must be obeyed and enforced. These reminders become so frequent that the sight of an official envelope gives him a chill. Then for a few days the correspondence ceases. The officer flatters himself that his case has been laid aside, and he breathes more freely.

Some morning (they always appear early in the day) a stranger enters the office of the collector, and delivers to him another official envelope. It contains his suspension from office, and an order to turn over to the bearer the entire contents of the office, the duties of which will be discharged by Special Agent Roe or Doe, pending an investigation. From that day the growth of the delinquent's troubles begins, and proceeds beyond anything he ever imagined. With the sharpness of an expert the agent finds every dollar of the money of the United States, and follows it to its illegitimate disposal. Higher and higher mounts the balance, until it reaches a sum which the officer might as well undertake to discharge the national debt as to pay. The climax of misery is reached when the agent points the collector to the statute which declares the misappropriation of each of these dollars a felony, punishable by imprisonment at hard labor. All this happened to General Stannard in an incredibly short space of time. He was really guilty of no crime but negligence. He had not squandered the money among evil companions, nor in riotous living, nor in the payment of his own debts. In fact, he could not tell why or whither the money had gone. But it had taken to itself wings, it had departed, it was not where it should have been, in the Treasury, and he was a defaulter, a ruined bankrupt, a disgraced man. It was even doubtful whether his sureties could make up the loss. Some of them were certainly ruined. His reputation as a citizen was gone forever, and even his hardearned fame as a soldier was stained and tarnished.

Those who visited the Ladies' Gallery of the House of Representatives in Washington during the Forty-first and Forty-second Congresses may have noticed, seated at the door, a silent, sad-faced man who had lost an arm. He was attentive to his duties, very courteous to every visitor. But he did not often speak to any one, and a smile seldom dispelled the sadness of his face. There he remained until he died. No one asked for his place or sought his removal. Even the fiercest of the applicants for office appeared to concede his right to retain this one until he surrendered it of his own will.

When I first recognized him there, it was a long time before I could break through his reserve and engage him in conversation. At last it gave way. "If I had followed your advice," he said, "I might have remained poor, but I should at least have preserved my own self-respect, and the respect of my friends and bondsmen. I must have been insane when I treated you as my enemy!"

There is no reason for giving further details. This poor, discouraged, ruined man, a doorkeeper in one of the legislative branches of the republic, was all that remained of a gallant general of division, who had led armies over the walls of forts, against thrice their number, to victory. He it was who many times had wrested triumph out of the iron jaws of defeat. It was his flashing eye which had faced the rush of an army as it hurled itself upon the Union forces; and, seizing the critical moment, it was his hand that delivered the decisive blow in the greatest battle of the century, his genius that won the victory which restored a divided union and made ours the greatest republic of the world.

I hope, and I believe it is true, that under the operation of the civil-service system, the rush after clerical positions under the government has been checked, if not wholly arrested. Thousands, who might have been active and useful citizens in private life, have condemned themselves to lives of anxiety and misery by their success in securing one of these positions. A man is buried in them. His duties become routine, he is soon incapable of doing anything better; in an incredibly short time he has lost all connection with the world, he is in peril of removal with every change of administration, and as he has forgotten how to do anything else, removal is his ruin. No men better deserve the attention of philanthropists than the clerks in the government service.

In the few salaried offices not subject to the civil-service system, the situation is no better. These necessarily change with the administration. The term of service is so brief, the demands upon the incumbent are so numerous, that no active man can afford to accept one of them, unless for a brief honor he is willing to pay a large price. It will be a fortunate day for the country when the civil-service system is extended to all the government offices, except the Cabinet and those immediately connected with Congress.

While a few have managed to keep their heads above water, how many of my contemporaries have gone down beneath the waves of government service! Some, sent to Washington as members of Congress, have degenerated into claim agents, and thence into the depths of political pauperism. Some, appointed to small offices, have bartered their independence for insignificant salaries, and have become the hacks of either party which will give them employment. Others, losing their offices, have sunk into poverty, a few, alas! into crime. I am unable to recall an instance where one of my friends, having become dependent on a small office for a livelihood, proved afterwards of any considerable value to his country or mankind.

XLI.

WAS GENERAL THOMAS LOYAL?

GENERAL GEORGE H. THOMAS is dead. Since his death, and that of nearly all his witnesses, it has been alleged that he was disloyal. Some Southern historical society claims to have discovered proofs that he at first decided to cast his lot with his own people; in other words, to follow the example of other officers of Southern origin.

Colonel Henry Stone, of the Army of the Cumberland, has recently, in a vigorous article, published in the *New York Tribune* of June 7th, 1890, given this unfounded statement its quietus. General Thomas was slow to anger, but if anything would cause him, "in complete steel," to revisit "the glimpses of the moon," and blast the slanderer with a look, it would be such a charge as this against his memory.

I am able to contribute one or two facts on this subject. Even before the inauguration of Mr. Lincoln, General Scott was very anxious about the safety of the public property of large value in Texas, which was under the control of General Twiggs. The Second U. S. Cavalry, of which Thomas was major, was stationed there, and it was upon information communicated by him that General Scott insisted upon the transfer of General Twiggs to another post. But Twiggs was a favorite of President Buchanan. General Scott's wishes were disregarded, and on the 23d of February Twiggs delivered himself, as many regular soldiers as he could control, and public property valued at one million two hundred and nine thousand five hundred dollars, to the state of Texas. After the horse was stolen the stable was locked. On the first day of March, Secretary Holt issued an order dismissing Twiggs from the army "for his treachery to the flag of his country."

Early in April the men who declined to be surrendered by Twiggs began to arrive in New York. Thomas, though on sick leave, received and disposed of them, and from that time was one of the most active and reliable assistants of General Scott. April 21st was a lively day in Washington. Lee sent to General Scott a notice of his resignation. The Baltimore committee were in Washington, protesting that no more Northern regiments should be permitted to pass through Maryland. They brought information that the authorities of Maryland had ordered the railroad bridges to be burned and all the railroads broken up. General Scott undertook to restore and maintain railroad communication with the North. He did not hesitate for a moment. He ordered a detachment, which he could scarcely afford to spare from the few regulars in the city, to disperse the Plug-Uglies who were threatening the destruction of the railroad between Baltimore and Harrisburg, and Major Thomas was the officer selected by him to command the detachment.

All this occurred on Sunday. There were loyal men from Baltimore in active communication with the President, and it was at their suggestion that the force was ordered to protect the Northern railroad. They objected to intrusting so important a matter to Major Thomas, and insisted upon the appointment of Colonel Mansfield. The President referred them to General Scott.

"Why do you object to Major Thomas? What do you

know to the prejudice of Major Thomas?" demanded the old chieftain.

They had nothing against Major Thomas, except that he was a Virginian. All the Virginians were resigning; even Colonel Lee had gone over to the rebels. They feared that Major Thomas would follow his example.

"I am more fortunate than you are. I know Major Thomas; he is incapable of disloyalty. I would intrust him with what is to me the most precious thing on earth —my country's flag! I know that some Virginians have deserted it. But there are Virginians whom I am not afraid to trust, for I also am a Virginian!" said the old hero, proudly.

I never heard the loyalty of General Thomas questioned after this endorsement. He was understood to be a worker, one of the most efficient organizers of his time. He was more quiet and unassuming than Colonel Mansfield, but equally reliable and true. He had a peculiar mental organization. He was cautious and deliberate; he would not fight until he was prepared. His military career was an unbroken success. From Mill Springs, before the capture of Fort Henry, to the crushing defeat which he administered to Hood before Nashville, I do not remember that he lost a battle. His tenacity was unyielding. "You must hold Chattanooga!" General Grant had telegraphed to him, when Longstreet held him at bay. "We will hold the town until we starve!" was his reply. And his animals did starve, and his men came very near doing likewise before his communications could be opened. But he gave no sign of surrender. In all his campaigns he never moved fast enough to satisfy Grant. When the "March to the Sea" was decided upon, Grant and Sherman were both of the opinion that Hood would move northward to recover

Tennessee and Kentucky. They left him to the care of Thomas, intending to reinforce his small army, so as to enable him to cope with Hood and all the rebel force north of Atlanta. It was a perilous movement on the part of Sherman. If Hood was not arrested before he took Nashville, the result might be fatal. Sherman must have had great confidence in Thomas, since the success of the whole campaign would depend upon the result of a single battle, which Thomas was to win against a veteran army larger than his own.

Sherman left Atlanta on the 15th of November. Thomas abandoned all the intervening positions, and Hood apparently forced him back, step by step, into the defences of Nashville, which he reached on the 3d of December.

Hood attacked Scofield at Franklin, but was compelled to draw off after an indecisive battle. Thomas sent no reinforcements to Scofield, rightly judging that the latter would be able to hold his own, and also because he preferred to choose his own ground for the decisive struggle.

General Grant misunderstood the deliberation of General Thomas's policy, and, from the day Sherman left Atlanta, pressed him to attack the enemy. As Thomas made no answer, but continued to retire, Grant became more emphatic, and finally, when the former was apparently forced back to Nashville, the orders to attack became peremptory. As Thomas gave no sign in reply, Grant became anxious, and, being satisfied that further delay would be fatal, directed Logan to relieve Thomas, and take the command of his army. His solicitude increasing, he left his camp before Richmond and started for Nashville. He reached Washington on the day when Logan arrived at Cincinnati.

I give these facts upon the authority of Captain Fox, whose relations with the President were at that time of the most intimate character. He related the incident immediately after its occurrence, as a strong proof of the accuracy of the President's judgment, and as showing how confidently he relied upon it in dealing with men. He said that General Grant informed the President of his anxiety about General Thomas, and of his purpose to relieve him and place General Logan in his command. The President suggested that, as General Thomas was one of the most cautious and prudent of the generals, whether it might not be that his judgment on the ground was better than that of others who were five hundred miles away; and that it might be better to wait for more evidence that it was erroneous before removing him. General Grant observed that that might be, if the consequences of his defeat would not be so serious—that he was a very competent officer, but habitually slow, and this time he had been slower than ever. "But has he not always 'got there' in time?" said the President. "Some generals have been in such haste that they have had to move in the wrong direction." However, the President declined to interfere or to influence the judgment of General Grant any further than to say, that "General Thomas acquired my confidence in April, 1861, and he has ever since retained it."

Fortunately, General Grant remained in Washington until the evening train for the West. Before he left, despatches were received from General Thomas, stating that he was ready, and proposed to attack Hood the next morning. General Grant decided to wait for results.

Possibly the finest trait in the character of General Grant was the freedom with which he admitted his own errors, and especially his misjudgment of others. His despatches to Thomas implied censure, and had culminated in an order relieving him from his command. We may now leave General Grant himself to describe the sequel.

In his Memoirs, Grant says, in substance, that he had directed Logan not to take the command if he found Thomas ready to fight—that Thomas did fight and "was successful from the start; and that he assailed the enemy in their intrenchments, and, after a desperate resistance, they fled in disorder, abandoning everything. In order to use his entire strength, Thomas had dismounted his cavalry, and fought them as infantry. This fact and some accidents prevented his effective pursuit of Hood. But the *morale* of the latter's army was destroyed, its fighting strength annihilated, so that it was rendered incapable of inflicting further injury to the Union cause."

The battle of Nashville crushed the Confederacy in the West, and made Sherman's "march to the sea" memorable in the annals of military science. The result was foreseen by Thomas, who pursued his plans with a deliberation which nothing could disturb, from the time he parted company with Sherman until, having collected and marshalled his forces for the final act, he dealt his annihilating blow to the rebellion before Nashville. Such a general could not fail to gain the complete confidence of his men. Well might General Grant send him from Washington his congratulations on "the splendid success of to-day." We who watched his career from that anxious Sunday in April, 1861, to its culmination before Nashville in December, 1864, should at least defend his memory, and see to it that, while we live, no spot or blemish shall stain the record of this modest, great soldier.

XLII.

THE IMPARTIAL JUDGMENT OF PRESIDENT LINCOLN.—THE RESIGNATION OF SECRETARY CHASE.—ITS CAUSES AND CONSEQUENCES.

THE endeavor now to write anything novel about President Lincoln is like gleaning in an exhausted field. While he has been gradually rising to the position he now holds in the world's esteem, it is not strange that those who had any acquaintance with him should each wish to contribute his mite to the aggregate of material concerning a man of such distinguished abilities. No American, possibly no public man anywhere, has had so many biographers; no biographers have ever written with a more imperfect knowledge of their subject than some of the authors of the so-called lives of Lincoln. Some of these writers have private griefs to ventilate, and, not courageous enough to oppose the general opinion of his sterling worth, have descended in a shamefaced way to make public assumed defects in his character; and others, claiming to be his old associates and friends, have hinted at scandals connected with his origin and early life which had no foundation, and which would never have been heard of but for their officiousness. Their poor excuse is a desire to exhibit Mr. Lincoln as he was, and not as the world would have him to be. There have been in the lives of all great men occurrences upon which friendship lays the seal of silence, and it would have been more to the credit of these writers if they had emulated the dignified silence with which Mr. Lincoln treated unfortunate circumstances which he could neither prevent nor control. Examples of both these classes will be found in any collection of the lives of Mr. Lincoln, and conspicuously in one collection claimed to have been written by the "distinguished men of his time."

One consequence of the *cacœthes scribendi* about Mr. Lincoln is that all the events of his life, the incidents of his professional career, the apt stories attributed to him, many of which he never heard, have been rewritten so many times, with such variations as the peculiar views of the writer at the moment suggested, that the points of some of the best have been lost and others so mutilated that they are no longer recognizable. The resignation of the Treasury by Mr. Chase in June, 1864, has not escaped the general mutilation. It was an important event; its incidents throw a flood of light over the characters of both the principals. As it has been sometimes described, it is a quarrel between two politicians, of little consequence to them, of none to anybody else. Some of the accounts begin with the nomination of Governor Tod, and omit the important events by which it was preceded. Except that of Messrs. Nicolay and Hay, all the accounts that I have seen attribute the resignation to Mr. Chase's desire for the Republican nomination for the Presidency in 1864, when, in fact, he had given up all hope of it for 1864, more than six months previously.

This aftermath of Lincoln material seems to increase as the living witnesses disappear. Soon its inventors will be able to exclaim, with a distinguished fabricator of history, "Who is there to dispute what I say?" What, then, is the earnest student to do? How is he to distinguish between the false and the true—the wheat of fact and the chaff of fiction? There can be but one answer to the inquiry. He will do it just as the works of great masters have always been distinguished from their counterfeits. There is a flavor about a genuine Lincoln sentence or story which is unmistakable—as different as possible from those of any other man. As the *connoisseur* in art identifies a Rembrandt or a Dürer at a glance, as the teller in the Federal Treasury casts out the defective coin by a touch, so will the earnest student become an expert in Lincolniana, in the sentences he has written, in all the events of his life. A single glance at a new fact or story will decide whether it has the ring of the true metal or the leaden sound of the counterfeit. By such experts must future lives and anecdotes be judged; to their judgment I submit the following version of one of the most important and striking events of his public career.

One of these old friends and associates declares that Mr. Lincoln had no faith. If Paul understood the subject, and faith is "the substance of things hoped for, the evidence of things not seen," then no man ever had a faith more perfect and sincere than Mr. Lincoln. Once, during a half-soliloquy in the Register's Office, while the register and his messenger were engaged in their work, and, as he liked them to be, paying no attention to him, he broke into a magnificent outburst—a word-painting of what the South would be when the war was over, slavery destroyed, and she had had an opportunity to develop her resources under the benignant influence of peace. Twenty years and more afterwards this scene flashed upon my memory with the vividness of an electric light as I recognized the word-picture of Mr. Lincoln in the following words of welcome by an eloquent Southerner to a Northern delegation: "You are standing," he said, "at this moment in the gateway that leads to the South. The wealth that is there, no longer hidden from human eyes, flashes in your very faces. You can smell the roses of a new hope that fill the air. You can hear the heart-beats of progress that come as upon the wings of heaven. You can reach forth your hands and almost clutch the gold that the sun rains down with his beams, as he takes his daily journey between the coal-mine and the cotton-field; the highlands of wood and iron, of marble and granite; the lowlands of tobacco, of sugar and rice, of corn and kine, of wine, milk, and honey." Such was the picture of the South presented to the eye of Mr. Lincoln's faith, and very similar were the words in which that picture was represented.

I have written the following account largely from personal knowledge, from what I myself saw and heard. The principal incidents were written in my journal about the time they occurred. It has been the regret of my subsequent life that I did not at the time know how great a man Mr. Lincoln was; that I did not at the time write out and preserve an account of many other things said and done by him. This occurrence was an exception. I felt at the time that Mr. Lincoln was revealing himself to me in a new and elevated character, and I undertook to record the words in which that revelation was made.

The resignation by Secretary Chase of his position as the chief financial officer of the United States closed his prospects as a Presidental candidate with the Republican, and did not improve them with the Democratic party. It was an act which was calculated to embarrass the President, for which there was no good excuse. He inferred from past events that his resignation would not be accepted; he hoped that it would demonstrate to the country that he had become a necessity of the financial situation, and thereby secure to him its more perfect control.

A question of forgery had arisen in the Assistant Treasury in New York. The auditor who signed checks for the payment of money pronounced two checks returned to him as paid, amounting to nearly $10,000, to be forgeries. The responsibility for the money lay between Mr. Cisco and the auditor. If the checks were genuine, the auditor—if they were forged, Mr. Cisco, must bear the loss.

Mr. Cisco claimed to *know* that the checks bore the genuine signature of the auditor. He so testified in an examination which took place before a commissioner of the United States. He declined to admit a possibility that he could be mistaken. His experience, he said, enabled him to identify a genuine, or detect a forged signature with unerring certainty. No one could imitate his signature so as to cause him to hesitate. He was as certain that the disputed signatures were genuine as though he had seen them written.

Friends of the auditor, who were confident of his integrity, finding that the mind of Mr. Cisco was closed to all the presumptions arising from the long service and the unblemished character of the accused, availed themselves of the assistance of experts and of photography. An expert wrote an imitation of the assistant treasurer's name, which that officer testified was his own genuine signature. He was as certain of it as he was of the genuineness of the disputed checks! The evidence of the expert who wrote the imitation, and an enlarged photograph of the signatures to the checks, made their traced, painted, false, and spurious character so apparent that the auditor was at once exonerated, notwithstanding the positive evidence of his chief. The result so intensely mortified him that he promptly resigned his office of assistant treasurer, declaring that nothing should induce him to withdraw his resignation.

Secretary Chase was fond of those who recognized his eminence, and were ready to serve him as their acknowledged superior. Those especially who were watchful of his convenience and of opportunities to contribute to his personal comforts secured a strong position in his esteem. Maunsel B. Field, an attaché in the office of the assistant treasurer of New York, was conspicuously a person of this class. From the first visit of the secretary to New York after he took office, Mr. Field had attached himself to his personal service. His devotion to that service was perfect; so that afterwards, as the visits of the secretary increased in frequency, Mr. Field attended to his social engagements, and became the authorized agent for communication with him. Mr. Field was a person of polished manners, who had the *entrée* into society. He was also a writer for the newspapers and a Democrat, without much position or following in his party. His service was so attentive that the secretary came to regard him as a kind of personal society representative. The office of Third Assistant Secretary of the Treasury was created for him. He was appointed to it, and removed to Washington, where he was afterwards employed in a confidential relation near the secretary's person. There were facts, of which it is impossible that the secretary long remained ignorant, which, though not reflecting upon his personal integrity, it was represented necessarily disqualified him for any position of trust or pecuniary responsibilty. From time to time he absented himself from the Treasury, sometimes for weeks together. No one seemed to know whither he retired, or to have any knowledge of the cause of his absence.

Mr. Cisco had filled his important office of assistant treasurer with great fidelity to the country and credit to himself. The fact that he was a member of the Democratic party, most earnest in his co-operation with the administration in all its measures for the suppression of the rebellion, had enabled him to contribute to the success of Mr. Chase's financial measures more powerfully, probably, than any Republican could have done in the same position, while his personal influence upon members of his own party had been strong, and always exerted to promote the cause of the Union. Very strong Republican influences were therefore brought forward to induce Mr. Cisco to reconsider his resignation, but he had apparently determined to return to private life, and peremptorily insisted upon its acceptance.

Always having great responsibility from the amount of public treasure intrusted to his care, the assistant treasurer at New York was at that time the most important civil officer in the republic, next after the members of the cabinet. The bank presidents of New York city, Boston, and Philadelphia then represented the money of the nation, and, acting together, as they usually did, they could promote the early success of or delay and obstruct the financial measures of the government. That they had always hitherto supported the secretary, and co-operated in the execution of his plans, had been largely due to the influence of Mr. Cisco. There had been occasions when these bank officers had attempted to defeat some of these plans, or, at least, to limit their success. But the strength of the secretary was re-enforced by the persistent influence of Mr. Cisco, always discreetly but constantly operating, so that when

Mr. Chase met these gentlemen in the assistant treasurer's office, as he so frequently did, his personal magnetism usually brought them to his support. It was, therefore, most desirable that Mr. Cisco's succcessor should, so far as practicable, possess his qualities, sustain his relations to the banks, and continue to exercise his good judgment. Such a man was not readily found. Ex-Governor Morgan, then a senator from New York, a financier of wide experience, and intimately acquainted with all the conditions which controlled financial movements in that city, took an active interest in the New York appointments. He was one of the most influential Republicans in Congress, who was upon every ground entitled to be consulted in regard to this appointment, He suggested Mr. John A. Stewart, the president of the oldest and wealthiest trust company in the city, an able financier of ripe experience, a pure and patriotic man, as Mr. Cisco's successor. Secretary Chase approved it, and the suggestion met with universal favor. But Mr. Stewart would not accept the appointment. He was unwilling to sacrifice his permanent position for one the tenure of which was uncertain, and this consideration was found to be controlling with other eminent financial men possessed of similar qualifications.

While it was generally understood that the Republican congressmen of New York were looking for a suitable successor to Mr. Cisco, they were amazed by the discovery that Secretary Chase had sent the name of Maunsel B. Field to the President for appointment to that responsible office. The fact became public through Mr. Field himself, who disclosed it to Republicans to whom he applied for recommendations. It produced something like an explosion of indignant opposition.

It seemed impossible to account for this nomination

upon the ordinary motives which control human action. It was one which Secretary Chase should have known was unwise to be made. The nominee had not one of the qualities which had made Mr. Cisco strong, or which had led to the selection of Mr. Stewart. He had no financial or political standing, and his natural abilities were of a literary rather than an executive character. It was not surprising, therefore, that Senator Morgan and other Republicans hurried to the President and indignantly protested against Mr. Field's nomination. They did not measure their words. They claimed that such an appointment would be an insult to the Union men of New York; that it would injure the party and disgrace the administration; and, finally, they offered to procure a written protest against the nomination, to be signed by every Republican senator and member of the House in the present Congress.

From the time the opposition to him was made public, the nomination of Mr. Field became impossible. The natural course obviously was for the President to assume that Secretary Chase had suggested him in ignorance of the objections now urged against him; to request the secretary to withdraw Mr. Field and make another nomination. But there had already been friction between the President and the secretary on the subject of nominations; the latter insisting that as he was held responsible for the administration of the Treasury, he should hold the unrestricted power of appointment and removal. The President conceded his claim, but maintained that it should be reasonably exercised, and that he should not be requested to make an appointment to an office in a state the whole congressional delegation of which opposed it, which would prove injurious to the party, or which was contrary to the traditions of the administration. In other instances the secretary had shown himself unwilling to admit even these restrictions, and in the case of one appointment made against the wishes of the Republicans of a state, and rejected by the Senate, he threatened to resign his office unless the President renominated the rejected candidate a second time. Although the difficulty in the case referred to was compromised, the President anticipated that Secretary Chase would insist upon Mr. Field's appointment, notwithstanding all the objections—an opinion in which he was confirmed by the fact that the secretary neither called upon nor communicated with him after some of the New York Republicans had remonstrated against the nomination to Mr. Chase in person.

After twenty-four hours' delay the President, waiving all ceremony, sent a polite note to the Treasury asking his Secretary *to oblige him* by sending him the nomination of some one who was not objectionable to the senators from New York. Instead of withdrawing Mr. Field's name, Secretary Chase replied by note, asking for an interview. When two parties are seated actually in sight of, and begin to write formal notes to each other, they are neither very likely nor very desirous to agree. The President declined the interview, on the ground that the difference between them did not lie within the range of a conversation. In the meantime the ingenuity of Mr. Field himself devised a way out of the difficulty. Finding that he would lose the appointment, he brought certain Democratic influences to bear to induce Mr. Cisco temporarily to withdraw his resignation, so that he (Field) might take a place in the New York office, nominally under Mr. Cisco, but really to prepare the way for his own appointment after the adjournment of Congress, and when the defeat of Mr. Lincoln should have been indicated by the early fall elections. Mr. Cisco unexpectedly complied, and the subject of contention was for the moment apparently removed.

Secretary Chase had many subordinates who regarded it as their duty to magnify his office and exalt his name. He was firmly of opinion that no one but himself could maintain the national credit; these subordinates assured him that such was the prevailing opinion, and it had become an article of faith in the department. He had no doubt whatever that the President had embraced it. He believed that his offer of resignation would create a general public demand that he should continue at the head of the Treasury, and upon a recent occasion the President had confirmed his belief in that respect by urgently requesting him to change his purpose to resign. Although there was no adequate occasion for it, he thought the present an excellent opportunity to repeat both the resignation and his former experience. He, therefore, again tendered his resignation, accompanying it with an intimation that the failure to nominate Mr. Field had rendered his position one of embarrassment, difficulty, and painful responsibility.

The resignation was written and forwarded on the 29th of June. It was not unexpected to President Lincoln, and he dealt with it with wise deliberation. During the day he requested me to call at the White House at the close of business. I found him undisturbed, and apparently in a happy frame of mind.

"I have sent for you," he said, "to ask you a question. How long can the Treasury be 'run' under an acting appointment? Whom can I appoint who will not take the opportunity to run the engine off the track, or do any other damage?"

I was too much troubled and surprised to answer him directly. "Mr. President," I exclaimed, "you will not let so small a matter as this New York appointment separate yourself and Governor Chase? Do not, I beg of you! Tell me where the trouble lies, and let me see if I cannot arrange it."

"No; it is past arrangement," he said. "I feel relieved since I have settled the question. I would not restore what they call the *status quo* if I could."

"But," I continued, "think of the country, of the Treasury, of the consequences! I do not for a moment excuse the secretary. His nomination of Field was most unaccountable to me. But Secretary Chase, with all his faults, is a great financier. His administration of the Treasury has been a financial wonder. Who can fill his place? There is not a man in the Union who can do it. If the national credit goes under, the Union goes with it. I repeat it—Secretary Chase is to-day a national necessity."

"How mistaken you are!" he quietly observed. "Yet it is not strange; I used to have similar notions. No! If we should all be turned out to-morrow, and could come back here in a week, we should find our places filled by a lot of fellows doing just as well as we did, and in many instances better. As the Irishman said, 'In this country one man is as good as another; and, for the matter of that, very often a great deal better.' No; *this government does not depend upon the life of any man,*" he said, impressively. "But you have not answered my question. There"—pointing to the table—"is Chase's resignation. I shall write its acceptance as soon as you have told me how much time I can take to hunt up another secretary."

"The Treasury can be run under an acting appointment

two or three days," I answered. "It ought not to be run for a day. There is an unwritten law of the department that an acting secretary should do nothing but current business. No one whom you would be likely to appoint would consciously violate it."

"Whom shall I appoint acting secretary?" he asked. "I have thought it would be scarcely proper to name one of the assistant secretaries after their chief is out."

"If you ask my opinion," I replied, "I should advise the appointment of the first assistant. I fear the effect of this resignation upon the country, and it would be unwise to increase its evils by departing from the usual course. An intimation from you that nothing but current business should be transacted will certainly be respected."

"That seems sensible; I thank you for the suggestion," he said. "But I shall have to put on my thinking-cap at once, and find a successor to Chase."

"Where is the man?" I exclaimed. "Mr. President, this is worse than another Bull Run defeat. Pray, let me go to Secretary Chase and see if I cannot induce him to withdraw his resignation. Its acceptance now might cause a financial panic."

I shall carry the memory of his next words as long as I live. Every time I think of them Mr. Lincoln will seem to grow greater as a man—to be the greatest American who ever lived. Consider the circumstances. The country was in the fiercest throes of civil war; the President was weighted with the heaviest responsibilities; his Secretary of the Treasury was tendering his resignation when there was no good excuse for the act, manifestly to embarrass him and to increase his difficulties. Then weigh these words:

"I will tell you," he said, leaning back in his chair,

and carelessly throwing one of his long legs over the other, "how it is with Chase. It is the easiest thing in the world for a man to fall into a bad habit. Chase has fallen into two bad habits. One is that to which I have often referred. He thinks he has become indispensable to the country; that his intimate friends know it, and he cannot comprehend why the country does not understand it. He also thinks he ought to be President; he has no doubt whatever about that. It is inconceivable to him why people have not found it out; why they don't, as one man, rise up and say so. He is, as you say, an able financier; as you think, without saying so, he is a great statesman, and, at the bottom, a patriot. Ordinarily he discharges a public trust, the duties of a public office, with great ability—with greater ability than any man I know. Mind, I say *ordinarily*, for these bad habits seem to have spoiled him. They have made him irritable, uncomfortable, so that he is never perfectly happy unless he is thoroughly miserable, and able to make everybody else just as uncomfortable as he is himself. He knows that the nomination of Field would displease the Unionists of New York, would delight our enemies, and injure our friends. He knows that I could not make it without seriously offending the strongest supporters of the government in New York, and that the nomination would not strengthen him anywhere or with anybody. Yet he resigns because I will not make it. He is either determined to annoy me, or that I shall pat him on the shoulder and coax him to stay. I don't think I ought to do it. I will not do it. I will take him at his word."

Here he made a long pause. His mobile face wore a speaking expression, and indicated that he was thinking earnestly; but, with perfect coolness, he continued: "And yet there is not a man in the Union who would make as good a chief justice as Chase." There was another pause; his plain, homely face was illuminated as he added, "And, if I have the opportunity, I will make him Chief Justice of the United States."

I thought at the time, and I have never since changed the opinion, that a man who could form such a just estimate and avow such a purpose in relation to another who had just performed a gratuitous act of personal annoyance intended to add to his responsibilities—already the greatest which any American had ever undertaken —who seemed wholly incapable of any thought of punishment or even reproof, must move upon a higher plane and be influenced by loftier motives than any man I had before met with. In the entire interview there was not an indication of passion or prejudice; there was a complete elimination of himself from the situation. There was nothing but the impartiality of a just judge, the disinterestedness of a patriot, the stoicism of a philosopher. I was silenced, and about to take my leave, when he said:

"Well, then, I understand I can take three days of grace. In that time I shall find somebody who will fit the notch and satisfy the nation. Perhaps I shall find him to-night. My best thoughts always come in the night. As soon as I find him, you shall know. I must first write my acceptance of Chase's resignation."

On the following day, June 30th, the President sent the nomination of ex-Governor Tod, of Ohio, as Secretary of the Treasury to the Senate for confirmation. There is no occasion now to inquire after his motives. Undoubtedly, his first thought was of an Ohio man, his opinion being settled that it was better not to select a secretary from any of the Atlantic states. The nomination was not well received, and it was a relief to his friends when, during the evening, Mr. Tod, by telegraph, peremptorily declined it.

Before sunrise the next day I was again sent for. I rode to the White House in the dawning light of an early summer morning, and found the President in his waistcoat, trousers, and slippers. He had evidently just left his bed, and had not taken time to dress himself. As I entered the familiar room, he said, in a cheerful, satisfied voice:

"I have sent for you to let you know that we have got a Secretary of the Treasury. If your sleep has been disturbed, you have time for a morning nap. You will like to meet him when the department opens."

"I am, indeed, glad to hear it," I said. "But who is he?"

"Oh, you will like the appointment, so will the country, so will everybody. It is the best appointment possible. Strange that I should have had any doubt about it. What have you to say to Mr. Fessenden?"

"He would be an eminently proper appointment," I answered. "The chairman of the Senate Committee on Finance; perfectly familiar with all our financial legislation, a strong, able man, and a true friend of the Union. He is also next in the direct line of promotion. But he will not accept. His health is frail, and his present position suits him. There is not one chance in a thousand of his acceptance."

"He will accept; have no fear on that account. I have just notified him of his appointment, and I expect him every moment."

At this moment the door suddenly opened, and Mr. Fessenden almost burst into the room, without being announced. His thin face was colorless; there was intense excitement in his voice and movements.

"I cannot! I will not! I should be a dead man in a week. I am a sick man now. I cannot accept this appointment, for which I have no qualifications. You, Mr. President, ought not to ask me to do it. Pray relieve me by saying that you will withdraw it. I repeat, I cannot and will not accept it."

The President rose from his chair, approached Mr. Fessenden, and threw his arm around his neck. It may seem ludicrous, but, as I saw that long and apparently unstiffened limb winding like a cable about the small neck of the senator from Maine, I wondered how many times the arm would encircle it. His voice was serious and emphatic, but without any assumption of solemnity, as he said:

"Fessenden, since I have occupied this place, every appointment I have made upon my own judgment has proved to be a good one. I do not say the best that could have been made, but good enough to answer the purpose. All the mistakes I have made have been in cases where I have permitted my own judgment to be overruled by that of others. Last night I saw my way clear to appoint you Secretary of the Treasury. I do not think you have any right to tell me you will not accept the place. I believe that the suppression of the rebellion has been decreed by a higher power than any represented by us, and that the Almighty is using his own means to that end. You are one of them. It is as much your duty to accept as it is mine to appoint. Your nomination is now on the way from the State Department, and in a few minutes it will be here. It will be in the Senate at noon, you will be immediately and unanimously confirmed, and by one o'clock to-day you must be signing warrants in the Treasury."

Mr. Fessenden was intellectually a strong man, one of

the last men to surrender his own judgment to the will of another, but he made no effort to resist the President's appeal. He cast his eyes upon the floor, and murmured, "Well, perhaps I ought to think about it," and turned to leave the room.

"No," said the President, "this matter is settled here and now. I am told that it is very necessary that a secretary should act to-day. You must enter upon your duties to-day. I will assure you that, if a change becomes desirable hereafter, I will be ready and willing to make it. But, unless I misunderstand the temper of the public, your appointment will be so satisfactory that we shall have no occasion to deal with any question of change for some time to come."

At this point the conversation terminated, and all the persons present separated. The result is well known. Mr. Fessenden's appointment was entirely satisfactory, and the affairs of the Treasury went on so smoothly that no change in the financial policy of Secretary Chase was attempted; and from this time until the resignation of Mr. Fessenden there was no further friction between the Treasury Department and the Executive.

Chief Justice Taney died in the following October. The friends of Secretary Chase immediately put forth the strongest effort possible to secure for him an appointment to the vacancy. They were assured that no such effort was necessary; that he would receive the appointment without asking for it. They would not, and could not, accept the assurance. They said that Mr. Chase had made some very harsh observations about Mr. Lincoln, which must have come to his knowledge; that nothing would induce him to overlook those remarks, unless there was practically a united demand from all the leaders of the Republican party for the appointment.

I am sincerely grateful that I had at that time so true an appreciation of Mr. Lincoln's character that I knew that such remarks would make no impression whatever upon his mind. I was confirmed in my opinion by the information I received of the experience of the friend of another candidate who attempted to improve his chances by repeating to the President some of these remarks of his former secretary. The President at first replied that the secretary was probably justified in his observations, but when the advocate pressed the point more earnestly, he received a reproof from the President which permanently suppressed further effort in that direction.

The appointment was made in November, as speedily as was appropriate after the vacancy occurred. The only direction of the President I ever consciously violated was when, after the appointment, I had the satisfaction of informing the chief justice that his appointment had been decided upon on the 30th of the previous June, after which the President had never contemplated any other. Not many days afterwards I was shown a copy of a letter to the President, written by Mr. Chase, in which he expressed his gratitude for the appointment, which, he said, he desired more than any other. Thus was the *entente cordiale* restored between these two eminent Americans, never again to be broken or interrupted. Among the sorrowing hearts around the dying bed of the republic's greatest President, there was none more affectionate than that of his chief justice and his first Secretary of the Treasury.

XLIII.

THE CAMPAIGN AGAINST WASHINGTON IN 1864.—THE BATTLE OF MONOCACY.

THE demonstration against the city of Washington by a Confederate army under General Early in July, 1864, was one of the important events of the war. It has originated so many issues of fact that the search for its true history has become obstructed by serious difficulties. There were reasons at the time why the Federal authorities did not wish to magnify the danger with which it threatened the capital, and after the retreat of his army General Early seems to have been influenced by motives acting in the same direction. Since the close of the war, the event has caused an extended discussion. On one side, the tendency has been to treat the fights on the Monocacy and before Washington as lively skirmishes rather than real battles, while General Early has persistently denied that the capture of Washington formed any part of the plan of his campaign.

I was in the Treasury of the United States and had a lively interest in the movements of General Early. I saw as much as any civilian of the movements of our own forces. I witnessed the fighting in front of Fort Stevens, and I know whether the terror and consternation existed which General Early supposes his so-called *feint* to have created. I think I am able to give pertinent evidence upon several issues which the Confederates have raised.

In June, 1864, all the available troops in the vicinity of Washington had been sent to General Grant, who was pressing Richmond by the slow and sure processes of a siege. A mixed collection of home-guards, convalescents, and department employés, with a very small number of veterans, was left in the defences of Washington and Baltimore, which was intended to hold them until reinforced from the Army of the Potomac, in case either city should be threatened by a Confederate army. At Point Lookout, below the capital, on the Maryland bank of the river, was a camp of about twenty thousand rebel prisoners, all veterans made vigorous by rest and Federal rations, who were much wanted by General Lee to recruit his army.

The signal service between the Confederates within the city of Washington and their friends outside the defences was perfect. Flags by day, lights and rockets by night, kept General Lee fully advised of everything important for him to know. He was as thoroughly informed of the defences of Washington, and the number and effectiveness of the forces by which they were garrisoned, as General Grant or any officer of the Federal army. Grant having undertaken a regular siege of Richmond which would occupy much time, General Lee represented to President Davis "the great benefit that might be drawn from the release of these (rebel) prisoners," and his ability to "devote to this purpose the whole of the Maryland troops." "I think I can maintain our lines against General Grant," he had written, "but I am at a loss where to find a proper leader." "Of those connected with this army, I think Colonel Bradley Johnson the most suitable." Colonel Johnson was a native of Maryland, perfectly familiar with the country between the lines of the Baltimore and Ohio, and Northern railroads, with Point Lookout, and in fact with the entire topography of Maryland.

It was supposed at the time that General Lee, having a full knowledge of the details of the situation, devised from his point of view an effective campaign, and that he determined to send a third of his army, under General Early, down the Shenandoah Valley by forced marches, across the Potomac, into Maryland. There a division of cavalry, under Colonel Bradley T. Johnson, would press on to Point Lookout and release the prisoners, guarded by a few colored soldiers; destroying the Baltimore and Ohio and the Northern railroads on his way. Early with his army would swoop down upon and capture Washington before any troops from the Army of the Potomac could reach it. He would clothe and arm the prisoners from his captured plunder, and with his army thus raised to over forty thousand veterans inside the defences, he could compel Grant to raise the siege of Richmond, and would be able to hold Washington against the whole Army of the Potomac.

We also supposed that this campaign only failed of success by a narrow margin. It was thought that of his three corps of infantry, General Lee sent the second, or Stonewall Jackson's veterans, with forty field-guns, a large body of cavalry, and Breckinridge's division of infantry, in all not less than twenty-five thousand men, under General Early, on the mission. That the latter, moving down the valley without resistance or delay, crossed the Potomac into Maryland, and on the 7th of July was within forty-five miles of Washington; that up to this point all went well with the Confederate army. We believed that Early then sent Bradley T. Johnson, from his left wing, on the mission to Point Lookout; but the stubborn resistance of General Lew. Wallace, and less than six thousand men at the Monocacy River, cost General Early a loss of over two thousand men, and, what was of infinitely greater consequence to him, the loss of two days, the 8th and 9th of July, after which, abandoning his wounded on the morning of the 10th, he moved to Rockville, where he halted within a few miles of the defences of Washington. But instead of assaulting them on the morning of the 11th, he postponed the attack until daylight of the 12th, when, finding the veterans of the Sixth Corps in the trenches, he abandoned the campaign, recalled Johnson on his way to Point Lookout, and lost no time in withdrawing his invading army to the south side of the Potomac.

It was not until some years after the close of the war that the Confederate leaders undertook to correct what had been up to that time the general conclusion of students of our war history. In 1877, General Long, Early's chief of artillery, and later the biographer of General Lee, published his account of Early's campaign, from which we learn that the capture of Washington and the release of the prisoners at Point Lookout were not its objectives. "Its object was simply a diversion in favor of General Lee's operations about Richmond," and "General Early was too prudent and sagacious to attempt an enterprise with a force of eight thousand men which, if successful, would be of temporary benefit." The account also informs us that, "after spreading dismay for miles in every direction, . . . Early proceeded to within cannon-shot of Washington, remained in observation long enough to give his movement full time to produce its greatest effect, and then withdrew in the face of a large army and recrossed the Potomac," thus ending "a campaign remarkable for having accomplished more in proportion to the force employed, and for having given less public satisfaction, than any other campaign of the war."

Sixteen years after the war, General Early made public his "version of the facts" of this campaign. His article of fifteen printed octavo pages does not once mention the prisoners at Point Lookout, and is largely devoted to an effort to show that his army was so very small, and the Union force opposed to him so very large, that, using his words, "an attempt to capture Washington at any time after my arrival was simply preposterous. If I had been able to reach Washington sooner, Grant would have sent troops to its rescue sooner, and hence there was never any prospect of my capturing that city. It was not General Lee's orders or expectation that I should take Washington. His order was that I should threaten the city, and when I suggested to him the probability of my being able to capture it, he said that it would be impossible."

There are several other statements in General Early's article which we shall hereafter compare with undisputed facts, and leave others to form their own conclusions. Enough has been quoted from it to present the principal issue. Was the real object of this campaign the release of the Confederate prisoners and the capture of Washington, or was it merely a scare, a diversion in favor of General Lee, restricted both in plan and execution to a mere threat against the capital?

The strongest witness against the General Early of 1881 is General Early in 1864.

On the 14th of July, only two days after his retreat from the defences of Washington, General Early, at Leesburg, made his first report to General Lee. It was before any question had arisen, when all the facts were fresh in his mind. In it, after giving his reasons for retreating, he says: "He (Johnson) *was on his way to Point Lookout*, when my determination to retire made his recall necessary. . . . *I am sorry I did not succeed in capturing Washington and releasing our prisoners at Point Lookout*, but the latter was impracticable after I determined to retire from Washington." After this statement, it seems a waste of words for General Early to deny that the capture of Washington and the release of the prisoners were seriously intended, and that they were the substantial objects of the campaign.

The importance of a battle is determined by its ultimate consequences rather than its immediate results. If that fought on the Monocacy did delay General Early, so as to save the capital from his assault and probable capture, it was one of the decisive battles of the world, and, with the events which immediately followed it, deserves a more complete account than it has hitherto received. In his "Personal Memoirs," referring to Early's retreat, General Grant says: "There is no telling how much this result was contributed to by General Lew. Wallace's leading what might well be considered almost a forlorn hope. If Early had been but one day earlier, he might have entered the capital before the arrival of the reinforcements I had sent. Whether the delay caused by the battle amounted to a day or not, General Wallace contributed on this occasion, by the defeat of the troops under him, a greater benefit to the cause than often falls to the lot of a commander of an equal force to render by means of a victory."

It is singular that the numerical strength of General Early's army has never been given. General Early must know what it was. He argues at great length to show that it was very small; why does he not give the figures? It was an army of veterans, trained by Stonewall Jackson; it was opposed by raw and undisciplined forces, with the single exception of the Sixth Corps. In such a case numbers are a secondary consideration. General Geary joined Sherman in Tennessee leading a division 12,000 strong. On the "march to the sea" its numbers were only 3300, and yet in General Geary's opinion the effective strength of his division was never greater than when it marched into the city of Savannah. As the Confederate leaders, in speaking of the strength of Early's army, deal only in the most general statements, and we are never to know from them what it was, we are compelled to rely upon estimates and secondary evidence. Where numbers are given on all occasions previous to 1864, the Second Corps was the largest of the three comprising the Army of Northern Virginia. With its high reputation there is no reason for supposing that its strength was relatively reduced. In addition to the Second Corps, General Early had Breckinridge's division of infantry, forty pieces of artillery, and a body of cavalry large enough to serve the purposes of his army, after he had detached Johnson with a force deemed sufficient to release the prisoners at Point Lookout.

The information received from General Sigel by General Wallace was that Early was advancing with an army of 30,000 men. After fighting him the whole day of the 9th, in part for the purpose of developing his force, General Wallace was of opinion that it numbered over 18,000, exclusive of Breckinridge's infantry and the entire force of artillery and cavalry. Medical Inspector Johnson, who was within the Confederate lines at Monocacy during the 9th and 10th of July, reported that they estimated their strength at 25,000, exclusive of a cavalry force of 5000 to 6000. Until the Confederate officers, who know, give the details of their own forces, no injustice will be done by placing the strength of this invading army at 25,000 men.

The Monocacy is a crooked river, which runs in a southerly direction into the Potomac. About three miles west of it is the city of Frederick, and three or four miles farther west is a range of hills extending from the Potomac in a northerly direction, called the Catoctin Mountains. The Washington Pike crossed the river by a wooden bridge, and the Baltimore Pike by what was called the "stone bridge." The railroad crossed within a quarter of a mile of the lower of these two bridges, which were about two and a half miles from each other.

As soon as Wallace learned that a Confederate army had entered Maryland, and that its cavalry was approaching Frederick, he removed his little force so as to delay the Confederate advance. He knew that every hour of such delay was an hour gained for reinforcements to reach Washington from the Army of the Potomac. Accordingly, on the 5th of July, he pushed his 2600 men out of Baltimore by railroad to the east bank of the Monocacy, hoping to hold the bridges against any attack of cavalry.

On the 5th of July, General Grant had sent the Third Division of the Sixth Corps, under General Ricketts, to reinforce General Wallace at Baltimore. When this division reached the place of embarkation, on the James, Quartermaster General Pitkin, as a favor to his friend and fellow-Vermonter, Colonel Henry, of the Tenth Vermont, gave his detachment, which also comprised the One Hundred and Sixth New York, the fastest steamer, a favor which also secured to the two regiments severe service and hard fighting. The detachment reached Baltimore in advance of the rest of the division, and hurried on board a train of freight cars, which arrived at Frederick at daybreak on the morning of the 8th.

General Wallace informed Colonel Henry that the

Confederate signal officers were watching from the Catoctin hills, behind which Early was gathering his forces for an advance, and that his object being delay, he desired to make a show of as strong a force as possible. Colonel Henry, therefore, advanced beyond Frederick to the foot of the mountain, where he marched and countermarched from hill to hill, threw up mock breastworks, withdrew his men under cover, and marched them to other positions, showing his regiment in different places until his men, who were not in the secret, thought he must have become insane. About six o'clock General Wallace was informed that a heavy body of infantry was moving in a direction to obtain control of the Washington Pike and endanger his lines of retreat. He accordingly withdrew from Frederick to the line of the Monocacy River. Before the Tenth Vermont could be withdrawn the Confederate cavalry had possession of the pike between Frederick and the river, only three miles distant, and Colonel Henry was compelled to make a long circuit until he reached the stone bridge, and then march down the river to the wooden bridge, where he was ordered to report. This march of twelve miles in the night so delayed him that it was daybreak before he reached his position.

The second detachment of the Sixth Corps had, in the meantime, arrived. The cowardly desertion of the railroad agent and the telegraph operator left the rest of the division at Monrovia, eight miles away, where orders could not reach them, and they were thus prevented from participating in the battle.

At early dawn General Wallace made his dispositions for battle. His right formed an extended line, two miles long, from the railroad bridge to the stone bridge, and was placed under the command of General Tyler. Colonel

Brown, with his command of ten companies from the One Hundred and Forty-ninth and One Hundred and Fifty-ninth Ohio, and the company of mounted infantry under Captain Lieb, was posted at the stone bridge, with orders to hold it; for upon the holding of that bridge depended the security of the right flank and the line of retreat to Baltimore. The remaining portions of General Wallace's original force were posted along the river above the railroad.

On the left, where the principal attack would probably be made, were placed the 3350 veterans under General Ricketts, in a line which reached from the railroad to a point below the wooden bridge. The end of the line was held by the Tenth Vermont, under Colonel Henry, and next to it was its companion regiment on many bloody fields, the One Hundred and Sixth New York, under Colonel Seward. Colonel Clendenin's cavalry were still farther down the river to watch the ford.

A line of skirmishers, seventy-five men of the Tenth Vermont, under Captain Davis, and two hundred men of the Potomac Home Brigade, under Captain Brown, extended in a semicircle on the west side of the river, below the wooden to a point above the railroad bridge. It should have been under the command of a lieutenant-colonel, whose name is not mentioned by Vermonters, because on that day he kept away from his command. Captain Brown and his men were wholly inexperienced; he surrendered the command to Captain Davis, whose men held the centre of the line where it crossed a hill, from which the field on the left was in full view.

The battle opened early. At half-past eight a body of Confederates came down the pike, directly upon the Federal skirmish line. Captain Davis and his men opened upon them as soon as they came within range, and the enemy were handsomely repulsed.

The Confederates now brought up their artillery, and firing and sharp skirmishing began all along the line. About half-past ten the first charge of the enemy was made. A body of Confederates moved around the left flank of the Northern army, forded the river, and advanced up the eastern bank, appearing from the woods in line of battle. General Ricketts was compelled to change front to the left, with his right resting on the river, thus bringing his line under an enfilading fire from the enemy's artillery. Although he formed his whole force into a single line, that of the enemy was so long that it overlapped it. Every man on the left was thus put into the fight, not one being held in reserve.

The enemy's first line was met with a heavy fire from the Tenth Vermont and the One Hundred and Sixth New York. Several times the line was broken, and their colors fell. The efforts of the Confederates to rally and re-form their line were ineffectual, and they were compelled to retreat into the woods, defeated. Within an hour the enemy advanced his second line, stronger and more numerous than the first, and with the steady step and firm bearing of veterans. But they could not move the veterans of the Sixth Corps. Partially protected by the Thomas house and the cut through which the road passed, they poured a fire into the Confederate line which nothing human could withstand. For a half-hour the line held its position until the ground was covered with the fallen, and then again retreated.

General Wallace and his staff witnessed the battle from a hill in the rear of the line opposite the railroad. He knew that he was blocking the way of an army which must push him aside at any cost, and that the next advance would be in force large enough to be irresistible. But he was there to stay, to obstruct the Confederate advance as long as he possibly could, and the conduct of Ricketts's veterans showed him that all that could be done by three thousand men they would do. His order to retire was not given.

There was now the hour or two of sharp skirmishing and artillery fire which usually precedes a charge. General Gordon, with his entire division, had crossed at the ford, and moved up the river, bringing with him the shattered remains of the defeated brigades. About three o'clock they again began to emerge from the woods. First came a heavy line of skirmishers, followed by a first, and shortly by a second, line of battle. For a full hour the fight went on, over one of the bloodiest fields of the war. The Confederate loss was by far the heavier, for they were on the open field, while the Sixth Corps veterans were in part protected. As the first and second were successively repulsed after stoutly maintaining the fierce contest, the third and heaviest Confederate line came out of the woods down the hill behind which they made their formation.

General Wallace saw that it was time to go. He gave the order to retire on the Baltimore Pike, and the greater portion of his left wing slowly obeyed the command. But the Tenth Vermont and One Hundred and Sixth New York, on the extreme left of the line, were shut off from Wallace's view by an intervening hill, and the order did not reach them. Several men were sent to them with orders, but were all shot down by the fire which swept the entire distance to be crossed. The regiments were out of ammunition, except as they borrowed it from the boxes of the fallen, and there was no ammunition train from which they could be supplied. But they stood their ground, fighting and checking the advance of the enemy, until their fire slackened, and the advancing line had almost encircled them.

At last a mounted orderly dashed over the hill in their rear, galloped within speaking distance of Colonel Henry, and shouted, "General Wallace says, 'For God's sake, bring your regiment out, if you can, to the Baltimore Pike.'" It was a difficult order to obey. In their rear was a high board fence, at the foot of a steep hill covered by a corn-field. On all the other sides were lines of advancing Confederates. The Vermonters scale the fence and ascend the hill, swept by screaming shells and showers of bullets. Near the top the color-sergeant gives out, and declares that he can go no farther. Strong arms seize both sergeant and colors, and bear them onward. The Confederates, yelling to the Vermonters to halt and surrender, follow them half-way up the ascent, but they cannot stand the pace, and give up the pursuit. Colonel Henry re-forms the remnant of his regiment, safe for the time, outside the line of fire. Their comrades of the One Hundred and Sixth New York, placed in the line on their right, pass around the hill through a tempest of missiles hurled upon them from three sides, and those who do not fall escape to the rear, where for the time we leave them, and turn to the right of the Federal line.

When the order to retreat is given, the stone bridge on the Baltimore Pike becomes all-important, for its loss is the loss of Wallace's line of retreat. A large body of Confederates are charging down the Pike from the west, to hurl themselves against Colonel Brown and his ten Ohio companies. General Tyler, without waiting for orders, gathers up a few men along the river, and rushes to Brown's support. The Confederates halt and recoil before the hot and heavy fire. General Wallace gallops up, and shouts to Colonel Brown, through the roar of musketry, that the bridge "must be held until his last regiment has cleared the country road by which the army is retreating, and has passed down the Pike towards Newmarket and Baltimore." Brown and Tyler, with their men, keep the bridge until five o'clock, when the rear of the last retiring regiment is well on its way down the Pike to Newmarket. By this time the Confederates have surrounded them. By the ordinary rules of fighting, they are captured. But the men keep their ranks, and, with Colonel Brown, fight their way through the encircling line. Then Tyler and his staff dash into the woods and escape.

The army has now all retreated, except the skirmish-line on the west bank of the river. These skirmishers have had a lively day. Their line of retreat was by the wooden bridge, but this was burned about half-past ten, and, before it was fired, such of Captain Brown's men as were on the left crossed to the east bank. During the long day of fighting, nearly all of Captain Brown's command on the right of the line quietly passed over the railroad bridge without waiting for orders, leaving a few of their comrades with Captain Brown and Captain Davis, with his seventy-five Vermonters, to hold the Pike and do the fighting. Captain Davis, in the centre of his line, occupies the crest of a hill, from which he sees all the fighting on Ricketts's left. During the skirmish which precedes the last attack, he sends a soldier to his lieutenant-colonel, who should be present for orders. The soldier finds him far in the rear, and returns with the inspiring message that that officer "supposed Captain Davis got off before the bridge was burned."

Earlier in the day an incident has happened here which had a share in the safety of the capital. When General

Ricketts changed front on the left, to meet the first Confederate charge, he opened a gap in the line of defence opposite the railroad bridge. Wallace has no force which he can send to fill it. About eleven o'clock General Wallace, from the hill on which he overlooks the field, discovers a body of Confederates stealing down the river under cover of the bushes towards the railroad bridge. It is a very exciting time. He has no men to despatch to the bridge—in a few minutes a stream of the enemy will be pouring over the bridge through the gap, which will cut his line in the middle, and inevitably cause his defeat. The Confederates are perfectly concealed from the skirmish-line, and are within a hundred yards of the bridge. They are about to make the rush, when a volley of musketry seems to rise out of the ground, and is poured into their very faces. Many of them fall, others reel and hesitate; another volley is fired into them; they turn and rush to the rear. Davis has had his eye on the bridge, for he may have occasion to use it. He has anticipated this movement, and sent a small detachment from his little force to lie concealed in the bushes and watch it. They have watched it to a purpose.

Late in the afternoon the position of Captain Davis becomes (to use his own expression) "peculiar." He has seen the colors of his own regiment borne up the hill and over it to the rear, followed by the regiment and a crowd of pursuing Confederates. As far as he can see, the entire Federal line has retired. He was ordered to hold the position where he was placed; it is not the custom of his men to change position without orders. But the enemy is pouring down the railroad, and in a few moments will sweep him into the river. No man of his seventy-five will move without an order. The moment has come when he has no alternative. He gives the order, his men form, and march on the double-quick to the railroad bridge, which has no floor, and across which they step from tie to tie. The pursuing Confederates press after with shouts of "Halt and surrender!" They pour their volleys into the backs of the Vermonters from a distance of fifty yards. The dead and wounded fall into the water forty feet below, one of the latter to survive the battle and the war. The Confederates overtake, and actually seize and capture four or five of the little company. The survivors reach the eastern bank and rush into the bushes. But they keep together, and follow the retreating army, leaving more than a third of their number upon the bloody field. Davis, who is a man of slight physique, has used up all his strength, and is marched to the bivouac of his regiment, *sound asleep*, between two stronger soldiers.

Twelve miles from the field all the detachments of the army have come together. They wheel into a convenient field and encamp for the night. Wallace lies down upon Henry's blanket, and before both fall asleep finds time to tell him that he is "as cool and brave a man as ever stood on a battle-field."

There were no prisoners in this battle except such as were captured by the actual laying on of Confederate hands. But Wallace left fully one third of his entire force on the field, and the thirty-three hundred and fifty veterans lost sixteen hundred of their number. Early reported a Confederate loss of only six or seven hundred. But there is strong circumstantial evidence that it was much heavier. In all the fighting the Union veterans were protected by natural defences, while the attacking Confederates had to advance for seven hundred yards over the open field. More than four hundred, so severely wounded that Early - could not move, but left them behind in Frederick, indicate a greater loss; and a Virginian, with whom Early made his headquarters at Leesburgh, declared that the Confederate general told him that his loss exceeded three thousand.

Perhaps no Southern leader could better judge of the severity of a battle from personal experience than General Gordon. In his report, made within two weeks after the battle, he said: "I desire to state a fact of which I was an eye-witness, and which, for its rare occurrence and the evidence it affords of the sanguinary character of this struggle, I consider worthy of official mention. One portion of the enemy's second (?) line extended along a branch, from which he was driven, leaving many dead and wounded in the water and upon the banks. This position was in turn occupied by a portion of Evans's brigade in the attack upon the enemy's third (?) line. So profuse was the flow of blood from the killed and wounded of both these forces that *it reddened the stream for more than one hundred yards below.*"

Although General Early had a heavy force of cavalry, he made no attempt to pursue the retreating army of General Wallace. His objective point was Washington. The fighting had occupied the day. In his report from Leesburgh, he wrote that he was "compelled to leave about four hundred wounded men in Frederick *because they could not be transported.*" He had no lack of transportation at this time, for he had captured horses and wagons enough to supply his army. He left these four hundred because they were too severely wounded to endure transportation, and took with him such as could bear the journey. There was no force now to obstruct his march. The Washington Pike was open—a good road through a country teeming with abundance. He compelled the small city of Frederick, under threat of

26

the torch, to pay him two hundred thousand dollars in good " Northern Federal money," and " brought off over one thousand horses." " On the morning of the 10th [we use General Early's words], I moved towards Washington, taking the route by Rockville, and then turning to the left, to get on the Seventh Street Pike. The day was very hot, and the roads exceedingly dusty, but we marched thirty miles," which must have brought him, on the night of Sunday, the 10th of July, within sight of the defences of the capital. " On the morning of the 11th we continued the march, but the day was so excessively hot, even at a very early hour in the morning, and the dust so dense, that many of the men fell by the way, and it became necessary to slacken our pace; nevertheless, when we reached the right of the enemy's fortifications, the men were almost completely exhausted, and not in condition to make the attack. Skirmishers were thrown out, and moved up to the vicinity of the fortifications." Here we leave him saying, "I determined at first to make an assault"—to observe that there were good grounds for the general conclusion from his forced marches, hot haste, and other indications, that General Early was not engaged in a mere theatrical display, but that he did seriously intend to attack Washington, and that the men who barred his advance for forty-eight hours performed a signal service, and earned the enduring gratitude of their countrymen, although they fought a losing battle on the Monocacy.

XLIV.
EARLY BEFORE WASHINGTON IN 1864.—BATTLE OF FORT STEVENS.

DURING Saturday and Sunday, July 9th and 10th, the Confederate sympathizers in Washington were anxiously listening for the sound of Early's guns. They knew his purpose, his strength, and the weakness of the city, of which he was expected to take possession without much resistance. The War Office certainly had all the information that Wallace could give them. It was a part of that information that about 25,000 veteran Confederate soldiers had passed the Monocacy on the pike leading to Washington, that they were marching rapidly in the direction of, and on Saturday evening were within thirty-five miles of, the capital. Of all this the loyal citizens knew nothing. The week closed on Saturday without their imagining that the city was in any danger, or that any thought for their personal safety was necessary. The story of Early's further movements will be given as its Washington aspect was presented.

It is true that for some days the summer atmosphere had been full of rumors of Confederate invasion. Every few hours a newspaper "extra" was announced. One had certain information that the Confederates had entered Maryland in force—that Washington and Baltimore were to be cut off from the North and captured—that the capital would be attacked within twelve hours. The next issue declared the rumor to be an idle scare, and that the only Confederates north of the Potomac were a few cavalrymen on a raid. It was the general opinion that the authorities would not expose the city to any danger, and that any considerable portion of the army of Northern Virginia would not be detached and sent on an expedition northward without the knowledge of General Grant. If he knew that such an expedition had been undertaken, he could certainly have sent a force to protect the capital against it. It was the third year of the war. In 1861 such reports would have disturbed us. Now, citizens had become in a measure rumor-proof, and went about their business as coolly as if there had not been a Confederate within a week's march of the city.

I had closed my house, and my family were living with me at Willard's for a few days before sending them to New England to pass the season of oppressive heat. On the morning of Monday, the 11th of July, we were taking a late breakfast. The morning papers had accounts of a *skirmish*, two days before, on the Monocacy, above Baltimore. They all agreed that it was only a skirmish, with no very important consequences. But the details appeared to indicate that several thousand men had been engaged, and that General Wallace had been severely handled.

Three army officers breakfasted with us; two of them were on their way to the front. They ridiculed the suggestion that any considerable force had been detached from Lee's army and sent northward without the knowledge of General Grant. If he knew it, he had acted accordingly. The rebels had quite enough to do in the vicinity of Richmond. Washington, they said, was in no more danger than Boston. I was inclined to the same opinion. So much had been said about the importance of protecting Washington, so many veteran regiments had been detained there when they were needed in the field, that it seemed impossible that the city should now be exposed to danger.

The third officer was the brigadier in command of the Invalid Corps, who had taken but little part in the conversation, and expressed no opinion. As we were about to separate, he observed to me that he was going to visit the outposts, that the morning was pleasant, and if I had nothing better to do, perhaps I would like to join his party. If so, he would have a horse ready for me at his quarters on Fifteenth Street opposite the Treasury at ten o'clock, at which hour he intended to start. I cordially accepted his invitation, and reported at his quarters at the appointed time.

The first part of this excursion was delightful. Mounted on spirited animals, preceded by a small escort of cavalry, we took the road towards Georgetown. The air was fresh and cool, the roses and flowering plants loaded the reviving breeze with their perfume, and the birds were singing in the trees which shaded the broad avenue, which was as quiet as I had ever seen it on the Sabbath. Bright-eyed children at play, ladies taking their morning walk, and all the other indications of summer life in the city, suggested thoughts of restful peace, which for the moment divested the mind of all remembrance of the miseries and anxieties of war.

We rode over the venerable pavements of Georgetown to its outskirts, now ascending a slight hill, now going down into a wooded valley, bathing our horses feet in the clear brooks which we forded. We passed through Tenallytown and out a short distance on the road beyond. On the summit of the highest ridge thereabouts we were halted by a picket-guard of a dozen men. The necessary words and salutes passed, the officer in command appeared and entered into conversation with our brigadier. To the latter's question whether this was the last picket, the officer gave an affirmative reply.

Sweeping the northern horizon, my eyes rested on the broad cleared hillside across the valley. It appeared to be the camp of an army. There were army-wagons, pieces of artillery, caissons, unharnessed horses, tethered near by, a few shelter tents, and all the paraphernalia of a camp in which the men were at rest. I could not clearly make out any of the flags. Very little calculation was necessary to show that the men numbered some thousands.

"Whose corps is that, general?" I asked, pointing in the direction of the camp.

"We think it is Early's, but do not certainly know. It may be Breckinridge's," he answered.

"Great heavens!" I exclaimed. "Do you mean to say that those are Confederates!"

"There is no possible doubt of that," he replied. "If you doubt it, you can satisfy yourself by riding down to their picket at the bottom of the valley. I am not sure that you will be permitted to return. I am going to show you another and a larger camp, if we can get within sight of the Blair mansion at Silver Springs."

"Thanks," I said, "I am not at all curious. General, I must ask you to excuse me for leaving you so unceremoniously. It has just occurred to me that I have a most important engagement at Willard's at this hour. I must keep it. I do not care to take a look at Silver Springs. Yonder view satisfies me, fully."

"I thought it would," he observed. "I saw that you did not comprehend the situation, and therefore invited you to ride out here and judge for yourself. I would like to have you make the circuit on the north side of the city. But that will take time, and I shall very probably find some of the roads obstructed. I can guess your appointment at Willard's. This may yet be a good day to send your family north—if they can get there? Yesterday would have been better."

"They would have gone three days ago if I had had any suspicion of that," I said, indicating the Confederate camp. "But tell me, what is your estimate of the Confederate force now before the city?"

"For some reason the War Office does not care to have that subject discussed. At daylight this morning I had reports from three independent sources. They agree substantially that Early has Ewell's old corps entire, and a part of another, numbering over 20,000 infantry, and forty guns, with about 6000 cavalry. The infantry and guns were counted by a scout before they left Maryland Heights. Wallace developed their force at Monocacy. He estimated it at over 20,000, besides the cavalry. One squadron under Bradley T. Johnson has gone around Baltimore to strike the railroads on the north. McCausland's and Rosser's cavalry are roaming over the country between this city and Baltimore. They can take the railroad any time they choose."

"Then the city is in great danger!" I said. "What good can come of concealing it?"

"There is but one way that it can be saved," he responded. "Grant must have sent men by steamer. The only question is whether they will arrive in time. I supposed Early would have attacked this morning. He is at Silver Springs now. We think he must have had a hard battle with Wallace day before yesterday, and is giving his men a rest. He will certainly attack to-night or to-morrow morning."

It was time for me to leave; I stood not on the order of my going. I did not draw rein until I reached the Treasury, whence I returned the tired horse to its quarters by a messenger.

The report at the close of business on Saturday lay on my office table. A glance at it showed me that every note and bond in the office had been sent to its destination by the mail of Saturday evening. I closed the door of my room again and started to leave the building. On my way out I called at the treasurer's office, which a man was just entering with a package of empty canvas mail-sacks. I found General Spinner, the treasurer, Mr. Tuttle, his cashier, and three or four of his principal clerks, engaged in filling mail sacks with Treasury notes and other securities. All were working with great earnestness and expedition.

"You are busy, general!" I observed. "I have just seen what convinces me that you are not wasting your time, that you are engaged in a work of necessity."

"I have not time to be angry!" he exclaimed. "Did the authorities give you any notice of our danger?"

"None whatever," I answered. "I have only this moment discovered it for myself."

"Nor did they to me. I have a small steamboat—no matter where. I can take any bonds or money you may have. I think it better to move in light-marching order, and to carry nothing but money or securities—if we decide to move!"

"Thank you, I have nothing of that description. I shall try and move my household by rail. I shall stay myself, and take whatever comes."

At the hotel our effects were literally dumped into our trunks by my direction, and my family prepared for instant movement. At the Baltimore and Ohio Railroad station, I learned that a train, just arrived, reported the road uninterrupted. Another train would leave for Philadelphia within an hour. Within less than two hours from my first view of the Confederate force we were all, together with two friends to whom I offered the opportunity, speeding northward at the rate of forty miles an hour. At Baltimore I left the rest of the party, having first written a despatch in cipher, which they were to send me if they reached Philadelphia. In due time I received it at the Fountain Hotel and knew they were out of harm's way.

This was the last train that passed over the railroad northward until the burned bridges were rebuilt after Early's retreat. The next train that left Washington was looted by Harry Gilmor's detachment of Johnson's cavalry. He had been a conductor on the railroad, and knew where to strike it. Upon this train were General Franklin, General D. W. C. Clarke, Executive Secretary of the Senate, with his family, and other prominent persons. Their trunks were rifled, and everything of value taken or destroyed. General Franklin adroitly escaped from the Confederates the same day of his capture.

During that evening I learned more about the fight on the Monocacy. There were wounded men at the station, and among them I found some Vermonters. They said that their regiment (the Tenth Vermont) had had some heavy fighting—had been compelled to retreat by sheer force of numbers, and was then at the Relay House, on the road to Washington. They could form no idea of the enemy's force except that it was very large, and as they were not pursued and the principal fight was in defence of the pike to Washington, they inferred that the Confederates were on the road to that city.

I called upon some acquaintances and spent the evening in walking about the city. I saw no evidences of "dismay or consternation." No one was fleeing northward. The train on which my family went received no rush of passengers, as would have been quite natural. But I did see many evidences of preparation and stern determination to fight and defend the city. The street windows of stores and dwellings were barred and being made secure. It was reported that General Wallace had returned to the city, that he was organizing and arming the volunteers for its defence, who were presenting themselves in great numbers.

Towards midnight I went to the Fountain Hotel, but not to sleep. The danger to the capital of the nation was too imminent; and at dawn I arose, went to the crowded station, and took the first train for Washington. I was the only passenger. At the way stations and road crossings the mounted Confederates were numerous, but as we were running into the city, which they regarded as already virtually in their hands, we were not molested.

At the depot in Washington a surprise awaited me. From the direction of the intersection of Pennsylvania Avenue and Seventh Street came the sound of enthusiastic cheering. I should not have been more surprised by an outburst of cheers from a funeral procession.

"What does this cheering mean?" I asked of the first colored cab driver I encountered.

"I reckon it's Gen'l Sedgwick's ole army, massa!" he replied. " Dey'se goin' out to hab a little talk with Gen'l Early dis mo'nin'. I reckon Gen'l Early can't wait for 'em. He's done gone souf, I reckon."

I made my way to Seventh Street and partially through the crowd. There was no mistake. Those sturdy veterans were marching with furled banners, to the beat of a single drum at the head of each regiment. Standing on the top of my carriage, I not only recognized the cross of the Sixth Corps, but also the faces of a lot of Vermonters. It was gratifying to see the citizens rushing into the ranks, as they rested on their arms, with baskets of eatables, buckets of water, and a hearty welcome to their deliverers. A Vermonter assured me that a large portion of the Sixth Corps was already at the front, and a part of the Nineteenth Corps, just returned from New Orleans, was to follow them. They marched with swinging stride out on Seventh Street, and with a lighter heart I made my way to the Treasury.

The arrival of the Sixth Corps removed our anxiety for the safety of the capital. Even the Confederates regarded these redoubtable veterans as invincible. Still, I hoped that Early would not retire without a battle, which, if possible, I intended to see. Directing the clerks in my office to make everything snug, I gave them the rest of the day for a vacation, and ordered my horses and light wagon to be at the Treasury promptly at one o'clock. I sent to Secretary Stanton for a pass to the front, which he accorded me, with, however, an earnest warning not to use it, as a heavy battle now seemed imminent on the north side of the city.

As I hope to give not only the first, but an accurate account of the battle of Fort Stevens, a sketch of the topography of the locality seems necessary. The extensions of Seventh Street and Fourteenth Street united in a single highway about three miles north of the city limits, which, after crossing two ranges of hills, extended still northward, passing the residence of the elder Blair at Silver Springs. On the crest of the first of these ranges, about one hundred yards west of the road, was

Fort Stevens, with Fort Reno about the same distance east of the highway. There were other forts in close proximity. Beyond these forts the road descended into a valley, where, about a third of a mile from the forts, were farm-houses with their outbuildings, around which the land was under cultivation. Passing these, the road ascended the opposite slope for a half-mile or more, and then crossed the second range of hills. This slope for about a mile on either side of the highway had been cleared, but was now covered with a thick growth of bushes. Farther on the right and left of the road the hillside and valley were broken by wooded ravines. The two forts had just been connected by a trench, the earth from which had been thrown up on the outside into a breastwork, which crossed and effectually obstructed the highway.

I invited Edward Jordan, Solicitor of the Treasury, and H. C. Fahnestock, of the banking-house of Jay Cooke & Co., to drive out to the front with me. The road was crowded with soldiers. They had passed scores of rum-shops, but not a man was intoxicated, and they made way for us to pass, with some good-natured badinage about "home-guards," and going into battle with a "pair of horses and a Concord wagon." On the last rise to the forts, the road was unobstructed, and the horses carried our light wagon up to the trench at a lively pace. The trench was well filled with men of the Sixth Corps, most of them lying down and taking matters very coolly. A tall, angular captain came out as we approached, slowly walked around and surveyed my team, then placing one foot on the hub of the fore wheel of the wagon, in the broadest Yankee dialect observed,

"Got a good pair of hosses there, judge. Them's

Morgan hosses. You don't often see 'em gray. They are most always bay."

"I do think they are a pretty good team," I said, pleased with his commendation.

"Naow, I wouldn't wonder if them hosses might be wuth a couple of hundred apiece—that is, if they was sound and kind, and hadn't no tricks about 'em."

"They cost more than that—I consider them worth three or four times the sum you name," I said.

"No? Yew don't say so!" he exclaimed. "Wall! I don't know but they be. Hosses—that is, good hosses—well-matched and good steppers, is hard to git." He seemed to be pondering the subject, again walked around them, looked them over, and continued with the same deliberation:

"Judge, if I owned a good pair of gray Morgan hosses, sound and kind and good steppers, wuth, say, twelve or fifteen hundred dollars, I wouldn't let 'em stand right there, not very long! Because a hoss was shot plumb dead right there not a half-hour ago."

To turn the team around and move from that exposed elevation was the work of a moment. I had not the slightest idea that we were under fire. The captain had been so entertaining that I had not looked over the earthwork. Now, looking down into the valley, though not a rebel was visible, I saw from the bushes and behind the logs frequent little jets of white smoke spurt out in a vicious manner; and in spite of the opposing wind I could now hear the crack of rifles, and the buzzing sound over our heads, dying away in the distance, I knew was the *ping* of minie bullets. The captain followed us. He called a colored man out of the ditch, told him to take my team to a place he indicated, and look after them until I returned, and he, possibly, might earn a quarter. Upon my expressing some surprise, he said :

"Oh, I know them hosses, judge. You bought 'em of William Drew, at the Burlington Fair! And I know you too, judge. I've heerd you in the old Court House in Middlebury, lots of times. Don't you remember the 'Cornwall Finish' Merino Case? I was on that jury. I am ———, of Starksboro'. That darkey is all right. He has froze to me. He'll take good care of the team."

"But you may be called into action!" I said.

"No such luck as that!" he replied. "Early is pulling foot for Virginia. These fellows are his rear guard. He didn't count on meeting the Old Sixth. He found we had come, and soon after he left. I wish Wright would let us go in. We'd get a sight of his coat-tails, if we didn't overhaul him."

I recognized the captain as an Addison County farmer. My friends left me here, and it was hours before I saw them again. The darkey drove my wagon into a ravine in the rear of a building used as a hospital, and I returned to the ditch. I was crawling up to look over the earthwork, when the captain called me down. "That won't do!" he said. "There's too much lead up there! You'd better watch the boys, and do as they do."

He took me to a place where a large stick of square timber lay on top of the earth-work, raised a little above it, thus leaving a space through which the whole region beyond was visible. "You'll be safe there, if you don't forget and raise your head too high," he said; then left me and returned to his company.

I lay there and watched the movements of the Confederates for half an hour. They were all under cover, and nothing could be seen of them but the smoke from their guns. In the early morning, when they had intended to storm the forts, they had occupied the opposite hill, and had filled the clusters of buildings of which I have spoken. There had been a sharp-shooter behind every stump and log and boulder, up to within a hundred yards of our lines. From all these places they were firing at every man exposed on our side. The captain said that before the Sixth Corps came their fire had been effective, and the loss on our side heavy.

I was interested in watching our own men. Only a few of them were firing, and after each shot they dropped back into the ditch to reload their rifles. One of them had a target-rifle which would weigh thirty pounds, and a field-glass. How he contrived to bring such a piece of heavy artillery into action, I do not know. He was as deliberate as if firing at a mark. After one discharge he continued looking through his glass for a long time. He then dropped back into the ditch and quietly remarked, "I winged him that time!" He pointed to a fallen tree, behind which, he said, a particularly dexterous sharp-shooter had been firing all the morning, killing two men and wounding others. He had borrowed the target-rifle to stop him, and thought he had done it, "for he didn't show up any more!"

Leaving the ditch, my pass carried me into the fort, where, to my surprise, I found the President, Secretary Stanton, and other civilians. A young colonel of artillery, who appeared to be the officer of the day, was in great distress because the President would expose himself, and paid little attention to his warnings. He was satisfied the Confederates had recognized him, for they were firing at him very hotly, and a soldier near him had just fallen with a broken thigh. He asked my advice, for he said the President was in great danger.

"What would you do with me under like circumstances?" I asked.

"I would civilly ask you to take a position where you were not exposed."

"And if I refused to obey?"

"I would send a sergeant and a file of men, and make you obey."

"Then treat the President just as you would me or any civilian."

"I dare not. He is my superior officer; I have taken an oath to obey his orders."

"He has given you no orders. Follow my advice, and you will not regret it."

"I will," he said. "I may as well die for one thing as another. If he were shot, I should hold myself responsible."

He walked to where the President was looking over the parapet. "Mr. President," he said, "you are standing within range of five hundred rebel rifles. Please come down to a safer place. If you do not, it will be my duty to call a file of men, and make you."

"And you would do quite right, my boy!" said the President, coming down at once. "You are in command of this fort. I should be the last man to set an example of disobedience!"

He was shown to a place where the view was less extended, but where there was almost no exposure.

It was three o'clock. General D. D. Bidwell's brigade of five veteran regiments now marched through Fort Stevens out upon the open space in front, where they were extended into two lines, threw out skirmishers, and then all lay flat upon the ground. The Confederate fire was so hot that in the little time required for this manœuvre one third of the men of this brigade were killed or wounded. I had supposed that a battlefield was filled with the shrieks and groans of the wounded and the dying. There was nothing of the kind, scarcely a spasmodic action, and in the majority of cases those who had been struck by the enemy's balls seemed rather to be lying quietly down. These veterans, under this heavy fire, went about their work as coolly as though on parade.

There was a flag raised, and thirty guns from four forts opened fire at the same instant. Six guns from Fort Stevens simultaneously hurled their shells against the clusters of buildings in the valley. We heard the shells strike, and saw them explode, throwing up a mass of dust and lime. A body of Sixth Corps men came out from the rear of the fort and poured their fire at short range into the crowd of rebels that rushed from the buildings like bees from a hive, across the open space to the bushes. In less time than is required to write the fact, there was a winrow of fallen men heaped entirely across this space. Now thick and fast the shells dropped into the bushes on the hillside. Hurrying crowds of Confederates rushed from either side into the highway and packed it full. Into these living masses the artillerymen now directed their galling fire. They had just returned into a fort which they had previously garrisoned for a year, and knew the range of every tree and object. One could follow the course of the shells by their burning fuses. They rose in long, graceful curves, screaming like demons of the pit, then descending with like curves into the crowds of running men, they appeared to explode as they touched the ground. The men swayed outward with the explosion, but many fell, and did not rise again. After the retreat of the last Confederates, the bodies lay so near each other that they almost touched. It was beautiful artillery work, but its results were horrible.

The shelling ceased. Instantly, the brigade lying on the ground was up and away. Over fences and other obstructions, dashing through the bushes, here and there halting a moment to re-form their broken lines, they went over the hillside, clearing away every Confederate, until they reached the summit of the ridge, where were buildings in which many of the enemy were captured. They then halted and formed in line of battle at right angles to the highway.

Every Confederate not captured, killed, or wounded, had now retreated over the hill, out of our view. I supposed the battle was over, when one of the officers standing near me exclaimed, "There they come!" and a squadron of cavalry, appearing over the crest of the hill, charged upon what seemed to be our doomed line of battle. They were dashing onward to the sound of the famous rebel yell. It looked as though that rushing mass of men and horses would brush away that thinned line of men like the dew. But now the jets of smoke darted from them in rapid succession, and riderless horses dashed out from the cavalry. Slower and slower still became its advance, more frequent were the jets of smoke from the line of infantry, until the horsemen came to an actual halt, seemed to quiver for a moment, then wheeled and disappeared over the hill to be seen no more. Again had a charge of cavalry been resisted and defeated by infantry in line of battle, and the last armed rebel who was ever to look upon the figure of liberty on the dome of the Capitol had disappeared forever.

The fighting was over, but the experiences of the day were not yet ended. I went back to my horses, found them well cared for, and then went on to the field of battle. Men with stretchers were already carrying off the wounded and collecting the dead. A few yards beyond our works I met two men. One, tall and powerful, was leaning heavily upon the other, a boy who was carrying the guns of both. The former asked me if I knew where the field-hospital was? After directing him to it I inquired where he was hurt. He replied by opening his shirt and exposing the path of a minie-bullet directly through his chest. I took his name, and afterwards traced him, found that he recovered, and was, when last heard from, a healthy man. His surgeon said that the wound was received during the exhalation of the air from his lungs. Had the ball entered the lungs during inhalation, the wound must have been fatal.

The buildings in the valley, which had been fired by the shells, burned very slowly, and were only now fully aflame. On all the floors, on the roofs, in the yards, within reach of the heat, were many bodies of the dead or dying, who could not move, and had been left behind by their comrades. The odor of burning flesh filled the air; it was a sickening spectacle!

Near a large fallen tree lay one in the uniform of an officer. His sword was by his side, but his hand grasped a rifle. What could have sent an officer here to act as a sharp-shooter? I placed my hand on his chest to detect any sign of life. It encountered a metallic substance. I opened his clothing, and took from beneath it a shield of boiler-iron, moulded to fit the anterior portion of his body, and fastened at the back by straps and buckles. Trusting to this protection, he had gone out that morning gunning for Yankees. In the language of a quaint epitaph in Vernon, Vt., upon one who died from vaccination,

"The means employed his life to save,
Hurried him headlong to the grave!"

Directly over his heart, through the shield and through

his body, was a hole large enough to permit the escape of a score of human lives.

I had not forgotten the sharp-shooter "winged" by the target-rifle. There, behind the log, he lay, on his back, his open eyes gazing upwards, with a peaceful expression on his rugged face. In the middle of his forehead was the small wound which had ended his career. A single crimson line led from it, along his face, to where the blood dropped upon the ground. A minie-rifle, discharged, was grasped in his right hand; a box, with a single remaining cartridge, was fast to his side. The rifle and cartridge-box were of English make, and the only things about him which did not indicate extreme destitution. His feet, wrapped in rags, had coarse shoes upon them, so worn and full of holes that they were only held together by many pieces of thick twine. Ragged trousers, a jacket, and a shirt of what used to be called "tow-cloth," a straw hat, which had lost a large portion of both crown and rim, completed his attire. His hair was a mat of dust and grime; his face and body were thickly coated with dust and dirt, which gave him the color of the red Virginia clay.

A haversack hung from his shoulder. Its contents were a jack-knife, a plug of twisted tobacco, a tin cup, and about two quarts of coarsely cracked corn, with, perhaps, an ounce of salt, tied in a rag. My notes, made the next day, say that this corn had been ground upon the cob, making the provender which the Western farmer feeds to his cattle. This was a complete inventory of the belongings of one Confederate soldier.

How long he had been defending Richmond I do not know. But it was apparent that he, with Early's army, during the past six weeks had entered the valley at Staunton, and had marched more than three hundred miles, ready to fight every day, until now, when in the front, he was acting as a sharp-shooter before Washington. He was evidently from the poorest class of Southern whites. I detached his haversack and its contents from his body and carried them away.

I noticed many of the Confederate dead who were clothed in blue, and had it not been for the hats, which were of many shapes and sizes, they would have closely resembled our own men. Where the brigade had formed which afterwards charged the Confederates and drove them over the hill, there were many Federal dead. It was subsequently reported that our loss here exceeded two hundred and fifty. The time could not have been longer than ten minutes before they were all lying flat on the ground.

It was after nightfall when we started to return to the city. The soldiers on their way to the front, having been notified that the fight was ended, had bivouacked in the fields, and left the road clear, so that we made rapid progress. On our left, a single heavy gun from a fort at intervals sent a shell, with a screaming rush, in the direction of the retreating Confederates, like some wild animal growling his anger at the escape of his prey. It was the last gun of the attack upon Washington. We carried the news of the retreat of the Confederates to the city, and that night its inhabitants slept soundly, free from alarm or anxiety.

In order to show the disparity between his own and the Union forces on the 12th of July, General Early has made a singular combination of figures. It is said that figures never lie, but sometimes they come closer to a false impression than the Confederate general did to the capture of Washington. Although such was not the fact, let it be assumed, as he claims, that within the circle of the defences of the capital there were about 20,000 men—quartermasters; laborers, who had never had a gun in their hands; district militia, of doubtful allegiance; department clerks, and soldiers only half cured of their wounds. No one then familiar with the state of affairs in Washington will doubt that the condition and forces of the defences were accurately known to General Lee. It was upon that knowledge that Early's campaign was projected and executed; that he came before the city; that he had disposed his forces; that he had ordered the assault at dawn on Tuesday morning. We must believe this, for General Early so wrote down the facts only two days afterwards. Of what avail, then, to take the census of males in the city? General Early intended to strike the capital before Grant could reinforce it, and to that end he had made a march of almost incredible swiftness and severity. When he ordered the assault, he believed he had reached Washington with its situation unchanged, and so had accomplished his object. Such facts cannot be refuted. They establish the ultimate fact by circumstantial proof, which is declared by the common law to be more satisfactory than the positive evidence of witnesses, who may be mistaken, while circumstances are always consistent with each other. It must therefore be accepted as a fact of history that the capture of Washington and the release of the Confederate prisoners at Point Lookout were the objectives of Early's campaign.

Nor is the exact hour of his arrival before Washington any more important. At Frederick he was only thirty-five miles from the capital. In his report of July 14th he says, "On the morning of the 10th, I moved towards Washington, taking the route via Rockville, and then turning to the left to get on the Seventh Street Pike.

The day was very hot, and the roads exceedingly dusty, *but we marched thirty miles.*" He passed the night of the 10th within five miles of Washington. Presumptively, he could have attacked next morning, when a considerable portion of his force was at Silver Spring and above Georgetown, within two miles of the defences. His own statement of the positions of his force on the 11th is very indefinite. The first detachment of the Sixth Corps did not reach the defences until after four in the afternoon. Had he made the attack on the morning of the 11th, he would have found the city in the condition supposed by General Lee when the campaign was projected. The Confederate army would have met with no resistance except from raw and undisciplined forces, which, in the opinion of General Grant, and it was supposed of General Lee also, would have been altogether inadequate to its defence. Its capture and possession for a day would have been disastrous to the cause of the Union. Early would have seized the money in the Treasury, the archives of the departments, the immense supplies of clothing, arms, and ammunition in store; he would have compelled General Grant to raise the siege of Richmond; he would have destroyed uncounted millions in value of property, and he would have had the same opportunity to retreat of which he availed himself next day.

But with his veterans behind the defences, he would have had no occasion to retreat. The released prisoners at Point Lookout in two days would have added 20,000 to the strength of his army. The Confederates of Maryland would have swarmed to his assistance, and he could certainly have held the capital long enough to give Great Britain the excuse she so much desired, to recognize the Confederacy and break the blockade. After the danger had passed, when its magnitude became apparent, there was but one opinion among the friends of the Union. It was that we had escaped a loss of prestige and property, compared with which previous disasters would have been trifling, and probably a blow fatally destructive to the Union cause.

And there is another record which will be held in honor so long as and wherever courage is held to be a virtue among men. It is the page which is filled with the story of Monocacy, where the streams ran blood, inexperienced men fought like veterans, and veterans like the legionaries of Cæsar. When the children of the republic are asked what it was that brought Early's campaign to naught and saved the capital, let them be taught to answer, " General Wallace and his command at the battle of Monocacy, and the arrival of the Sixth Corps within the defences of the capital."

As promised, I proceed to compare other statements of General Early with facts which no one has ever questioned. Possibly they may have a bearing upon the credibility of other statements of his which are controverted. In his report of July 14th, after stating that he had "moved his force up to the vicinity of the fortifications" (of the capital), he says: " Late in the afternoon of the 12th, the enemy *advanced in line of battle* against my skirmishers (of Rode's division), and the latter being reinforced, *repulsed the enemy three times.*"

No other account of the proceedings of that day makes any mention of any repulse of Federal troops, nor of any advance by them "in line of battle." In his article published long after the war, General Early referred to this advance as an affair which occurred late in the afternoon of the 12th, between some troops sent out from the works and "a portion of the troops in my front line."

General Long has omitted all mention of such an event. The account which I have given of the fighting before the works on that afternoon could be confirmed by two thousand witnesses. The only line of battle that afternoon was formed by Bidwell's brigade, after they had charged over the valley and up to the crest of the hill, opposite the fort, and driven every Confederate over the hill and out of sight of Washington. And this brigade was not repulsed; on the contrary, it went up the hill at a speed scarcely outstripped by the pursued Confederates. On the top of the hill these veterans did form in line of battle, and were charged upon by the Confederate cavalry. But it was the cavalry, and not the Union force, which was repulsed and retreated. If the subject were open to argument, it might be asked for what possible purpose a force, attacked when it was behind breastworks, went out to form a line of battle in front of them! No, this is a statement that cannot possibly be true.

General Early frankly confesses that some of his men who were captured before Washington "did some very tall talking about my (his) strength and purposes." He says that he himself told a "sympathizer" that he "would not mind so small a force as 20,000 in the earthworks of Washington." Such observations are so very difficult to explain, that we may leave them with the comment that they do not increase our confidence in the evidence of the witness who made them.

Both General Early and General Long have asserted frequently, and with great apparent satisfaction, that the Confederate advance " threw the authorities, civil and military, at the Federal capital, as well as the whole population of Washington, into a wild state of alarm and consternation." Similar statements have been so frequently made that they have been countenanced by some

Union writers since the war, who have no personal knowledge on the subject. General Early even claims that the universal "wild dismay" so upset the Northern judgment as to disqualify it from forming any reliable conclusions, and that it led to the most exaggerated estimates of the Confederate forces.

These statements are destitute of the least shadow of foundation, for a reason which is conclusive. The Union men in Washington had not the slightest knowledge of the existence of the danger. No confidence was placed in the press, which as often contradicted as it asserted the fact of Early's advance, and all its statements were upon rumor. It may be assumed that those who had the custody of the money and securities would have been informed as early as others, but until the Sixth Corps was in sight of the capital on Monday, neither the treasurer nor the register had any knowledge on the subject. Had I supposed there was even danger of possible delay on the railroads, I should have sent away my family, who were staying with me at a hotel. When they finally left the city on Monday, I offered to a party of acquaintances the opportunity of going by the same train, and told them what I had seen above Georgetown. But they were so confident that only cavalry raiders were around the city that they declined, and consequently Major Gilmor relieved them of their luggage at the Gunpowder River the next morning.

There was indignation in Washington when the facts were known, but there was no scare and no fear. And the indignation was directed against our own authorities, and not against the Confederates, the former being charged with the defence of the city. It was claimed that they should not have permitted its exposure to any danger. Even now, when we learn from the Memoirs of General Lee that, within four hours after the despatch of the Sixth Corps by General Grant to the defence of Washington, a courier was on his way from General Lee to General Early with a letter giving its numbers and destination, we may consider it somewhat remarkable that one third of Lee's army could have been detached on the 13th of June, and marched over two hundred miles into Maryland, and no knowledge of the movement have reached Grant until the 5th of July, when he sent the first reinforcement of a part of the Sixth Corps to Baltimore.

The effect produced by the mere presence of this corps was a grand tribute to the reputation of its soldiers. No one asked what its numbers were. They had come, and the capital was saved. The friends of the Union at once assumed that the city must have been in danger, or General Grant would not have sent the Sixth Corps to its defence. The inhabitants resumed their ordinary avocations: one went to his field, another to his merchandise, with perfect confidence that the Sixth Corps would take care of Washington; and from his instant and precipitate retreat the belief was universal that General Early was of the same opinion.

XLV.

THE JUDGMENT OF PRESIDENT LINCOLN.—HIS COOLNESS IN TIMES OF EXCITEMENT.—HIS FAITH THAT THE UNION CAUSE WOULD BE PROTECTED AGAINST SERIOUS DISASTER.—FOUR OF HIS LETTERS NOW FIRST PUBLISHED.

THOSE who were with the President upon the three occasions when the capital was supposed to be in danger of capture know that in neither of them did he exhibit any evidence of excitement or apprehension. The loss of the capital he regarded as a disaster that would probably be fatal, because it would give Great Britain a pretext for intervening in our affairs, of which she would certainly avail herself. For that reason he did not believe it would happen. He made no parade of his faith, but upon proper occasions he spoke of our ultimate success as one of the designs of the Almighty, and that he would protect the country against any disaster from which it could not recover. He kept General McClellan in command in the campaign which ended at Antietam, because, as he said, he clearly saw that that was the surest way to insure the defeat of General Lee. The despatch which first announced the victory at Gettysburgh did not produce in him the slightest emotion. He read it, passed it to a civil officer, and directed him to read it to those who stood around him, with the quiet observation, " It is no more than I expected." The following letters will show the state of his mind during Early's invasion, and I submit them without further comment.

On the 10th of July, at 9.20 A.M., after he had received

General Wallace's telegraphic report, which stated his defeat, and his losses much heavier than they proved afterwards to be, for he then supposed that the Tenth Vermont and the One Hundred and Sixth New York were captured, the President wrote to ex-Governor Swann, at Baltimore, as follows:

"Yours of last night is received. I have not a single soldier who is not disposed of by the military for the best protection of all. By latest accounts the enemy is moving on Washington. They cannot fly to either place. Let us be vigilant, but keep cool. I hope neither Baltimore nor Washington will be sacked. A. LINCOLN."

At two o'clock P.M. on the same 10th of July he wrote to General Grant, at City Point, as follows:

"Your despatch to General Halleck, referring to what I may think in the present emergency, is shown me. General Halleck says we have absolutely no force here fit to go to the field. He thinks that with the hundred-day men and invalids we have here we can defend Washington, and scarcely Baltimore. Besides these, there are about eight thousand, not very reliable, under ——— at Harper's Ferry, with Hunter approaching that point very slowly, with what number I suppose you know better than I.

"Wallace with some odds and ends, and part of what came up with Ricketts, was so badly beaten yesterday at Monocacy that what is left can attempt no more than to defend Baltimore. What we shall get in from Pennsylvania and New York will scarcely be worth counting, I fear.

"Now what I think is, that you should provide to retain your hold where you are, certainly, and bring the rest with you personally, and make a vigorous effort to destroy the enemy's force in this vicinity. I think there is really a fair chance to do this if the movement is prompt. This is what I think upon your suggestion, and is not an order. A. LINCOLN."

There are some important interlineations in this letter. Speaking of Halleck's opinion, he first wrote that the hundred-day men and the invalids "may possibly but not certainly defend Washington," and then erased these words and interlined, "can defend Washington." As the letter was finally sent it expressed his opinion that both cities could be defended with their then present forces, and that Early's army could be captured by a prompt movement of General Grant. It contained no expression of fear.

The President's next letter is dated July 11th, and is to General Grant:

"Yours of 10.30 yesterday is received, and very satisfactory. The enemy will learn of Wright's arrival, and then the difficulty will be to unite Wright and Hunter, south of the enemy, before he will re-cross the Potomac. Some firing between Rockville and here now.
"A. LINCOLN."

General Wright with the advance of the Sixth Corps began to arrive in the afternoon of the 11th, and the last detachment went to the front on the morning of the 12th. President Lincoln was in Fort Stevens at two o'clock P.M., and remained there until the fighting was over. At 11.30 A.M. of the 12th he wrote to General Grant:

"Vague rumors have been reaching us for two or three days that Longstreet's corps is also on its way to this vicinity. Look out for its absence from your front. A. LINCOLN."

These letters show that while the situation was perfectly comprehended by the President, it did not disturb the serenity of his mind nor excite his apprehension. Neither on this occasion nor upon either of the Confederate campaigns north of the Potomac, did he have the slightest fear of the capture of Washington.

CHAPTER XLVI.
ABRAHAM LINCOLN.—A SKETCH OF SOME EVENTS IN HIS LIFE.

I CANNOT conclude this volume of disconnected sketches more appropriately than by a brief account of some events which exerted a powerful influence upon Mr. Lincoln's character, and indirectly upon the fortunes of the republic. I shall attempt no connected biography, but confine myself strictly to an account of the events to which I have referred.

On the 12th day of February, 1809, were born two men who each exerted a more powerful and permanent influence upon mankind than any of their contemporaries. The name of one was Charles Robert Darwin. He came of an old English family, renowned for its contributions to physical science, which was able to give to its young representative all the advantages of wealth and position. From the university, young Darwin went as naturalist on board the British ship *Beagle*, engaged in explorations in the Southern Ocean. Returning from this voyage in the year 1845, he published the scientific results of his labors, in a large illustrated volume, and also that charming book, "The Voyage of a Naturalist," so well known to students of physical science. Then for many years he was engaged in his private investigations, and cut no figure in scientific literature. But in the year 1858 (and synonymously with the "divided-house" speech of Mr. Lincoln) he convulsed the world of science by the publication of his "Origin of Species."

For this publication Mr. Darwin was denounced by the whole Christian world. He was called a heretic, a pagan, a scoffer at the Bible, a knave or a fool, who had invented a theory which led straight to atheism.

But Mr. Darwin lived to see his theory adopted by the leading Christian thinkers of his time, as not irreconcilable with the Bible, and when he died, "by the will of the intelligence of the nation," he was buried in Westminster Abbey, "the fitting resting-place," said Dean Stanley, "and the monument of the heroes of England."

On the same 12th day of February, 1809, in one of the new settlements of Kentucky, Abraham Lincoln was born. With none of the advantages of wealth, education, and position, which assisted the eminent Englishman, the young Kentuckian rose to greater eminence, and exerted a more powerful influence upon his country and his race, than his English contemporary. The object of this sketch will be fully accomplished if it shall direct the student of American history to the events and processes by which such an extraordinary result was attained.

Mr. Lincoln once wrote his own biography in these words:

"Born, February 12th, 1809, in Hardin County, Kentucky.
"Education defective.
"Profession, a lawyer.
"Have been a captain of volunteers in the Black Hawk War.
"Postmaster at a very small office; four times a member of the Illinois legislature, and was a member of the lower House of Congress."

If he had not survived the year 1857, he would not have required a more extended biography. It is a singular but impressive fact that all the events which have given him such an honorable place in American history were comprised within the last seven years of his life. In his youth and early manhood there was nothing very different from the common experiences of young men of poor parents and his position in life. He had served through four sessions of the state legislature of Illinois, without any taint upon his reputation—he had an average position as a member of Congress in his second term; he may have ranked as the leading lawyer of his county, and, what is perhaps more to his credit, he had acquired among those who knew him most thoroughly, the name of "Honest Abraham Lincoln." But he had done nothing to distinguish himself above many of his contemporaries, or to give his name a place in history. Had his life ended before the new year of 1858, he would have left to his children a fair reputation as a lawyer, a good name as a citizen, a small estate, and the credit of no remarkable achievement.

But in that year, when he was already past middle life, he suddenly appeared above the political horizon, and so strikingly challenged the public attention that he was taken out of private life, and, without any intervening step, placed in the presidential chair. This was an extraordinary occurrence. It had not happened before, to a really able man, since the adoption of the Constitution. There must exist a reason for it in some act of his own or with which he was prominently associated. An act which produced such a result should assist us in the interpretation of his character, and ought to be discovered without great difficulty. The inquiry for it involves some recapitulation.

It appears from the story of Mr. Lincoln's youth that his early education comprised less than a year of very ordinary school instruction, and that the only books accessible to him were the Bible, "The Pilgrim's Progress," " Burns's Poems," and Weems's " Life of Washington." His study of these books was very thorough, for they were in large part committed to memory. The mental exercise involved taught him how to think. During his public life, all his great ideas, his sentences that will outlive the spoken language, have been wrought out of his own brain with few or no adventitious aids. Thus, his first inaugural address is said by those who know to have been composed with no assistance but the Federal Constitution and one of Henry Clay's speeches. But his entire public life testifies how thoroughly he had learned the power of thought, a lesson which few men completely master. Judged by their relations, some of his most matured mental conclusions must be referred to those years of quiet home life which intervened between his retirement from Congress, in 1849, and his nomination to the Senate of the United States in the summer of 1858.

The decade which ended in the year last named covered the aggressive campaign of slavery. The original slave states had been content to abide by the Missouri compromise line, and made no attempt to carry their domestic institution beyond it. But their representatives in Congress, aided by Northern votes, secured the passage of the act for the return of fugitive slaves; and encouraged by that act, and their short-lived victory in the Kansas controversy, they broadly claimed the right to carry their slave property into free territory. The decision of the Supreme Court of the United States, in the case of Dred Scott, very nearly confirmed their claim, and well-nigh broke down the last geographical barrier between freedom and slavery.

The friends of human freedom had never asserted any right to legislate touching slavery in the slave states or south of the compromise line. Within those limits slavery was conceded to be a continuing evil, entrenched in the Constitution. The most ultra-abolitionists had restricted their labors to the attempted abolition of slavery in the District of Columbia and its exclusion from the territories. No public man had proposed to attack slavery within its consecrated limits. Had the advocates of the institution abided by the line to which they had for a good consideration agreed, there is no reason to believe that it would have ever been disturbed except by themselves. But they would not abide by it. They charged the North with an agitation for which they alone were responsible. They made every success the pretext for some new aggression, until the halls of Congress became the theatre of a conflict which was renewed with every session with increasing intensity.

In the quiet of private life Mr. Lincoln was a thoughtful observer of this controversy. He had taken note of the aggressions of the slave power, and he reached the conclusion that they would continue until they became intolerable. In the Kansas outrages they had almost reached that point, and when the point was passed he believed that the fate of slavery would be determined. He hated slavery, because it was oppressive and cruel—he loved freedom, because it was the natural right of all men, ordained by the Almighty. Freedom had been fighting a losing battle, but it would triumph in God's own good time. He saw where his own party had erred, and he worked out in his own mind the lines upon which the next battle—the fight for freedom, could be won.

Mr. Lincoln's mind was not secretive, but it was his habit not to disclose the problems upon which it was engaged until all his own doubts were removed and his conclusions settled. This peculiar quality now received a marked illustration. On the 17th of June, 1858, the Republicans of Illinois, at their state convention, in Springfield, nominated him as their candidate for the Senate of the United States. He anticipated the nomination, and had written out his speech upon its acceptance. This speech seems to have been the most effective of his life, and as momentous as was ever delivered in this republic. Its theme was the insatiable demands of the slave power. Upon the incontestable authority of the Saviour of men, that "if a house be divided against itself that house cannot stand," he avowed his own faith in these words: "I believe this government cannot permanently endure, half slave and half free."

It is now more than a quarter of a century since Mr. Lincoln himself gave an unpretending account of the occasion and circumstances of this speech. He spoke of it as an example of the thoroughness of his own convictions. It wrought upon his hearers a conviction equally thorough, that for the first time it put the issue between freedom and slavery upon its true ground. We know now that it made Mr. Lincoln President and drove the bolt of death straight to the life of human slavery.

The announcement of this bold prediction almost produced a convulsion among the Republicans. It came upon them like a burst of thunder from a cloudless sky. His friends were shocked—his party leaders were appalled. They declared that it destroyed his chances of an election; that unless he retracted or modified it, his defeat was inevitable. The issue, as he proposed it, they said, involved the destruction of slavery or the government. It was a declaration of open war. "I cannot change the fact, nor can I escape the conclusions of my own judgment," said Mr. Lincoln. "The statement is a truth confirmed by all human experience. It has been true for more than six thousand years—it is still indisputably true. I cannot retract it without resorting to subterfuge, and that I will not do. I would rather be defeated, with this expression held up and discussed before the people, than to exclude it from my speech and be victorious." And so the message went forth. It was the result of his calm deliberation—by it he would stand or fall!

Judge Douglas was already his opposing candidate. He seized upon what he believed to be his opportunity to destroy Mr. Lincoln. In his reply to the prediction, he assumed an air of lofty superiority—and scornfully declared that Mr. Lincoln's speech had been "prepared for the occasion." "I admit the charge," said Mr. Lincoln. "I have not a fine education like Judge Douglas, and I cannot discourse on dialectics as he can, but I can be honest with the people, and tell them what I believe." Then he challenged Judge Douglas to a public discussion; the challenge was accepted; the debate followed, which is now historical. Instead of destroying the Republican party, it drew to it a majority of the voters of Illinois, and left its candidate, although defeated by the legislature, the most conspicuous of its leaders.

The influence of this debate has not yet passed away. Men still remember and refer, as an epoch in their lives, to the first discussion of the new issue by these two candidates, in the city of Chicago, on the 9th and 10th of July, 1858. Mr. Lincoln was an auditor when Judge Douglas, on the 9th, delivered a speech of such power that his admirers believed it unanswerable. But on the following evening Mr. Lincoln made an answer, in which he established a national reputation as an orator, and the "little giant of the West" found his peer as a logician and his master in eloquence.

What was it which drew such crowds of plain men to every one of the seven meetings for this debate? Neither speaker indulged in oratoric flights or descended to the common level of the hustings. Mr. Lincoln even disdained his ordinary anecdote and humor. Both sought to address the sound reason of their auditors by fair argument alone. Yet the public interest in the debate increased as it proceeded, and was never greater than on the evening when it closed. Mr. Douglas had not been an ultra pro-slavery man—he had opposed his own party in the trick by which it sought to force the Lecompton Constitution upon the people of Kansas; he now took very high ground. He claimed that he was the champion of constitutional rights. He declared that he would maintain and enforce these rights for all the people, and when these rights were recognized he said he "did not care whether slavery was voted up or voted down."

In his reply Mr. Lincoln spurned all half-way measures and men. Was slavery right? If it was, then Judge Douglas ought to be sustained. If it was wrong, then Judge Douglas and his party had no claim to the support of good men. But slavery was not right. Slavery was degrading—it was cruel, brutal—it was unjust and wicked. Therefore it was wrong, and Judge Douglas and his party ought to care, and ought to vote, to put it down. Freedom was the opposite of slavery. It was noble, just, godlike—and it was right. It was the gift of the Almighty to all men. He would see that his children were not robbed of their birthright. Freedom was truth, it "was mighty, and would prevail!"

To this plain issue of the wrong or right of slavery Lincoln held his adversary with an inflexible hand. Douglas plied him with questions—he answered them fully, always coming back to the wrong of slavery. He put questions in return, which his opponent answered evasively, and then strove to retreat under cover of the evasion. Lincoln was the victor in every encounter. Finally, he drove his adversary into the corner, where there was no escape, and where he extorted from him the admission that his party was committed to the doctrine that slavery was right. Then, with the earnestness of Paul, he demanded, What true man would uphold slavery and wrong against freedom and the right and justice?

The great contest was half won when it was to be fought to its termination in the light of day on its real issue. Slavery had declared the war. It was not in its nature to recede or to lay down its arms until it was victorious or defeated. It was Lincoln who had forced the fighting to its true issue, and he, therefore, became the natural leader of the party of freedom.

In the new departure of the "divided-house" speech, and in his powerful demonstration of the inexcusable wrong of slavery, lay the secret of Mr. Lincoln's power. He was at once in great demand as a political speaker. In the Ohio campaign of 1859—in the Cooper Institute in New York—in Connecticut, New Hampshire, Rhode Island, and in Kansas—everywhere he went, he drew large audiences. His style of speaking was changed. He no longer told witty stories; his speeches were so solidly argumentative that a few said they were dry, and the same critics decided that their length made them tiresome. But the great audiences heard them delighted, and complained only of their brevity. No theme had ever made so many permanent converts to his party faith as his, touching the wrong of slavery—no speaker had laid it bare with the strong sense of Abraham Lincoln.

As the day appointed for the national nominating convention for the presidency approached, the name of Mr. Lincoln was mentioned as one of the candidates of the great West. But he was not regarded as a strong candidate in comparison with Mr. Seward, Mr. Chase, Mr. Cameron, or Judge Bates, of Missouri. The Republican party was under a great obligation to Mr. Seward. His ability was conceded; his long and brilliant services deserved recognition. It was supposed by his friends that he would poll the largest vote on the first, and be nominated on the second ballot. But the convention witnessed a demonstration in favor of Mr. Lincoln which left no doubt of the place he had secured in the hearts of the people. At the right moment the enthusiasm for him was lighted, and it ran over the convention like a prairie fire. It not only gave him the nomination, but it secured a solid, hearty union of all the members in his support.

The presidential canvass of the year 1860 was unique in our political experience. It required none of the accessories of the "log-cabin" campaign of "Tippecanoe and Tyler too." The pseudonym of "Railsplitter" was the gift of his enemies. The name of Abraham Lincoln was an inspiration. Enthusiasm for his election pervaded the country like an electric influence. It was everywhere the same. In the crowded city or at the country cross-roads; up in the mountain hamlets, or out on the Western prairies; among the fishermen of the Atlantic, and the miners of the Pacific coast, the political orator was heard with quiet consideration until he spoke the name of Lincoln. At that name, cheers such as never welcomed king or conqueror supplied his peroration. That was the only campaign in which every voter who deliberated voted for the same candidate, in which every highest estimate for the successful candidate was exceeded by the counted vote.

From his nomination to his election Mr. Lincoln calmly awaited events. He came and went among his neighbors, received delegations and dismissed them delighted, but ignorant of his intentions. He seemed to be less interested in the result than his supporters—he received the news of his election without exultation. He had promised no rewards, made no pledges, and was free to follow whither his judgment pointed the way.

From October, when his election was assured, until the end of February, the mind of Mr. Lincoln was devoted to his coming work. He laid it out with the care of an architect planning a building. He studied the situation. He determined the general policy of his administration with the greatest care. He prepared his inaugural address—he decided upon the tenor of his speeches to be made on his journey to Washington—he well considered the temper of mind in which he should first meet the supporters of slavery. Nothing was left to accident which he could possibly foresee.

His first public address was his farewell to his Springfield friends on his departure for the capital. That address was the microcosm of his future. It was an avowal of his own undoubting faith in, and purpose to be guided by, the wisdom of the Almighty. That faith and purpose he repeated upon every proper occasion as long as he lived. In conformity with it, in all the addresses he made upon his journey, there was no threat, no harsh word, nothing but kindness for the whole people. To the friends of the South he extended the hand of affection. His inaugural address was full of peace, kindness, and good will. On one point only he was inflexible. He would perform his duty, enforce obedience to the laws, and keep his oath to support the Constitution.

The advent of the war was no surprise to him. He knew that slavery was so woven into the national life that it could not be wrenched out of it without violence and blood—as he said afterwards, that "every drop of blood drawn by the lash must be repaid by another drawn by the sword." But in all the pressure of public duty and excitement of warlike preparation his mind was engaged upon measures, not to punish, but to protect those who had brought war upon the country as the consequence of their own reckless acts. Slavery, which had taken the sword, must perish by the sword— it was the cause of the war, and war would only cease with its destruction. Yet he advocated payment by the nation of the full value of the slaves, and would even have removed the slaves into a far country at the national expense. It was not until his kindly proposals had been rejected by those whom they would have relieved, with curses, that he ceased to make them, and the patience of the loyal North had been twice exhausted when he issued the decree of emancipation.

He came to his great office inexperienced in government—no modern ruler was ever surrounded by so many difficulties. Yet he brought the nation through them all into the harbor of permanent peace; and, looking back over his term, it is very difficult to say where he took a wrong course or committed an error. Finally, when he was strongest in the love of a loyal people, had won the friendship of his former enemies, and had gained the respect of mankind, he sealed his faithful service with his blood, and was slain by an insane assassin.

Nor was the intellectual growth of Mr. Lincoln any less remarkable. We have seen that his education scarcely deserved the name. His course of reading was restricted to a few good books, but his thoroughness of study more than compensated for their lack of numbers, if any such existed; for he has written many paragraphs which, in force, elegance, and beauty, are not surpassed in our language. Except Shakespeare, no writer of English has produced so many that will outlive the spoken tongue. His farewell to his Springfield neighbors—the closing paragraph of his first, and the last third of his second inaugural address—the last sentence of his message to the third session of the Thirty-seventh Congress—his Gettysburg speech of Nov. 19, 1863, are examples from his pen which will not suffer by comparison with anything written by Addison or Irving, Daniel Webster, or that scholarly master of English composition, George P. Marsh. And where in our language is a finer antithesis than this, thrown off, *calamo currente*, in the middle of a letter in answer to strictures on the conduct of the war?—" When peace with victory comes, there will be some black men who will remember that with silent tongue, and clenched teeth, and steady eye, and well-poised bayonet, they have helped on mankind to this great'consummation; while I fear there will be some white ones unable to forget that with malignant heart and deceitful speech they have striven to hinder and prevent it." A collection of his public addresses and letters, commencing with his farewell to Springfield in February, 1861, and ending with the last made by him on April 11, 1865, will be read hereafter with an interest as absorbing as any volume in the literature of the rebellion.

Some of his written compositions may be classed as literary curiosities. In August, 1862, Mr. Horace Greeley had written to him an impatient and dictatorial letter, charging him with culpable delay in the emancipation of the slaves, and their employment in suppressing the rebellion. Mr. Lincoln knew the force of short words and crisp sentences—he never used those of many syllables or pretentious sound. His answer was all the more effective in that it took no note of Mr. Greeley's temper—while its conclusive statements were embodied in four hundred and thirteen words, of which three hundred and two, or more than seventy-four per cent., were words of a single syllable.

In the campaign of 1864, the friends of General McClellan, in Tennessee, presented to him a protest against the oath of loyalty prescribed by Governor Johnson, to be taken by the voters. It was an adroit political attempt to connect the President with a subject over which he had no authority, which he detected at first sight. They wanted an answer. "I expect to let the friends of George B. McClellan manage their side of this contest in their own way, and I will manage my side of it in my way," he said. They were not satisfied, and wanted an answer in writing. A few days later he sent them his written reply. It occupied one and a half printed octavo pages; in fifteen paragraphs, none of them more than three lines. But every paragraph was an answer which struck the protest like a rock from a catapult.

He never hesitated to sacrifice euphony to strength. "This finishes the *job*," he said, when Illinois had voted, making the number of states requisite to ratify the amendment of the Constitution abolishing slavery. Cuthbert Bullitt and other citizens of Louisiana had written to him, protesting against the severity with which the war was waged. "Would you prosecute the war with elderstalk squirts charged with rose-water, if you were in my position?" he demanded, and there was no reply. In his message to the extra session of Congress of July 4, 1861, he wrote of Southern political leaders, that, "with rebellion thus sugar-coated, they have been drugging the public mind of their section for more than thirty years." Mr. Defrees, the public printer, advised the omission of the compound word, on the ground that it was not dignified. "Let it stand!" said the President; "I was not attempting to be dignified, but plain. There is not a voter in the Union who will not know what sugar-coated means."

His heart was as tender as ever beat in a human breast. Those who saw him standing by the coffins of young Ellsworth and the eloquent Baker knew how he loved his friends—how he sorrowed over their loss. In his companionship with his boys, and particularly with the younger, there was a most touching picture of parental affection; in his emotion when he lost them, a grief too sacred to be further exposed. "He could not deny a pardon or a respite to a soldier condemned to die for a crime which did not involve depravity, if he were to try," said an old army officer. He shrank from the confirmation of a sentence of death in such a case, as if it were a murder by his hand. "They say that I destroy all discipline and am cruel to the army, when I will not let them shoot a soldier now and then," he said. "But I cannot see it. If God wanted me to see it, he would let me know it, and until he does, I shall go on pardoning and being cruel to the end." An old friend called by appointment, and found him with a pile of records of courts-martial before him, for approval. "Go away, Swett!" he exclaimed, with intense impatience—"tomorrow is butchering day, and I will not be interrupted until I have found excuses for saving the lives of these poor fellows!" Many pages might be filled with authentic illustrations of his tenderness and mercy, for they were prominent in his official life. Three times I assisted in procuring their exercise, each to the saving of a soldier, and each time he shared our own delight over our success, though he knew not how his face shone when he felt that he had spared a human life.

In the presidential campaign of 1864 there were sullen whisperings that Mr. Lincoln had no religious opinions nor any interest in churches or Christian institutions. They faded away with other libels, never to be renewed until after his death. One of his biographers, who calls himself the "friend and partner for twenty years" of the deceased President, has since published what he calls a history of his life, in which he revives the worst of these rumors, with additions which, if true, would destroy much of the world's respect for Mr. Lincoln. He asserts that his "friend and partner" was "an infidel verging towards atheism." Others have disseminated these charges in lectures and fugitive sketches so industriously that they have produced upon strangers some impression of their truth. The excuse alleged is, their desire to present Mr. Lincoln to the world "just as he was." Their real purpose is to present him just as they would have him to be, as much as possible like themselves.

It is a trait of the infidel to parade his unbelief before the public, and he thinks something gained to himself when he can show that others are equally deficient in moral qualities. But these writers have attempted too much. Their principal charge of infidelity, tinged with atheism, is so completely at variance with all our knowledge of his opinions that its origin must be attributed to malice or to a defective mental constitution.

His sincerity and candor were conspicuous qualities of

Mr. Lincoln's mind. Deception was a vice in which he had neither experience nor skill. All who were admitted to his intimacy will agree that he was incapable of professing opinions which he did not entertain. When we find him at the moment of leaving his home for Washington, surrounded by his neighbors of a quarter of a century, taking Washington for his exemplar, whose success he ascribed "to the aid of that Divine Providence upon which he at all times relied," and publicly declaring that he, himself, "placed his whole trust in the same Almighty Being, and the prayers of Christian men and women;" when, not once or twice, but on all proper, and more than a score of subsequent occasions, he avowed his faith in an Omnipotent Ruler, who will judge the world in righteousness—in the Bible as the inspired record of his history and his law; when with equal constancy he thanked Almighty God for, and declared his interest in, Christian institutions and influences as the appointed means for his effective service, we may assert that we know that he was neither an atheist nor an infidel, but, on the contrary, a sincere believer in the fundamental doctrines of the Christian faith. In fact, he believed so confidently that the Almighty was making use of the war, of himself, and other instrumentalities in working out some great design for the benefit of humanity, and his belief that he himself was directed by the same Omniscient Power was expressed with such frankness and frequency, that it attracted attention, and was criticised by some as verging towards superstition. His public life was a continuous service of God and his fellow-man, controlled and guided by the golden rule, in which there was no hiatus of unbelief or incredulity.

Here I might well stop, and submit that these charges do not deserve any further consideration. But I know how false they are, and I may be excused if I record one of my sources of knowledge.

The emphatic statement made by the President to Mr. Fessenden, that he was called to the Treasury by a Power higher than human authority, I have already mentioned. His calm serenity at times when others were so anxious, his confidence that his own judgment was directed by the Almighty, so impressed me that, when I next had the opportunity, at some risk of giving offence, I ventured to ask him directly how far he believed the Almighty actually directed our national affairs. There was a considerable pause before he spoke, and when he did speak, what he said was more in the nature of a monologue than an answer to my inquiry:

"That the Almighty does make use of human agencies, and directly intervenes in human affairs, is," he said, "one of the plainest statements of the Bible. I have had so many evidences of his direction, so many instances when I have been controlled by some other power than my own will, that I cannot doubt that this power comes from above. I frequently see my way clear to a decision when I am conscious that I have no sufficient facts upon which to found it. But I cannot recall one instance in which I have followed my own judgment, founded upon such a decision, where the results were unsatisfactory; whereas, in almost every instance where I have yielded to the views of others, I have had occasion to regret it. I am satisfied that when the Almighty wants me to do or not to do a particular thing, he finds a way of letting me know it. I am confident that it is his design to restore the Union. He will do it in his own good time. We should obey and not oppose his will."

"You speak with such confidence," I said, "that I would like to know how your knowledge that God acts directly upon human affairs compares in certainty with your knowledge of a fact apparent to the senses—for example, the fact that we are at this moment here in this room."

"One is as certain as the other," he answered, "although the conclusions are reached by different processes. I know by my senses that the movements of the world are those of an infinitely powerful machine, which runs for ages without a variation. A man who can put two ideas together knows that such a machine requires an infinitely powerful maker and governor: man's nature is such that he cannot take in the machine and keep out the maker. This maker is God—infinite in wisdom as well as in power. Would we be any more certain if we saw him?"

"I am not controverting your position," I said. "Your confidence interests me beyond expression. I wish I knew how to acquire it. Even now, must it not all depend on our faith in the Bible?"

"No. There is the element of personal experience," he said. "If it did, the character of the Bible is easily established, at least to my satisfaction. We have to believe many things which we do not comprehend. The Bible is the only one that claims to be God's Book—to comprise his law—his history. It contains an immense amount of evidence of its own authenticity. It describes a governor omnipotent enough to operate this great machine, and declares that he made it. It states other facts which we do not fully comprehend, but which we cannot account for. What shall we do with them?

"Now let us treat the Bible fairly. If we had a witness on the stand whose general story we knew was true, we would believe him when he asserted facts of which we had no other evidence. We ought to treat the Bible with equal fairness. I decided a long time ago that it was less difficult to believe that the Bible was what it claimed to be than to disbelieve it. It is a good book for us to obey—it contains the ten commandments, the golden rule, and many other rules which ought to be followed. No man was ever the worse for living according to the directions of the Bible."

"If your views are correct, the Almighty is on our side, and we ought to win without so many losses—"

He promptly interrupted me and said, "We have no right to criticise or complain. He *is* on our side, and so is the Bible, and so are churches and Christian societies and organizations—all of them, so far as I know, almost without an exception. It makes me stronger and more confident to know that all the Christians in the loyal states are praying for our success, that all their influences are working to the same end. Thousands of them are fighting for us, and no one will say that an officer or a private is less brave because he is a praying soldier. At first, when we had such long spells of bad luck, I used to lose heart sometimes. Now I seem to know that Providence has protected and will protect us against any fatal defeat. All we have to do is to trust the Almighty and keep right on obeying his orders and executing his will."

I could not press inquiry further. I knew that Mr. Lincoln was no hypocrite. There was an air of such sincerity in his manner of speaking, and especially in his references to the Almighty, that no one could have doubted his faith unless the doubter believed him dishonest. It scarcely needed his repeated statements that

" whatever shall appear to be God's will, that I will do," his special gratitude to God for victories, or his numerous expressions of his firm faith that God willed our final triumph, to convince the American people that he was not and could not be an atheist or an infidel.

He has written of the Bible, that "this great Book of God is the best gift which God has ever given to man," and that "all things desirable for man to know are contained in it." His singular familiarity with its contents is even stronger evidence of the high place it held in his judgment. His second inaugural address shows how sensibly he appreciated the force and beauty of its passages, and constitutes an admirable application of its truths, only possible as the result of familiar use and thorough study.

Further comment cannot be necessary. Abraham Lincoln accepted the Bible as the inspired word of God —he believed and faithfully endeavored to live according to the fundamental principles and doctrines of the Christian faith. To doubt either proposition is to be untrue to his memory, a disloyalty of which no American should be guilty.

There are a few persons whose perverted minds experience a satisfaction in imputing to Mr. Lincoln a love for coarse, erotic stories and a habit of repeating them, which, if he had, would indicate a vulgar stratum in his mental structure. If these persons were conscious of the contempt with which those who really knew him listen to their statements that they have heard Mr. Lincoln relate these stories, they would never repeat them. No occupant of the Executive chair knew better the exaltation of his office or how to maintain its dignity. If he had been inclined to such practices, this knowledge would have effectually restrained him from their indulgence. But there is not a shadow of truth in these imputations. Major Hay and Mr. Nicolay, his secretaries, were members of his household during a large portion of his official term—Mr. Carpenter, the artist, lived in the White House during six months—Professor Henry sought every opportunity to be with him, and these four witnesses, who saw him in his unconstrained private life, agree that neither of them heard from Mr. Lincoln's lips any sentence or word which might not have been repeated in the presence of ladies. The subject is one upon which I can and must give evidence. It was a great pleasure to me to listen to him, and I have several times sought to excite his propensity for anecdote with success. In my own office, where no one but a messenger was present, he was under no restraint. Yet I never heard him relate a story or utter a sentence which I could not have repeated to my wife and daughters. The story of young Webster and the schoolmaster, related elsewhere, was the least refined ever told in my presence.

What may have been his habit, in this respect, before his election, and his coming to Washington, is unimportant. It is of his public life of which I am speaking. A vulgar story in the mouth of the President of the United States would have been offensive—to none more so than to Mr. Lincoln. It is time that the statements in question should cease. They originate in the prurient imaginations of their authors. The friends of Abraham Lincoln, who revere his memory, should protect his reputation. They should resent such imputations in a manner which will impress his calumniators if it does not reform them.

I am asked, and more frequently as time moves on,

which is the best biography of Abraham Lincoln? Where is the most reliable account of his life and services to be found? I am able to answer these inquiries without hesitation. In my opinion, the noble work of Messrs. Nicolay and Hay must always be the standard life of Lincoln. Their opportunities for observation and the collection of authentic facts were exceptionally good —their labors have been diligent and faithful. Their volumes constitute a great storehouse of facts well arranged and digested. It would be faint praise to say that their history is a work of rare merit.

For those who deem the work of these authors too comprehensive, and wish to know what can be comprised in a single volume, his life by Mr. Arnold will have no competitor. Mr. Arnold was Mr. Lincoln's associate at the bar, and his friend of many years. The two friends were unlike each other, and yet I think Mr. Arnold possessed many of the qualities which made Mr. Lincoln so attractive. His book was a labor of love, and is everywhere worthy of its subject and its author. Although Mr. Arnold did not survive to witness its publication, and it lacks the final polish of his hand, it is one of the most reliable of American biographies.

My pen lingers over this paragraph, the last I may ever write about a good man whom I honored, respected, loved. I do not hope to make it worthy of its theme— or to employ it to better advantage than to commend the history of Abraham Lincoln to the careful study of all my countrymen. He came to his great office inexperienced and almost unknown—his responsibilities were heavier, his difficulties greater than were ever encountered by the head of any civil government—he was the object of the unrelenting hostility of his enemies, of the fiercest criticism of many of his former friends.

His final triumph was not long delayed. An hour came of universal victory, when the nation was swelling with a mighty joy over peace restored to a reunited nation. It was the last hour of his noble life. In the very climax of his career, when his mind was filled with sympathy for the vanquished and with plans for their relief, when those who had borne arms against him had been overcome by his noble generosity, when he had not a personal enemy in all the republic, he was stricken down. It is an honor and a consolation to his countrymen, South as well as North, that he fell by the hand of a crazed assassin.

I venture the hope that what I have written in this volume will tend to suppress the aspersions of a very small number of writers upon Mr. Lincoln, and increase the interest of his countrymen in the study of his life and character. The time has not yet come to measure his services, or to compare him with other public men. We must leave that duty to those who come after us, when Abraham Lincoln shall have ceased to grow in the world's esteem, and we, who saw his face and heard his voice, and felt the warm grasp of his kindly hand, have passed away. For the present, we may say of him as his biographer wrote of Cicero, that, "though violent, his death was not untimely," for, like another noble man and martyr, he was ready to be offered, he had fought a good fight, he had finished his course, and he had kept the faith. Until we shall follow him where he shall receive his crown, let our hearts be his shrine, and our prayer without ceasing be, "Lord, keep his memory green!"

INDEX.

Adams, Charles Francis, American minister in London, his efforts to prevent sailing of Confederate iron-clads, 198; his confidential despatches, 199; his agreement to indemnify the liberal Englishman, 202; prevents the sailing of the iron-clads; value of the service, 210, 211.

Anderson, Major Robert, favors armored vessels, from experience with armored battery at siege of Fort Sumter, 212.

Armored vessels: Messrs. Laird contract to build two for the Confederates, 197; their destination and intended use, 198; how their delivery was prevented by noble act of an Englishman, 198–211; they are sold to Eastern powers, 208, 209; iron-clads first suggested by Major Anderson after fall of Sumter, 213; their use opposed by naval officers, 214.

Assassination conspiracy: Republicans refuse to believe in its existence; two members of Conference secretly visit Baltimore, February 17th, 58; Baltimore Republicans give details of the plot, 60; cool statements of an Italian, who had betrayed his associates, 61; conspiracy at first believed to be confined to the criminal classes; meetings of its members; who provided the money? an actor connected with it, 60–63; police in sympathy with the plot, 63; the schooner and tug purchased, 61–63; Mr. Lincoln declines to pass through Baltimore except in open day, 63; the facts communicated to E. B. Washburn, who replied that Mr. Lincoln had finally put himself in the hands of his friends, who would insure his safety, 64.

Baird, Professor Spencer F., secretary of the Smithsonian, 238; suggests the Potomac Club, 239; his energy and scientific work, 240; discusses the octopus, 249.

Baker, L. C., made chief of the detective service, 345; his lawless proceedings, 346; one of his illustrative methods, 347–349; his method of dealing with "bounty-jumpers," 350.

Baltimore city: obstructs passage of Northern forces; public meetings to prevent passage of troops, 120; authorities favor secession, 121; the "Plug-Uglies," 125–130.

Bates, Edward, nominated for attorney-general, 104.

Baxter, General H. H., with ex-Gov. Hiland Hall, Levi Underwood, B. D. Harris, and the author, delegates from Vermont to Peace Conference, 19.

Bellows, Rev. Dr. H. W., principal organizer of the Sanitary Commission; tenders its services to the Surgeon-General, who rejects them, 155; his indignation; fortunate results of his appeal to the President, 156, 157.

Belgian muskets condemned, purchased by War Department at a low cost to arm the first volunteers, 150.

Benjamin, Judah P., a Secession leader, meets other leaders at house of Davis, Jan. 5, where final plans were agreed upon, 29.

Bidwell, General D. D., charge of his brigade at battle of Fort Stevens, 416.

Black, Judge, transferred from attorney-general to State Department on resignation of General Cass, 28; his opinion that Congress had no power to make war upon a state, 179.
Blair, Montgomery, nominated postmaster-general, 104.
Blair, Colonel Frank, his services in the Lincoln campaign of 1860, 9; prefers charges against General Fremont, 174.
Blatchford, R. M., with General Dix and George Opdyke, authorized to expend $2,000,000 for public defence in April, 1861, 177.
Bonds of the United States: how $10,000,000 were issued, 194; necessity for their issue in seventy hours, 195, 196; Mr. C. F. Adams's agreement to deposit them as security for the noble act of an Englishman, 201; severe labor of their issue within the time required, 204; success of the undertaking, 208; statistics of the magnitude of Treasury issues, 209; more than half of this issue returned to the Treasury in original packages, 209.
Bradley, John, a Vermont contractor, offers to remove the colored race to Texas, 337; his opinion of the President, 338.
Breckinridge, Vice-President, promises co-operation with General Scott to secure count of electoral vote and declaration of President Lincoln's election, 38; his dignity and firmness, 43; declares the election of Lincoln and Hamlin, 44; his fidelity until the end of his official term, 46; his division forms part of General Early's army, in the campaign against Washington, in July, 1864, 391.
Breech-loading guns: none in use at commencement of the war, except Colt's revolvers for the cavalry, 150.
Bright, John, one of the few friends of the United States in Great Britain, 134.
Buchanan, President: determination of Secessionists to drive out loyal men and control his Cabinet, 28;

receives the Peace Conference, 32; his intense anxiety; urges members to make great concessions to the South, 33; does not refer to incoming administration, 34; his return to private life, with less credit than he deserved, 91.
Bushnell, Cornelius S., presses passage of bill authorizing iron-clads, and builds the *Galena*, 215; shows Captain Ericsson's plans to the President, 215; the President favors and the Board of Construction consents to their adoption, 216; secures the contract for the *Monitor*, which is built principally through his energy, with Messrs. Winslow, Corning, and Griswold his associates in the contract, 216; energy of her construction, 217.
Butler, Benjamin F., Colonel of the Eighth Massachusetts Regiment; on steam-ferry *Maryland*, from Havre-de-Grace to Annapolis, 125; saves the *Constitution* by towing her out of Annapolis; awaits a rebel attack at Annapolis Junction, 126–128.

Cabinet officers: principle of their selection by President Lincoln, 104.
Call for men: first call for 75,000, April 15, 107.
Campbell, Hugh, appointed on commission in Department of the West, 173.
Cameron, Senator Simon, announced as a prospective member of Mr. Lincoln's Cabinet, 81; nominated as Secretary of War, 104; applied to for rifles for First Vermont, 151; his resignation as Secretary of War, 168; success as a manager of corporations, 169; reasons for his resignation; retains the confidence of the President, 176; House of Representatives censure him by resolution; his prompt vindication by the President, 177.
Campaign, political, of 1860: a glimpse of, 8; Vermont first pronounces for Lincoln, in September, 8; speech-making in Pennsylvania with Colonel Blair, 11; the "Wide-awakes," a meeting in Southeastern New Jer-

sey, 12; excitement over the election returns from Pennsylvania, Ohio, Indiana, and other states, 13; election of Mr. Lincoln practically decided in October, 14; Republican gains; election of Judge Kelley; counting in a candidate, 15, 16.
Cass, General, to be forced out of Buchanan's Cabinet by Secessionists, 29-34.
Chase, Salmon P., 5; selected by Mr. Lincoln for Secretary of the Treasury; approves the Republican caucus of members of Peace Conference, 104; his opinion that civil war was inevitable; appoints a collector of customs for Vermont; offers the author a bureau in the Treasury, 105; wishes to have loyal men about him, 109; orders the Treasury to be defended, 112; chairman of Republican caucus of members of Conference, 35; announced as a prospective member of Mr. Lincoln's Cabinet, 81; directs issue of $10,000,000 in coupon bonds to comply with a pledge of Minister Adams, 195; decides that the secret of the English friend of the United States must not be disclosed except by his authority, 210; frauds under his administration and their detection, 285; opposed to internal-revenue system until compelled to adopt it, 342; decides in favor of employing detectives in the internal-revenue and customs service, 344; evil consequences of his decision, 346; his resignation as Secretary of the Treasury; its inadequate causes; his nomination of M. B. Field, 370 et seq.; Mr. Lincoln's just estimate of him, 377 et seq.; Mr. Lincoln makes him chief justice, 383; his gratitude and subsequent affection for President Lincoln, 384.
Cisco, John J., resigns as assistant treasurer of New York, 370; his fidelity and value, 372; withdraws his resignation, 376.
Clarke, General D. W. C., Executive Clerk of the Senate, captured, with his family, and robbed by Harry Gilmor, on the Baltimore and Ohio Railroad, July 12, 1864, 409.

Clay, Cassius M., forms a company for defence of the White House, 115.
Clay, James B., member of Conference from Kentucky, 31; his cordial reception by Mr. Lincoln, who expresses his admiration for Henry Clay, 72.
Cobb, Secretary Howell: premature acts of, and those of Secretary Floyd, postpone proposed seizure of Washington, 28; assists in driving General Cass from the Cabinet, and destroys the public credit, 179.
Colored race, the: their strong desire to learn to read; a colored preacher, 161; his discussion of the superiority of the white race and confidence in the President, 162-165; four gray-haired colored scholars taught by a boy, 166; sources of early news of the colored people, 167; procession of their children from Sunday-school reviewed by the President, 331; enthusiasm of the colored children for him, 332.
Congress: extra session called for July 4, 1861, 107; passes the act for Board of Construction, and authorizes armored vessels, 214.
Cumming, Alexander, with Governor Morgan, authorized to transport troops and provide for public defence, in April, 1861; defended by the President, 177.
Curtin, Andrew G., Republican candidate for Governor of Pennsylvania in 1861; his canvass and election, 9-14.

Darwin, Professor Charles, born on the same day with Mr. Lincoln; their advantages and personal influence compared, 431 et seq.
Davis, Captain, with Admiral Smith and Commodore Paulding, formed the Board of Construction, and approved armored vessels for the navy, 216.
Davis, captain of Tenth Vermont, holds the skirmish line at Monocacy all day with seventy-five men, 394 et seq.; defeats attempt of Confederates to cross the railroad bridge and break Wallace's line, 398 et seq.; narrow escape and courage of his men, 399.

458   INDEX.

Davis, David: his appointment on commission in the Department of the West, 173.
Davis, Jefferson, to be president of Confederacy to seize the government, Feb. 13th, 28; head of new plot to seize Washington, March 4th; meeting at his house, Jan. 5th, 29; his long enmity to General Scott, 94-96; opposes conferring upon General Scott the rank and pay of lieutenant-general, 96; opinion of General Taylor, his father-in-law, of Mr. Davis, 95; commissions officers of armored vessels to be built in England, 199.
"Demand notes," their redemption and destruction, 289; their origin and issue, 297; extraction of written signatures upon, 298.
Department of the West: excessive claims upon the Treasury in; their disposition, 175; Secretary Stanton refuses to approve them, 187; efforts to influence him to allow them, 188; how they were paid, 189; claimants accept payment of allowance by commission, and then bring suit, 189; they fail to recover, 190.
Detectives, professional: arguments for and against their use in the Treasury, 342-344; Secretary Chase decides to employ them, 344; evil consequences of their employment, 346; necessity of continuing their use, 347-351.
Dix, General John A., brought into the Cabinet by misdeeds of Secretary Cobb, 28; his despatch to Hemphill Jones, 34; his influence in the Cabinet, 79, 80; on the quiet of the inauguration, 91; with George Opdyke and R. M. Blatchford authorized to expend $2,000,000 for arms and supplies, in April, 1861, 177.
Dodge, William E., member of the Conference from New York, presses Mr. Lincoln to yield to the demands of the South, and not go to war on account of slavery, and so prevent the grass from growing in the streets of Northern cities, 74; Mr. Lincoln's expressive reply, 75; its influence upon the audience, 76.

Douglas Democrats praise the inaugural, 103.
Douglas, Stephen A., moves omission of formal parts of certificates during count of electoral vote, 44; his debate with Mr. Lincoln in 1858, 437 et seq.

Early, General Jubal A., denies his intention to attack Washington in 1864, 385; his supposed force and intentions, 387 et seq.; his denial that he intended to attack Washington, and his report of July 14th, 1864, 388 et seq.; declines to give his numerical force, 390 et seq.; presses for Washington after the battle of Monocacy, 401 et seq.; is before Washington with his army on the morning of July 11th, 405 et seq.; his retreat, 408 et seq.; leaves four hundred of his wounded at Frederick, 400 et seq.; confesses a loss of three thousand at the Monocacy, 401; before Washington, 403; he does not give the strength of his force, 421; denies that he expected to capture Washington; his statements about the battle in front of Fort Stevens, 424; the statements of himself and his men, 425; his statements that "dismay and consternation prevailed in Washington," 426 et seq.
English citizen, an: his great service to our government; offers to provide £1,000,000 sterling as security for an order to arrest Confederate iron-clads; his secret; obligation to keep it, 194-210.
Ericsson, Captain John, approves plans of the Galena, and furnishes C. S. Bushnell with plans for an invulnerable armored vessel, 215; his plans rejected by Board of Construction; visits Washington; the President favors his floating-battery, and the board reverses its decision, 216; Monitor built on his plans, and her draught less than he calculated, 217; Captain Fox calls him the inventor of the Monitor, 234.

Fairbanks, Governor Erastus, appoints delegates to Peace Conference, 19;

INDEX. 459

offers First Vermont Regiment, April 15th, 107; applies for Enfield rifles for First Vermont Regiment, and offers to purchase their guns in preference to arming them with Belgian muskets, 151.

Fessenden, Senator, is appointed Secretary of the Treasury, 381; declines the appointment, but yields to the influence of President Lincoln, 382 *et seq.*

Field, David Dudley, member of Conference from New York; final vote of New York on resolutions of the Conference by unfair advantage taken of his absence, 82.

Field, Maunsel B.: his relations to Secretary Chase; is made Assistant Secretary of the Treasury, 371; is named to President Lincoln by Secretary Chase for assistant treasurer of New York; opposition to his nomination, 373 *et seq.*

Floyd, Secretary J. B.: his disloyalty in President Buchanan's Cabinet; leaves the Cabinet charged with crime, 180.

Foot, Senator, of Vermont: esteem of Vermonters for him; he regards the Conference as a trick; his bold denunciations of Secessionists, 20; suggests to delegates to arm and defend themselves, 21.

Fox, Gustavus V., a favorite of President Lincoln; Assistant Secretary of the Navy; his impressions about armored vessels, 213; favors building the *Galena*, 215, and the *Monitor*, 216; watches progress of the *Merrimac* and predicts her success, 217; warns the President that she may prove effective, 218; despatch from, after first battle with the *Merrimac*, 223; his praise of Captain Worden for his handling of the *Monitor;* attributes the *Monitor* to President Lincoln, 234.

Fractional currency: Its origin and utility, 303; large amounts issued and redeemed; profit of the United States upon, 304; wholly made in one Treasury bureau, 305.

Franklin, Captain W. B., appointed to organize and drill the Treasury regiment, 113; captured by Gilmor's cavalry, July 12th, 1864; his escape on the day of his capture, 409.

Frederick, city of, compelled by General Early to pay $200,000 in Federal money, 401.

Fremont, General, appointed to command the Department of the West; his extraordinary powers, 171; his want of business ability, 172; he manumits slaves of rebel owners, and the President reverses his order, 173; his susceptibility to praise; gives contracts to all; General Blair's charges against him, 174; his removal by the President, and his loyal action thereupon, 174.

Galena, the, first armored vessel, built at Mystic, Conn.; doubts of her success; her plans approved by Captain Ericsson; public outcry against her; the President and Captain Fox her friends, 215.

Gault, J., invents encased postage stamp; extent of its use as currency, 301-303.

Gooch, Hon. D. W., of Massachusetts: his report to 38th Congress on condition of exchanged Union prisoners at Annapolis, 325; says the prisoners were intentionally starved by the rebel authorities, 325.

Grant, General U. S.: simplicity of his first visit to Washington, 317; his call on the President before advance of the Army of the Potomac, 319; his views of the Union and Confederate armies, 321; his celebrated telegram of May 11th, 1864, 322; decides to remove General Thomas from command of the army operating against Hood, 363; waits, and Thomas defeats Hood, 364; finally does Thomas justice in his "Personal Memoirs," 365; his estimate of the battle on the Monocacy, 390; sends part of Sixth Corps to Wallace in Baltimore, 392; intended to reinforce Washington if attacked, 407.

Great Britain favorable to the North at beginning of the war, 132; becomes hostile — reasons therefor, 133; contemptuous treatment of the American minister, 134; de-

mands surrender of Mason and Slidell, and prepares for war, 137; repudiates her former claims, 139; attributes the surrender to cowardice, 146; unfriendliness of crown officers to the United States, 198; demands security in £1,000,000 for preventing departure of iron-clads, 199; waives the demand on notice that Mr. Adams would give the security, 208.
"Greenback:" army name for legal-tender notes; its origin, 311. *See Legal-tender.*
Greene, Lieutenant, fired the guns during first part of the battle with the *Merrimac*, 231; his youth and modesty; takes command of the *Monitor* when Captain Worden was disabled, 226; his modest account of the last part of the fight, 232.
Gregory, C., describes encased postage-stamp in *Philatelic Journal*, 301.
Griswold, John A., Corning, & Winslow, co-contractors with C. S. Bushnell to build the *Monitor*, 216.
Gurowski, Adam: his sources of information of events; his origin unknown, 26; his address to Northern members; details alleged conspiracy to seize the government, 26-30; urges members to go home and organize regiments, 27; declares that Lincoln's election determined the South on war, 29; seizure of Washington on February 13th prevented by indiscretions of Cobb and Floyd, 28; postponement of seizure to March 4th; new conspiracy confined to leaders; to be managed by Jefferson Davis, 30; Peace Conference a part of the plot, 30; declares his personal knowledge of the plot to assassinate Mr. Lincoln, 58.

Hall, Hiland, ex-Governor of Vermont, delegate to Peace Conference, 19; surprised by conversation with Senator Foot, 20; shocked at suggestion of carrying arms, 22; his reply to a Kentuckian on the subject of the courage of New England men, 56.
Hamilton, Alexander: his creation of the Treasury system of the United States, 4; no account of the Treasury to be found in his writings or elsewhere in print, 4, 5; his checks against frauds, 285.
Harrington, George, First Assistant Secretary of the Treasury, 109; invites heads of bureaus to meeting for defence of the Treasury, 112; announces that Captains Shiras and Franklin will drill the Treasury regiment, 113.
Henry, Colonel William W., commands Tenth Vermont, which is sent, under General Ricketts, to reinforce General Wallace at Baltimore, 392 *et seq.*; gets fastest steamboat, reaches Baltimore, hurries to the front, where he arrives on July 8th, 392; deceives the Confederates, and reaches the Monocacy on morning of July 9th, 393; receives General Wallace's order to retreat, 397; brings off his regiment, 397; General Wallace's opinion of him, 400; his regiment at the Relay House, 409.
Henry, Dr. Joseph, secretary of the Smithsonian Institution; his character; his esteem for President Lincoln, 235; his conversation with the President, 237.
Herald, New York, compelled by the people to display the "Stars and Stripes," 107.
Hicks, Governor of Maryland, elected as a Union candidate; opposes passage of regiments through Baltimore, 121; his interview with the President, April 20th, 1861, 122; the President's answer to him, 123.
Histories of the war, their inaccuracies, 3.
Holt, Judge, of Kentucky, a loyal member of Mr. Buchanan's Cabinet; his influence, 79, 80; assists in the order of Mr. Lincoln's inauguration, 91; appointed on commission in Department of the West; his justice and equity, 173; his fidelity and loyalty in President Buchanan's Cabinet, 181.
Hospital notes: the wounded from the Wilderness; their sufferings and exposure, 251; charities of the colored people; "mammy" and her pickles, 255; the Catholic sisters,

258; anæsthetics and their merciful effects, 261; the wounded Dane, 263.

Inauguration of President Lincoln, March 4th; a bright day, the city orderly, soldiers not visible, 84; procession starts from Executive Mansion, with President Buchanan in an open carriage; takes up Mr. Lincoln at Willard's, and moves through a great multitude of spectators to the Capitol, 85, 86; strong contrast of the two presidents, 86; Senator Baker introduces Mr. Lincoln, 87; his voice distinctly heard; its opening received in silence; his declaration that the laws should be executed in all the states excites great applause, 89; beauty of his peroration; impressive dignity of his oath to defend the Constitution, 90, 91; return to the Executive Mansion without disorder or disturbance; departure of ex-President Buchanan to private life; the undisturbed dignity of the impressive ceremony due to the influence of Mr. Buchanan, Secretaries Dix, Holt, and Stanton, and General Scott, 91, 92.

Johnson, Colonel Bradley T., selected by General Lee to command expedition to release Confederate prisoners at Point Lookout, 386; commands division of cavalry in Early's campaign in July, 1864, 387; moves against railroads and for Point Lookout, 389; is recalled by General Early, 390.

Johnson, Waldo P., member of the Conference, afterwards a Confederate brigadier, wants to know how Mr. Lincoln got through Baltimore; Mr. Seddon's reply, 66.

Kelley, William D.: first meeting with him at the Astor House, in September, 1861, 8; his first canvass and election to Congress, 8-15, 16.

Laird, Messrs., ship-builders, contract with Confederates to build two iron-clad vessels at Birkenhead, 197; how their departure was prevented by Minister Adams, 198-203.
Lamon, Ward H., Mr. Lincoln's friend and prospective Marshal of the District, not present when he received the Conference; a member supplies his place, 71.
Lane, Colonel, of Kansas, forms a company to defend the White House, in April, 1861, 115.
Lee, General Robert E., a colonel in 1861; arrived in Washington from Texas about March 1st; General Scott's high estimate of, 97; condemns secession in a letter to his son, January 23d, 1861, in very strong terms, 98; rumor early in April that General Scott would resign and Colonel Lee be appointed to command, 99; resignation of members of his family; resigns his own commission, April 20th, 99; his only reason that he did not desire to draw his sword against Virginia; was this reason adequate? 100; influence of his family; its probable effect if exerted in behalf of the Union, 101; his splendid genius, military abilities, high character, and otherwise stainless life admitted, but his claimed justification for taking up arms against his country and his flag denied, 99-102; he is informed of all events in Washington, 386; plans the movement against Washington in 1864, 387; statements of Colonel Long, his biographer, 388.
Lefferts, Marshal, colonel of the Seventh New York Regiment, 125, 128, 131.
Legal-tender notes: their origin a necessity, 306; President Lincoln's opinions of their legality, 307; description of, 310; amounts issued and outstanding, 311; amount reduced by Secretary McCulloch, 313; Congress prohibits further reduction, 314; opinion of Secretary Chase on their constitutionality, 315; portraits of living men upon, prohibited, 306.
Lewis, Walker, a colored man; his experiences as a slave; his appointment as a messenger; his fidelity,

159; rules for his own observation, 161; his industry and success, 160.
Lincoln, Abraham: decease of his financial officers, 2; his charity, 7; the campaign of 1860, 8; his election assured in October, 14; electoral vote counted, and declared elected, 40; his peaceable election, and its announcement secured by General Scott and Vice-President Breckinridge, 46; threats against his life by Southern newspapers, 48; conspiracy for his assassination in Baltimore in February, 58; consents to follow advice of his friends on his journey through Baltimore, 64; arrival in Washington, and his alleged disguise, 65; disappointment caused by his arrival to Southerners, 66; contempt of Secessionists for his supposed coarseness and vulgarity, 67; receives members of Peace Conference on the evening of his arrival, 68; desires acquaintance with Southern members, 69; his frankness with them, 71; his reception of Mr. Rives, James B. Clay, George W. Summers, and others, 72; his answers to Mr. Seddon, 74; to William E. Dodge, 75; his determination to enforce the provisions of the Constitution, 73; declines to discuss the slavery question, 76; opinions of Mr. Rives, Judge Ruffin, and other Southerners of Mr. Lincoln, 77; influence of his arrival in Washington in checking growth of secession, 80; his procession to the Capitol on March 4th; his introduction to the audience by Senator Baker, of Oregon, 87; his opening address received in silence, 88; effect of his announcement that he would use the National powers to recover the forts and property of the nation, 89; subsequent enthusiasm of the audience; his oath to support the Constitution, 90; his return to the Executive Mansion, 91; hated by the Secessionists, 93; his novel selection of his Cabinet officers, 104; his first call for seventy-five thousand men on the fall of Fort Sumter, 106; popular enthusiasm for him, 107; his interview with Dr. Wynne, 118; the governor of Maryland and mayor of Baltimore solicit an order that no more Northern regiments be permitted to pass through Maryland, 122; his answer to them, 123; his reception of the New York Seventh and Eighth Massachusetts regiments, 129; his prompt decision that Mason and Slidell, captured on the British steamer *Trent*, must be surrendered; his reasons therefor, 147; his influence in overcoming prejudices of the War and Navy departments against the volunteer service, 149 *et seq.*; orders the surgeon-general to co-operate with the Sanitary Commission, 155; confidence of the colored people in him as their chosen emancipator, 163; appoints Davis Commission on claims in the Department of the West, and removes General Fremont, 173; his confidence in Secretary Cameron, 176; overlooks Mr. Stanton's discourtesy and appoints him Secretary of War, 185; his attachment to Secretary Stanton, 186; his reply to resolution censuring Mr. Cameron, 177; his trust in Secretary Stanton, 192; consultation with him about issuing bonds on pledge of Minister Adams, 195; early opinions in favor of armored vessels, 213; favors construction of the *Galena*, 215; approves Captain Ericsson's plans for the *Monitor*, 216; his confidence that the *Merrimac* would not prove irresistible, and his faith in the favor of the Almighty, 219; his confidence in Captain Worden and the *Monitor*, 220; his cheerfulness over news of the *Merrimac's* first victories, 222; receives news of the battle between the *Monitor* and the *Merrimac*, 224; not elated by the *Monitor's* victory, 225; hears Captain Worden describe the fight on the deck of the *Monitor*, 227; Captain Fox attributes the adoption of armored vessels to President Lincoln, 234; his interviews with, and high opinion of, Professor Henry, 236; the par-

don of the sleeping sentinel, 265; Scott's death at Lee's Mills; his message to the President, 280; his opinions of the constitutionality of legal-tender notes, 307, 310; his love for ballad poetry, 309; his interest in returned prisoners at Annapolis, 323; his sympathy for them, 327; unwilling to believe they were intentionally starved by the rebels, 328; his review of the colored children, 332; his story of Daniel Webster and the school-master, 333; favors paying for slaves, 335; his interview with a Vermont contractor, who would remove the slaves to Texas, 337; advises General Grant not to relieve General Thomas and give his command to General Logan before the battle of Nashville, 364; his faith, 368; he accepts Mr. Chase's resignation; his just estimate of Secretary Chase; he appoints him chief justice, 371 *et seq.;* his opinion that the republic did not depend on the life of any one man, 377; nominates Mr. Fessenden as Secretary of the Treasury, who declines and finally accepts the appointment, 381; his influence upon Mr. Fessenden, 382; witnesses battle at Fort Stevens, 416; his calmness in times of excitement, and confidence that Washington would not be captured, 428; letters of, to Governor Swann and General Grant now first published, 429, 430; sketch of some events in his life, 436 *et seq.;* writes his own biography, 432; his power of thought, 434; origin and powerful influence of his "divided-house" speech, 435 *et seq.;* his debate with Senator Douglas and Chicago speech of July 10th, 1858, 436; his nomination and election, 440 *et seq.;* his faith in the Bible, 447 *et seq.;* the best histories of his life, 453.

Logan, General John A., ordered by General Grant to supersede Thomas in command of the army against Hood; waits at Cincinnati until Thomas defeats Hood, when the order is rescinded, 363 *et seq.*

Logan, Stephen T., member from Illinois, moves that the members of the Conference call in a body on the President-elect; motion carried by the influence of President Tyler, 67.

London *Times,* the, opposes secession before the commencement of the war, 132; favors secession and disunion, 133; statement of practice of Great Britain in cases like that of the *Trent,* 138; attributes surrender of Mason and Slidell to American cowardice, 146.

Long, General: his account of Early's campaign against Washington, 388.

Lowndes, Francis, a clerk in the Register's office, seventy-five years old, the first to sign a pledge to defend the Treasury, 114.

Lyons, Lord, British minister, friendly to the North; his person and character, 140; his interview with Secretary Seward, 141; indifferent when Mason and Slidell are surrendered, 141; sends a steamer to Provincetown, 146.

Maryland: Governor Hicks and authorities oppose passage of troops; public meetings in, 120, 121.

Mason and Slidell, captured on British steamer *Trent* by Captain Wilkes, of the *San Jacinto,* 134; their delivery demanded by Great Britain, 137; Mr. Seward agrees to surrender them, 140; they are sent from Fort Warren to Provincetown, Cape Cod, and delivered to a British steamer, 146; their mission a failure, 147; their complaints of accommodations, 147.

Mason, J. M., and John Slidell, Secession leaders, present at meeting at Davis's house, January 5th, 29; Mason to arrange for Peace Conference; Slidell and Mallory to call convention at Montgomery, 29.

Massachusetts Sixth Regiment fights its way through Baltimore; its dead and wounded, 116; its gallantry, 117.

McClellan, General George B.: baggage train for his headquarters described, 317.

McClure, Colonel Alexander, conducts

the Republican campaign in Pennsylvania in 1860, 9; his efficiency, 9-13.

Merrimac, the: Confederate Congress plans her conversion into an armored vessel in May, 213; Captain Fox reports her completion and predicts her success, 217; sinks the *Congress* and the *Cumberland*, 222; her fight with the *Monitor* reported, 224; described by Captain Worden, 228.

Minnesota, the, runs aground in Hampton Roads when the *Merrimac* first came out of Norfolk, 222; it is decided to burn her, and she is stripped for that purpose; timely arrival of Captain Fox saves her, 223; the *Monitor* arrives and is laid alongside, 224.

Monitor, the: Captain Ericsson's plans for, favored by the President, 215; contract for, awarded; energy of her contractors, 216; sent to sea before she was completed, 217; the President's confidence in her before the battle, 220; Captain Fox telegraphs her arrival at Newport News, 223; his account of the battle on his return to Washington, 225; she comes to Washington, 225; Captain Worden describes her fight with the *Merrimac*, standing on her deck, 227; her success, 234.

Monocacy, the battle of: its importance underrated by Union authorities and by General Early, 385; battle of, described, 391 *et seq.;* its incidents, importance, and results, 391 *et seq.;* General Grant's opinion of its importance, 390; General Gordon's opinion of its sanguinary character, 401; Tenth Vermont Regiment, its account of, 409; its place in history; it saved Washington from capture, 424.

Morning Chronicle, the, declares that Congress must "eat the leek brandished in British faces," 137.

Morrill, Lot M.: his altercation with Commodore Stockton in the Conference; his character; his coolness under excitement, 52-55; impresses Southern members with a better opinion of Northern courage, 56.

New York city: excitement in, over the fall of Fort Sumter, 106.

New York Seventh Regiment reported cut to pieces in Baltimore, 116.

Nixon, John T., appointed judge of the Federal Circuit Court in New Jersey, 8; his election to Congress in October, 1861; his canvass, 12, 13.

Noyes, William Curtis, states determination to protect rights of members of Conference, 25.

Office-seeking, its discouragements, 18; it has no possible profits; its evils and dangers, 353 *et seq.;* its influence upon men of ability, 359.

O'Neill, Charles, his report on a monument to Secretary Stanton, 191.

Opdyke, George, with General Dix and R. M. Blatchford, authorized to expend $2,000,000 for public defence in April, 1861; accounts for whole amount, 177.

Paulding, Commodore, reports government property at Norfolk safely protected on the 18th of April, 114; chairman of Board of Construction, favors construction of iron-clad vessels, 215.

Peace Conference, the: delegates from Vermont, appointed to, 19; meets at Willard's Hall, 23; a device to keep the North quiet, 29; members witness count of electoral vote, 41; altercation between Senator Morrill and Commodore Stockton; its suppression by President Tyler, 52-56; Mr. Seddon's opening speech, 51; change of Southern opinions of courage of Northern men, 56; report of Committee on Resolutions a complete surrender by the North to slavery, 50-56; influence on members of Mr. Lincoln's arrival in Washington, 66; motion that the Conference call on Mr. Lincoln opposed by the Secessionists; President Tyler declares it eminently proper; it passes, and the president is to ascertain when Mr. Lincoln will receive the Conference, 67; adjourns February 27th; its resolutions adopted by a majority of one state, secured by refusing to accept the vote of New York, as agreed by a majority of its delegates, by the unfair ruling of President Tyler, 81; its resolutions not considered in Congress, except by way of amendment to those of Mr. Crittenden; its results, except to unite the Republicans and loyal Democrats, *nil*, 82.

Pennsylvania: six hundred men, the first troops under the call, arrive in Washington, April 18th, 114.

Phelps, J. W., colonel First Vermont, declines discarded Belgian muskets and wants Enfield rifles for his regiment, 151; his recognition by General Scott, who sends his regiment where active service was expected, 154.

Pitkin, Parley P., Grant's quartermaster on the James, favors Colonel Henry with fastest steamer for Baltimore, 392.

"Plug-Uglies," the, of Baltimore: their character; their connection with the plot to assassinate President Lincoln, 63; attack on the Sixth Massachusetts in Baltimore, 125; burn the bridges and destroy the railroads, 127; prepare to attack the Northern forces at Annapolis Junction, 128; their final departure from Washington, 129.

Postage-stamps: first used as currency by General Spinner, treasurer, 300; are encased in copper and used as coins, 301; extent of their use, 301.

Potomac Naturalists' Club, the: its origin, meetings, and membership, 239, 246; Robert Kennicott, William Simpson, Count Pourtalis, Baron Osten-Sacken, Theodore Gill, Dr. Newberry, Agassiz, and other members and guests, 240–245; discussion of the giant octopus, 246–250.

Prisoners, Confederate: General Lee proposes to President Davis to send Colonel Bradley T. Johnson to release twenty thousand at Point Lookout, 386; General Early's report concerning, 389.

Prisoners, Union: exchanged at Annapolis, 323; their horrible treatment and desperate condition, 326; its effect upon their minds, 327; sympathy of the President and a lady of Boston for them, 324, 328.

Public men, to be estimated by final results, and not by single errors, 5.

Register's office: cringing address of employés corrected, 110; in excellent working order in April, 1861, 111; issues $10,000,000 in coupon bonds between Friday and Monday, 195; necessity for it and how it was done, 203–211; severe consequences to the register, 205, 210; process of signing and issuing bonds, 205; entries of the $10,000,000 on the register's books, 211.

Register of the Treasury: proposes to pay balances to resigning army officers by checks on Richmond, 98; excitement resulting therefrom, 99; takes the oath of office, 109; declines to pay deserters from the Treasury for fractions of the month, 111; invites his clerks to promise to defend the Treasury; their excuses, 113.

Regular service, war and naval: antipathy of, to volunteers; heads of bureaus old men, 149; Chief of Bureau of Ordnance, his anger at a proposal to change his order, 152; declares the old Springfield musket best for volunteers, 153; his reasons, 154; regular officers oppose the Sanitary Commission, 155; required by the President to give reasons, 156; overruled by the President, 157.

Republican members of Peace Conference: decide to take action, 24; alarmed and united by call on President Buchanan, 34; resolve to invite loyal Democrats to a caucus, then subsequently form union, 35.

Ricketts, General, sent by General Grant with Third Division of Sixth Corps to defence of Baltimore in July, 1864, 392; his defence of the left at the battle of Monocacy, 394.

Rives, William C.: Mr. Lincoln desires to meet him, 69; his high character and courtly bearing; Mr. Lincoln's cordial reception, 72; the conversation between them, 73; Mr. Rives a close observer of the conduct and conversation of Mr. Lincoln, 75; his declaration that Mr. Lincoln had been misjudged by the South, that he would be the head of his administration, and that much fault could not be found with the opinions he had expressed, 77.

Ruffin, Judge Thomas, of North Carolina, a member of the Conference whom Mr. Lincoln wished to meet, 69; his conversation with Mr. Lincoln, 76; regrets Mr. Lincoln's pronounced opinions against slavery, but otherwise could not find much fault with his views, 76, 77.

Sanitary Commission tendered to Surgeon-General, and rejected, 155; just indignation of its officers, who appeal to the President, 156; Surgeon-General called to account, and ordered to accept and co-operate with Commission, 156; inestimable value of the Sanitary Commission to the soldiers, 157.

Saturday Review, the: opposes secession before the war; declares conquest of the South a hopeless task, 133; charges the North with cowardice, 146.

Scott, Colonel Thomas A., Assistant Secretary of War, requires application for rifles of First Vermont to be made to Bureau of Ordnance, 151; but on refusal of that bureau overrules it, 154; reasons for his selection as Assistant Secretary, 169; his efforts to reform the management of the War Office, 170; his ill success; reasons for his return to private life, 171.

Scott, General Winfield: opposes and breaks up first conspiracy to seize Washington; collects regulars there in January, 28; facility of access to him in February; his opinion of Vermonters, 37; his declaration that the electoral vote should be counted, and that there should be no revolution in Washington, 38; Vice-President Breckinridge promises to co-operate with him, 39; his numerous visitors, 39; his precau-

tions on February 13th, 41; excites anger of Secessionists, 43; peaceable declaration of Mr. Lincoln's election due to him and to Mr. Breckinridge, 46; his reply to Wigfall, 46; refuses to temporize with secession, 79; secures a dignified and orderly inauguration, 92; hated by Secessionists; urges President Buchanan to reinforce Southern forts in December; proposes to send two hundred and fifty men, with supplies, to Fort Sumter without informing Secretary Floyd, 93; his stern reply to a senator who urged his desertion; enmity of Jefferson Davis, 94; its origin; his severe expressions against Davis, 95; declares that no cause can prosper of which Davis is a leader, 95; opposed to the Abolitionists; hopes of a great Union party on the basis of the Crittenden Resolutions; declares that the North was the stronger in resources, the equal of the South in courage, but could not subjugate the South with less than three hundred thousand men, 96; declared in favor of young generals —that he was too old and worn-out for the command; his high estimate of Colonel Robert E. Lee—that he was, and would remain, loyal to the Union—that he was equal to the command of the army, 97; grounds of his faith in Colonel Lee, 98; directs that Northern regiments must pass through Baltimore, 119–121, 122; orders First Vermont Regiment to Fortress Monroe, 151.

Scott, William, a private of Company K, Third Vermont, condemned to be shot for sleeping on his post, 271; interest of his comrades, 272; pardoned by the President, 276; his death at Lee's Mills and message to the President, 280, 282.

Secession: blindness of the North to its progress; transfer of money and supplies to the South; South Carolina first secedes, 18; leaders assume control of Peace Conference, appoint its officers, and exclude the press, 23, 24; refuse to have a recording secretary, 25; oppose any

INDEX. 467

record of proceedings, 25; convention to form confederacy to be held at Montgomery, Ala., by February 14th, 29; rumors of revolution before counting of electoral vote, 36; Washington crowded with disorderly Secessionists, 36; leaders hope for a disturbance during count of electoral vote, 42; their angry denunciations of General Scott for his preventive measures, 43-46; depressing influence upon Southern members of Peace Conference of Mr. Lincoln's opinions at his reception, 77; ripens during the last week but one of the old administration; six states secede, 79; growth of, in the Border states, 80; suddenly checked by Mr. Lincoln's arrival, 80; effect of influx of young Republicans to see their President inaugurated, 81; they fill Washington and overflow to neighboring cities; a paralysis for the time falls upon secession, 82; it condemns inaugural address as fatal to the Union, 103; opens fire upon Fort Sumter, April 14th, 106; an angry Washington judge, 109; he leaves for the South, 109; clerks in register's office infected with, 111; Secessionists threaten Harper's Ferry in April, 116; premature rejoicings over destruction of New York Seventh and Eighth Massachusetts regiments, 128.

Seddon, James A., Southern manager of Peace Conference, 24; opposes making proceedings public, 26; leader of Southern members; his opinions, ability, and resemblance to John Randolph, 51, 52; his servant gives him a note of Mr. Lincoln's arrival, which he hands to Johnson, of Missouri; his contempt for the unguarded inquiry of that gentleman, 66; his charges against the North, and Mr. Lincoln's dignified answers at the reception of the Conference, 73.

"Seven-thirty" notes: their issue; they did not circulate as currency, 298.

Seward, William H., with Mr. Washburn, takes charge of Mr. Lincoln's journey through Baltimore, and escorts him safely to his hotel, 65; announced as a prospective member of Mr. Lincoln's Cabinet, 81; his speech to a body of his constituents which disclosed none of Mr. Lincoln's purposes, 83; selected by President Lincoln for State Department, 104; his negotiations with Lord Lyons for surrender of Mason and Slidell, 140; his masterly reply to Lord Russell, 142; approved by the American people, 145; consultation with the President and Secretary Chase on the necessity of keeping the faith of Minister Adams to a noble Englishman, 195.

Shiras, Captain, appointed to organize and drill the Treasury regiment, 113.

Sigel, General F., informs General Wallace of General Early's advance, with thirty thousand men, past Maryland Heights, 391.

Silver coins, fractional: their sudden disappearance from circulation, 299; necessity of a substitute for them, 300.

Sixth Corps: Third Division, under General Ricketts, sent to reinforce General Wallace at Baltimore, 392; its position on the Monocacy, 394; its bravery and desperate fighting there, 396; its heavy losses there, 400; the remaining divisions reach Washington, July 11th and 12th, 410; its part in the battle of Fort Stevens, 416; Early's sudden retreat upon its arrival, 427.

Smalley, Judge D. A., of Vermont, defines the crime of treason in his charge to a grand jury in New York, 47; declines to interfere with seizure of arms about to be shipped to Charleston, 49.

Smith, Admiral, member of Board of Construction with Commodore Pauldingand Captain Davis, 215; approves construction of the Monitor, 216.

Smith, Caleb B., nominated Secretary of the Interior, 104.

Spinner, General Francis E.: his fidelity as a Treasury officer; his suffering from disease, borne heroically; his death, 3; suggests payments to resigning officers by drafts on Southern assistant-treasuries, 98; prefers to take his secession from the outside of the Treasury; proposes vigorous defence of the Treasury, 112; Cornwell, a clerk in his office, abstracts "demand notes;" his detection and punishment, 290-295; uses postage-stamps in place of small coins, 300; collects money and securities of the Treasury, and prepares for leaving Washington when it was threatened by General Early in 1864, 408.

Stannard, General George J.: his brilliant record in the war, 354; he is appointed collector of the district of Vermont, 355; he is ruined by it, with some of his sureties, 357; he becomes a door-keeper in the gallery of the House of Representatives, 357.

Stanton, Secretary Edwin M.: enters President Buchanan's Cabinet, 28; his influence there, 79; declares that the surrender of the forts in Charleston harbor would be criminal, 80; promotes the quiet of the inauguration, 91; public opinion of him less favorable than it should be, 168; his character and qualities, 178; his physical and mental vigor in 1861, 178; his first act in President Buchanan's Cabinet; declares surrender of Fort Sumter a crime, 181; his hatred of cant and hypocrisy, and of speculative patriots, 183; his strong prejudices and caustic criticism, 185; his love for, and eulogy of, President Lincoln, 186; his appointment as Secretary of War, 187; his refusal to sanction improper claims; his firmness, 188; his patriotic character, 190; report of Charles O'Neill's committee to House of Representatives on appropriation for a monument to Mr. Stanton, 192; present at battle of Fort Stevens, 415.

Stars and Stripes: enthusiasm for, April 15th, 105; love for it abides forever, 108; affection for, of an old Carolinian, 114.

Stevens, Fort, location of, 411; battle of July 12th, 1864, 412 *et seq.*

Stewart, John A., is proposed by Senator Morgan as assistant-treasurer of New York; he declines the appointment, 373.

Stimers, Alban C., chief-engineer of the *Monitor*, managed the turret during the fight with the *Merrimac*, 231.

Stockton, Commodore: his character; his interruption of Senator Morrill in the Conference; vigorous action of a Northern delegate, 53-56.

Summers, George W., member of Conference from Virginia, 31; his cordial reception by Mr. Lincoln, 71; his approval of Mr. Lincoln's statement that he would obey and enforce the Constitution and the laws, 73.

Sumter, Fort, fall of; its effect on the North, April 14th, 106.

Taney, Chief Justice, death of, October, 1864, 384.

Thomas, George H.: his loyalty questioned and defended, 360; he assists General Scott in April, 1861, and protects the railroads to Washington, 361; he "will hold Chattanooga until we starve," 362; moves against Hood; his slowness; General Grant proposes to remove him and give his command to Logan; he waits under the President's advice; Thomas fights and defeats Hood's army; Grant's justice to him, 362 *et seq.*; his unflinching loyalty, 365.

Tod, ex-Governor, of Ohio, nominated for Secretary of the Treasury, and declines, 380.

Treasury notes, did not circulate as money, 296.

Treasury of the United States the creation of Mr. Hamilton; no written history of; its expansiveness, 285; three frauds upon, and their detection, 287-294; frauds upon by the warrant clerk of the secretary, 347-351; the end of the dishonest clerk, 352.

"*Trent* affair," history of, 132; fortunate conclusion of, 146; Great Britain's action upon it, 169.

Trumbull, Senator Lyman, a teller during count of electoral vote in February, 1861, 43.

INDEX. 469

Tyler, ex-President John, president of Peace Conference, 24; enforces rights of Northern members, 26; suppresses an altercation and restores order in the excited Conference, 55; instead of calling on Mr. Lincoln, sends a note of inquiry when he would receive the Conference—Mr. Lincoln's prompt reply, 68.

Tyler, General, commands right wing at the Monocacy, 393; goes to the assistance of Colonel Brown at the bridge; assists in holding it until Wallace's army has passed; is then surrounded by Confederates, but escapes, 397 *et seq.*

Vallandigham, Clement L., introduces resolution in House of Representatives opposing surrender of Mason and Slidell, 138.

Van Brunt, Captain, commands the *Minnesota* when attacked by the *Merrimac*, 224; his joy at the arrival of the *Monitor;* informs Captain Worden that the *Merrimac* will probably attack at daylight, 228.

Vermont regiments: First Regiment, Colonel Phelps, tendered to the President, April 16th, 107; objects to Belgian discarded muskets, 151; applies for Enfield rifles, 152; how it got them, 153; its colonel commended by General Scott, who orders regiment to Fortress Monroe, 154.

Vermont Tenth Regiment holds the left of Union line in the battle of the Monocacy; its desperate fighting, 394 *et seq.*

Virginia: invites a Peace Conference of the states on the 4th of February, 19; her delegates assume its control, 24; Gurowski's opinion of the mother of Presidents, 27; to provide forces to seize the Capitol, 36; one of her members proposes "to have some music" before count of electoral vote, 42; influence of Lee family in, 101; rumors that Virginia has seceded, April 18th, 114; threatens Harper's Ferry, 116.

Volunteers: antagonism of regular service to, 149–157, 169–171.

Wadsworth, James S., a leading Republican, 30; his criticism on Gurowski's speech, 31.

Wallace, General Lew.: General Grant's opinion of the battle of the Monocacy, 390; prepares to check the Confederate advance, 391; is reinforced by Ricketts with a part of the Sixth Corps, 392; forms his line of battle on the Monocacy, 393 *et seq.;* fights the battle, 394 *et seq.;* orders retreat, 396; his opinion of Colonel Henry, of the Tenth Vermont, 400; his resistance on the Monocacy saves Washington from capture, 390 *et seq.;* with the Sixth Corps saves Washington from capture, 424.

Wallach, ex-Mayor, introduces Walker Lewis, a colored man, to the register, 158.

Washburn, Elihu B., a teller during count of electoral vote in February, 1861, 43; with Mr. Seward takes charge of Mr. Lincoln's journey through Baltimore to the Capitol, 64; they attend him to Willard's Hotel on the early morning of February 23d, 65.

Washington city: isolated from the loyal states in April, 1861, 115; rumors of rebel attacks, 117; disappearance of the "Plug-Uglies," 129; its condition and defences well known to General Lee in 1864, 386; Early's campaign against, in 1864, 387 *et seq.;* not supposed by its citizens to be in danger, 404; saved from capture by the battle of the Monocacy and arrival of the Sixth Corps, 424; no dismay or consternation there on account of General Early, 426.

Webster, Daniel: President Lincoln's story of his boyhood, 333.

Welles, Gideon, nominated Secretary of the Navy, 104; congratulates Captain Wilkes on the capture of Mason and Slidell, 135; his report to Congress on the capture, 135; his claim that he favored and Secretary Seward first opposed the surrender, 147; this claim unfounded, 148; an early friend of armored vessels, 213.

Wilkes, Captain: his capture of Mason and Slidell on the *Trent*, 134; secures the thanks of the House of Representatives, 135; his capture without instructions, 136; Lord Russell demands his dismissal from the navy, 137.

Winslow, Corning, & Griswold, joint-contractors with C. S. Bushnell to build the *Monitor*, 216.

Wood, Fernando, mayor of New York: his distress over the charge of Judge Smalley; his apology to Senator Toombs for not interfering with the police for want of power, 48, 49.

Wool, General John E., heads the call in Troy to promote enlistments, April 15th, 107.

Worden, Captain John S.: President Lincoln appoints him to command the *Monitor*, 220; the President's confidence in him, 221; his prompt attack on the *Merrimac*, 224; his high praise from Captain Fox, 225; boards the *Monitor* at Washington Navy-yard; his wounds; affection of his men, 226; the first naval officer to volunteer for the *Monitor;* his energy hastens her completion, 228; his description of the fight with the *Merrimac;* points out where the *Monitor* was weak, 227–231; his first inquiry when, after his injury, he recovered consciousness, 233; Captain Fox ascribes the victory of the *Monitor* to Captain Worden, 234.

Wynne, Dr. James: his escape from New York; his exaggerated reports of the loyalty of the North, and danger to persons and property of Southerners; escapes across the Potomac, 118.

Zollicoffer, F. K., a member of the Conference from Tennessee; cordially received by Mr. Lincoln, 72.

THE END.

www.ingramcontent.com/pod-product-compliance
Lightning Source LLC
Chambersburg PA
CBHW051854300426
44117CB00006B/394